Praise for *Are You Getting Enligh*

Dr. David Gersten is a healer in the h: supplemented his technical skills with and love, which shine through on every p
Excerpted here from the ...y Dossey, M.D., author of *Prayer Is Good Medicine*.

I was enthralled with *Are You Getting Enlightened or Losing Your Mind?* Dr. Gersten's courageous, heartfelt, and practical look at the interface between enlightenment and mental distress is inspiring, authentic, and life-changing. I couldn't put it down. The deep understanding and healing that Dr. Gersten brings to his psychiatric patients is available, through this book, to each of us—regardless of our current state of health.
Christiane Northrup, M.D.,
author of *Women's Bodies, Women's Wisdom*.

Dr. David Gersten courageously incorporates spirituality into the practice of medicine, bringing alive the true essence of healing.
Judith Orloff, M.D., author of *Second Sight*.

A psychiatrist openly and honestly shares his life's experience. Read what he has lived and learned so that you can liberate yourself and live fully.
Bernie Siegel, M.D., author of *Love, Medicine and Miracles*.

Dr. Gersten masterfully moves readers straight into the day-to-day arena of spiritual transformation. This is a profound guide that spiritual seekers will celebrate?
Bradford Keeney, Ph.D. author of *Everyday Soul: Awakening the Spirit in Daily Life*.

Some very simple truths and techniques from a caring author. David steps in and out of "reality" with ease. A brave, courageous book that challenges our assumptions and teaches in the same breath.
Peter Jensen, Ph.D., author of *The Inside Edge: High Performance Through Mental Fitness*.

In this comprehensive and highly accessible book, Dr. Gersten shares his passion for the healing potential inherent in a spiritual orientation to life. His thirty years of experience ... have taught him that both mystical experiences and mental illness are real ... and, most important, discernible even to the average lay person. This book can change your life.
Janet Quinn, Ph.D., R.N., author of *I Am A Woman Finding My Voice: Celebrating the Extraordinary Blessings of Being a Woman*.

The current medical industry has no models to aid a clinician in distinguishing, assessing, and helping patients with spiritual experiences. By speaking out and providing integrative language, Dr. Gersten is helping to transform the excesses of an exclusive, narrow, biological model.

Scott Walker, M.D., Assistant Professor of Psychiatry,
College of Medicine, University of New Mexico.

ARE YOU GETTING ENLIGHTENED OR LOSING YOUR MIND?

A PSYCHIATRIST'S GUIDE FOR MASTERING PARANORMAL AND SPIRITUAL EXPERIENCE

By David Gersten, M.D.

Wisdom Moon Publishing

2012

ARE YOU GETTING ENLIGHTENED OR LOSING YOUR MIND?

A PSYCHIATRIST'S GUIDE
FOR MASTERING PARANORMAL AND SPIRITUAL EXPERIENCE

Revised & updated Edition, 2012

Copyright © 2012 Wisdom Moon Publishing, LLC
All rights reserved. Tous droits réservés.

No part of this work may be copied, reproduced, recorded, stored, or translated, in any form, or transmitted by any means electronic, mechanical, or other, whether by photocopy, fax, email, internet group postings, or otherwise, without written permission from the copyright holder, *except for brief quotations* in reviews for a magazine, journal, newspaper, broadcast, podcast, etc., or in scholarly or academic papers, *when quoted with a full citation to this work.*

Published by Wisdom Moon Publishing LLC
San Diego, CA, USA

Wisdom Moon™, the Wisdom Moon logo™, *Wisdom Moon Publishing*™, and *WMP*™ are trademarks of Wisdom Moon Publishing LLC.

www.WisdomMoonPublishing.com

ISBN 978-1-938459-09-2 (softback, alk. paper)
ISBN 978-1-938459-11-5 (eBook)

LCCN 2012941854

9 8 7 6 5 4 3 2 1

Dedication

I dedicate this book to the memory of my father, Dr. Jerome Gersten, a true healer, a physician who was the embodiment of brilliance, compassion, and humility ... and to Sri Sathya Sai Baba, my spiritual teacher: the embodiment of full consciousness, for whom no challenge is too great and no person too unworthy to shower love upon in abundance.

Table of Contents

Foreword

"The deepest passion of the western world is to reunite with the ground of its being," wrote Richard Tarnas in his 1991 book *The Passion of the Western Mind*. This unquenchable desire to touch the Divine is universal. It is the source of the most sublime music, art, literature, and architecture of every culture.

But if our most intense drives are toward the transcendent, why do references to "the spiritual" create such emotional and intellectual indigestion in modern medicine and psychiatry? Over the past century, health care professionals have avoided religion and spirituality like the plague. This has created problems not only for patients but for physicians as well. As a result of this avoidance, medicine has become one of the most spiritually-malnourished professions in our culture.

The reason why the healing profession has avoided spiritual issues is rooted in the history of science. Only through great struggle did science finally escape the constraints and confines of the Church. Scientists discovered early on that a hands-off approach to religion worked best for both sides. They learned to leave "the spiritual" to religion as they claimed "the physical" for themselves.

This separation has been disastrous. It has led to the belief that there are basically two ways in which we can live our lives. We may, on the one hand, choose to be rational, intellectual, analytical, and scientific. On the other hand we can choose the path of intuition, religion, and spirituality. These paths are divergent; they cannot possibly be brought together. The failure to harmonize these two vectors in the human psyche has created immense emotional pain for millions of people in our culture, as they have attempted the unhealthy task of dividing their minds. Dr. David Gersten shows that this choice is false and artificial. We *can* have it both ways; we can honor both our spiritual and intellectual impulses, and heal the hurt that so many feel.

There are pitfalls, to be sure, as Gersten points out. Madness is real and not every vision of God or Goddess is authentic. Self-deception is alive and well, as it has always been. Gersten makes clear that the path toward transcendence is not easy; the spiritual path is not for wimps. But many have gone before us and the path is well described. Through this book, Gersten becomes a guide.

Medicine and psychiatry are changing. We are gradually learning to lighten up where spiritual issues are concerned. The pressure to do so comes not just from patients, who are hungry for a spiritual spark in healing, but also from science itself. For example, there are currently over 130 controlled experimental studies examining the effect of prayer and the ability of an empathic, caring, loving person to intervene in the function of a distant, living being; over half of these studies show statistically that prayer works. In addition, more than 250 studies reveal that religious practices, including prayer, are correlated with better health and a lower incidence of a broad variety of diseases. We need to admit what our research shows: that spiritual practice is *good* for health, both physical and mental. Today we can say that it isn't just nice or humane to include spiritual concepts in medicine and psychiatry; it's bad science *not* to do so.

Gentle rains have begun to fall on some of the spiritual deserts of medicine. The Office of Alternative Medicine, established in 1992 within the National Institutes of Health, has funded a study testing the effectiveness of distant, intercessory prayer in a program of drug and alcohol rehabilitation. A few years ago this study would have been unthinkable.

Not everybody agrees that these developments are a good thing. There are skeptics and cynics who believe that spirituality is ruinous for the human race, and that our best hope is to pull ourselves up by our intellectual bootstraps. While we can honor these opinions, we can observe nonetheless that this is the old-style thinking that creates deep and painful divisions in the lives of human beings. We must honor *all* we are, not just isolated parts, and we must learn to harmonize, not fragment, our psyche. The fact is, most people do not function well when they are deprived of spiritual experiences. There are spiritual deficiency syndromes, just like vitamin and mineral deficiencies.

André Malraux, France's great novelist and former minister of culture, said, "The twenty-first century will be spiritual or it will not be at all." There is urgency in the spiritualization of modern life; time may *not* be on our side. But the movement has begun.

It gives me great personal pleasure that a physician has written this book, because it tells me there still are physicians who deeply sense the spiritual dimension of healing. Dr. David Gersten is a healer in the highest sense of the word. He has supplemented his technical skills with uncommon wisdom, compassion, and love, which shine through on every page. It is an honor to add my endorsement to his vision.

Larry Dossey, M.D.
Author of *Healing Words:*
The Power of Prayer and the Practice of Medicine

Introduction

Samantha had not always been joyous. Her mother suffered from bipolar illness, and kept Samantha's younger brother locked in a room with the windows painted black so that he wouldn't know if it was day or night. Eventually, her mother murdered Samantha's father, for which she was put in a psychiatric hospital. Samantha had every reason to be as psychotic as her mother. But she wasn't.

Samantha traces the reason for her happiness and mental stability to something that happened one day when she was fourteen. The agony of her home-life had brought her to the edge of suicide. She could find no point in living. An inexplicable urge tugged at her to leave the house before killing herself, and guided her to sit on the front lawn. Suddenly Samantha felt immersed in a state of complete bliss and extraordinary peace, as if she were one with all of nature. She knew with certainty that there was a reason and a purpose to her life, a God without a name, a loving force that chose to remain anonymous, but completely and instantly pulled her out of her suicidal state of mind and gave her the joy that has been a part of her nature ever since.

Pamela, another patient of mine, was hospitalized after making a very serious suicide attempt. One evening one of the nurses in the hospital called me and said, "Pam is hallucinating. She claims to be seeing auras around us." I replied, "She probably is! Don't give her any more medication." Pamela had other experiences that fell beyond the traditional reach of psychiatry. Immediately after her mother died Pamela became terrified by a "huge, dark, menacing, terrifying force or being" that was trying to break through the windows of her bedroom. Her windows were violently shaking and Pamela feared that her mother, with whom she had been on very bad terms, had come back to menace, harm, or haunt her. The meaning Pamela gives this experience would be strange and perhaps totally unbelievable, except that that same night, Pamela's brother, who lived in another city, had the identical experience. Perhaps Pamela's mother's spirit needed to get in one more good last scare before moving on to a more peaceful afterlife.

James is a 25-year-old who had been schizophrenic for many years when I first met him in a V.A. clinic. Stelazine made it easier for him to cope in the world, allowed him to think more clearly, and cut down on his auditory hallucinations. I'd see James every few months to re-evaluate his medication needs, until he came in one day, and looked totally different. "What's going on, James? I've never seen you look so good." James said, "I started meditating, joined a spiritual organization called Self-Realization Fellowship and quit taking my medicine. I feel great." Schizophrenics aren't supposed to do that—suddenly recover—because schizophrenia is a nasty brain disorder with serious bio-chemical imbalances. Almost invariably they live a life of torment, hearing voices, and having paranoid thoughts and periodic episodes in which they completely lose touch with reality and may have to be hospitalized. I continued to see James every few months to see how his meditation was going. He continued to blossom and seemed to have no need of medication, for about a decade. Although I never suggested that James discontinue his medication, and in fact disagreed with his decision to do so, I was happy for him but still remained cautious.

Recently, however, his brother phoned me to tell me that James wasn't doing so well—he'd "gone off his medication again." Sometime in the last ten years, many years after I had stopped working at the V.A. Clinic, James had gone back on his medication. I felt as if the universe were telling me something. "Get James' story straight," I said to myself. "The meditation and spiritual path helped, but he's not cured. Don't glorify the situation. He's schizophrenic and needs medication. Meditation is not enough." James' decade of wellness was miraculous, but people with schizophrenia almost always require medication. The ideal combined treatment would have been medication and meditation.

A friend of mine, Norma, walked into church one day and began to see "golden rain" falling through the air. The sight filled her with awe, reverence, and extraordinary happiness. Her priest told her that she was indeed blessed to have had such an experience, a rare spiritual experience, recognized and acknowledged by the Roman Catholic Church. Because she still had doubts about the reality of the "'golden rain," Norma visited a psychiatrist who had treated her in the past for depression. He had wanted to put her into a psychiatric hospital immediately and start her on anti-psychotic medication to help her get rid of the "hallucination." This psychiatrist was unable to ask "medically-taboo" questions about God, spirituality, visions and higher states of consciousness. Thankfully, her priest was able to reassure her that she was not losing her mind.

Pepe Romero, widely regarded as the greatest living classical guitarist, says that, "God plays most of my concerts. When he does that, I am in a state of total and complete ecstasy. I am one with the audience. There is not an audience and me. There is only one. There is only music. There is only love. There is only God. Really they are one and the same."

I have been fortunate to share in a few special, synchronistic experiences with Pepe. On one occasion, upon returning from Vienna, he told me he knew how Mozart had written the Magic Flute. Pepe had stood in Mozart's studio and heard birds singing and he recognized the melody of the birds to be that of the Magic Flute. This in itself is not a stunning revelation, since Mozart himself wrote about how he used bird songs. Yet as we talked in Pepe's backyard in Del Mar, jokingly, I said, "I wonder if Vivaldi's guitar concerto was inspired by the birds." At that moment a bird in a tree overhead began singing the exact melody of Vivaldi's concerto. Now, granted it was only one bird. We didn't hear the full orchestration, but the rather complicated melody of Vivaldi's concerto was identical to the bird song.

What do these people, these experiences, have in common? They all share a quality that some might call "spiritual," and others would call "crazy" or dismiss as mere coincidence. These few introductory stories illustrate miracles and madness, grace and skepticism. Many medical doctors and scientists would agree with Karl Marx who said, "Religion is the opiate of the masses," and Sigmund Freud who regarded it as a crutch. Freud's attitude was recently reaffirmed by the American Psychiatric Association (APA) as a necessary "scientific pessimism." Further, an APA panel in 1991 agreed that people have an "innate tribalism and need for conflict." The doctors all agreed: "There will always be enemies. For there to be 'us' and 'them' is human nature." In response to the

APA position statement, the San Diego Union newspaper ran an article with the headline, "Wanted: Enemy to Unite America's Allies."

As a psychiatrist, I am embarrassed by the APA quote and general mindset. How arrogant for a profession that is less than a century old to make such sweeping, negative statements about human nature! We are doomed if happiness can only be attained by fulfilling our personal desires, and if we are motivated only by finding and defeating an appropriate enemy.

History is replete with heroes who disregarded their own self-interest, people who would surrender their lives for the good of others: Mother Theresa, or Boris Yeltsin, who stood on top of a tank to make one of the boldest statements of the twentieth century: "I will give up my life rather than allow Communism to stand," the lone man in Tiananmen Square in Beijing who stood in front of a brigade of tanks, for freedom. Thousands of unknowns rise above their own needs for a greater cause every day—just watch "Rescue 911" on television for people who risk their lives to help total strangers. In the average family, anywhere in the world, parents risk their lives for their children. Call it love, call it spirit, call it courage, but there is no doubt that the urge to rise to something higher, to follow a higher cause, is inherent in humankind.

We cannot become what we cannot conceive of. We cannot realize the dream we cannot dream. Where can we look for our Vision? Perhaps to the world's great teachers who, throughout history, have all taught that we do not need enemies! Only limited minds need enemies. Every human problem will not be solved by investing money in drug research to "fix" the brain's various moods and organic problems. The saints, sages, and wise men and women throughout history have experienced, lived, and taught the need for a "higher vision." They have taught that truth, right action, peace, love, non-violence are the guideposts to human life—that all of life is one, that the entire physical, mental, and spiritual universe is one interwoven tapestry. They have taught that life has a purpose: to love all and serve all.

Experiences of Spirit in a Secular World

Theresa was a beautiful, gregarious Catholic girl and a brilliant student who, by the time she was a teenager, was so popular she could have started her own fan club. Her parents adored her and she was her teacher's pet. Her vivacious personality, her curly dark hair and pitch-black eyes made her the dream of many young men's imaginations. She had a zest for life, an extraordinary exuberance, and the ability to throw herself into any activity with complete abandon.

Theresa's carefree life suddenly changed at the age of sixteen, when she began to receive love letters from her cousin. Part of her was falling in love and another part was wracked with guilt. Finally, after resisting the advances from her cousin, she confided her troubles to her father, who promptly sent her away to a convent for one year. Although Theresa was quite religious, a life of disciplined prayer was not what she had in mind for her life. Nonetheless, she spent the next year trying to respect her father's wishes that she be a responsible member of the convent. Although she fit in quickly, as she had previously adapted to every other situation in life, she was unhappy.

Theresa anxiously awaited the end of her year in "confinement." Just prior to returning home, she suffered an attack of severe weakness, followed by agonizing pains that started in her chest and abdomen, and then filled her entire body. Theresa's face, which had always been cheerful and upbeat, became flaming red and took on the look of someone who fears death is imminent. The attack subsided, but left Theresa with a life-long fear that the attacks would return, which they did over and over again.

Theresa's interest in boys vanished, as did every other "normal" desire. Theresa began to crave God alone and focused all her energies on "pleasing the Lord." She prayed incessantly. And then Theresa began to hear voices and to experience visions. At first, she began to feel a "presence" around her, which she "knew" to be God. And then began a lifetime of experiences similar to one Theresa described: "One feels that one has been wholly transported into another and a very different region from that in which we live, where a light so unearthly is shown that if during one's whole lifetime one would be trying to picture it and the wonders seen, one should not possibly be able to succeed." Theresa began to experience ecstasies: "An upward flight takes place in the interior of the soul, and this with the swiftness of a bullet fired from a gun." She began to have visions of Jesus, initially brief episodes, which later on would last for days at a time. She saw angels, and "a light far brighter than the sun." She saw one angel of such exquisite beauty that she was unable to adequately describe it. The angel "threw a dart" into Theresa, which resulted in a state of supreme ecstasy.

Not only did Theresa begin experiencing extraordinary visions, but those visions spoke to her. She heard God say to her, "I do not want you to converse any longer with humans, but only with angels." During one period of extreme emotional anguish, she felt that the devil was tormenting her. Then she heard a voice that said, "Do not fear, daughter, for it is I and I will never abandon you. Do not fear." Theresa took the voice to be that of God.

Theresa sounds as if she were suffering from a major mental illness, most likely schizophrenia, in which brain chemistry drives a person crazy, and the individual's psychological and social pressures, in turn, throws brain chemistry out of whack. Or perhaps, she suffered the euphoria of mania, which is caused both by a severe disturbance in brain chemistry as well as by a severe disturbance in one's psychological make-up. But this Theresa was Saint Theresa of Ávila, the great Spanish mystic of the sixteenth century.[1]

Saint Theresa was no schizophrenic. She learned how to live in two worlds, the world of the spirit and the world of men and women. She developed an iron will and commanded the respect of kings and popes, a feat that is impossible for a psychotic person. And, unlike the schizophrenic who loses the ability to cope with the world, Theresa continually grew in those abilities. She founded an order of nuns, corresponded with officials, including San Juan de la Cruz, known in English as John of the Cross, and was a major organizing force of the Roman Catholic hierarchy. After Theresa came to realize the spiritual truth of her voices and visions, her emotional suffering was transformed into joy and peace. Her attacks of pain and physical weakness continued throughout her life but she learned how to live with them and how to understand them in spiritual terms. For Theresa, happiness was the hallmark of spiritual progress.

At the age of 63, four years before Saint Theresa died, she wrote of herself, "an aged woman, good for little now, very old and weary. Yet my desires are still vigorous." Despite her physical frailty, she worked tirelessly until she died, trying to reform the church. So strong were her will and her spiritual convictions that near the end of her life she pronounced, "If you faint on your way, if you die on the road, if the world is destroyed, all is well if you reach your goal." Clearly, these are not the words of a person defeated by mental illness, but rather are the triumphant words of a victorious soul, a person who has been able to distinguish the voice of God and the voice of conscience from those voices that arise out of insanity and the whims of imagination.

If the signs, symptoms, and experiences of mysticism and enlightenment can be confusing and upsetting to a saint, imagine how others feel when the inexplicable happens to them.

More and more people are having spiritual, mystical experiences. Millions of us believe in and have experienced altered states of consciousness, have had visitations from deceased relatives, and have had strong premonitions that came true. These inexplicable experiences, these glimpses beyond the grasp of time and space, are always regarded as among the most meaningful and powerful experiences in people's lives. Such experiences are not always blissful and pleasant; sometimes people find them frightening. Spiritual experience can bring on true spiritual emergencies that are not effectively treated with Xanax, Zyprexa, or Paxil. Invariably, people begin to look at life differently after having glimpses of a different reality. They sense with a deep conviction that there is something greater than themselves, that there are ways of seeing that have nothing to do with the eyes, ways of hearing that have nothing to do with the ears, and ways of knowing that have nothing to do with the five senses or with "reason."

The average American already believes that modern science cannot yet explain many human experiences. Most of us already believe in a higher invisible order. In 1987 the National Opinion Research Center of the University of Chicago found that 67% of

Americans have experienced extrasensory perception, 42% have had contact with the dead, and 29% have had visions. Gallup Polls in the late 1980s showed that 43% of us have had an unusual spiritual experience; 46% of us are convinced there is life elsewhere in the universe; 15% of us have had a near-death experience, and 23% of us believe in re-incarnation. According to a 1976 Gallup Poll, 94% of us believe in God, 90% of us pray, and 88% of us believe that God loves us. One survey reported in *Brain/Mind Bulletin* (August 1990)[2] revealed that 79% of psychiatrists accept the reality of psychic phenomena, and that 33% have had a life-changing religious experience. A recent study reports that 60% of Americans believe in angels. A 2001 Gallup Poll showed an increase in every category with the exception of possession by the devil. In this most recent poll, 54% of Americans believe in psychic power or spiritual healing or the power of the mind to heal the body. This is an increase of 8% since a 1990 Gallup Poll. 42% of us now believe in haunted houses, which is a 13% increase over the same time period. 25% believe in reincarnation, up 4%. 28% of us now believe it is possible to communicate with the dead, an increase of 10%. 32% believe in the power of the mind to see into the past and know the future, an increase of 6%.

Although nearly half of us have had an unusual spiritual experience, most of us don't realize that the average person has ordinary as well as unusual states of consciousness every day. We need to pay attention to other states of consciousness. Half of all Americans will experience at least one major clinical depression during their life; and a little less than one percent of the world suffers from schizophrenia. Several books have already examined, at least partially, some of the altered states of consciousness and the "Varieties of Religious Experience." *Are You Getting Enlightened Or Losing Your Mind* looks at varieties of human experience. It seems that Americans believe in a "normal" state of consciousness, one kind of consciousness only. Everything else is considered to be abnormal whether it's "nirvana" or "depression."

Besides my intention to elaborate on the different kinds of experiences—"normal," "abnormal," and "super-normal"—one goal of this book is to describe a new system of classifying human experience, a view that includes the whole spectrum of consciousness. Altered states of consciousness are not mental states that only a few people experience. We all, in fact, experience at least a half-dozen different states of consciousness every single day. It scares most of us to death just to consider that we spend any part of our day in anything other than "logical, linear, goal-oriented" consciousness. But we do. My goal is to help you grow more comfortable with these different, sometimes disturbing, states of mind, so that you may embrace each experience in life more completely without fear and without judgment.

Before plunging headfirst into this book, a few words about my background are in order. I write from the perspective of a medical doctor trained in psychiatry, but who works in nutritional and mind-body medicine. Much of my clinical work involves treatment of chronic physical conditions, such as chronic fatigue syndrome, fibromyalgia, irritable bowel syndrome, cardiovascular disease, some brain disorders, allergies, and a host of other symptoms and illnesses. I specialize in amino acid therapy in dealing with physical illness and mental imagery as my main mental fitness tool. I also do work with peak performance, in particular working with professional and high level amateur golfers. All of my work is done within a spiritual context. I am a doctor who has himself had numerous miraculous events in his own life, some of which I will share with you. I also will share a number of stories of patients, friends, and acquaintances that they have shared with me about their mystical experiences and other miraculous phenomena they have seen. And I write as a psychiatrist who has worked with literally thousands of severely mentally-ill people, people I see in my office, people who have fallen apart and need treatment in a psychiatric hospital for a few weeks, people who are permanently psychotic and have spent years in state mental hospitals. The world's great religions have demonstrated that spiritual experiences, visions, angels, and a variety of higher states of consciousness are not only normal but also desirable and attainable through spiritual practice.

Based on my own experiences, I can say with confidence that the difference between a miracle and madness, between an angel and a psychotic vision, between clairvoyance and psychotic delusion is vast. In general, it is easy to tell them apart as long as you believe in both. And it is essential that we become able to sort out what is a miracle—and what is madness. The agony of not knowing if one is having a nervous breakdown—or getting enlightened—is a terrible worry that can be lifted just by knowing the diagnosis.

If you're looking for evidence of a miracle proven by double-blind controlled studies, you won't find it in this book. You'll never find a miracle in a test tube and you won't be able to count the number of angels dancing on the head of a pin. Some day scientists will be able to tell us exactly what the brain chemistry of depression or schizophrenia is, but they'll never be able to put the "experience" of depression into a test tube. Likewise, scientists will, I believe, identify brain wave patterns and various blood chemistry parameters that are associated with samadhi or the highest state of consciousness, but you can't put samadhi into a test tube and measure the experience any more than you can put God or the Infinite into a test tube, or under an electron-microscope. You will, however, find ways to find meaning in your miracles.

As a psychiatrist, I have come to a new and different understanding of my "job description." I work with strong medications to treat depression and psychosis. I work with powerful mind-body tools such as meditation and guided imagery that have rapid and profoundly deep healing potential. And I work with what I believe to be the essence of our humanity—our striving for excellence, our yearning to be immersed in the moment, our ability to love, our quest to travel on our own personal mythological journeys, and our ability to rely on God as our primary healing ally.

Physicians may feel unsettled as more and more people share with them these glimpses into other realms of consciousness. But many of the greatest doctors and scientists of our time have been deeply spiritual. Here are a few of Albert Einstein's thoughts about God and the Spirit:

"That deeply emotional conviction of the presence of a superior reasoning power, which is revealed in the incomprehensible universe, forms my idea of God."

"The principal art of the teacher is to awaken the joy in creation and knowledge."

"The most beautiful and profound emotion we can experience is the sensation of the mystical. It is the sower of all true science."

I believe that the next quantum leap for psychiatry will be the integration of spirituality into clinical practice. Psychiatry needs to begin addressing a new order of questions, such as: "How do you differentiate insanity from mystical ecstasy?" "How do you know if someone is hallucinating or seeing auras?" "When are antipsychotic medicines required?" "Should we be treating auras at all?" "How do one's attitudes about life after life or a higher dimension affect the way we live life?" How do our attitudes as psychiatrists about these issues affect our ability to empathize with our patients? And how can you find out if you're getting enlightened or losing your mind? These are questions that psychiatrists are afraid to ask, but need to ask. And we urgently need to figure out how we can utilize the faith and beliefs of the average American—your faith—to help you heal your mind and body.

Although my role as a psychiatrist is not to try to exorcise so-called "dark" or "evil" experiences nor to teach people paths to spiritual wisdom or enlightenment, I and others in my profession—and lay people in all walks of life—need to listen respectfully to spiritual experiences and not discount them. We need to provide a safe place for people to talk about their deep experiences in a way that helps them come to grips with the meaning and significance that these experiences may have for their lives. An open, nonjudgmental attitude will help people accept the magical, mystical side of their personality and let it flourish. To modify slightly one of Einstein's quotes, I believe that the principal art of the psychiatrist is to awaken the joy in creation and knowledge and to help clarify what is a miracle and what is delusion.

Finding Meaning in Your Own Miracle

Of course, this book is not a book just for psychiatrists. In fact, this book is primarily written for you, the average person, who is not a psychiatrist and doesn't need to see one. You, someone in your family, or a friend is likely to have had a spiritual experience.

Maybe you're still "in the closet" about your mystical experience, worried about the reaction your loved ones would have if you told them what you believe you've experienced. By understanding that spiritual experience is normal, you and those you love will feel freer to open up to each other in a deeper, more meaningful way, sharing your most profound experiences without fear of ridicule. I hope that through the information in this book you will come to embrace your spiritual experience, and by the time you've finished reading this book, you'll know more about it as others have experienced it, and will learn how to make it uniquely your own. I hope you will also know what to call your experience. Being able to name the experience is a priceless treasure. When you know that you've had a mystical experience, or a kundalini awakening, or a true vision of the departed, you'll feel comforted and reassured in the knowledge of its normality and united with others in a commonality of experience. You're not crazy. For the vast majority of the people reading this book my message to you is, "Most people have had a mystical experience, ESP, a vision, or a visitation from the dead: you're normal!"

By my mere act of listening to Pamela's frightening story of her mother's spirit, "the ghost at her window," for instance, I gave her permission to share and relive this experience. My acceptance and interest were very healing for her. She was not "crazy," and my nonjudgmental attitude calmed any fear she may have had about this strange experience. You too deserve the peace of mind that arises when you embrace your own spiritual experiences, and can share them with your loved ones without fear of judgment.

I recently treated a man in a mental hospital who claims to be God. He claims to have millions of minds, that in fact all minds are his because he is God. Carl is a 40-year-old street person who has been diagnosed schizophrenic for many years. He mumbles, hears voices and becomes frightened when I ask him direct questions about being God. Carl is so dysfunctional I have had to apply for a conservatorship, which means he will have a person appointed by the court to help him out, find him a board-and-care facility to live in, and help re-hospitalize him if that is necessary. When I told Carl I was applying for a conservatorship, he got very upset and said, "How can you do that? All of my minds are perfect.

How can you put God on a conservatorship?" I told him that was indeed a good question and I would have to let the judge decide that question. Other people who claim miraculous or divine experiences really are having those experiences. That's part of what this book is about—helping you find out what your unusual experience is or was. This book is your own diagnostic manual of mystical experiences. It will help you recognize: when you're having a universally-recognized experience that augurs spiritual development, how to distinguish visual disturbances from spiritual vision—or auditory distortions from oracles—or auras from a migraine headache. Chances are, if you're reading this book, you're not going crazy, yet you're in a culture that—with all its beliefs in God, religious practice, and higher purpose—does not believe in or accept a range of different experiences the way some cultures do. For all our protestations of belief in God, we are on, as Joseph Campbell put it, a "terminal moraine" of the fall of our traditional religious institutions and many of us experience a spiritual void in our materialistic, competitive workaday lives. We need to make time to listen to what we already know—that love, faith, God, and spiritual experience are real and are the cornerstones of a meaningful life.

There is a huge gap between what the average person believes and the way the average psychiatrist practices. I wrote *Are You Getting Enlightened...?* to provide a bridge between patient and psychiatrist, a bridge that allows spirituality to become a viable issue for patient or doctor to bring up. It is my hope that we can de-stigmatize spirituality, altered states of consciousness, visionary experiences, extra-sensory perception, paranormal phenomena, and other important experiences so that patients can discuss them without being labeled "crazy" by their psychiatrists. I hope this book helps you recognize your miracles and feel comfortable sharing them, even with your psychiatrist. But I hope you don't use this book to "beat up" on your doctor or spouse for being "backward."

This book is written in part for the millions of misunderstood patients, the ones who were called "crazy" and put on Zyprexa or Haldol because they told their psychiatrist they were having visions. An honest diagnosis is an incredibly healing tool in itself. I cannot express to you the relief and hope patients feel when they believe they are deeply understood, when I can clarify for them that they have a clinical depression that I need to treat with anti-depressants, or that the vision of Mary they had is not part of their depression but is, in fact, a part of them that is turning them toward the light. I may not need to treat "Mother Mary." I may need to inspire the patient to develop her relationship with Mary, at the same time that the Prozac or Paxil is alleviating her depression.

It is my deep hope that we can begin to recognize the distinctions between mental illness and enlightenment. Some ecstatic rapture is mania and some is samadhi, a mystical state of consciousness in which one experiences a sense of unity with God and all of creation. Some is drug-induced, a temporary "high" caused by amphetamines, cocaine, LSD, or ecstasy, which may produce a permanent "low". We need to learn how to sort out these different mental states so that we're not treating "samadhi" or "nirvana" with Zyprexa. I invite you to dive in and find out if you're getting enlightened and to become comfortable with the different states of mind and body. I invite you to explore more deeply the many threads in the web of life—spiritual experience, enlightenment. And miracles.

What is a miracle? Like love, it is that which is not measurable. It is that which occurs beyond our five senses. It is that which is not limited by time or space. And yet a miracle is something we all have a sense about; it's something that a huge number of us have direct experience with. A miracle is the healing from the "untreatable illness." It is the extraordinary courage in the face of immense adversity. It is the subtle knowing of things that we're not "supposed" to know. And a miracle is a peaceful death.

Like dreams, the meanings of spiritual experiences may not be apparent until after much probing and thought. Like any life experience the full import is not instantly known (and sometimes may never be fully understood). We need to explore gently our spiritual experiences, our synchronicities, and our miracles and hold them lovingly up to the light of inquiry. And yes, there may be uncertainty in that inquiry. Not all prophetic dreams come true the next day. Some may take years before one realizes that the dream was a true prophesy and not the whims of the unconscious mind.

When one holds experience with openness, humility, and the ability to tolerate uncertainty, the deeper mysteries of life reveal themselves to us.

Life is filled with experiences that have no name, ecstasies that are not insanity, love that is incomprehensible, knowings of the unknowable, and miracles that are commonplace. It is within this context that I work with people, hoping to coach them, inspire them, give them faith and hope to keep them going. My goal is to help people gain access to all their strengths—mental, physical, and spiritual—and to help them not only get "back to normal" but to dream their grandest dreams, seek their higher vision, and go beyond the limited thinking that says, "We will always need enemies. That's our nature."

Our real enemies are internal and are the most difficult foes of all. We must move beyond this kind of thinking that puts the enemy on the outside. This is the very thinking that makes change so difficult for people. It is our recognition of the real enemies that puts the power of change in our own hands. We often see the heroes of history as invincible people with few personal struggles, as if they had nothing left to do but transform society. In fact, even the great Mahatma Ghandi spoke candidly of his struggle with his "demons," reporting that his strong spiritual beliefs gave him his strength to drive the British out of India. That is why, even as he lay dying from a fatal gunshot wound, he was able to recite the name of the form of God he worshipped.

By his example, we see Ghandi's lesson to the world that non-violent resistance can conquer the "enemy" with greater strength than can fire power. We can easily deduce that without having lived a personal life consistent with his public message, all the strength and power he wielded would never have existed. Likewise, as a physician, it is my personal self-work that has lent me the strength to take so seriously the essential message of the Hippocratic Oath that teaches doctors the same message Ghandi taught, namely, "Do no harm."

In the spirit of doing no harm, I have taken great care that the strange, wondrous, and perhaps scary stories found in the pages of this book have been carefully researched and to the best of my knowledge are 100% true. Nothing has been sensationalized, dramatized, sanitized, or altered. Only the names of my patients have been changed.

So you see, this book was written with several hopes and goals in mind:

1) To develop a new system of classifying all of human experience. This book describes a four-step system of Psycho-Spiritual Assessment, a valuable tool for diagnosing spiritual experience, which adds, what I believe to be a missing element in the body-mind-spirit equation, namely "energy." In other words, a future holistic approach might be to evaluate a patient based on body, mind, spirit, and energy. This then could be considered the new holistic medicine.

2) To build a bridge that allows doctors and patients to better communicate with each other about spiritual experience, and,

3) Most of all, I wrote this book to give validity to the power and the importance of profound experiences which our society does not yet feel comfortable discussing. The truth is that even though you most likely already know you're not crazy, it is very easy to feel exposed, insecure, and misunderstood if you've had an experience that even comes close to any of those you'll find in these pages. After reading this book, you should be able to diagnose your experience, your visions, your hunches, and your intuitions and know what to call them.

There is no replacement for psychiatric training and the experience of diagnosing and treating patients for decades, but there still is no reason why you cannot have a more empowering understanding of your life experience. For the vast majority of you, merely finding out what to call your experience will be liberating. Knowledge, by itself, is a powerful tool. For too long the medical profession has maintained its mystique of secrecy, elitism, and technological knowledge as if the non-physician were not capable of understanding his or her own health. The mystique of psychiatry has prevented its most fundamental concepts from being adopted in the everyday thinking process of the average person, and so has prevented the merging of the spiritual outlook with the psychiatric outlook.

Every week in churches and in temples everywhere in the world, the clergy stand in front of a congregation expounding upon principles that they hope their listeners will absorb. Now it is time for psychiatry to do the same. This book attempts just that. It lifts the mystique of medicine and psychiatry so that you can have an insider's view. After all, information should be shared, not hoarded. Information is meant to lead to transformation.

I wrote this so that you could recognize and embrace your miracles and not chase them back into the recesses of your mind. I hope this book inspires you and assists you in a practical way in your daily life. I hope it helps you recognize your miracles, strengthens your faith, and helps you find deeper (and higher) meaning in your life. Through this book I hope to help you come closer to your own sense of spirituality and God, tap your own healing power, and become comfortable with mystical or spiritual experience. I want to help you bring sacred awareness more fully into each moment and each experience in life.

---

1. Giorgio Papasogli, *Saint Theresa of Ávila* (Boston: St. Paul Books and Media, 1990).
2. Marilyn Ferguson, *Marilyn Ferguson's Book of Pragmagic*. Adapted and updated by Wim Coleman and Pat Perrin (New York: Pocket Books, 1990). Also reported in *Brain/Mind Bulletin*, August 1990.

PART I

OPENING THE MIND TO SPIRIT

Chapter 1

Opening to the Possibilities

During the 'sixties, when much more experimentation was going on with hallucinogenic drugs, some researchers wanted to see how LSD would affect Indian Yogis. Would they hallucinate and lose touch with reality like everyone else?

An astonishing thing happened when the yogis took LSD. Nothing. Nothing happened at all. How can that be? They have the same brains that we have, the same central nervous system. How can they not be profoundly affected? Perhaps the spiritual disciplines the yogis practice are doing more than lowering metabolic rates and producing deep relaxation—physical, or bodily effects. Maybe LSD and other mind-altering drugs literally act on the mind. Can this mind of ours that thinks, feels, imagines, and affects our physiology also be directly acted upon by drugs and medications?

Is it possible to go beyond the mind that hallucinates under the influence of LSD? Is it possible to uncover our "true nature"? Is there a "true nature"? That's what Eastern religion teaches—that the mind is not our reality, that the mind helps obstruct reality. But the mind can also be used to lead us to the heights, to reach God, and to realize that our own soul is not unlike God or even different from God. Each soul is a wave, while God is the ocean.

The mind can even be used to "go beyond itself." That is the ultimate paradox. Yes, we can actually use our minds to slow down our minds, even to stop our minds. When the mind finally stops, we become not just loving, truthful, or peaceful; we become love, truth, and peace. Our small minds disappear and we become completely one with love, truth, and peace.

How does the mind slowing down or stopping relate to yogis and LSD? My theory about the yogis and LSD is that because their minds had been so tamed, so disciplined, the LSD had nothing to work on. And that implies that the mind is more than just a philosophical construct that helps us communicate, but has real biological parameters. Thus, the mind is the biological level at which certain drugs such as LSD work. These drugs have no effect on that part of us that is divine, that is beyond time, space and matter, that is also beyond the reach of medicine or chemicals.

A Powerful Mystical Experience

By the time I was in my psychiatric residency, I had been meditating quite a bit every evening after I'd come home from the hospital. One night I got out of bed and went to sleep on the living room couch. I dreamt that somebody was asking me about forensic psychiatry. Forensic psychiatry deals with psychiatry and legal issues. In the dream I said, "Yes, I believe in forensic psychiatry." Then I took a step back and said, "No, I don't. I don't believe psychiatrists should play God."

I still don't totally understand why that dream preceded the most powerful spiritual experience of my life, but it did. I was suddenly hit with a gigantic blast of light, that immediately threw me into a state that was neither wakefulness nor sleep. It was a state that transcended all states of mind I'd ever known before. The light blasted through me as if shot out of a fire-hose about three feet wide. The energy moved from my feet up through my head.

The force of the energy was thousands of times greater than any force I ever before had experienced. If the worst anger I ever had experienced in life was like being pulled around by a strong St. Bernard dog, the force of the light was like being pulled by 100 wild horses.

All of this was quite instantaneous and, as I mentioned, started while I was fast asleep. For one tiny fraction of a second, I was able to think and make a decision. I had heard about something called "kundalini energy" or "serpent fire," an immense energy dormant in us. The core energy of our existence lies at the base of the spine and in our solar plexus. I recognized that in that instant. I didn't say to myself, "I am going crazy." But I did have a decision to make. "Do I fight this thing or surrender?" The decision was quick and easy. If I didn't surrender, I felt like this energy would destroy me. So I said to myself, "O.K., here we go." I never enjoyed roller coaster rides. I like being in more control than that. And I wasn't initially thrilled to be hit by this intense energy.

But I surrendered. And all of this still within a fraction of a second. The light, the awesome energy moved upward and literally dissolved my mind. I could hear the light blasting through. It was loud. I could feel the substance of my mind dissolving. It was scary for a moment. I was rapidly moving into that state of being that allows yogis to be unresponsive to mind-altering drugs. I moved to where there is no mind to alter.

Up and up I went above this earthly existence. "Up and up" may not even be the correct way of describing where I went. In fact, one thing that was clear to me was that the experience was completely ineffable, completely beyond any description in words. My being, my consciousness, expanded further and further, higher and higher, until I discovered that I was "next to" Michelangelo's sculpture of David. I don't know if I was in Italy or if The David and I met in some other time and space beyond time and space.

It was a divine experience. I studied the magnificent face of David, glistening white. I was with him for many minutes of "real time." Slowly the face of David faded, but I remained in this altered state for hours. It was a state of complete bliss. I could see that the normal way I live, that almost all of us live, is totally unnecessary. I live in the world of the mind all the time, the ups and downs, the highs and lows, the joys, sorrows, and depressions. I always thought that was life. But up there in the stratosphere I could see that all of that was absolutely and completely untrue. It felt more real than anything I'd ever experienced in life.

Several hours passed before the experience faded and I slowly came back to normal awareness. My mind assumed its old form, but I was forever changed. My mind still has many of its rough edges but I have had a beautiful glimpse of another way of looking at life. Finally, when I was back on planet Earth, I woke up my then-wife. It was a bit strange trying to explain it to her. She didn't panic, nor was she thrilled for me. It was more like, "That's nice, dear. Now go back to sleep."

That morning I had a meeting to attend. It turned out that the address was Vision Drive. After the meeting I drove from San Diego to Los Angeles. I could sense that everything living in the world, human and non-human, animal and plant, was filled with the same energy hidden in me and in everyone else. I could sense that every blade of grass had true "atomic energy" within it, and that the entire world contained an infinite amount of this energy. That day my energy was as normal as ever. Nobody ever could have guessed what I had just been through.

I also came to believe that many people must go completely insane when they are hit by the kind of energy I experienced. I already had an idea what it was all about. If I hadn't known, I would have fought, struggled, and lost. You can lose your mind in a good way and in a bad way. Great athletes like golfer Tiger Woods, basketball legend Michael Jordan, cyclist Lance Armstrong (7-time winner of the Tour de France), and Brazilian soccer legend Pelé when "in the zone," have lost their minds in a good way. So does Pepe Romero when he feels God is playing through him during a concert. When in the zone, perception changes. Golfers "see" the cup as being larger than it actually is. Michael Jordan experienced the hoop as being quite large. Pelé described the zone as, "a strange calmness; it was a type of euphoria; I felt I could run all day without tiring, that I could dribble through any of their team or all of them, that I could almost pass through them physically." A patient in the back wards of a state mental hospital has lost his mind in a bad, destructive way. Losing the mind in a good way implies that you have a mind to surrender.

Did the experience make me a totally different person? I don't think so. But it gave me a glimpse into a reality that seemed much more real than normal awareness. Life is a journey and that intense experience was one very bright lamppost on my journey. And that lamppost is as clear and bright in my memory now as it was in 1976.

I had another interesting experience a few years ago, in 1991. All my most vivid spiritual experiences have come in the middle of the night, as if God has to sneak up on me when my mind is quiet and reveal new levels of truth and experience. The experience I had in '91 also began with a sudden burst of intense energy, although the energy was not cranked nearly as high as it had been in 1976. I felt myself entering a state of bliss and peacefulness. It had the quality of being one with God, with the quality of total effortlessness. I didn't have to do anything—just be and exist in the bliss, in the moment.

This kind of intense energy surge is called kundalini by many spiritual explorers. It is often depicted as a fiery surge up the spine, an energy moving up through the body in a rush toward enlightenment or insight. Although most commonly called kundalini, it is a universal human experience. In fact, as I was writing this book, it occurred to me that one of the earliest spiritual references to a burning, fiery energy is in the story of Moses and the burning bush, which "burned and was not consumed." Perhaps there was no burning bush at all. Maybe Moses was having a kundalini experience, an experience in which the enormous power of kundalini was burning inside him, but he was "not consumed."

Consider what might have happened if Moses, the great, revered leader of thousands of Jews, had returned from Mount Sinai and said, "I have just had the most incredible kundalini experience." Rather than looking upon him as a great spiritual leader, they may have looked upon him as a lunatic. So he found a way of telling the story that would make sense. That's what Jesus did, also. He taught in stories, in parables.

How many people do you know who may have had equally legitimate, profound spiritual experiences that sound as ridiculous to us as it would have sounded to the Jews if Moses had said he'd just had a fiery rush of energy through his body and heard an inner voice through it all? At that point in human spiritual history, it was more believable to the dejected, fleeing tribe that Moses had heard the voice of God from a miraculous source. Moses was able to re-frame his experience in a way that was understandable and empowering to the Jews. Many "normal" people are also having such experiences but don't have the ability to convey them in such a skillful way. We may call them crazy, when in fact they've had profound experiences that they cannot describe coherently or approximately in ways that make any sense to us.

I am not promoting this story of Moses in any way. Maybe it's correct and maybe not. But notice how it may have changed your view of the history of the Bible. Maybe your thinking shifted slightly away from the worldly image of a "burning bush," and toward the mystical idea of a powerful lightning force that shot up the spine of Moses and gave him an experience of "samadhi." Consider this idea for a moment and see how this idea may influence your concept of Moses and the Bible, and other cultural attitudes toward unusual experiences.

Most of us have ideas about religion that are sealed in cement, locked into a dogma. We act as if we really know Moses, or Jesus, or the Bible. Likewise, when we look at the spiritual experiences of others, we peg them as if we really know what they are. But we don't consider how vast each and every person's experience may be, which is why it is so essential that we expand our view. Even the "average" person doing his laundry or the dishes can have an experience like Moses.

We all have life-force energy within us and we all have access to higher states of consciousness. Chinese call this energy "chi," the Hindu "prana." It is "yesod" in the Kabbalah; "baraka" to the Sufis, "orenda" to the Iroquois; and "megbe" to the African Ituri. We can all come to understand and manage our energy better. The ability of a woman with terminal cancer to live far beyond her "expected life-span" in order to see her "daughter's wedding day" is one example of a conscious control over life-force energy. In the experience I had, the life-force energy was dramatically focused and released in a powerful and new direction.

The range of experience in life is infinite, as is the range of mystical or spiritual experience. I do not want to imply that having intense rushes of energy is anything to strive for. If I could strive for anything, I would pray to be able to love more people, be more forgiving, and be of more service. I am not trying to have any special kind of experience. But my awareness of this potential of spiritual energy makes it possible for me to help my patients find and move along on their own personal journey.

Before I tell you how I bring this understanding of spiritual energy and its human potential into my practice of spiritual psychiatry, let me tell you a bit more about myself, so you have a better idea of your guide through some of the strange territories we're going to enter.

Psychic Beginnings

A spiritual view of life and psychiatry was not part of my training, although the way I practice psychiatry and the lessons I try to impart to my patients come from my medical and psychiatric training as well as from personal experience. My transformation from "normal doctor" to "spiritual psychiatrist" was gradual and was helped along by personal pre-cognitive and extra-sensory experiences, several extraordinary teachers, a bout with a severe case of chronic fatigue syndrome/myalgic encephalopathy (CFS/ME), and lessons my patients taught me.

I began on my fast track to medicine at the age of four, and later charged through high school and college, not enjoying life much except for sports. In high school, I was a real supporter of good old Denver East High's great basketball and track teams, and a big fan of the University of Colorado football team, the Buffaloes, for whom I spent many days with snow falling onto my already shivering bones in the hope of seeing a long bomb caught or the half-back running 85 yards for a touchdown.

I was raised a Jewish atheist. At synagogue I was one of two atheists and I argued the case vehemently. I had no respect whatsoever for what was going on. My friend David and I used to sneak out of synagogue between classes and the Saturday morning service. We'd go to the local drugstore and read Playboy Magazine. Sometimes we'd return to synagogue during the service and hide somewhere in the back where it was dark and play cards. We were smart, very careful, and never got caught. I was not interested in God.

It is amazing to me to look back at the rebellious Jewish child at Temple Emanuel and to realize how important God has become to me. It has been a strange and slow process of opening up to spirituality. I started to come out of my shell of disbelief during college as I began to have intuitive perceptions and psychic experiences that showed me there was something greater than myself. I began to know that there were ways of communicating that went beyond space and time. By the time I had become a young psychiatrist, these intuitive or psychic events were simply "the way the world was." There was nothing terribly unusual about these garden-variety experiences that well over 50% of Americans have. I still didn't believe in God or a Higher Power, but I was coming to believe that the mind is not limited to the complex physical organ called the brain.

Medical school was the same nightmare for me that it is for many doctors. I forced my brain to remember more facts than any poor brain should ever have to. I became a mere piece of furniture in my home, affixed to my comfortable blue chair, day and night, only to rise at the end of a school quarter to walk in the park for a day before the whole misery started again. Medical school was like living in and under a dark black cloud, a level of emotional coldness I had never experienced.

My class literally had a 6% mortality rate. Six of the 100 medical students I started with were dead by the time I finished: suicides, freak accidents, cancers, and drownings. As far as I was concerned, medical school was not a very healthy place to learn to be a doctor. It was a place where the human spirit was systematically trampled and destroyed. That any doctor produced by this system recovers his love, humanity, and ability to touch the heart of a patient is a miracle.

After two years I quit. I just couldn't take it anymore and turned professional photographer, but realized after six months that it was not the life for me, and re-applied to med school. Getting into med school had been a piece of cake. Getting back in was a nightmare. I had started psychoanalysis my second year of med school so I could begin uncovering and chasing away some of my demons of unhappiness and disillusionment. When I re-applied, the medical school dean told me that "psychoanalysis was not compatible with being a medical student!" I didn't know what to do and would not quit analysis to please the dean. My mother came through with a brilliant insight for me. "They want to hear that medicine is the only thing in your life that matters, that you're only in analysis to make you a better doctor. Tell them that you will quit analysis in an instant if it begins to interfere with your training." I repeated her words almost verbatim and was re-admitted to school the next day. But what was the message the medical school was giving me? "Understanding yourself, exploring your feelings, coping with your inner demons is not important."

Yet medical school did not knock me out of being a little bit psychic. Even as a small child I had extrasensory perceptions. When riding in the family car, I would often hear the next song to be played on the radio, a few seconds before it was actually played. I just assumed there was some kind of technical error with the radio or radio station that produced this phenomenon. I had no mental framework that allowed me even to guess that I was experiencing something beyond what my five senses could perceive.

The most intense example of altered perceptions during my childhood took place when I was three or four during a family car trip from Denver to the Southwest, to Mesa Verde and the Grand Canyon. I knew things that no four-year-old had any business knowing. I knew the names of the composers of music on the radio. "This piece is by Tchaikovsky, this one's by Corelli." My father at one point was discussing lung physiology and he mentioned the word, "vital capacity." My mother said, "What's that?" I said to her, "He just explained it." My father replied, "No, I did not explain it." I then proceeded to discuss how the term referred to the amount of air one has in the lungs, what one's breathing capacity was.

On and on it went during that two-week period. We were walking through the Painted Desert when I picked up an odd-shaped stone and proudly said to my father, "Look, Dad. This is a fossil clam." He looked at it, tossed the stone as far as he could and said, "No, it's just a rock." Later that day we went to a museum at the edge of the Painted Desert, and there was a collection of fossil clams that had been found nearby. My father, rather distraught, went back to the place where I had found it. He searched and searched with no luck. Thirty-five years later my father said, "Do you remember that fossil clam? I bought you one to replace it."

One day after I had become a psychiatrist, I woke up in a state of absolute panic. I knew deep down in my soul that it was going to be a tragic day. I went to work that day at the Veterans Administration Hospital and shared my fear with one of the nurses, telling her, "Something terrible is going to happen today. I think someone high up in government is going to be shot." I wanted to "go on record." That day President Reagan was shot. I don't report this as some kind of new discovery or some earth-shattering insight into the nature of reality. This is the kind of event in which the vast majority of Americans already believe. I was finally catching up!

In my twenties I began to look back at those early childhood experiences and realized that something had been unusual about them. Like millions of other people I had seen and heard things without using my eyes or ears. These odd and inexplicable experiences began to pique my curiosity, began to help me look at the world a little differently, and to re-define what "reality" is. I do not consider these experiences important in the overall context of my life—and there are certainly thousands or millions of people who have these abilities developed far more than I, but I mention them to help explain how and why I began to look at life and ultimately psychiatry in a new light.

A Spiritual Teacher Remakes a Psychiatrist

I did my psychiatry residency in San Diego, where I now live. I had been working at the La Jolla V.A. Hospital for only two weeks when one of the nurses with whom I was working handed me a photograph of an Indian holy man. She simply said, "I know you need to know about this man. His name is Sai Baba." A week later my chief resident in psychiatry told me about a psychiatrist in San Diego, a Doctor Samuel Sandweiss, who incorporated spirituality into his practice and who was also a follower of Sai Baba. And shortly after that the ward chief also told me about Sai Baba, and about Sandweiss!

Although I was certainly developing an interest in spirituality, I did not have the time or energy to look into it during my first year of psychiatric training. I had my hands full learning how to diagnose and treat severe mental illness; learning how to tell if someone was really going to kill themselves if they said they were suicidal; learning to treat extremely violent patients; learning how to sit and talk with schizophrenic people who thought they were John the Baptist and had been standing in the middle of the street before they were hospitalized, letting everyone know it. Emergency psychiatry included learning what to do when a veteran walked into a V.A. hospital emergency room to talk to the psychiatrist—me—and opened his briefcase, which contained a loaded revolver.

It was truly fascinating work, challenging, difficult, scary, and fun. Yes, it was fun. Although medical school had not been fun, when I arrived in San Diego to do my psychiatric residency, I felt I had finally come home, that I was finally studying to be what I had wanted to be for so long. A decade before I would begin psychiatric training, I thought it to be a truly noble profession, one in which a medical doctor could probe the depths of the mind and the brain to relieve human suffering. I am not happy that my field has become one in which the prescribing of medication is most of the "job" and the quest for healing the mind and recovering the soul has been discarded or relegated to "counselors" of various sorts.

I even felt at home working in the psychiatric ward of the Veterans Administration Hospital, where it was sometimes dangerous, noisy, and frightening. But by the end of that first year, I was ready to jump into something entirely different, something that was not part of the regular psychiatric curriculum.

Without really knowing what I was getting into, in the second year of my psychiatric residency I called up Doctor Samuel Sandweiss and asked him to supervise me, to teach me about psychiatry and spirituality. My budding interest in spirituality was really quite cerebral. I knew that there was something more to life, something beyond what you can see and touch, but I didn't have any real experience other than those past moments of intuition. My meetings with Dr. Sandweiss changed all that. We spoke about God as a living presence that applied to everyday life, as a divine presence that was part of every person, a presence that was with us and around us. We talked about miracles, the power of love and faith, and the role of spirituality in psychiatry. We talked about consciousness and kundalini. And we talked about Sai Baba.[1]

Three years later, I was in India meeting with Sathya Sai Baba, who has become a great teacher and resource for me. Through his teachings I came to know how important it is to help my patients on all levels—mentally, physically and spiritually. Through his teachings, I came to know the importance of love and service to others.

Sai Baba slowly taught me how to bring spiritual principles into everyday life. He taught me to try to see everything and everyone as a spark of divinity, that the highest good, the greatest peace is to be attained through serving our fellow men and fellow women and fellow living creatures on this wonderful, singular planet. I learned practical principles that helped bring happiness, and the feeling was contagious. Experiencing a deeper sense of peace and love spread to the people around me. While Sai Baba passed away in 2011, he remains in my heart, and his teachings guide me.

Although I have a spiritual teacher, I rarely guide people in his direction. How do I safeguard against such a "prejudice"? Sai Baba has said in his writings, "Who are you to publicize me? I have no need of publicity." I try to put into action his teachings without invoking the teacher. One of his teachings is pertinent here: "There is only one language, the language of the heart; there is only one religion, the religion of love; there is only one race, the race of humanity; there is only one God and He is omnipresent." I am concerned with trying to live the message: to be loving; to treat all races, all religions, all people with love, respect and equality; to open my heart so I can respond to the suffering of others; to try to limit my ego and personal needs and allow my higher qualities to shine through; to value service and personal sacrifice; to face my inner demons, hold on to the vision, be persistent, reach the goal; to respect awe, mystery and uncertainty; to learn to experience the moment more fully.

The core of the spiritual teaching I have learned is to help people deepen their own convictions and their own faith in what they already believe in. With my Muslim patients, we speak about Allah; with Christians I am very happy to talk about Jesus. One of my patients brings in his Bible, picks out a passage or two, reads it, and then tries to apply the principle in his life in a practical way. Believing in Jesus is quite a stretch for someone raised as an atheistic Jew, yet through the guidance of my spiritual teacher, I have come to love Jesus. Not only Jesus, but also the teachings and teachers of all religions.

Illness:
A Doctor Learns Compassion the Hard Way

The third major twist of fate that shaped my thinking and my practice of psychiatry came out of my own struggles with chronic fatigue syndrome (CFS). CFS is called ME (myalgic encephalopathy) in the U.K. and Australia, and many pioneers now refer to it as CFS/ME.

In October 1984, I got pneumonia. I'd never had that before and it really knocked me out. I went to the doctor, who listened to my lungs, took my temperature, and made the diagnosis. I took antibiotics for ten days and the pneumonia cleared up. But after the pneumonia departed, I was not the same old "me." I was exhausted. I could hardly get out of bed. By the time I had made breakfast, showered, and reached my car, I was already wiped out.

Those of you with CFS/ME or any other serious chronic illness will instantly relate to my story. To the rest of you, I ask you to remember what it's like having a severe case of the flu. Now imagine that it never goes away. That's CFS/ME. By the way, exhaustion and feeling tired are entirely different. When you have severe exhaustion, often you can't sleep. You're just too exhausted to sleep. I used to pray to feel just plain-old tired.

It is impossible to convey the agony of that year. Being a psychotherapist is not easy when you are drained to the bone. By Friday every week, I was so exhausted that I could hardly move. Sometimes, I would be on the verge of convulsions. Every muscle in my body would start contracting randomly, as if the normal modulation that the brain provides over such functions were completely gone. I would start to see halos of light around things and around lights. I couldn't even walk straight. CFS/ME was like living in quicksand. No matter in which direction I turned, no matter where I looked for help, I sank.

During 1985 I avoided any socializing whatsoever. I could not predict a day in advance if I would be able to function the next day. On a rare occasion I'd go out for dinner. One time a friend of mine said to me, "You know, there is no life left in your eyes anymore. Your eyes look really dead." I didn't need her to tell me that. I knew it. I felt it. I lived it. The exhaustion took a toll on my body and my mind. I couldn't think straight, couldn't concentrate. My memory was a fraction of what it had been. My IQ dropped by 30 or 40 points. I felt like I was "losing it" physically and mentally.

I will not bore you with the details of what I did to recover over a ten-year period. My journeys to medical doctors, homeopaths, nutritionists, Chinese acupuncturists, Indian ayurvedic doctors, and Mexican faith healers would fill a book. But I am including this sketch of my bout with chronic fatigue syndrome to show how it deepened my faith, helped shape the way I incorporate spirituality into my life and my work, and helped me to help others in sorting out their miracles and their madness.

CFS/ME gave me a real crash course in being a patient and being a doctor. It has taught me more than any university could have. I have much greater compassion and empathy for people with chronic illness. As a human being I have changed enormously as a direct result of my illness, and lost the moodiness I used to have. My illness leveled out my moods completely. I am much happier and more alive than ever. CFS/ME has helped me open my heart. It's helped me love and accept myself more and to love and accept others.

CFS/ME taught me about surrender. When animals get sick, they have excellent instincts about what to do to recover. A bat with a broken wing will stay put and not try to fly for weeks until the wing is mended. Humans tend to go right on pushing and pushing, abusing ourselves in the face of illness. But finally I began to learn about surrender. I could just lie there, sometimes in real agony, and say, "Dear Lord, I don't know what I'm supposed to be learning, but help me surrender to whatever I am supposed to learn. Help me realize that everything is a gift from you, whether it brings me joy or pain. Help me stop resisting. Help me stop fighting this thing the way I do." Now this idea may sound pretty weird and cowardly: "Stop Fighting." It doesn't mean giving up hope. It means learning to feel what you feel without trying to push it out of your consciousness. It means learning to let feelings, thoughts, and pains just enter your consciousness, arising and dissolving. Sometimes, this is also the best advice in the face of unfamiliar or uncomfortable spiritual experiences, too.

Surrendering means "allowing yourself to fully experience your current condition." Surrender is profound acceptance. It's the ability to embrace the good and bad in life, and accept before moving quickly into action mode. Before we can change, we must learn to experience where we are right now. Sometimes we need to give up struggling and be like that bat with the broken wing. We need to just let it mend, in its own time. In the process of surrendering, we learn great lessons in patience. Illness, like enlightenment, mystical callings, or strange visions, can be terrifying, upsetting, and painful. But they also can be a real gift, if we open our hearts to the full experience, pain and all.

Some might consider my illness a spiritual failure. If I have such faith and belief, why can't I heal myself? Spirituality is a source of faith, hope, and comfort. It is a clinical and technical error for any healer or therapist to tell a patient, "They're sick because they're not praying hard enough, or they're not doing their imagery techniques correctly, or sticking to their diet 100%." That attitude constitutes medical malpractice in my opinion.

Illness helped me reach out to God and say, "Help me make it through another day." Spirituality helped allow me to see meaning, purpose, and lessons in illness. And spirituality gave me the strength to keep going.

Spirituality helped me feel as if my divine friend were always by my side, holding my hand, picking me up when I fell, inspiring me to smile while in the grip of the lion's jaws. I never felt alone through this illness. Perhaps most importantly, I learned that healing is not just what happens to the body. It's also what happens to the heart. While I had full-blown CFS/ME for ten years, my healing journey eventually took me far beyond the illness. It was exhilarating when the day came in the early 1990s when I was strong enough to risk going for my first jog in 10 years, and after running that first mile, I knew I had come a very long way.

Thus, the transformation of my life and my professional outlook took hold. From extra-sensory perceptions, from extraordinary teachers, and from CFS/ME I learned that love, faith, hope, spirituality, God, joy, surrender, forgiveness, compassion, and self-acceptance were essential tools of a healer. All of these experiences, the pain of chronic fatigue syndrome, and the psychic experiences were part of my preparation to write this book.

I write this brief history of my health out of awe and gratitude, to encourage you to keep going, to keep searching, to keep hoping, never to give up unless you choose to give up. I write to encourage you to dig deep inside yourself and look for and find reserves of strength and courage that you never dreamt could exist in you. They are there, waiting to be tapped.

Don't ever let anybody take away your hope or tell you that "nothing more can be done." There is no illness from which somebody has not recovered. Even AIDS survivors are not news. A lot of us have known about them for years. They survived the same way I did: by experimenting, by changing their life style, by doing mental imagery and meditation, by diet, vitamins, herbs, prayer, hope, and by miracles.

A word of caution: You must be your own doctor to some extent. If you expect your doctor to have all the perfect answers, you are not taking enough responsibility. Do your own research. Libraries and the Internet are not out-of-bounds for patients. Search the medical literature. Doctors are forced to know more and more technologically. In addition they are overwhelmed with ever-increasing piles of paperwork, and ever-more complicated bureaucracies, HMOs, PPOs, rising overhead costs, and the ever-present threat of lawsuits.

This book is not about us against them. It's about us and them. Help out your doctor. Help educate him or her. Help educate yourself and try to have some compassion for why he or she may lack compassion. Remember your doctor is human, and don't expect him to be perfect. We have come to expect and to demand so much from our doctors. We demand to be fixed, and fixed quickly. The "quick fix" is the American way of doing things, but most Westerners do not yet comprehend that most illness cannot be fixed.

Western medicine can be proudest of its ability to treat bacterial infections, to treat trauma, and to use extraordinary surgical techniques. That's treatment of acute illness. But Western medicine does not yet have a single cure for any chronic illness: heart disease, kidney disease, brain disease, etc. And most doctors have no idea how to deal with spiritual emergencies and other psycho-spiritual symptoms that do not respond to quick fixes.

That is one of the great lessons I learned from CFS/ME: how to cope with chronic illness, how to go beyond the notion that everything can be instantly fixed. Look for the lessons in your own suffering. Look for the hope that is there, and embrace your sense of spirituality. CFS/ME provided me another amazing gift. In order to heal myself, I became a specialist in amino acid therapy, and later developed a much broader comprehensive approach to all chronic illness. I forged my own way of being a holistic physician, and, in the process, have saved many lives and alleviated the suffering of many.

Through illness, God was teaching me to surrender, and was preparing me to serve.

---

1. Samuel Sandweiss, M.D., *Sai Baba: The Holy Man and the Psychiatrist* (San Diego: Birth Day Publishing, 1975).

Chapter 2

Twenty-Five Spiritual Questions
Psychiatrists Are Afraid to Ask

Comedian Lily Tomlin has asked, "Why is it we're said to be praying when we talk to God, but we're called schizophrenic when He talks back to us?" Many of my seemingly ordinary patients of whom I ask questions about their spiritual experiences give me extraordinary responses. A 60-year-old man who was hospitalized for treatment of alcoholism began to cry in telling his story: "When I was 13, I was riding my bike one day when something amazing happened. I came around a corner and suddenly right in front of me was the Father and the Son. I've never mentioned this to anybody in my whole life, not my wife, not my minister." I said to him, "By the Father and the Son you mean God the Father and Jesus?" He said, "Yes, that's who I saw. I know it sounds really crazy and that's why I never told anybody, ever." What a relief he felt after 47 years to finally be able to share his most extraordinary experience in life. And by sharing his experience, his recovery from alcoholism was accelerated.

Was it really the Father and the Son? I didn't feel qualified to say, "Yes, or No." It was his experience and I respected that. He felt heard and understood by me and cried tears of joy and relief that he had held inside for 47 years. I don't believe that God only comes every few thousand years, parts the Red Sea or heals the blind—and the rest of us are left out. God is for ordinary people, and He is here, all the time. As a psychiatrist I evaluate every patient in terms of traditional psychiatric diagnosis, which I did with my alcoholic patient who had met Jesus. There was no evidence whatsoever that at the time of his vision he was psychotic, delirious, or physically or mentally ill. If that were the case, it would have been a lot more difficult for me to diagnose the vision accurately. My patient's vision had a spiritual message for him, however, that he needed to explore, not suppress or try to forget.

Spirituality is a complex concept with many definitions. As widely used as the word is, it is surprising how difficult it is to find an adequate definition. It is much easier to define "spiritual quest," "spiritual qualities," or "spiritual practices." For some, spirituality is the pursuit of a moral life. To others, believing in angels may be spirituality; for still others, it is their relationship with God. I have found no dictionary definition that I find worth sharing with the reader, so I will provide the broadest, most inclusive and understandable definition of spirituality that I can. It is important for you to have a conscious understanding of your own spiritual beliefs. Your basic view of the world as benevolent or threatening and your own place in the world are key to self-understanding.

Spirituality is the heart of religion, much as the soul is the spiritual heart of the human body. Spirituality is "sacred awareness." It is the awareness of sacred ways of being, of our relationship to something sacred, something greater than ourselves. It is the awareness of sacred forms of action. Spirituality refers to our relationship to God or a Higher Power, or our belief in something larger than ourselves. One might logically ask, "If spirituality is sacred awareness, why are there people who are aware of the sacred in life but don't act in a kind or sacred way?" If one has ultimate sacred awareness, he knows that all of life is one. Everything, everyone is interconnected. As a result of that deep knowing, one's actions will automatically become pure and sacred. Partial awareness leads to partial results, part-time spirituality, and part-time morality.

One of the most important aspects of "sacred awareness" is understanding the relationship between oneself and one's chosen form of God. To quote producer and composer Richard Del Maestro, "Spirituality is the relationship between the devotee and God. It is the relationship between himself and his higher Self. Just as in physics the observer becomes part of the equation, in spirituality the observer becomes part of the equation. If the person is a Buddhist and God is not the central theme in his spiritual life, then spirituality is about one's relationship to moral values and to society at large. On the other hand, if the person is a Christian, Muslim, Jew, or Hindu, spirituality is defined by the relationship with one's chosen form of God. The more you focus on God or on human values the more spiritual you become."[1]

Spiritual practices, such as prayer, meditation, fasting, charity, service are all intended to foster spiritual qualities such as love, service, sacrifice, detachment, honest speech, simple living, a sense of unity with all of life, the sense of sacredness in everyday life, and a deep, reverent connection with Nature and Mother Earth. The practice of spiritual psychiatry can do the same thing. Peace of mind through the ups and downs of life is a major goal of spiritual practice and psychiatry or other modes of self-inquiry, as is joy and happiness. The thread that unites these different terms is "love." Love is the goal of spiritual practice. Love is also the means of reaching that goal, for love is the way and the goal.

Spirituality, or sacred awareness, helps us address life's most profound questions: "How do I fit into this universe? Who am I? Where did I come from? What is my real purpose here? Is there a purpose? Where do I go when I die? Can I do anything here to make my after-death experience (if there is one) better?" Spirituality helps us understand why "bad things happen to good people" and "why good things happen to bad people" and what "good and what evil are." Spirituality is awareness of God or something greater than ourselves. For the sake of custom, I will refer to God as "He" as opposed to He/She. By "God" I mean the "God" and the "Goddess," the Male and the Female, the Yin and the Yang, the Absolute. I look at God as a force, a presence that is not separate from us, not far away, and the universe as the body of God or a manifestation of God. Spirituality asks higher questions. These are just a few of the questions that psychiatrists are afraid to ask.

Spiritual "qualities," such as faith and belief in a purpose, give us the courage to persevere in a world that we really don't understand. They give us the hope that some Higher Being is taking care of business, because, as human beings, most of us truly do not know what we are doing. Doctors tend to believe that truth can be measured, stored in a bottle, and replicated in controlled, double-blind studies. But the truth that Western civilization clings to is temporary, for each technological advance displaces the old truth or modifies it. Thus we cling to ever-changing explanations of reality. Spirituality deals with that which is unchanging, eternal, and true. It helps us learn to seek unity rather than distinctions, to realize that the spark of life, and of God, is contained within each living creature.

Because the word "spirituality" seems so obvious, yet is so difficult to define, I want to summarize what you've just read.

Spirituality is sacred awareness. Spiritual practices are intended to help us develop spiritual qualities so that we may lead a more sacred or spiritual life. One's sacred awareness increases or expands with conscious practice. Sacred action arises out of sacred awareness and out of spiritual practice.

In a book about spirituality it is important to clarify the difference between spirituality and religion. Religion consists of rites, rituals, and structures, such as churches and synagogues. Religion is like a container. Spirituality is the "juice" that the container of religion should be filled with. That spiritual juice is a blend of our thoughts and feelings about God, our personal quest to understand life's key questions, namely: "Where did I come from?" "Does life have meaning or purpose, and if so, what is it?" and "What happens to me after death?" Spirituality is sacred awareness, and that awareness leads to a quest, a hunger to discover the answer to these questions. More than just questions and answers, spirituality includes our experience of and with the Divine, and our ability to merge with Nature, to feel one with God, Nature, and all living things. Most of all, spirituality teaches us how to love. Spirituality includes experience, and it is the "juice" that may or may not fill the container called "religion." Spirituality does not need a container. It is free to flow in, around, and through you. When the container of religion is filled with the juice of spirituality, you have a marriage made in heaven. But because so many churches and synagogues are empty containers, people have been leaving their religions in huge numbers, often turning to Eastern spiritual philosophy in order to obtain the sustenance their souls require.

Many years ago I heard psychologist Ram Dass talk about how we approach relationships. We see others as "potentials" (i.e., opposite sex; attractive; or potential business opportunity), "not-potentials" (not attracted to the person), "competitors" and "irrelevants" (people who are too old or too young for us to be interested in). We tend to categorize everyone we meet in this way and that means that there are a lot of people to whom most of us pay no attention whatsoever because we don't "need" them.

Spirituality, sacred awareness, helps us see that the most lasting thing, the only lasting thing about any of us is the soul—that spark of divinity that has been present in all of us from birth. Even though our bodies, minds, and personalities undergo tremendous transformation, the soul remains unchanged, for it is that part of us that is directly connected to God.

In the West we tend to believe that God is distant, above us, up in heaven. We pray by looking up to God. In the East, the belief is that God is everywhere—outside us, inside us and around us. He is the very center of our own being. Eastern religious traditions ask us to look within for God. Many Christian mystics throughout the ages also have used the approach of finding God within. Thomas Merton, a well-known Trappist monk and teacher, sought out the truth of spiritual mysteries through the practices of solitude, meditation, prayer, and silence. In fact, this form of Christian mysticism is not at all unlike Eastern mysticism. If one believes that God is present everywhere and in everyone, including within oneself, it becomes natural to "look" for God within—by visualizing your personal form of God, by repeating or chanting your personal name of God, by trying to visualize that form of God within yourself and within others. Whether one sees God through the eyes of Eastern or Western teaching is not important. However, spiritual qualities, such as love, truth, peace, non-violence, faith, hope, moral conduct, truthful speech, and devotion—which arise from spiritual practice—are important.

Most of us are comfortable with the normal trappings of religion. But as we begin to try to understand God and life's deeper meaning, we can wind up exploring phenomena that some consider pretty strange. Spirituality can be associated with strange, esoteric practices, such as trances, channeling, healing with crystals, psychic phenomena, stigmata, faith healing, working with pyramids, speaking in tongues, and shamanic journeys.

Spirituality is not only awareness of God, or the Absolute; it's also awareness of human values. His Holiness, the Dalai Lama, the leader of Tibetan Buddhism, never talks about God, but only about human values and human character. Spirituality makes you aware that your actions count, every one of them. Even rationalists believe their actions count, but there is a difference between spiritually-motivated action and rationally-motivated action. Reason may tell us that good actions are in our own best interest. Spiritually-motivated actions arise out of a desire for a pure heart. Action creates character, and character guides our actions. Our actions help form our character and through our character we can each add something positive to the world. Positive actions build character. Negative actions destroy character.

I do not have any absolute answers about God or spirituality. I am writing from my own experiences and background, my personal spiritual experience, and from the writings of the world's great spiritual teachers. I hope that this bringing together of idea and experience will help you see the many routes to spiritual awareness, the many paths of spiritual practice, to an understanding of the many ways of experiencing God.

A psychiatrist's job is to help patients identify their spirituality, their source of hope and faith and then help them use that higher source to heal themselves physically and mentally. My purpose is not to judge an individual's beliefs as good or bad, correct or incorrect. Each patient and each reader needs to find the light that leads him or her out of the tunnel, whatever he or she calls that light and whatever form it takes.

Though I firmly believe in God, I cannot begin to say how or why He sheds His Grace. I believe that happens and that His Grace can override anything—any illness, any problem. I believe that it is a power that I simply cannot ignore as a psychiatrist. As a doctor, I want to help my patients find everything that will alleviate their suffering and in my practice, faith has proven to be a powerful and essential part of healing, as well as a way to cope with pain and suffering.

Is there a "correct" God or a "correct way" to approach God? Perhaps a theologian might say there is, but for a psychiatrist trying to bring hope and inspiration into clinical practice, there is no room for notions of correct and incorrect. Each religion has a different name for God and some religions have many Gods. Pantheism has existed in many forms from the ancient Greeks up to the present time. For some religions everything is God. For Native

Americans all of nature is an embodiment of God—the trees, the sky, the rivers, the animals, the thunder, and the rain. Native Americans, from Cree to Cherokee, believe that even hunting is a sacred activity and they offer a prayer to the animal to be killed, a prayer acknowledging the spirit of the animal.

In many ways the Hindu philosophy is similar to most Native American religions. God is felt to be everywhere, in everything. Although there is one very heavy-duty singular God, named Brahman, there are thousands of other Gods and Goddesses of rain, prosperity, wealth, health, etc. This can be a very confusing notion for a Westerner to whom it may seem that the Indians are worshipping stones and trees. They are actually worshipping the God or divine principle that they believe exists even in the stone and the tree.

Buddhism does not rely on the notion of God, but rather teaches mindfulness and non-attachment, living in the now. Spirituality for the Buddhist is sacred awareness of each moment, sacred awareness that all suffering on earth must be alleviated, for if one person suffers, all people suffer.

Psychiatry in the light of spirituality is about God, faith hope, truth, right action, and miracles. It's not about what feels good at the moment, or how one can milk the most from the system. It's about love. It's about the therapeutic role of service. It's about how one can lead the most meaningful, happy life, whether one is rich or poor, sick or healthy. It is about learning to share, to love, to care—to take a real interest in the people and the world around you. It's about learning "giveness" and forgiveness.

Spiritual practice teaches a kind of love that asks us to respond to another person's pain and reach out in any way we can. It teaches us to rejoice at others' good fortune—whether we are the beneficiaries of good fortune or not. This is also the aim of spiritual psychiatry. Any practice of awareness and kindness is, in effect, spiritual psychiatry.

The essential message of the sacred Hindu texts, the Vedas, has been summed up as "Speak the truth and act righteously, or with moral conduct." Telling the truth is essential to psychological and spiritual growth. And it's far easier to tell the truth than lie and then have to "cover one's tracks." But how often do we try to get away with a "little lie"? And how many of us cheat on our husband or wife? Cheating is a lack of the sacred awareness of the power of truth. It is almost impossible to make progress if one is lying. My job is to help people feel safe enough to look at their own pain, to dive into their own pain, to embrace their pain, to swim through it, and to get to the other side. But when people lie, they completely short-circuit the process. The lie hides the pain and makes it impossible to bring one's life into harmony.

The entirety of the ancient Indian sacred texts, the Vedas, can be summed up in one phrase—"Sathyam vada dharmam chara," which means, "Seek to know the truth and the Truth. Speak the truth. After you know the truth, practice dharma, or powerful right action." Once you know the truth (sathya or satya) and the dharma of a situation, all that is left is courage. All of us can discover our personal truth and dharma fairly easily. In fact, as soon as you come to grips with the truth of a situation, right action becomes obvious. You are then left to decide whether or not you will take right action. It often takes courage, but the more you flex the muscles of taking dharmic action, the easier it gets. In the process, you become a much more powerful and centered person, a more peaceful and loving person. I have offered this simple life equation to many of my patients over the years, and much of the time I have skipped the Sanskrit and just explained things in English. People find the simplicity amazing and empowering, and they find that they can make changes in their life very quickly, when previously they had been paralyzed by indecision. I once evaluated a woman who had been kicked in the jaw by a horse. The trauma unleashed mental pain, physical pain, and brought up memories of trauma. At the end of the first session, she asked, "So, Doc, what are my chances?" I replied, "How much do you want to know the truth. Truth with a small "t" and truth with a big "T?" Her response was immediate: "I want to know the truth no matter what." I told her, "Then you will do very well. I don't know the time-table, but you will do well." It did take years of counseling followed by years of just living, but she did heal at a profound level —mentally, physically, and spiritually.

In my struggle and search to define spirituality, I read numerous books, spoke with experts on the subject, and also asked one of my patients, Amanda, who shares these insights with me: "Spirituality is letting go of everything you thought was true, so that the Truth may embrace you. It is the practice of becoming unhitched from illusions and fleeting distractions, and awakening to eternal Truth, breathing through life, enlivened and supported by boundless love. Spirituality is arriving at the realization that salvation, satori, mercy, samadhi, enlightenment, and the omnipotent and benevolent beingness that suffuses this moment, this universe and beyond, lies nowhere outside of, but within all animate and seemingly inanimate manifestations. And spirituality is a rising up of empathy, compassion, selflessness, equanimity, and unconditional love, and acquiring a stance of being here, now, and always. Spirituality is bringing daily life into concert with the cosmos." Amanda shares the view of Buddhist nun and writer, Pema Chödrön, in *The Wisdom of No Escape*, that "spirituality is coming into profound knowing by releasing what you 'think' you know."[2] Amanda's idea of spirituality is shaped by her Buddhist practice, her love and practice of Navajo teachings, and her Indian spiritual teacher. I find her definition as compelling as any I've run across. I believe that the thread that runs through her definition is "awareness."

Spirituality, sacred awareness, includes "sacred vision," the desire or ability to have faith in that which cannot be seen or measured, to "see" with one's inner eye, with one's intuition. That is one reason modern medicine and modern science don't have too much respect for spirituality, why psychiatrists are afraid to ask these questions, and why it's hard to get an honest diagnosis that includes your body, mind, and spirit. Science cannot say anything about love, or about God. Yet so much of the world believes in God or a Higher Power. And what about love? Who in the world denies the existence of love? Yet, love is entirely invisible. Oh, there are certain physiological signs, measurable phenomena that go along with love. We know that when people watch a film of Mother Theresa administering to sick people with her extraordinary love, their immune functions are enhanced. But that is not love. That's a by-product of love.

In looking back over my career and my training, it is absolutely astounding that love was never seriously mentioned by my professors or in the textbooks. How to cultivate love was never discussed. It was important as a psychiatrist to take a good "sexual" history, or a history about our patient's work-life, but not a "spiritual" history. Taking a spiritual history can get you labeled "weird" in a hurry, so psychiatrists are naturally a little timid about asking some very important questions.

Modern psychiatry has become so Cartesian in its outlook, now that we are developing a body of technical knowledge, some of us are calling our work a "hard" science. But many of us are focusing so exclusively on the brain that we're starting to ignore feelings! A psychiatrist friend of mine recently attended a psychiatric meeting that focused on psychopharmacology. The word "feeling" never came up once during the entire conference. Psychiatry has tried to wear the mask of science at a great price.

As a psychiatrist, I try to be open to all the possibilities, open to psychiatry as art and science. In psychiatry, you tend to get information for which you are looking or for which you have formulated questions. If you think you need to find out about a patient's work history or sex-life, you'll find out. If you're a Jungian, your patients will start to have Jungian dreams. If you're a Freudian, your patients will start having Freudian dreams. Likewise, a spiritual history will always elicit specific spiritual information.

My belief in the usefulness of integrating God, spirituality, and psychiatry has led me to stop beating around the burning bush. I confront issues about God as directly as I deal with anything else in my practice. Here are some of the questions that I may ask when taking a spiritual history:

25 Spiritual Questions Psychiatrists Are Afraid to Ask

1. In what religion were you raised?
2. What religion are you now?
3. What do you believe in? Is there a God?
4. What's God's job description?
5. Is God an important part of your life?
6. Is He nearby or far away?
7. Do you feel there is a purpose to your life?

8.   Is there life after death? What is it?
9.   Do you pray or meditate? If so, how often?
10. What do you call God?
11. Have you had any experiences in life that you couldn't explain? Have you ever known things that you simply had no way of knowing?
12. Do you go to church, synagogue, or some other organized religion? If so, how often do you attend?
13. Is God a man or a woman? Or both? Or neither?
14. Are there saints or other holy figures who have special meaning to you?
15. Are you and God on good terms?
16. Does He or She scare you? How do you feel about God?
17. Do you deserve God's love?
18. Is God critical, watching every move you make, looking for mistakes?
19. Do you have a sense of purpose or meaning?
20. Have you ever had a mystical or spiritual experience?
21. If so, how has that experience changed your life? (Did it change your life?)
22. Do you believe there is a heaven or a hell? If so, where do you believe you'll be going?
23. Do you have any particular spiritual practices?
24. If you met God, what would you ask for?
25. Do you believe in miracles? If so, do you deserve a miracle?

These questions are both spiritual and religious, for religion is the structure within which spirituality may flow. Religion is the rites, rituals, and beliefs, the external or expressed form that spirituality takes. The term "spirituality" relies on one's direct and immediate experience of God or Spirit, and the rites and rituals can facilitate that experience.

Unfortunately for some people, the rites and rituals of their first religion have lost their power. Their spiritual challenge is to rediscover the tremendous depth, power, love, beauty, awe, and divinity these rituals can convey or to find a new spiritual direction. Currently, I am treating a Catholic woman who told me that on one occasion she experienced a blazing light piercing the glass of the church and passing through the Eucharist. For her, religion and spirituality came together in a beautiful visual way. Her container was full.

Of course, most of you reading this book don't need to visit a psychiatrist to have your vision or your miracle diagnosed accurately. You need to know what to call your vision, and you'll know that by the time you've finished reading this book. I know that what is sacred to me may not be what is sacred to you but I invite you to explore your spirituality, your sacred awareness, so that your life and the lives of those you love may be richer and more miraculous.

Who Is God and Where Does She Live?

While more than 95% of Americans believe in God, I have found that the word "God" often triggers a negative response in my patients. I usually begin a discussion of God when I am helping to create a mantra that is tailored to that individual. A mantra is based on whatever word or words they use for God. I may ask, "Who do you pray or talk to? Male and female forms of God are open territory here."

A frequent response is, "Well, I believe in something greater than myself, a force, a universal energy, but I don't believe in the God of the Bible, an old bearded man." I never imply that my idea of God is that old bearded man, but this response is very common. I open up the conversation by saying that I am only interested in what word they use, not what they think I am thinking.

So many people raised in traditional Jewish or Christian families, who went to synagogue or church as children, have a toxic relationship with the word "God" and many of these people have left their religion of origin in search of spirituality rather than religion. It is important for all doctors, and all who do spiritual counseling, to realize how deep and profound the fear of the word "God" is. But it is my job to open up the discussion about God and spirituality.

I understand the problem. Many were raised with the belief of a wrathful, angry God, a supreme being who was very far away. This God sits in judgment after we die and decides if we go to heaven or hell. Some believe in purgatory, which actually makes death less frightening, because people feel that they have more than two options.

For these people, which is most of us, God is not a loving God. As politicians love to say, "America is a God-fearing country." The word "God" is associated with fear for millions of people, rather than a source of refuge, comfort, consolation, love, and miracles. It is hard to describe how deep this fear is, but I have watched the reactions on my patients' faces for decades when I mention the G-word, and that reaction is fear.

I lighten up the conversation and share my understanding of God. It's not the complete Truth, but it is my honest experience of God and spirituality and not just something I read in a book. I don't ask anyone to agree with me. In fact, arguing for your viewpoint is a divine right, and arguing from your conscience is a duty.

Here is how I might discuss God with patients (or large audiences):

> After decades of soul-searching, of a serious spiritual quest, and of day-long spiritual practice, it has become obvious to me that God is either everywhere and in everything, or he does not exist at all. How can our puny human minds confine God to some territory and call it heaven? How can a minister, priest, or rabbi tell you where God is, or that the only way to have contact with him is through a priest?

> Science has amazingly been able to trace back the origins of the Universe to the Big Bang. They actually are pretty clear what happened up to a millionth of a second before the Big Bang, but they haven't been able to go back any further. To me, it is a miracle that scientists have been able to help us understand the very moment of creation. It is phenomenal. But science will never be able to tell us what was going on one second before the Big Bang, because there was virtually nothing in existence. There was nothing. Then there was a Big Bang, which started with sub-atomic particles and ended up with this immense universe.

My understanding from studying the Vedas, the ancient Sanskrit texts, is that the universe was created through expression of the sound "AUM" (or OM). God was hanging out for God knows how long. And that is for sure. Maybe for billions or trillions of years, but then there really weren't years, because time did not come into existence until space and the physical universe came into existence. So, even if God was waiting with a stopwatch, doing a countdown, "10 seconds to AUM, 9 seconds to AUM, etc," that stopwatch would not have even worked for there was no time.

But for the sake of argument, let's just say that God was hanging out for an eternity or so. He, She, or It, whatever you want to call this Cosmic Force, this Creative Energy, finally creates the sound "AUM," and out of absolutely nothing, suddenly there was a Big Bang, and then there was everything. What I am saying is not different from the Bible, which says, "In the beginning was the word." So AUM was the spark of the Big Bang. I don't know why this is obvious to me, but it seems quite natural to consider that the entire physical universe is inseparable from AUM. In other words, as AUM created the universe, every physical thing, every atom that exploded in all directions, was vibrating with the sound that created it, namely "AUM."

It is also my belief that the entire physical, seen universe, as well as the unseen universe is completely permeated by God. God and AUM are virtually everywhere, in everything, and in every one. How is it possible that God could be in one place and not another? So the body of God is this entire physical universe. There have been divine incarnations of God on this planet, and that is a separate issue. The point I want to make is that God is not sitting on a cloud, getting ready to give you a hard time and then scare the hell out of you when you die. That is not his job description and I don't know who came up with that idea.

When I say that the entire universe is the body of God, I mean everything we can see, as well as all the unseen realms, all of the angels, demi-gods, departed souls, and all those things we call "paranormal." There is nothing that is not God.

Since God is everywhere and in everything, it follows that He or She also dwells within us, permeating every cell in our body, and also existing as a much more palpable presence that we experience as the human soul. Our soul or spirit is separated from God only by our mind and imagination. In reality, there is no separation.

So, this is the context I would like you to consider, and it is very important that we discuss God, because spirituality and a spiritual connection to a Creator, or Loving Energy, is going to be important to your overall healing. If you want to call God "Bob," that's fine with me. If you are more in line with 12-step programs, then call him "Higher Power." Any way you look at it, we will need to help you deepen your spirituality and your connection to a Higher Power. Without deepening your spiritual connection, healing your problem or illness will be more difficult.

By now, my patient is laughing, and is comfortable with the whole subject. She knows I'm not going to cram God down her throat, but rather allow her to slowly awaken to her own truth.

I may talk about my spiritual teacher, Sathya Sai Baba, but I am not going to "sell" anybody on Sai Baba. There are times when I think it is appropriate for a patient to know where I am coming from, who my spiritual teacher is, and that my spiritual outlook is Vedanta, whose origins are in the Sanskrit Vedas. Through my spiritual teacher and Vedic teachings, I have become completely at home in all religions.

Whether my patient is Jewish, Christian, Muslim, Hindu, Sikh, Zoroastrian, Buddhist, or Native American, I am able to step into their spiritual shoes without any problem. I don't care what you call God, which makes it very easy for me to relate to you and whatever you call God. After awhile, I stop beating around the bush, using terms like "Universal Energy," or "Cosmic

Consciousness," and I will just use the word "God." It makes life easier as a spiritual psychiatrist. And after they've heard my view of God and the universe, and have begun to consider that God is everywhere and in everyone, they relax around the word "God" and I can just be free to be me, which is what is best for my patient—and for you too.

---

1. Richard Del Maestro, *Personal communication* (1996).
2. Pema Chödrön, *The Wisdom of No Escape: And the Path of Loving-Kindness* (Boston: Shambala, 1991).

Chapter 3

A Day in the Life of a Spiritual Psychiatrist

By calling myself a "spiritual" psychiatrist in this chapter title, I would not want to be misread as saying that I am "more spiritual" than other psychiatrists. In the professional world, I do not actually call myself a "spiritual," "holistic" or "New Age" psychiatrist. Because I treat mental, physical, and spiritual illness, I call myself a physician specializing in Integrative Psychiatry and Nutritional Medicine. The general labels of "doctor" and "psychiatrist" are noble and lasting ones that need no embellishing. For the purpose of this book's inquiry into human experience, however, thinking of me as a spiritual psychiatrist may be useful to you.

Nature helps some people connect with the sacred. For others, surfing the California waves brings a sense of peace and spirituality, or contemplating Jesus, Allah, Mazda (not just a car, but also a deity), the Buddha, the Torah, the Bible, the Koran, or the Bhagavad-Gita. Some find the "sacred" in jogging, swimming, gardening, or fly-fishing. One way is no better than another. All paths lead to the mountaintop, and to God, and he/she answers by a thousand different names. I have my own set of spiritual practices, techniques, and attitudes, which I use to make not only my personal life more sacred, but also the way I practice psychiatry.

In order to make healing and psychiatry sacred, the healer makes an effort to turn his or her mind from the material world and direct it inward to a place of peace, love, and truth. Necessarily, one lives in the material world and there's no getting out of it alive! Yet, one needn't live in a cave in order to be "spiritual"; one needn't be poverty-stricken, renouncing life's physical pleasures and conveniences. The key to spiritual living in the world is practicing "detachment." One can be a billionaire, yet be detached from wealth, and be humble, loving, and honest. It's not what we do and what we own, but how we live and how we are. Bringing the sacred into your life changes everything, and the sacred awareness of a psychiatrist radically changes treatment.

Bringing spirituality to the everyday practice of psychiatry also means changing the therapist! A psychiatrist cannot practice sacred psychiatry if he is not first practicing what he preaches. Even when I am not succeeding in my own spiritual efforts, I am aware that I am not succeeding. My awareness of how difficult spiritual practices can be allows me to work with my patients compassionately. I do not expect them to change their lives overnight. When a patient drifts from the therapy I prescribe, I can respond nonjudgmentally. I know how easy it is to get caught up in the drama of our lives, whether that drama is about finances, romance, career, family, or health. My own spiritual efforts have shown this to me in great detail. Who I am, or who any psychiatrist is, is as important as what we do or which specific techniques we utilize in helping people. With the attitudes of love, peace, and reverence prescribing medication becomes as sacred as prescribing meditation. Paxil or Zyprexa can be administered in a holy way (and imagine the difference it makes). On the flip side, meditation and prayer can be prescribed in an unloving way, which defeats the purpose of using these techniques.

When healing techniques are given to patients in order to help them grow, embrace suffering, and live more meaningful lives, psychotherapy is being conducted in a holy way. If, on the other hand, a psychiatrist conveys the message, "You are creating your illness, and you can use these tools to create a new reality with complete health," he is not practicing in a sacred way, but rather is using some of the techniques associated with spirituality to the detriment of his patient, "beating him up psychologically," and making him feel guilty for being sick. It may be easier for you to see how the process works if I walk you through a "day in my life."

I try to follow the teachings of Sathya Sai Baba by practicing his message and his teachings every waking moment, whether cooking a meal, driving the car, writing a book, or seeing patients. Baba teaches that, "The goal of spirituality, and of life, is to always remember God and to live a noble life." I do not fully succeed in my daily spiritual goals and practices, but I try to walk the talk.

When I arise each day, I say this prayer: "Oh Lord, I am born again from the womb of sleep and I am determined to carry out the tasks of this day as an offering to you. May all my thoughts, words, and deeds be ever sacred and pure. Let me harm no one. Let no one harm me."

After I drag my body from the bed, I often will imagine my chosen form of God in the house with me. I will not share with you who my chosen form of God is. That is not important for you to know. It is only important for you to know who your chosen name and form of God is. It is as if I "carve God" out of thin air, until I can "see" his form. I try to remember to keep him with me all through the day. Even as I run up the three flights of stairs at Mercy Hospital on my way to the Behavioral Health Unit, I imagine God climbing the stairs beside me. I am truly filled with happiness as I mentally say to him, "O.K., God, let's go and help some people." Strangely, I find it easy to feel his presence and continue my inner dialogue with him in that craziest of places, the mental hospital.

Often I "Practice the Presence" (as this technique is called) as I sit with patients in my office. I'll imagine that God is sitting in one of the chairs, helping and guiding the session. Sometimes when I get "stuck," I will "ask" God what to do. I might silently say, "God, what does this person need right now?" Immediately I will always have a thought, feeling, or image that I convey to my patient, a concept or theme that guides therapy like an arrow flying toward the bull's eye of a target.

Occasionally, I will receive inner guidance through words. Beginning in 1994, I began to be able to hear the voice of my spiritual teacher on very rare occasions. When I have seen him in person in India, he usually speaks to me with one or two words. The same is true now when I hear the inner voice. Here's an example. I use a mental imagery technique called "Cutting the Ties that Bind," a powerful method that frees us from interpersonal conflicts and the invisible connections that bind us to others, especially family members, spouses, and anyone who lingers on in our mind as a problem. This technique takes one hour, but the individual needs to do preliminary work for two weeks, practicing the "Figure Eight" imagery once or twice a day for a few minutes. On one occasion, a woman asked if she could come in for an "emergency cutting the ties." Her daughter was arriving the next day for vacation, and my patient was very anxious about the visit.

The "Cutting the Ties" imagery was created 50 years ago, and it is one technique that does not need to be perfected, or messed with. I stick with the protocol as it was developed by

Phyllis Krystal. With the emergency "cutting" I had to modify it, adding a step that I felt would make up for the lack of two weeks of preparation. My patient had her eyes closed as I took her through this modification. I have a small photograph of my teacher, Sai Baba, on my desk in my office. While my patient was doing the modified imagery, I turned to Sai Baba's picture, and said, "I really need your help with this." I was very surprised when I heard him answer me very quickly, saying, "I bless!" I have come to distinguish the inner voice of Sai Baba from my own thoughts, so I was relieved by his words, and I knew that the emergency modification would work, and all would be well, which it was.

Along with "Practicing the Presence," the most important discipline I practice is the constant repetition of a mantra. In my case, I chant "Om Sai Ram," which I understand as "Divine Mother and Father." I am describing the ideal of my spiritual practice, not what I actually succeed at. We'll get to the reason for "repetition of the name" in a moment, but for now, let's continue with my day as it actually unfolds.

Much as the Native American Indian prays to Nature and thanks the Great Spirit that is present in everything, I pray before I eat. Then, while showering, I chant the Gayatri mantra, a prayer that God will illuminate our intellect. As I'm "soaping up," I say a prayer of surrender: "Think through me. Feel through me. Act through me. Love through me. Speak through me. Heal through me. Thy will be done. Help me remember your name. Help me see you everywhere. Help me see you in everyone." A few minutes of yoga follow.

And then I'm off and running with the usual morning tasks: dressing, fixing lunch, and feeding my cat. Work begins on the freeway for me. With cellular phone in hand I check in with my office and begin making calls from the car. There doesn't seem to be enough time in life, so the cell phone comes in very handy.

In the fall of 2003, I went to New Mexico on a Native American pilgrimage. I loved Native American spirituality from a distance but had not integrated anything tangible into my life. During that trip, one day I was driving the mountain road from Santa Fe to Taos. I saw a large bird soaring over the hills to my right. I sped up to make it around the next hill and catch another glimpse. The bird came closer and I saw white-tipped wings. I had seen my first bald eagle. Two hours later I was in Taos having a psychic reading done by an Anglo named Alan. He sat down across the table from me, reached into a bag, pulled out a bald eagle feather and gave it to me. He said, "As I was pulling out of the driveway to meet with you, an image flashed in my head. This eagle feather was given to me several years ago by a Native American elder. He told me that I would part with it one day and I would know who it belonged to. I knew it belonged to you." There were more experiences involving the bald eagle during my time in New Mexico. All I can say is that I was in awe when I was given the bald eagle feather. More importantly, Alan shared a great deal about the Native American way of being. I knew that the Native Americans were very connected to the Earth, but I did not have a concrete idea. Alan shared that, when a man wants to pick a flower, he will take out his knife, cut the flower just above the ground, leaving a living plant in the ground that could grow again. He does not simply pluck the flower.

Alan shared much more, which I put into practice as soon as I returned to California. For years I had gone to work in a rather automatic, unconscious way. But things changed. As soon as I leave my house and am heading for the car, I stop to feel Nature. I notice the wind and what direction it is coming from, and I thank the wind. I smell the air for whatever odors or aromas are on the wind. I consciously notice the air temperature on my skin, my feet making solid contact with the ground, and I take in all of the sights and sounds. I have added this way of being into my life in a profound way. When I go shopping, I will first get out of my car, take a few steps, and then just stand there, mindfully taking in the world through all of my senses. This is the way we all are as children, rolling around in the grass, and feeling very connected to Nature. I had certainly lost that over the years, even though I drive by the Pacific Ocean every day on the way to work. I had stopped really seeing the ocean, but that has all changed. This aspect of the Native American way is not different from Buddhist mindfulness meditation. I will have connected to Nature as best I can before I arrive at my office.

Before I see a patient, I try to remember to dedicate the session to God. Now, if you were a new patient of mine, you wouldn't know that I had "prepared" myself in this way. Let's say this imaginary patient is Mrs. Diamond. She has some problems that are common in the Western world. Here is what her experience—or your experience—might be like:

"Hi, Mrs. Diamond. I'm Doctor Gersten. It's very nice to meet you. Please come this way. (I show her to my office)." As she enters my office, I ask her to please sit in the chair on the left. But before she can sit, she takes a good look around my office. I have many plants and statues from most of the world's main religions: a crystal statue of Mary holding Jesus, a Native American kachina called "Eagle Dancer," with long feathers with blue tufts at the end of each feather; a statue of the Buddha, another of Shiva, and one of Quan Yin.

We get down to business as I ask why she has come to see me, what her problems are, etc. I'll want to know about her whole life: her mental life, her social life, her marriage, her kids, her work, her stresses, her sex life, and her finances. I'll want to know about any physical problems and will probe deeply into subtle metabolic problems, such as those associated with chronic fatigue syndrome, candidiasis, digestive disorders, or adrenal insufficiency that are often overlooked by psychiatrists as well as internists. I may or may not ask about her childhood. I'll ask about creative outlets, special talents. I'll ask about her religious upbringing as well as her current spiritual beliefs. In the first session, I will have some idea about her life as a whole, not just the reasons she came in to see me. I want to know how her symptoms fit into the fabric of her life.

Mrs. Diamond is stressed-out. She's having trouble making ends meet. She's a wreck by the end of her workday and the tension is spilling over into her marriage. She gets frustrated and angry with her husband over trivial matters—and she's not sleeping very well. She could go on like this for a long time, but she knows something just isn't right in her life. My most important goal is that I "connect" with Mrs. Diamond. If I ask all the "right" questions but don't connect with her, I have failed and have not helped her.

Thought Watch
Mental Fitness Technique #1

During the first session, I will teach her the importance of getting perspective on how her mind works. "Mrs. Diamond, I now want to do a 30-second exercise. Close your eyes and simply observe your thoughts. Remember what comes into your mind. Don't try to change or alter your thoughts. Just watch them. I'll tell you when we're starting."

Why don't you try this exercise now, too? Set a timer for 30 seconds. Close your eyes and observe your thoughts.

"O.K. Go." After 30 seconds have passed, open your eyes.

I would say to Mrs. Diamond, "O.K., let's review your thoughts." I write down her thoughts on my notepad and tell her the purpose of this exercise. You can write yours down, at this point, too, according to the following format:

Write down every thought, image, feeling, or sensation that floated through your head during those 30 seconds. If you had the same thought five times, write it down five times.

After you've written down each thought, go back to the top of the list, and indicate if that particular thought was negative (-), positive (+), or neutral (±).

The next step is to figure out how many thoughts you're having in a single day. Let's say, for example, that you had five thoughts in 30 seconds. That's 10 thoughts per minute, or 600 per hour. When you're working, your mind is probably fully engaged in the work. However, when you're not working, that's when your mind, and every mind, begins to fly. How many hours per day are left after you add up the hours you sleep and the hours you work? For example, if you sleep eight hours and work eight hours, you have eight hours left. If that is the case, multiply 600 thoughts per hour times 8 hours. You have 4,800 random thoughts per day.

Now make your own calculations:

How many hours per day are you neither working nor sleeping? This figure is the number of hours per day your mind is free to wander.   _____

A.   Total thoughts in 30 seconds X 2 = thoughts
          per minute   _____
B.   Multiply A by 60 minutes = thoughts per hour   _____
C.   Multiply B by number of hours per day your mind
          is free to wander = total number of random
          thoughts per day   _____

How many thoughts were negative, how many positive, and how many were neutral? If you're like most people, the majority of your thoughts are neutral. Almost every thought you've thought hundreds of times before. Rarely does an original, creative, useful thought arise.

Review your list of thoughts and determine if a thought was about the past, present, or future. To the left of the list, write "P" for past, "PR" for present, and "F" for future. If you're a worrier, you'll have a lot of thoughts about the future, such as "What if there's not time to prepare dinner" or "I'm afraid I won't survive the IRS this year." If you tend a bit toward the depressed side, your thoughts will be more about the past, such as "If only I had done such-and-such," "I still feel so guilty for ..."

People whose thoughts are predominantly about the future need to work on spiritual issues of faith, trust, and surrender. Those whose minds are in the past need to work on forgiveness, letting go of resentment, overcoming blame, and releasing guilt.

This simple technique gives you an overview of what your mind is doing and why it's doing what it's doing. We all think too much, except for advanced, skilled meditators who have learned how to turn off the mental noise.

I have worked with people who had 35 thoughts per minute. Can you imagine? And what is your mind doing all day? The mind is like a two-cylinder engine that's driven by attraction and repulsion. Think for a moment about what your mind is doing all day long. You see a beautiful house and you wish you owned it. You see a little extra fat when you look in the mirror and you wish it would go away. We want to gain one thing and want to get rid of another, and believe it or not, we spend most of our lives thinking like this.

Mantra Meditation
Mental Fitness Technique #2

The next step with Mrs. Diamond would be teaching her how to slow down all of that mental noise and find some peace. That can be accomplished through the use of a mantra. A mantra (itself a Sanskrit word) is a word or phrase that is repeated. Mantra also means "that which takes us across this sea of illusion, that which saves when repeated in the mind." A mantra is generally between two and seven syllables. To find an effective mantra, think about when you pray. Whom do you pray to?

A mantra takes your mind to the highest realm it can dwell in, and for that reason, most mantras are names of God or saints. In Christian tradition, the most common mantras are: Jesus, Jesus Christ, Jésu, Heavenly Father, Mother Mary, and Holy Spirit. In the Jewish tradition, God is referred to as: Jehovah, Yahweh, Elohaynu, Baruch Hashem or Shechina (the Goddess). In Islam, God is referred to as Allah or Rahim. And in Buddhism, "buddha" (one who is awakened or enlightened) is often used as a mantra.

In Zoroastrianism, Mazda is the name of God. And in Hinduism, there are literally hundreds of names, including: Rama, Shiva, Vishnu, Brahma, Krishna, Ganesha, Sai Baba, Saraswati, and Parvathi. Sanskrit mantras usually include the word, "Om" before the name of God, for example, "Om Namah Shivayah."

If none of these feels right for you, try "Lord God," "Loving God," or "Universal Intelligence." Remember, your mantra has to be more than one syllable, so the word "God" does not suffice as a complete mantra. Or you may want to consider "Higher Power" or "Higher Self."

If you still haven't found a mantra you like, you may want to combine some human values and turn them into a mantra, such as: "Love and Peace," or "Truth and Compassion." Or if nature takes you to a higher realm, a nature mantra might be "Golden Eagle," "Rocky Mountains," "Pacific Ocean." I don't often recommend a "nature mantra" for they have not yet proven that they stand the test of time, and do not accurately represent ancient spiritual wisdom. They will, nonetheless, help you relax.

Take a moment and write down in your notebook some of your favorites from those I've listed, or make up your own.

Now, let's practice. Let's say, for example, that "Heavenly Father" is your chosen mantra. Close your eyes. Make yourself relaxed. Take a few deep breaths. As you inhale, silently say the first half of your mantra ("Heavenly"). As you exhale, silently say the second half of your mantra ("Father"). Practice your new mantra for one minute.

Don't try to change your breathing while you're silently repeating your mantra. Rather, allow your breathing to change on its own. Keep repeating your mantra in time with each breath.

If any other thoughts enter your mind, simply allow them to pass through your mind like clouds passing through the sky. Do not try to push away "bad" thoughts, nor hold onto "good" thoughts. If your mind drifts, slowly bring your mind back to the mantra. People often will get upset with themselves when their minds drift. Please remember that "mental drift" actually is part of meditation. You drift, and then you re-focus. Drift, and then gently re-focus. When you understand that meditation involves both the focus and the drift, you can't do it wrong!

Rx for Your Mantra

Practice two or three times a day for five minutes each time. Practice when you wake up, at noon, and before going to sleep. Stick with one mantra for at least a week. If it doesn't feel right, change to a new one. Eventually, however, it is essential that you settle on one mantra. Otherwise, no progress will be made.

If you do this simple exercise for one month, you will notice a difference in your life. You'll feel calmer, less hurried, less worried, and better centered. After practicing for one year, your personality will solidify at a new level of wholeness. And after you've practiced for ten years, you'll hardly recognize the person you had been. The essence of you will always be there, but your rough edges will have been smoothed out.

The mantra has three important purposes. One of these is to "slow down" the always-buzzing mind. There are many ways to look at the mind. We've already looked at how the mind is a two-cylinder engine that runs on attraction and repulsion. Another analogy is that the mind is like a fan that's furiously buzzing around all day. Every time you say your mantra—every time—it's as if you have turned off the switch to that fan, and it turns a little slower. So if you practice your mantra five minutes twice a day, which is what I recommend, your "mental fan" will begin to turn more slowly, and you'll begin to feel less stressed-out. But you don't have to limit your mantra to twice a day. When you're driving and come to a red light, recite your mantra until the light turns green. Do it with your eyes open. But when the light turns green, please focus your attention back on the road. When you're walking from your car into the supermarket, recite your mantra. Maybe even when you're sitting on the can! These are all opportunities to slow down the mind.

The second purpose of the mantra comes from the mind's need to do work. If we do not give it work, it will simply run itself, lurching this way, then that. In ten days you will have had 60,000 random thoughts; in 100 days, you will have had 600,000 thoughts. That is an incredible thing to think about (there's another thought!). So you see, you don't want your mind running you around. You have to be your mind's master—or else you will be its slave. And it has nothing to do with whether you're depressed, and living in poverty—or if you're a successful billionaire. The mind does the same thing to everyone. So give it something positive to do. And there's nothing more positive for your mind to do than remembering the name of God.

And the third point of the mantra? The mantra is a "mental home base." It's the place in your mind that you can come home to over and over again. Even if you've been frazzled and haven't chanted your mantra in five hours, you can come back home to your mantra. Where do you go mentally without a mantra? There's simply no mental home base for the vast majority of people. This can be your anchor, if what I'm saying makes sense to you, and you begin to practice.

I can guarantee you that you will feel more peaceful after just a few days of practicing your mantra. In a few months you'll begin to be a different person. It will start to affect you in a profound way. And if you practice for years, your whole life will change. It's the simplest, most effective technique in the world and it's free. But although it's simple, it's not as easy as you might think. Your mind has years of momentum built up. That's a lot of spinning of that mental fan, that mental flywheel. You're going to have to throw that mental switch over and over again. I've been practicing my mantra since 1979. I find that it gets easier with practice, almost effortless. In the beginning, I could go days without remembering my mantra. My mind was just running so fast and so far. But now, I can always return home to my mantra within seconds, no matter what's going on in my life. It's been absolutely transforming for me, and has helped me become a lot more peaceful.

You—and Mrs. Diamond—might worry that a mantra will make you so peaceful that you won't get anything done, but the amazing thing is that the quieter our minds become, the better we are at what we do. We don't get lazy. We don't become worse at what we do. We become better. We clear out the mental clutter in life that interferes with our purpose and happiness.

Here's something else I do to help me get rid of the clutter: I carry a three-by-five card with me on which I write down all the things I have to do, people to call, things to buy. Once I write it down on the card, I don't have to worry about it and have it clutter up my mind.

As I help my clients learn about mantras and meditation, I'm periodically "checking in" with God. Sai Baba teaches that work is worship. One needn't retire to a cave and meditate in order to progress on a spiritual path. By regarding my work as worship and remembering to dedicate every session to God, the work of psychotherapy is transformed. I continue to remember God throughout the session. Sometimes he's in "sharp focus" and sometimes in "soft focus." I believe that divinity is present within everyone, that all of creation is not only made by God, but is permeated by God. Now how does that concept translate into clinical psychiatry? I try to see God in the patient I am working with. And sometimes God is hard to see. Sometimes when I'm looking at someone, I will mentally say, "Yoo hoo. You who. Hello, God. Are you in there? I know you're in there!" Surely, all of this must appear as sheer madness to most psychiatrists, but to me, it is all part of an integrated approach to life.

How different this approach is! Imagine if Mrs. Diamond's psychiatrist were saying to himself, "She suffers from a fixation at the Oedipal stage of development. Her depression reflects repressed rage, which is a reaction formation. She secretly hates her mother for stealing away her father, but she is not aware of her hatred. Her current problems with her husband, who works too late, is triggering early feelings of abandonment and re-activating her Oedipus Complex." Mrs. Diamond wouldn't know what one psychiatrist or another is thinking, but I think that the therapist who regards psychotherapy as a sacred process and keeps God in mind throughout the process, uplifts the patient—instead of confusing, or (worse) making her feel officially pathological or psychologically defective. A spiritual therapy process can help take the patient to a new level of consciousness. Imagine that Mrs. Diamond had never felt loved and her psychiatrist was quietly considering God to live inside her and treating her with respect and compassion. That alone will help her heal.

After my first five or six years as a psychiatrist, I discovered that my medical, psychiatric theorizing about my patients' problems was actually getting in the way of therapy. My theorizing got me and my patient stuck at the level of the mind. My thoughts and theories were an emotional wall between my patient and me. I spent years tearing down the wall that my formal training built up.

Therapy is most effective when engaged on levels of consciousness much higher than the mind. Through the years, as my own mind became quieter as a result of spiritual practice, that quietness began to carry over into my clinical work. Finally, I reached the point where I just stopped the whole process I learned while I was in training to be a psychiatrist. Once I threw out the theories, I was left with a different experience in which I was there with the patient with nothing between us. In place of those theories, I now have a much quieter mind, a mind that is seeking the divinity in my patients.

I do not come right out and say to my patients, "You are God. I can see divinity within you. You are a divine light. No need to be depressed or anxious anymore. Just let that God that is in you, that you really are, just come right out." No! On the outside I maintain a professional, doctorly manner. I do not need to narrate my inner workings to my patients, but those inner workings are the therapy. Therapy is not just the talking, the listening, the guided imagery, the mantra meditation, the exploration of spiritual experience, the use of nutritional supplements, the use of anti-depressant medication, the variety of strategies and suggestions. Therapy is the moment. The therapist is not merely a dispenser of drugs. He is the dispenser of the moment. The therapist helps create the atmosphere in which healing will, or will not, take place. Therapy is what you do and who you are. Eventually, the patient becomes his or her own therapist or inner authority, just as you, the average person reading this book who is or is not in therapy becomes his or her own therapist. In many ways, I am a consultant to my patients, and, here, I am your consultant, providing information that may lead to transformation, information that you choose how or if to integrate into your life. I want you to find your own inner healing resources.

Mrs. Diamond almost certainly has had her spirits lifted by her first session. She has understood a bit more about how her mind works and how it gets her into trouble. She will take home a mantra that she can use to help her today, tomorrow, and I hope for the rest of her life. Our first session ends with an overview of her problem.

"Here's what I think is going on: You have a number of life stresses that are leaving you depressed, anxious, and worn out. I believe I can help you feel less moody and anxious quickly. I wouldn't worry about the marriage right now. Once you're more relaxed, you will probably experience many positive changes in your life. Your marital problems may simply go away. If not, we'll deal with your marriage in the future. The mantra should begin helping you soon.

Most people I see with this degree of stress have a variety of metabolic imbalances caused by the stress. We'll go into this in more detail next time. But let me outline this briefly. Nothing in our life exists in a vacuum. Your moods are not confined to your brain or mind. In my experience, I have found that there are four major systems within us that are very inter-dependent: our brains and nervous system, the immune system, the endocrine system—consisting primarily of the adrenals, pancreas, gonads, and thyroid glands—and the digestive system. So when you're stressed out over a long period of time, your immune system suffers. People begin to get sick more often. Constant stress drains the adrenal glands, and when the adrenals begin to get exhausted, the pancreas and thyroid get out of balance. Basically, the endocrine system helps maintain our energy level. And stress begins to impair digestion. I do not see this as a serious problem for you, but in this society of high stress, high pollution, pesticides, foods with hormones, and land that has been leached of its nutrients, most of us simply are not running at our metabolic best."

In general, I recommend that my patients try to enhance their nutritional health by avoiding junk food, eating a wholesome balanced diet and taking a variety of nutritional supplements, depending on the individual's particular needs determined by lab testing. In this high-stress society, I generally recommend high doses of vitamin C, spirulina (a high-protein food made from plankton, and which is an immune system booster), anti-oxidants, such as vitamin A, selenium, zinc, pycnogenol, co-enzyme Q-10, and a multivitamin. I'll also recommend specific amino acids, depending on the particular need (tyrosine or tryptophan for depression; taurine for nervous system instability and anxiety, alanine and serine for problems with blood sugar, lysine for a stressed immune system and frequent viral infections). I'll also advise them to take pyridoxal-5-phosphate (P-5-P), the active form of vitamin B-6, if they're taking any amino acids, because P-5-P is needed in order for amino acids to work.

Over decades, I developed a 3-Level Health Map to facilitate diagnosis and treatment. Level I is the Primary Causes. Level II is How the Body Responds to Primary Causes (namely through inflammation and the stress response). Level III deals with Total Body Biochemistry. I will be looking for all the primary causes of her problem. Every chronic symptom or illness has a minimum of seven primary causes and as many as fifteen. Some examples of primary causes include: acute stress, Epstein-Barr Virus, Candidiasis (a yeast infection throughout the body), mercury or lead toxicity, intestinal malabsorption, leaky gut syndrome (another common digestive problem), food allergies, damaged detoxification pathways (especially depleted glutathione), physical trauma, and more. Imagine that each primary cause is a domino and that behind each primary domino there are 10,000 dominos lined up. When, for example, the "mercury" domino falls, 10,000 dominos behind it fall. If you have ten primary causes, 100,000 dominos will fall. The 100,000 dominos represents metabolic chaos. Let's say that with healthy metabolism, your biochemistry is running clockwise. When you have metabolic chaos, the biochemistry is running counter-clockwise, which results in what we call "symptoms" and "illnesses." Most of the metabolic chaos is amino acid chaos, because our bodies by dry weight are 60-70% amino acids. First we are water. After that, we are mainly amino acids. I will explain to Mrs. Diamond that mental/emotional factors are also primary dominos, and I classify those five ways: 1) acute overwhelming stress, 2) chronic stress, 3) unresolved conflict, 4) long-term effects of child abuse or neglect, and 5) trauma at any time in life.

I may or may not tell Mrs. Diamond if I am considering using medications, but I will have assessed that need. Mrs. Diamond has been hit with a heavy dose of information and transformation. Most of all, I want to see her walking out of my office with a sense of hope. I want her to feel that she can talk about anything with me, from sex to samadhi (mystical ecstasy).

I specialize in the use of guided imagery techniques and usually begin using imagery in the second session. If my patient and I are working on a relationship, say with her husband, rather than simply talking about him, I'll ask her to close her eyes and imagine that he's right in the room so that she can tell him things mentally that she may not have thought of daring to say at all. It's far more powerful than simply talking about him.

Another way to look at how the imagery process works is by using the analogy that our minds are like a garden. When you use your mantra, you're weeding the garden. After you've done some weeding, further imagery work is like planting seeds into that fertile ground. If you haven't cleaned up the garden, then flowers and weeds will be growing once we start imagery work.

For instance, here's a brief imagery exercise for helping you deal with little stresses in your life that rob you of energy:

Magic Box Imagery
Mental Fitness Technique #3

Imagine you have a magic box beside you. Now get in touch with any worry, fear, or problem that is bothering you. Imagine that you allow the problem to flow out into your hands. Notice what the problem feels like in your hands. How big is your problem? What color is it?

Toss your worry or problem into the magic box and leave it there. Your magic box can hold an infinite number of worries, fears, and problems.

If imagery is new to you, this technique may seem foolish. Please suspend judgment about this, and all other techniques you read in this book. Try them and see which ones work for you. Simply tossing your worries into an imaginary magic box actually does help relieve stress. Now that you know how to de-stress, you can "carry" your imaginary magic box with you wherever you go. Put it in your office, and another one at home.

This simple imagery technique will go a long way toward reducing stress. Furthermore, when you combine breath techniques with imagery, you can relax at an even deeper level.

Regulating Energy with Breath
Mental Fitness Technique #4

The ancient Hindu texts, the Vedas, described a complex system of breath control called "pranayama." We won't go into the details here, but will show how the breath can either raise or lower our energy, depending on how we choose to breathe.

If you want to lower your energy, and become calmer, practice this method of breathing:
1.   Inhale to the count of four.
2.   Hold your breath to the count of four.
3.   Exhale to the count of eight.

If, on the other hand, you want to bring your energy up, the method you'll want to use is the opposite:

1.   Inhale to the count of two.
2.   Hold your breath to the count of two.
3.   Exhale to the count of one.

If you're always exhausted, this "energizing" breath is for you. If, on the other hand, you have too much energy, or are anxious and stressed out, practice the first technique. A general rule is to practice one minute four times a day.

These techniques not only affect your energy level, but also your consciousness and state of alertness and activation. If you are extremely energized, you may become over-activated, and, as a result, your focus will begin to narrow. You'll see less. You'll only be fully aware of what's right in front of you. We can illustrate this by looking at a variety of sporting events. If you're a football defensive tackle, you need to have high energy with a narrow focus of attention. All you need to do is knock down the guy in front of you and then try to tackle the quarterback or whoever is carrying the football. If, on the other hand, you're the quarterback, you need to have a much wider focus of attention. You don't want to be as pumped up as the defensive lineman. You want to "slip into the zone," like quarterback Joe Montana and be able to see everybody on the field, all your receivers and everyone defending against your receivers. A quarterback in a high-pressure game, like the Super Bowl, usually needs to practice the first kind of breath technique, the relaxing kind.

The same principles holds true for any event in which you're participating. If you're about to give a speech in front of 1,000 people, you'll want to bring your energy down so you're centered and relaxed. But you don't want to be "flat." You don't want to be too calm, for a certain degree of tension is necessary in order for you to deeply connect with your audience.

Whatever situation you're in, you can consciously use your breath to optimize performance and make yourself feel better.

Now, back to Mrs. Diamond. She will have a good idea after that first meeting about the direction therapy will take. I want her to know that psychotherapy, as I practice it, actually is fun and inspiring, and she may feel that way now. She does have a lot of questions to mull over, for I've given her food for thought that she can "digest" for months. And she has received something that she doesn't consciously know about yet. By describing the way the mind works and the way our minds get us into trouble, I've conveyed a subtle but powerful message: We have a mind but we are not our minds. By meditating on a mantra, one begins to witness the mind. One witnesses the thoughts that pass in and out of our minds like clouds passing through the sky. But who is it that is doing the watching? There is an eternal witness within us, that part of us that has witnessed the drama in our lives since childhood, that part that stays the same despite the ever-changing landscapes of our lives.

Automatically, Mrs. Diamond will begin to get in touch with that part of her that is eternal, which is called the witness. As she becomes more aware of her witness, her mind will have less of its self-limiting control on her. She (the "real she") will be the master of her mind, and not its slave.

This attitude that I bring to therapy is radically different from a traditional approach because psychiatry does not recognize anything above or beyond the mind. Psychiatry gets stuck in the mind and stays there, mucking around sometimes for years. But when therapy is "launched" from a spiritual foundation, the trajectory from the moment of "launch" is set quite differently than it would be without such an approach. And the spiritual context continues even as my patient is walking out the door.

One patient with a particular New Age spiritual orientation, asked after the first session, "Would it be O.K. to use 'I am the Universal Intelligence' as a mantra?" I replied, "No, that's not a good idea for a mantra. It's a fine affirmation, but it's not a good mantra. When you say, "I am the ...," you're actually putting those words between you and the Universal Intelligence. When you simply repeat the words Universal Intelligence, you eventually can become one with it. Those few words, "I am the ...," actually create a distance between you and God or Universal Intelligence."

Traditional psychiatry deals with our dark side, our shadow, our unconscious, but it does not lead anyone toward the light side, the bright side. It is essential to deal with both sides. The dark side, the painful experiences, the anger, and the shame—all of this must be brought to the surface, expressed, and released. But released from what and to what? I believe spiritual psychiatry enables you to be released more easily because you are being released to something with God and spirituality in the psychiatric equation. Because of that "balanced equation," my patients realize that I want them to identify with their strengths, and not just dwell on their weaknesses. I want to help them develop those strengths, to be better than better. I want them to find their unique place on this planet.

Sometimes I act as a cheerleader to help someone see the light, to see their inner divinity, their love, their courage, and their positive side.

Spiritual psychotherapy can help people who already identify themselves with a spiritual practice but it can also help others. My patients are Jane and John Doe. They're your next-door neighbors. They are you. They are doctors, nurses, lawyers, musicians, beauticians, private investigators, businessmen, salesmen, and psychics. They come from all walks of life, all religions. They're very rich and they're unemployed. Amazingly, the approach I use seems to have a universal appeal. It resonates with almost everyone, because the human mind works the same way no matter who you are, no matter your sex, race, creed, color, or religion. Everyone has a mind, and almost everyone believes in God. Therefore, almost everyone is very happy to experience this spiritual approach.

After work, I try to get to the beach and go for a long walk. I silently chant my mantra. I re-connect with Mother Earth and Father Sky, smelling the fires burning on the beach, feeling the breeze, and "putting my mind into my feet," becoming more conscious simply of my bare feet making contact with the Earth. This is my Red Path Time, or time spent with Native American practices.

I won't bore you with the details of supper and some of my couch-potato behavior. I read from spiritual books for about a half-hour before turning off the lights. And then I begin a long prayer, starting with the Gayatri mantra (the prayer to illuminate my intellect) followed by: "Loka Samasta Sukhino Bhavantu—may all the beings in all the worlds be happy." Then I continue with, "Dear

Lord, the tasks of this day whose burden I placed upon you this morning are now over. It was you who made me think, feel, and act as I did. Now I offer all my thoughts, words, and deeds to you. Please receive me. I am coming home to you."

The first set of prayers is rather fixed and routine for me. Then I go on "talking to God" for a while. "Dear God, I pray that you fill me with your love and grace. I pray for liberation. I pray that you will work through me as a healer. I pray for (family, friends, the world)." I also bug the hell out of God. "God. Um. I know I've asked you this every night for the last ten years, but I'm going to ask again tonight ..."

God and I talk for a while. I talk. He listens. And then I begin reciting my "main" mantra over and over again: Om Sai Ram, Om Sai Ram, Om Sai Ram, Om Sai Ram, ZZZZZZ.

Chapter 4

The Healing Power of Human Values

Human values are fundamental to success in all arenas of life. Values form the core of character and the foundation of spiritual development. The Indian yogi and scholar, Patanjali, outlined an "eight-fold path" to enlightenment, for which the first step is the development of human values.[1,2] The second step has to do with man's relationship to society, and the duty to fulfill our obligation to society which gave birth to us and which continues to provide for us.

Patanjali's third step is "asana," the physical postures that we commonly think of as "yoga." The fourth step is "pranayama," or regulation and control of the breath. Step five is "pratyahara," or sense control. Through pratyahara, we learn detachment, how to be in the world, how to have objects but not be "owned" by them. Step six is concentration, which prepares us for meditation. It is a common misconception that meditation is the beginning of spiritual development. In Patanjali's view, meditation is actually the seventh step. Samadhi, or Nirvana, is the final step, the state in which all is one. All mental agitation ends. In Samadhi, we are more than peaceful. We are peace, and we are love.

True healing of mind, body, and spirit requires paying attention to your moral values. You can be cured of an illness through high-tech surgery or antibiotics, but you won't find out what led you to become vulnerable to the illness in the first place without attending to the life and spiritual issues at the source of the illness. In psychiatry, fostering human values is also the first step toward self-understanding and insight. Understanding a patient's values helps psychiatrists diagnose and treat. The goal of psychiatric treatment, however, is not samadhi. It is "healing"—healing of one's suffering, healing from illness, even healing into a good death.

Sathya Sai Baba illustrates the importance of human values on mental health, as well as politics, business, and education, and has created an entire educational system, from kindergarten through graduate school, based on the premise that the fostering of human values and character are the main goals of education. The Sathya Sai Education in Human Values (Sathya Sai EHV) system is not only prevalent in his native India, it is being taught all over the world. According to this belief system, the five core human values are: truth, right action (moral conduct), peace, love, and non-violence. Each human value evolves out of the one prior to it. For example, truth is the first human value. When one knows the truth, one proceeds with right action. When one has taken right action, one develops peace of mind. Where there is peace, love soon follows. Finally, non-violence evolves out of love.

All other values are sub-values of these five core values. For example, compassion is a sub-value of love. Sai Baba asks, "Are you practicing brotherliness, tolerance, equanimity, charity, compassion? These are the armors that guard the mind from the arrows of sorrow and pain."

The essence of Baba's teachings are essential to my practice of psychiatry, and I am convinced that tolerance and compassion really are medicines for the mind. Spiritual diagnosis and treatment is not just about gathering information or incorporating the latest data on mind-body medicine and the latest thoughts on spirituality. It's about transformation and goodness of the heart. In order for transformation to occur, I try to make psychiatry "sacred" by creating a "space" in which trust, healing, and even miracles, can take place, where truth and love can be shared and experienced. Compassion and trust are the essential healing ingredients in almost all doctor-patient relationships.

The exceptions include the approximately 40 percent of psychotic people who don't believe they have a problem. So, even if I have no doubts whatsoever that a person is a paranoid schizophrenic in the middle of a psychotic episode, the treatment may not be so easy. The patient will require powerful anti-psychotic medication, but since he doesn't think there's anything wrong with him, he's not going to trust me if I tell him he has schizophrenia and will often resist taking the very medicine that he needs. In these cases I often have to treat, even though no trust has been established. I order the Haldol or Zyprexa and, along with the nursing staff in the hospital, we gently try to persuade the patient to take the medicine. It can be a difficult disease to treat, even when the patient is cooperative, but the current state of the law makes involuntary treatment with medication almost impossible. If I can get them to take the medicine, however, they'll start to recover, and then they may begin to trust me. It's that rare situation where trust may come after treatment, not before.

Doctors must look at body, mind, and spirit—and diagnose and treat each aspect of every patient. You, the patient, need to become aware of your mind, body, and spirit, too. One of the easiest ways to do this is to reflect on your values, your code of behavior in the world. There is even more to us than body, mind, and spirit. But we'll start by discussing these components for now. In the East, six aspects of man have been explored for thousands of years: the physical body, prana or life force, the mind, the intellect, the "layer of bliss" and the soul. In Eastern medicine "chi" or "life force energy" is not the same as "spirit." Spirit or soul is eternal, unchanging, limitless, and not bound by time or space. The physical body is the densest form of energy, followed by "life force," mind, intellect, the layer of bliss, and finally spirit. So we'll limit our discussion to the body, mind, and spirit for now.

One of the main qualities of spirituality is morality, a word that is used as infrequently as "God" and "love" by psychiatrists. When I am working with a patient, I am not only looking for signs of mental illness and psychological stress, but I am also looking for "deficiencies in human values." After determining which human values need to be fostered, I incorporate those values into my treatment plan. It is extremely important to understand that mental illness and moral illness are not the same thing. I have worked with very sick schizophrenics who were quite moral, and I have worked with people who were normal psychologically, but severely impaired morally. I have also worked with people who were both mentally and morally ill.

An example of someone who I consider to be mentally healthy but morally impaired is a psychiatrist who practices in San Diego. One of the nurses in a hospital, a married woman, confided in me that Doctor T. had walked up to her, slid his hand inside the elastic belt of her pants and pulled the fabric four or five inches away from her waist-line, so that he could stare down at her underwear. Doctor T. shows no sign of mental illness to me, but his actions were immoral. Not a "great" sin, but immoral. Another San Diego psychiatrist, Doctor A. has been in prison for several years for hiring a "hit man" to murder a former lover. One may argue that you'd have to be mentally ill to plan such an evil deed. From whatever extent of mental instability Doctor A. suffers, his moral illness is by far more serious. I attempted to have this doctor removed from the residency program before he was licensed, but sadly my pleas fell on deaf ears. As one of the Chief Residents in psychiatry, I attended an administrative meeting to discuss Doctor A. I felt he was not competent and was immoral. Doctor A. was given a year of probation, a slap on the wrist, and completed his training.

Some people suffer from both mental and moral illness. Ben, a 35-year-old, is a case in point. He had requested psychiatric hospitalization because he was depressed and was hearing voices. After treating Ben for three weeks in the hospital, and preparing to discharge him, he asked me to read a note he had written. He slyly grinned and said, "You asked me to write down some goals, so here they are." I concealed my horror as I silently read Ben's 20 goals. They included entries, such as: "I plan to buy a semi-automatic rifle and kill as many people as I can." "I plan to blow up the police station." "I plan to carry a large hunting knife with me at all times and randomly attack people."

"What do you think, Doc?" Ben asked without a trace of guilt, shame, or fear.

"Ben," I replied. "What is the worst physical harm you've actually done to another human being, or to an animal?"

"Oh, one time, about ten years ago, I set a bum on fire. It was pretty funny to watch."

I pursued the details and learned that Ben had discovered a homeless person, smelling of alcohol, sleeping at the side of a building. Ben had doused him with lighter fluid and then set his big toe on fire, as if it were the wick of a candle.

"Did he die?" Ben.

"Yeah. I killed him," Ben responded.

I told Ben that he had given me some serious things to think about and that I'd have to talk to him further at another time. I went into the doctor's lounge and notified the Homicide Division of the San Diego Police Department, who met with Ben in the hospital, investigated the alleged murder, and called the city where the murder was alleged to have occurred.

I waited for a week without hearing back from the police department. When I spoke with them, they told me that the city where the murder was supposed to have occurred had no record on file that corresponded to the alleged murder. I informed the police that Ben no longer needed psychiatric treatment and that the police now needed to assume full responsibility for what I believed to be a severe case of moral illness. They said they'd get back to me. I kept Ben in the hospital for a few more days and then called the Homicide Division again. They told me they were dropping the investigation and that Ben was free to leave the hospital.

This story is a clear example of mental illness (borderline personality disorder with psychotic features) and moral illness. Ben was primarily lacking in the human values of non-violence, love, peace, and right action. It is my opinion that the police department may have also been exhibiting a degree of moral illness. I remain convinced that the murder did take place and believe that if the victim had been wealthy, powerful, or famous, the case would have been investigated and Ben would have been transferred to the county jail. Perhaps an unknown homeless person was the victim, someone who mattered to nobody in the world.

Amanda, a patient of mine, whose definition of spirituality you read in Chapter 2, suffers enormously, both mentally and physically. Her history of being abused is more like torture. Yet her honesty, her sincerity, her compassion, her urge to help others is immense. She and I have worked with her suffering as "part of her spiritual path," and a major part of her recovery has been assisting her in finding a highly-structured spiritual community. After a half-dozen over-doses in one year and even more psychiatric hospitalizations, I told Amanda, "We've reached the end of the line. We need to find a long-term facility for you, and that is either going to be a locked long-term mental hospital, or a spiritual community." Amanda was terrified but knew I was right. Both of us began researching spiritual communities, and based on her Buddhist leanings we found the ideal place for her, where she lived and worked for six months, trying diligently to practice the teachings of the Buddha every day. Amanda is no saint and few of us are. Everyone except for saints, sages, and enlightened masters have to overcome moral deficiencies, deficiencies in honesty, or love, or truth, or non-violence, or courage to do the right thing.

The practice of morality is essential to mental and spiritual healing. The practice of non-violence, loving speech, forgiveness, and forbearance will help you make progress with your emotional suffering. The practice of these virtues is essential to our progress as human beings, whether we are progressing from mental illness to "normalcy" or from "normalcy" to super-normalcy, or enlightenment. In politics, the word "values" is tossed around without much understanding. They are usually talking about social and cultural norms. The five core human values are universal and they are the foundation for character.

Much of the field of psychiatry is based on "healing through awareness or understanding." The greater the awareness, the deeper the healing. Of course, awareness must be followed by appropriate action. Once you are aware, once you know what to do, you have to do it. If you can't or won't do it, my job is to help you become aware of whatever obstacles are preventing you from taking right action. In a sense, my philosophy is an extension of traditional psychoanalytic thinking, which highly values understanding.

I believe that one of the primary goals of a physician is to encourage a patient to become aware of his own inner resources, to better understand what to call his experience, to know how he feels about it, and to discover what to do about it. Awareness must lead to action if real change is to occur. It gets back to the Vedic injunction: "Sathyam vada dharmam chara"—Discover and speak the truth, and then practice dharma, or powerful right action.

---

1.   Archie Bahm, *Yoga Sutras of Patanjali* (Berkeley: Asian Humanities Press, 1993).
2.   *The Path Divine: Sri Sathya Sai Bal Vikas Group III.* Education in Human Values Series (Prasanthi Nilayam, India: Sri Sathya Sai Bal Vikas Education Trust, 1981).

Chapter 5

Psycho-Spiritual Assessment (PSA)

You've already read about the simple Sanskrit phrase "Sath-yam vada dharmam chara," which means, "Speak the truth and practice dharma." Dharma means "powerful, super high-integrity, right action." Dharma is "doing the right thing no matter what." Doing the right thing often requires courage. "Truth, dharma, and courage" is a powerful and transformative way to live one's life.

I have shared that simple equation with many patients as a way to think about how to handle life's problems. More often than not, people find their solutions within "Sathyam vada dharma chara." First, ask what the truth and the Truth are for you. Once you know those truths, then dharma, or right action, automatically becomes clear to you.

Using the essence of the Vedas as a foundation, I spent fifteen years developing a four-step process called "Psycho-Spiritual Assessment" (PSA), to help people identify the issues in their lives and then map out a course of action.

Psycho-Spiritual Assessment (PSA) can be a powerful tool for transforming your life. It helps people understand their spiritual and life experiences so they can integrate them in a commonsensical way into their lives. Throughout this book, I show how Psycho-Spiritual Assessment has helped me zero in on a patient's core issues so that I could help him work through that issue or problem and move on to the next challenge in life. Because of the Psycho-Spiritual Assessment, many patients whom I treated have been able to meet their challenges courageously and feel empowered by the experience. Many of these patients had spent years in traditional psychotherapy without making much headway, but were able to "see the light" when they realized that there was a light to be seen. When spiritual questions are included as a viable and important part of therapy, both psychiatrist and patient gain a larger perspective on the patient's life, which, in turn, leads to faster personal growth, transformation, and healing.

There is great power, including healing power in "Sathyam vada dharmam chara." You know what the right thing to do is most of the time. You feel it in every cell in your body. When you go against your own intuition of right action, you feel confused, depressed, and off center. You have given away your power and no medication can give you back your power. The only way to empower yourself is by doing the right thing every day. Do your dharma, your right action. Dharma applies to minor issues that come up every day as well as major life decisions. Christina, one of my patients became quite depressed after breaking up with James, her long-term boyfriend. As she came out of her depression, she realized that she had to set boundaries and limits on James. It took the better part of a year to establish clear boundaries, which required that she have no contact with James. After months of stability and a positive outlook on life, she called me in a crisis. She was very depressed. I asked what, if anything, was going on in her life. She replied that James had called her at work, at a beauty salon, caught her off guard, and requested that she cut his hair, and Christina said, "Okay." But it wasn't okay. Christina had violated her own dharma, her own sense of right action, and had opened a hole in the solid boundaries she had set up. I suggested that she call James immediately to cancel his hair appointment and let him know that that would not be an option for him. All too often psychiatry neglects this very important question, namely, "What is the right thing to do?"

Psychiatry is the only medical specialty in which one is diagnosing and treating at the same time. A cardiologist, in contrast, will take a history and order an electrocardiogram in order to make a diagnosis, and then, after he has run those tests, will proceed with the appropriate treatment. A psychiatrist, on the other hand, should be "treating" his patient from the moment he first meets him or her.

In a sense, the major goal of all forms of therapy is to convey the message, "Everything is going to be all right." If we regard death and suffering as failures, it is impossible to give full reassurance to any patient, for every person will suffer and eventually die. I deeply believe that everything is going to be all right for all of us. The obstacles we face in life are challenges and opportunities for growth. They are not to be dismissed or frowned on. Even death can be a healing experience, a time of releasing, letting go, and completing unfinished business. To heal, in the sacred sense, means to convey hope at all times, even in so-called hopeless situations.

From the moment I first shake hands with a new patient, I am working to create hope. I am treating with a dose of "hope," and diagnosing to see what feels hopeless to my patient. For many people, hope is inspired and fear alleviated through compassionate diagnosis. People want to know if they've really seen a ghost or if they're crazy. On dozens of occasions, while writing this book, people have shared stories with me to find out if I think they're crazy. It's a kind of abbreviated therapy. They tell me their "ghost" story or spiritual experience; I tell them what I think their experience is called, and they feel better.

PSA (Psycho-Spiritual Assessment)
Guideline #1

1.   What is your Main Concern? *Name* it. Your main concern can be a symptom, problem, experience, or goal. A symptom or problem is something you want less of, such as: pain, depressed mood, or insomnia. A goal is something you want more of, such as: money, friends, peace of mind, or work-related or athletic success. When one's main concern is an experience, and is neither a symptom nor a goal, one doesn't need to "get rid of it," or "acquire more of it." Examples of experiences are: angels, near-death experience, and past-life memories. When you visit a medical doctor, he is always looking for what's wrong. That is how he is trained. When you tell your psychiatrist or family practice doctor that you saw an angel, he will go into "symptom mode" right away. He can't help it. For the vast majority of doctors, that is all they know. But PSA wasn't created just as an assessment tool for doctors and other healthcare practitioners. It is a tool that you can use on your own, many times a day.

Be as specific as possible in naming your main concern. For example, if you have cancer, your main concern may be pain caused by the cancer. What is your main concern *today*? Realize that your main concern may change from day to day.

This first step may seem elementary, but I cannot tell you how many people come to see me who are not clear about their main concern. I have to ask a number of questions just to find out why they are sitting in my office. So, clarify what your main concern is for today.

2.   How do you *feel* about your main concern?
3.   What does your main concern *mean* to you?
       (How does your main concern affect your belief systems or sense of meaning in life?)
4.   What is the *dharma*, the right action, to take regarding your main concern?

As I said at the beginning, sometimes, powerful solutions come with such simplicity that one says, "Well, of course. That seems obvious." And once people begin using PSA, it does seem obvious, and they wonder why they had not been using it before I taught it to them.

The most difficult step for you may be step 4, the action or dharma step. However, what is most important is step 1, determining and naming your Main Concern. What is it you want to work on? What is your symptom? What is your illness? What is your goal? What is your experience? Before moving from step 1 to step 2, it is helpful to reconsider the wording of your main concern if it is a problem or symptom. For example, your main concern may be "fatigue." You can state that as a symptom, but you can reframe your main concern as a goal, which would be "more energy." A positive starting point always works to your advantage. As a goal, you would say, "My goal is to have more energy." When stated as a symptom, you are saying, "I want to get rid of this fatigue." This wording creates a battle in your mind, a sense of struggling against something. When you re-state the main concern as a goal, you can martial all of your powers of intention and move toward the goal. This concept applies to all symptoms and problems. If your "problem" is that you are financially struggling, restate the problem as the goal, "I intend to make more money, or to allow more money to flow into my life." You get the idea. There are a million ways to take that small step from dealing with a problem, to working toward a goal.

Let's run through one PSA, using a "symptom" of pain as the main concern. Here are some possible answers to the four questions:

1.   What is your main concern? (symptom, problem, experience, goal).
        Name it.
"Pain." Almost everyone wants "less pain," but see if you can state the main concern as a goal, namely "more comfort."
2.   How do you *feel* about your main concern?
"I hate it!"
3.   What does your main concern *mean* to you? How does your main concern affect your belief systems or sense of meaning in life?
"The pain makes me question if God exists. If he exists, I think he has forgotten about me."
4.   What can you do about the main concern? What is the *dharmic* action?
        The action steps for pain are complex. You may want to see a chiropractor, acupuncturist, or orthopedic surgeon. You may benefit from getting massage, or learning to express anger at the person who has become your "pain in the neck." We can see, by looking at step 3, what the pain means, that this person needs helps with her spiritual connection, with her feelings about God, and her spiritual life in general.

Here's another PSA, which starts with an "experience" of angels as the main concern:
1.   What is your main concern? *Name* it.
"I saw an angel."
2.   How do you *feel* about your main concern?
"It made me feel ecstatic."
3.   What does the angel *mean* to you? How did the angel affect your belief systems or sense of meaning in life?
"I believe I'm losing my mind. I don't believe in angels. They're not real. Even though it felt real, I'm sure it cannot be real."

4.   What can you *do* about it? What is the *dharma*? What are some action steps you can take?

I might recommend some reading to someone with this main concern, suggesting that they read personal accounts of angelic visitations, as well as more scientific studies. I might quote the Gallup Poll or other survey. A recent survey showed that 60% of Americans believe in angels. That action step, namely hearing new information, might be all that is needed. I would also suggest that this person go back to the religious text of whatever religion he was raised in, and look for accounts of angels. Virtually every major sacred text makes reference to angels. I would reassure her that she is not losing her mind, and I won't be recommending anti-psychotic or other psychiatric medication for her.

If you've just seen your first angel, you will probably be startled, and will be wondering what it is and what it means. If, on the other hand, you've seen so many angels that you've lost count, then seeing one more angel, will not concern you any more than will going to the mailbox.

All symptoms, problems, experiences, and goals are worthy of our attention. Don't attempt to persuade yourself to dismiss an experience as insignificant. If something has grabbed your attention, that "something" is your main concern, if only temporarily.

The key to working with PSA is to become present and ask yourself what your main concern is *today*. Work through the four steps and transform the main concern. You may have a main concern that dominates your life, and you will want to deal with that. But over the course of a single day, you may have two or three other main concerns. Deal with them. You can move through many main concerns quickly, and with practice, in five minutes you can arrive at the truth of your situation and the dharmic action.

PSA is about making your life a conscious experience. Many of us don't even know what we want or what our biggest concern is. We push things aside and tough things out. Most of the time that is not the best strategy. We are all capable of checking in with ourselves throughout the day, noting the main concern, and taking a minute to deal with it. In this way, difficulties and strains won't build up.

Because people may dismiss things that are too simple, let me run through the PSA again. This time, take a minute to go through the process. Right now you are reading this book and this is your focus. During the rest of this day you have a main concern:

1.   "What" is your main concern? *Name* it.
2.   How do you *feel* about your main concern?
3.   What does your main concern *mean* to you?
4.   What is the *dharma*, the right course of action to take?

To go back to the Sanskrit phrase this chapter started with, steps 1, 2, and 3 deal with "Sathyam vada," or speaking the truth. It also has to do with "knowing" your truth. Steps 1-3 allow you to do a quick awareness check to find out your personal truth. Step 4 deals with the second half of the Sanskrit phrase, "dharmam chara," meaning "practice powerful right action."

For some people dharma may raise a question. You may feel that the solution has to do with, "What I WANT to do," and not necessarily with what is the RIGHT thing to do." The right thing to do is the thing that will bring no harm to anyone, including yourself. Dharma is action for the higher good. Because we are a society that is more concerned with our rights rather than our duties, dharma may be a challenge. Hollywood celebrities have great access to fame, power, money, connections, and sex. And they may like the status quo. As a general rule, you have to be very competitive and materialistic to rise to the top of the field in movies or music. It may be difficult, once you have all the material things you have, to adopt a different life strategy. You may "want what you want when you want it." In your case, PSA will bring you short-term relief, but will not lead to long-term positive life changes—if you opt out of *dharma* for step 4. Dharmic actions are those that lead to a win-win solution.

For the rest of you, who make up more than 99.9% of the world, PSA with *dharma* as step 4 will help you zero in on what your issue or main concern is. It will then help you find a solution, and will, over time, spiritualize your life, bringing greater harmony into all relationships, and more inner peace and joy into your heart.

And now, for the really abbreviated version of PSA, now that you understand the process, the 4 steps are: the *name*, the *feel*, the *meaning*, and the *dharma*.

Now let's look at Psycho-Spiritual Assessment in more depth by seeing how these four questions can help us, not only in overcoming problems, but also in attaining our goals.

Because PSA is so widely applicable, it can help you achieve a variety of goals, from mundane problems at work or home to physical challenges. Aaron, a 55-year old, came to see me at his wife, Penny's, strong urging. Penny had asked Aaron to move out after 25 years of marriage, mainly because he drank too much. I saw Aaron weekly for several weeks and then met with them together. When I asked Penny, what she wanted from Aaron, she replied, "I just want him to stop drinking."

Aaron replied, "But I have stopped drinking. I haven't had a drink in three months. You can check it out. There's not a can of beer or a bottle of liquor in my apartment." Penny didn't believe Aaron, but I did.

"What else is bothering you, Penny?" I asked.

"I'm really sick of the whole situation. I work 50 or 60 hours a week. I come home and the house is a mess and he expects me to do all the cooking. I've just had it."

"So tell me this, Penny," I asked. "Is this marriage 100% over for you? Is there a 50/50 chance? What are we dealing with here?"

"Well, Doctor, I'd say this marriage is 99% over."

"O.K., at least now we know what we're dealing with. We have 1% to work with here. It's not much. Do you two want to work on that 1%, or just call it quits? Frankly, it looks pretty bleak to me." Aaron was ready to give the marriage a good try, without hesitation. Penny took a little longer to answer, sighed, and then said, "We might as well try. I don't see much hope at all, but—whatever."

We now had clarified step one of the PSA. Their main concern was a goal, named, "We want to save the marriage." Aaron and Penny answered step two, how they felt about it, differently. Aaron was frightened that it wouldn't work out. Penny felt confused. She had been preparing herself for divorce and now had to face the uncertainty of her situation.

Here's how they answered step three, "What does your main concern, the goal of saving the marriage, mean to you and how does it affect your belief systems or sense of meaning in life?" Aaron was overwhelmed at the thought of completely losing Penny. He deeply loved her and felt that life would not have much meaning without her in it. Penny's beliefs were in greater conflict. She didn't believe the marriage could be saved, but at the same time, was willing to try something anyway. For Penny, trying to save the marriage meant taking a leap of faith. She too was scared.

Having assessed the situation as thoroughly as possible, it was time for step 4, taking dharmic action. The diagnosis was clear. The treatment soon would become clear. "You guys really have a lot of problems. Let's start with something small and try to solve one problem at a time. Let's start with anything. I don't care what it is. What would either of you like to see the other change?"

Both of them felt stuck and didn't answer, so I replied, "I have an idea. Penny says she's upset that you never cook. She hates coming home and feeling as if she has one more person to take care of, one more mouth to feed. Now, she wants to be taken care of. Aaron, I suggest you begin cooking for her."

"But I really don't know how to cook," Aaron replied. I grilled Penny and Aaron about their favorite foods. They both liked fish.

"O.K., Aaron, how do you feel about starting to cook fish?"

"I have no idea how to do that, Doc."

Patiently, I gave Aaron a "cooking lesson." "Aaron, here's a piece of paper and a pen. Take some notes. I want you to go to your grocery store. Go to the fresh fish section. Do you like sea bass?"

They both agreed on sea bass. "Ask your grocer to pick out two terrific sea bass steaks, let's say a half-pound each. Then buy a lemon, some olive oil, salt, and garlic powder. You can buy fresh garlic, but let's keep things simple." I went into details about how to prepare the fish and told him to cook the sea bass for four minutes on each side. We then ended the session and made an appointment for the following week.

When they returned, I asked them how the cooking was going. Penny was happy and was very pleased with how the fish tasted and with the fact that Aaron had made the effort. Aaron was happy and relieved. He hadn't been sure if he had the skills to cook, and now he knew he could. Step 4 in the PSA, the dharma, was for Aaron to learn to cook fish. Life's problems often can be solved by practical, simple, down-to-earth action steps.

This "fish story" actually was the turning point for the marriage. Immediately, hope and trust began to return to the marriage. I continued to help them with specific, detailed tasks, with more "fish stories." Within a few months, Aaron had moved back in with Penny. The marriage was saved and has grown even stronger over the ensuing years since I last saw them.

I still find this story amazing. Love was rekindled and a marriage restored simply because a man learned how to cook fish. This may not sound like spiritual psychiatry to you, but the "spiritual" thing to do is the "practical" thing to do, the "right" thing to do. For some, the practical thing to do, after completing Psycho-Spiritual Assessment, is intensive meditation and guided imagery work to assist them in deepening their faith in God, and in removing obstacles that prevent progress on one's chosen spiritual path. In the case of Aaron and Penny, the practical thing to do was to save a sacred bond, a marriage, through a mundane activity.

Psycho-Spiritual Assessment may not always provide you with the ultimate answers or relief you seek, but, at the very least, it helps you organize your thoughts, feelings, and experiences so that you can begin the process of understanding them and can start doing something about them.

I once had a "patient" referred to me by Peter Jensen, Ph.D., one of Canada's top sports psychologists,[1] to help prepare her for the Olympic Games. She was a Canadian sprinter who was training in San Diego.

Tammy's main concern (PSA step 1) was "wanting to run faster." I asked her how she was feeling about the Olympic trials (PSA step 2) and she replied that she felt fine, "just a little nervous." I was later to find out that she was more than a little nervous, but I didn't know it at first, nor did she. It would take a few weeks for me to understand PSA step 3, what the Olympics meant to her.

I visited Tammy at the Olympic training grounds, watched her practicing her race, and spoke with her coach. Tammy had been expected to be running much faster than she had been, but, in fact, her times were getting worse, rather than better. I taught Tammy a mantra to quiet her mind through the day, and especially before she started a race. I taught her a variety of imagery techniques to help her deal with every part of the race, as well as every part of the day. We developed a 24-hour-a-day "mental fitness" program (a term coined by Peter Jensen). In spite of these efforts, Tammy's times continued to worsen. I called Peter Jensen for advice and told him everything I had Tammy practicing. Peter replied, "You're dealing with overwhelming fear here. You're doing everything right, but since nothing's working, I can confidently say that she is terrified. A lot of athletes are like that. They start training for the Olympics when they're ten years old. In the back of their mind they're afraid they'll fail in their quest, but they're trained to hide the fear. I think Tammy is afraid that either she'll fail or that she won't give her best effort when it really counts. That's a big problem. An athlete may lose the big race but feel fine if she knows she's given it her best shot, but if she knows she didn't give it her best shot, it's very hard for her to live with." Peter added one final item, "You know, you've got a tough situation here. Many of the Olympic Gold Medalists have spent more than two years practicing mental fitness, but Tammy just started and the Canadian trials are only four weeks away." PSA step 3 was becoming clear to me. If she did poorly in the Olympics because she did not give it her best shot or was not able to for whatever reason, she might carry a sense of failure with her that could follow her for life.

Finally, Tammy and I were able to see the bigger picture and could successfully complete the Psycho-Spiritual Assessment. We focused on her feelings (PSA step 2) and uncovered tremendous fear, fear that she had blocked out of her mind for a decade. Understanding step two allowed us to understand step three (How does your main concern, a goal in this case, affect your belief systems or sense of meaning in life?). The Olympics were a "do-or-die" situation for her. It was everything. Making it to the Olympics was her meaning in life.

When we finally understood Tammy's PSA in greater depth, we moved on to PSA step 4, dharmic action steps. We knew what was wrong. Now we had to fix it. With time running out, we zeroed in on action steps. I used imagery techniques to help Tammy "embrace" her fear, rather than running from it. I asked her to allow an image to emerge that represented her overwhelming fear, and then I asked her to imagine that she was communicating with that image, and asking it what it wanted from her. I asked her to picture her chosen form of God (Jesus) beside her before each race.

Suddenly, Tammy began blowing away the competition. Her coach had pretty much "written her off" and was paying attention to two other athletes who had been improving must more rapidly than Tammy, and who had been consistently beating her to the finish line. Within two weeks of this change in strategy, Tammy had beaten two of the fastest women in America, in her particular race. Things were looking good. At the Canadian Olympic trials, Tammy ran very well in the first two races, almost guaranteeing herself a place in the Olympics, but she faltered in the third and final trial and didn't qualify for the Olympics. She was quite dejected but had every reason to hold her head high. She had nearly pulled off a minor miracle.

Some may regard this as a story of failure, and indeed I wished Tammy had qualified for the Olympics. But she had risen to such a high level of competition that she felt good about herself. We simply had not had enough time. If Tammy had prepared mentally for a year, rather than a month, I believe the results would have been great.

If PSA merely helps people identify their main concern, it has already provided a valuable service, for you cannot arrive at your destination without knowing what or where that destination is. You have to begin somewhere. Begin where you are this moment. And where you are this moment is your main concern.

This seemingly simple tool is intended to be all-inclusive. It is not intended merely for the spiritual aspirant, nor even for the theist. Atheists and agnostics equally benefit by using the same steps. Everything in life can be seen as part of one's spiritual process. To the spiritual seeker, the real challenge is finding meaning in the everyday things in life—in cutting a loaf of bread, doing the dishes, balancing the checkbook, investing wisely, planning vacations, and even learning to cook fish.

Peak Performance

No matter what your goal is, peak performance techniques will help you. We can't elaborate on a program so complete that we can address every aspect, from beginning to end, of every goal, every dream, every vision. Yet, by understanding the basic principles of peak performance, you can understand how Tammy almost made it to the Olympics after practicing these techniques for just a few weeks.

Concretizing the Goal: Long-Term Visioneering
Mental Fitness Technique #5

In your mind's eye, see yourself succeeding at your goal. Bring all your senses to the experience. Notice how you feel attaining your goal. What are the sights, sounds, smells, and physical sensations.

Fill in all the details of success as if you are painting a picture of life the way you want to see it, feel it, and live it.

Whether your goal is to win an Olympic Gold Medal in diving or become President of the United States, you must have a clear long-term vision, which is like a rope that pulls you into the future, into the place, situation, or person you want to become. After you've "seen" who or what you want to become or what you want to achieve, you'll want to practice "mental rehearsal" as your next step.

Mental Rehearsal
Mental Fitness Technique #6

In order to illustrate "mental rehearsal," let's use the example of a diver whose main concern is trying to win an Olympic gold medal. In order to make it to the Olympics, you'll need to do more than visualizing yourself on the winner's stand with the National Anthem playing in the background, although that is a necessary kind of imagery. You'll want to practice the dive in your mind thousands of times. According to Peter Jensen, Ph.D., one of Canada's top sports psychologists, Olympic and elite athletes need to be visualizing success 100% of the time. Peter instructs his athletes that if they dive incorrectly in their imagination, they must repeat the exercise correctly, no matter where they are. If they're in a grocery store and suddenly "see" themselves doing the dive incorrectly, they are instructed to stop right there, put down whatever they were about to place in their shopping cart, close their eyes and "do the dive correctly."

Visualizing success is not a part-time job. Even if you're dedicated to attaining your goal and are practicing imagery of this kind 30 minutes twice a day, it's still not enough, for the unconscious mind, with all its doubt and fear may continue to project images of failure. Therefore, if you want to win at the highest level, prepare yourself to visualize success every waking moment.

If your goal is to overcome cancer, you may choose to use mental rehearsal techniques the same way an Olympic athlete would, visualizing health on a continuous basis. This technique is certainly no guarantee of a cure. We don't have the data yet, but anecdotal reports abound regarding the power of the mind to assist in physical healing.

You'll want to mentally-rehearse every aspect of your event (or your recovery from illness). Run the race in slow speed, and then in "real-time." Rehearse the race using your sense of sight as the dominant feature of your imagery. Rehearse again using the sense of touch, feeling your feet hit the ground just right. Rehearse again using the sense of hearing, listening to the sound of the wind in your face, and the sound of your breath. Rehearse again using all of your senses together.

Throughout the day, if you think about your dive and picture yourself stumbling or making some other error, stop everything and mentally-rehearse the event correctly.

Facing Up To Self-Lies
Mental Fitness Technique #7

You may think you know what you want, what your goal is, and what your talents are. Yet, many of us are unrealistic with ourselves. We exaggerate, either telling ourselves we're worse than we really are, or that we're better at something than we really are. No matter what you want to succeed at, you've got to start with an accurate and honest self-assessment, brutally honest.

Almost all of us fail to tell ourselves the full truth about ourselves. We lie to ourselves. We pretend to be something we're not. We fool ourselves into thinking we're better at something than we actually are, or that we're worse than we really are. By facing our personal reality, free of lies and distortions, we become free. Every lie we tell ourselves requires mental effort to keep that lie in place. We have to keep telling the same lie.

For some people, it's not so much a question of lying to themselves, but rather is more a question of exaggerating or distorting the truth. This exercise is an opportunity for you to write down the lies you've been telling yourself, or those things you've been distorting or exaggerating.

This technique may reveal some obvious self-lies, or you may have to think about it to before you discover ways in which you may be hiding from the truth about yourself or your life situation.

Information can and should lead to transformation. By working with this technique, I am *not* encouraging you to beat up on yourself. Just tell yourself the truth. Write down your self-lies, exaggerations, and distortions in your notebook.

After you've written down your list, review each entry and ask yourself why you've been distorting that particular item. And then, if you really want to accelerate your personal growth and spiritual advancement, vow to stop lying to yourself about anything no matter how petty or small it might seem. This vow of truth will clarify some of the shadow parts of your personality, allowing you to shine some light on that area. Telling the truth is immensely powerful. Start by telling yourself the truth, the whole truth, and nothing but the truth. Once you have shared your soul with yourself, you can proceed toward your goal without being hindered by false notions. You'll know exactly how much higher you have to jump and how much longer you'll have to persevere in a particular endeavor. If you think you're going to be an over-night success as a rock-and-roll star, harsh reality will clash with your dream, and reality is likely to win.

Mood Words
Mental Fitness Technique #8

Mood words are verbs that we say to ourselves to assist us in achieving a particular goal. It's easier to illustrate mood words through examples than by lengthy discussion.

If you're an athlete, a sprinter, who needs to find tremendous reserves of energy when "coming out of the starting blocks," you may want to use a mood word like: "blast," or "explode." By silently saying "blast," one's entire system comes into better harmony. Thought, word, and deed come into closer alignment. Practice has shown that mood words work. Telling yourself to "blast" out of the starting blocks helps you run faster.

Let's say you have a serious physical problem, like cancer, with which you are battling. As part of your mental fitness program, you may want to incorporate mood words like: "conquer," "win," "overcome," "triumph." But don't just say these words in a repetitious way. Pour your heart into the words so that your own deep emotions empower the words.

If you're about to take an exam, you'll want to first calm yourself by using your mantra. Then you may use mood words throughout the exam, but not mood words that make you feel pressured. You want to be able to glide through the exam without getting hung up on any particular point. So "glide" or "fly" may help you do better and feel better while taking an exam.

If you're giving a speech, lecture, or sermon, first become clear about your intentions. Are you trying to inspire your audience, educate them, or move them into a particular course of action? Let's say you want to inspire them, in which case, you can inspire yourself with mood words like: "inspire," "breathe," "glorify," "unify."

Perhaps you work in some kind of production business with deadlines. Every month you're under the gun and there never seems to be enough time. Time is a big issue, which requires a broad approach. Mood words can play a part in "expanding time" and helping you relax as deadlines come and go. You may feel the need to "speed things up," but that attitude almost invariably makes you run out of time, so try mood words like: "slow down," or "expand." Yes, you can expand time, so by telling yourself to expand, you actually can expand psychological time.

I used mood words to assist one elderly woman who was recovering from a stroke. She had to learn how to walk again and was started with a walker while in the hospital. Because her feet no longer seemed to obey her wishes, mentally she was saying, "Damn these useless feet." I suggested she use the word "lift" every time she wanted to lift her feet. It made a big difference for her.

No matter what your situation, problem, goal, challenge, or experience, you can find a mood word that will improve your situation.

Overcoming Resistance
Mental Fitness Technique #9

Let's return to the main concern that you selected through Psycho-Spiritual Assessment. You *know* you want to attain your goal. You *know* you want to be free from pain, suffering, symptoms, and problems. You want to win that Olympic gold medal in diving and you've been practicing "mental rehearsal," and have been using "mood words." Yet, when I ask my patients (and you) if they are 100% ready and willing to work toward that goal (or away from that symptom), they usually pause and say, "Well, I pretty much want it. Even if they tell me they definitely want "it," I'll ask them how committed they are. "Are you 100% committed, 90%, 50%, 25%? I almost never hear, "100%."

That part of you that is not 100% behind success with your main concern is your "resistance." There is some part of you, maybe only 1%, that is sabotaging your "best laid plans." Until you are aware of your resistance, it will be nearly impossible to fully actualize your dreams, or resolve your symptoms or problems:

Get in touch with that part of yourself that is resisting, that is not fully committed to attaining your goal or overcoming a symptom—that 1, 5, 10, 25, 50% of yourself. Allow an image to emerge from your unconscious mind that represents that resistance.

Once you have seen, heard, touched that image of resistance, you will immediately have more information about how to proceed and about what obstacles you may be putting in your own way.

For example, when I asked one patient of mine to get in touch with her resistance to romance, she immediately "saw" and "felt" her elbows being pulled back into the chair as if drawn by ropes. She then had to work with those ropes in her mind. One month later, she resumed dating for the first time in many years.

Once you have visualized your resistance, you can gain more information and deepen your transformation by proceeding in this way:

Give the image of resistance a voice. Express your feelings toward the image of resistance. Ask what it needs and wants from you. Ask it why it wants what it wants. Ask it if is protecting you from anything.

The four mental fitness techniques you've just read are essential for peak performance. Let's review the steps required for attaining a goal:

1.   Identify your goal. Name it. Define it.
2.   Using mental imagery, mentally-rehearse success in attaining the goal.
3.   Face up to any self-lies. Tell yourself the truth. Is your goal realistic? Do you need to make any adjustments between who you think you are and who you really are?
4.   Identify the mood words that motivate you in the right direction, and then use them.
5.   Identify any pockets of resistance. Visualize the resistance and "talk to" an image of resistance.
6.   You'll also want to incorporate the mental fitness techniques which you already read about in Chapter 3, namely,
7.   "mantra meditation" and,

8.   "regulating energy with breath."

That's what I did with Tammy, the woman I helped train for the Olympics. Her 24-hour-a-day program included all seven of the above steps, plus a few more. She also had to learn how to embrace overwhelming fear. These tools take practice, both for clinicians, patients, and clients.

---

1. Peter Jensen, Ph.D., *The Inside Edge: High Performance Through Mental Fitness* (Toronto: Macmillan Canada, 1992).

Chapter 6

Belief Medicine

Most of us believe in God. Half us have been visited by the spirits of the dead. Most of us believe in angels and many of us have had close encounters with them. Even though millions of Americans have these experiences, we still consider these phenomena to be stunning and unusual, while the rest of the world has similar experiences, and most peoples take them in stride as part of every day life. Of course, there are cultural differences. Among the Hopi, and certain Japanese villagers, the dead always visit. The lack of such visitation is abnormal.

Healing through faith, magic, potions, spells, spirits, hexes, divination, "irrational" belief systems and non-scientific thought is prevalent throughout the non-industrial world. Some of these healing systems may appear as strange to us as our own spiritual practices appear to them. Yet cultural perceptions of mental derangement and miraculous occurrences can help us sort our attitudes to spiritual experience in our own culture.

One theme pervades the indigenous world: Everything, whether animate or inanimate, contains spirit. All of life is interconnected and we can communicate with it. So, even rocks and trees are believed to have some type of consciousness. And people can listen to the rocks.

Another commonly-held belief among indigenous peoples is the power to heal or harm through thought. The Balinese people have a curious courting ritual. If a man wishes to pursue a girl in marriage, he sends her a bouquet of flowers. If he is determined that she will answer in the affirmative, he places a pea-sized package in the bouquet. That package is made by wrapping a boar's tooth with a banana peel, and then wrapping that with boar's hair. If the girl discovers this addition to her flower bouquet, she believes she must marry him or else she will fall ill immediately and die. Up until the mid 1960s this practice was prevalent in Bali. Many women married because of this practice, and many women died because they refused to marry.

In India, spiritual experience, paranormal phenomena, and the power of thought have been accepted as commonplace for thousands of years, so commonplace that many Indians are distrustful of ochre-robed gurus with siddhi powers.

Not only is the power of the mind given considerable weight in India, but also the power of the Gods is accepted by hundreds of millions of people. It is believed that deities cause rain, fire, and every other natural event. Droughts and natural disasters are believed to be caused by nature's response to man's "evil deeds." In the American state of Hawaii, nature is worshipped and feared in the same way. Great care is given to propitiate Pélé, the Goddess of volcanoes, for her wrath can bring death. Every year, post offices in Hawaii receive vast quantities of lava, packages mailed back from tourists all over the world, tourists who had brought a little bit of Pélé home with them but became frightened by stories of Pélé's powers and returned the lava to its natural home.

In every culture, including our own, belief systems form the foundation of diagnosis and treatment of illness. People all over the world have visions and talk to spirits, and spiritual belief and practice are central to their ideas of health, illness, and treatment.

Shamanism and Sorcery

Every culture has its shamans and sorcerers. India is well known for its yogis and gurus. Yogis have the same powers as do shamans, but they do not use them in the same way. The shaman acquires power with a specific intention of healing, while the yogi acquires power as a kind of side effect of spiritual practice. The yogi is interested in spiritual liberation as well as the uplifting of his fellow humankind. But the yogi, unlike the shaman, rarely displays his powers, for such a display is considered a sign of ego and an obstacle to spiritual progress.

Shamans and sorcerers practice their craft in every inhabited continent. They work not only in the villages of Africa and Asia, but also in cities across America. In my own hometown, there are several shamans whom I am aware of and very likely others whom I am not aware of. In San Diego, there are Chinese healers, Thai healers, curanderas, kahunas, and, among the 18 Native American reservations in San Diego County, shamans.

Anthony is a psychiatric nurse with whom I work. You would not know by listening to his beautiful English diction that he comes from the Ibo tribe in Nigeria. Nigeria consists of three main tribes—the Ibo, the Yorba, and the Housa. Anthony's Ibo name "Chukwura" means "God is great." The Ibo's beliefs and practices, according to Anthony, include, "5 to 10% of my people who talk to the spirits and the spirits talk back. These are the traditional healers, and that's all they do: they talk to the spirits and heal people. Many of them throw stones, bones, or feathers in order to make their diagnosis. My village has between five and ten thousand people, and there's one major shaman in each village. There are no psychiatric hospitals in the villages. The crazy people are treated by the shaman who usually considers insanity to be caused by possession."

With "rational" psychiatry we spend billions of dollars on brain research, and treat psychotic people with powerful mind-altering drugs, and, of course, we keep looking for those genetic markers. The drugs are great. They work. But the collapse of traditional society has everything to do with why the schizophrenic no longer fits in and no longer functions. The schizophrenic is not an outcast in Anthony's tribe. He is considered sick, but is not discarded. Schizophrenia is not just a disorder of dopamine metabolism in the brain. It's a disorder of society itself.

Madre Sarita was an urban healer in San Diego, California, a shaman or curandera, who was world-renowned for her healing abilities.[1] She died in 2008 at the age of 98. Sarita was very ill with asthma for more than 20 years and had little relief from her years visiting traditional doctors. Because her own father was a medical doctor, it was certainly logical that she be treated allopathically. But at age 45, as a last resort, she visited a curandera, a Mexican folk healer, a shaman. During the psychic surgery that permanently cured her, Sarita intently observed two "medical assistants" who worked beside the shaman. When the healing was over, Sarita asked who the other two helpers were and the shaman responded, "Oh, you can see them? They are my spirit guides."

Because Sarita was restored to full health, she decided to learn the art of healing and devote her life to others. Sarita practiced a blend of Mexican folk healing and Native American practices. Through the years I discreetly referred three or four patients to her, one of whom she cured of a fatal, inoperable brain tumor. To a Western-trained psychiatrist, Sarita sounds like she was insane. In an altered state when she healed, she felt the presence of Pata de Águila Gris (Grey Eagle Foot), a spirit guide who assisted her, and she felt and saw "angels of light" pouring out of her fingers into the patient when she was doing her healing work. She claimed to be able to see into people as if she had "x-ray" eyes. She talked to the spirits; the spirits talked to her. Bright lights swirled around her while she was in trance.

Sarita was the daughter of a physician and had two sons who are medical doctors, surgeons. One of her sons is Don Miguel Ruiz, author of *The Four Agreements*. In her family, the ancient and the modern came together and were embraced fully and completely. There was no "either-or," no debates about which form of healing is better. The only questions they ask are, "Which type of healing is needed in a given situation?"

Sarita was unusual only in the extent of her healing gifts and in her generosity. She charged $50 for the entirety of treatment, whether it took one session or one year. Herbs cost extra. Sarita had an extensive out-reach program, routine follow-up care, and a devoted group of patients who visited from all over the world. But Sarita's beliefs were not unusual. They are part of healing in Mexico and throughout the Americas. Almost all Latinos in America are familiar with curanderismo, but few I know will admit it to me until I have asked specific questions that prove I already have some knowledge about curanderismo. Then, Latinos will open up to me about their beliefs, because they see that I respect the tradition.

The Ibo shaman of Nigeria and the curandera of Mexico both believe that spirit is present everywhere, that we can communicate, not only with the spirits, but also with all of creation. Both believe in the interconnected web of life.

In order to acquire special healing powers or the ability to predict the future, shamans like Sarita undergo a variety of spiritual practices, which may include: meditation, prayer, fasting, dancing, assuming yogic postures, chanting, drumming, and the use of natural hallucinogens, such as peyote. By contrast, sorcerers use these same techniques to acquire power, but then use those powers for malevolent purposes, or in difficult cases of tribal justice. In Panama and in many Central and South American countries sorcery is commonplace. Usually, the person who is about to have a spell cast on him is notified ahead of time, not so that he can repent, but rather so he might live in fear.

In one of the most highly developed types of sorcery practiced by the Kahunas of Hawaii, the spell is cast without the targeted villager being aware of this "attack." A group of Kahunas will meet in order to decide how to cope with a problem villager, and, on some occasions, will decide to kill him through spells and "black prayer." Illness and death proceed the same way in each case with the villager developing a progressive paralysis, which eventually leads to death. The symptoms and course of the illness are identical to a poorly-understood Western illness called Guillain-Barré Syndrome.

It is believed that the sorcerer has intense will power and supernatural powers and can use these powers to inflict harm on those who are spiritually unprotected. It is widely accepted that people who come under this psychic attack fall prey to accidents, fires, theft, illness, or death. Whether the afflicted individual is living out a self-fulfilling prophecy or is actually being attacked by negative thoughts cannot be scientifically determined. These beliefs are widespread throughout the world.

Eastern Healing Systems

Over a billion people live in China and almost a billion in India. That's 40% of the entire world population. Central to the healing system of those two billion people is the idea of chi, prana, or life force. Throughout the millennia they have shared the same philosophy of all pre-industrial people.

Acupuncture is based on an understanding of chi. Although Western medicine has begun to accept the efficacy of acupuncture for a variety of conditions, most Western doctors are not aware of the philosophy that underlies acupuncture. The Chinese understanding of mental illness is particularly interesting. According to some practitioners, mental illness is caused by problems of the liver, because, "the liver is the house of the mind." Rather than labeling mental illness with names like "schizophrenia" and "manic-depressive illness," the Doctor of Oriental Medicine looks for "an excess of fire in the liver," "ascending fire," "liver chi stagnation," "liver yin deficiency," or "liver yang deficiency."[2]

The liver is believed to be closely linked to the expression of anger. The kidney and spleen are also believed to be essential to mental health. The kidney is associated with fear, memory, and forgetfulness. According to Chinese medicine, "If someone with a mental problem complains of an episode of absent-mindedness, they probably have a liver-kidney problem." Worry is caused by problems with the spleen, so an emotional problem characterized by an "excess of worry," would be diagnosed as a liver-spleen problem. Many mental-emotional problems are treated by "reducing liver heat," and then balancing spleen or kidney "yin" and "yang" energies.

Because Chinese medicine involves an understanding of body, mind, and spirit, a Chinese doctor is not surprised by reports of visions of spirits or other paranormal phenomena. He will know that an angelic vision requires no treatment at all. If the patient desires deeper spiritual understanding or further spiritual experiences, the Chinese doctor may choose to use specific acupuncture points which encourage the flow of chi through the chakras, up toward the head, and out the "third eye," thereby encouraging spiritual experiences. If, on the other hand, a patient is troubled by "spirit possession," the Chinese doctor will treat by focusing on the patient's chi, helping him build up his own defenses, his own mind, body, and energy, so that the spirit can be overcome.

Even more ancient than Chinese medicine is Ayurveda, the ancient holistic medical system of India, which was first written about in part of one of the Hindu sacred texts, the Atharvaveda, and which has gained acceptance in America through the writings of Deepak Chopra, M.D.[3]

Like Chinese medicine, Ayurveda is based on an understanding of "chi" or "prana" as the life-force is called in India, as well as an understanding of three body types or doshas: Kapha (water), Vata (air), and Pitta (fire).[4]   The Ayurvedic physician decides whether his patient has too much fire, air, or water, and then prescribes herbs and a diet that will balance the three doshas. For more than 5,000 years Ayurvedic physicians have been practicing and perfecting their medical science. While Western doctors naturally want to know if Ayurveda really works, in time they will have to examine the source of Ayurveda. Ayurveda is believed to have originated in "Cosmic Consciousness," handed down from God to the ancient Indian rishis, who in turn, transmitted their knowledge and wisdom, by word of mouth, to their students.

Belief in something beyond the mind and body pervades Asia, and goes beyond the diagnosis of medical and psychological problems. In Burma, people who spend years meditating have visions of creatures that live in another dimension of consciousness. These pale creatures with large dark eyes fit the common description of aliens. According to the spiritual adepts who see these creatures, they are not aliens, but live right here next to us, although they generally cannot be seen without "spiritual sight."

By looking at the beliefs and customs of other cultures, we may initially be struck by the differences between "us" and "them." However, when we look beyond the obvious differences, we discover commonalities. Not only do body, mind, and spirit matter to people in every culture, from every religion and from every age in history. In addition, core healing principles are universal, common to Western medicine, Oriental medicine, Ayurvedic medicine, and even faith healing.

Universal Healing Principles

While these cultural medicines of spiritual beliefs may seem different from Western approaches, they actually share the key ingredients of every health care system in the world, which are: 1) hope, inspired by the healer, 2) trust in the healer, his diagnostic methods and his treatment modalities, and 3) a shared belief in the causes and cures of illness.

Even if penicillin is the right treatment for pneumococcal pneumonia, the treatment will work much more effectively if both doctor and patient share the same belief about bacteria and antibiotics. Shared belief inspires hope, deepens trust, and allows our built-in healing systems to kick in. Part of how penicillin works is through our deep belief in its awesome power.

Dr. Frank Lawlis spent years working with Native Americans in the Southwest, and learned some powerful lessons about the power of belief systems. After working with chronic pain patients for a number of years, he began to wonder why the Indians came into the clinic only three or four times a year to refill their Demerol, instead of every few weeks as the typical American would. Dr. Lawlis was amazed to learn that the Indians were not ingesting the Demerol tablets! They were placing them around the house to ward off the "pain spirits." This treatment was very effective but would wear off after a few months.[5]

Belief systems have everything to do with the onset of illness, the treatment course, the recovery rate, and every other aspect of health. When I was a resident in psychiatry, I met Chang, an 18-year-old Chinese man with clear-cut paranoid schizophrenia who knew he was sick. When I asked him why he thought he had developed the mental illness, he replied, "When my grandmother was buried, my back was to the sun and my shadow was cast across her grave. That is very, very bad luck." This deep belief, which is widespread among the villagers in the southern provinces of China, may have been the straw that broke the biochemical back of Chang's brain, bringing on the full-blown schizophrenic psychosis. This information did not entice me to ignore anti-psychotic medications, but it gave me a broader view of Chang's illness and how it fit into his life and worldview.

One's cultural belief system can trigger illness or at least greatly contribute to the onset. Culture can also determine the course of the illness. Remember that the schizophrenics in the Ibo village in Nigeria do not appear crazy. They fit in. Culture can trigger illness or prevent it!

Health and illness are intimately woven into the fabric of life in every culture on earth. We, in the West, believe that we can separate illness from the individual, from society, from culture. We try to separate the mind from the body and relegate the spirit to the clerics. However, a complete diagnosis must take into account body, mind, spirit (and energy), as well as the cultural beliefs, rites, and rituals. In a sense, all healing is "faith healing," even our own. American medicine men won't cop to being superstitious but they really are.

In Great Britain and throughout most of Europe, 50% of medical doctors either prescribe homeopathic medicines or refer patients to homeopaths. A homeopathic remedy is created by taking a substance, say the mineral phosphorus, and diluting it to the point where you can barely find a single molecule of phosphorus in the remedy. Well-controlled scientific studies performed around the world over the past twenty years have demonstrated that homeopathy works, at least sometimes.[6] Yet American doctors argue that, "homeopathy can't work because there's nothing in the medicine." Homeopathy is like chemical acupuncture. The molecule of phosphorus, or whatever the remedy is made from, "charges" the solution. Homeopathy works on the "energetic body," or chi.

The belief that spirit doesn't matter, or that it has no place in healing, is common in American medicine, but it is important that we realize that this is just a belief and not a fact. The fact is that the absence of spirit in medicine is a major cause of our disenchantment with medicine, with our sense of discomfort with some doctors, and with our shaken faith in the current healthcare system.

Folk Medicine of the American Tribe

Perhaps the strangest tribe I have had the privilege to study personally are the Americans. Anthropologist Horace Miner was one of the first to study, and write about, the Americans as if they were an indigenous tribe from a foreign land. In order to make his point about the "strange" habits of the Americans, he referred to this tribe as the "Nacirema" ("American" spelled backward).[7] To quote Dr. Miner:

> The Nacirema are a North American group living in the territory between the Canadian Cree, the Yaqui and Tarahumare of Mexico, and the Carib and Arawak of

the Antilles. Little is known of their origin, although tradition states that they came from the East.

Each family has a shrine. The focal point of the shrine is a box or chest, which is built into the wall. In this chest are kept the many charms and magical potions without which no native believes he could live. These preparations are secured from a variety of specialized practitioners. The most powerful of these are the medicine men, whose assistance must be rewarded with substantial gifts. However, the medicine men do not provide the curative potions for their clients, but decide what the ingredients should be and then write them down in an ancient and secret language. This writing is understood only by the medicine men and by the herbalists who, for another gift, provide the required charm.

In the American healthcare system medicine men are not actually the highest authority on healing. After the medicine man has poked, prodded, and stuck needles into the tribesman, he asks the client to wait before going to the herbalist.

The medicine man is now required by the tribal leaders to confer with a ceremonial leader who knows absolutely nothing about healing, but from whom the medicine man must get approval in a paper ritual dance in order not to violate tribal taboo. The natives give gifts several times a year to these ceremonial leaders, who then transfer these gifts in part to the medicine men.

The poorest of the American tribe are not required to give to the same ceremonial leaders, but a special leader allots gifts to the medicine men working with them. Both types of ceremonial leaders exert incredible control over the medicine men, telling them what herbs and potions they can dispense and how long it should take them to cure a particular patient. If the medicine man does not comply completely with the ceremonial leader, especially the leader involved with the poor, the medicine man will receive no gift at all.

Much like the healers of Bali who pierce their arms with arrows, the American medicine man undergoes brutal rites and rituals in a long, grueling apprenticeship under other medicine men. During this initiation the apprentice is shamed and humiliated repeatedly for many years. Part of the training is not unlike the Vision Quest of the Cherokee, who go into the desert or forest alone for days and days, until they have a vision. Usually they do not eat or sleep until they have their vision. That vision gives guidance about what they are to do in life and what their totem animal is. The Vision Quest of the American medicine man, however, goes on for years with extended periods of sleeplessness only briefly interrupted with sleep. The medicine man in training lives in a state of almost complete mental and physical exhaustion. The medicine men have told me directly that this method of training is ancestral. "It's the way it's always been done."

Dr. Miner writes as well about the healing temple, which is given the name of "latipso" ("hospital"):

The latipso ceremonies are so harsh that it is phenomenal that a fair proportion of the really sick natives who enter the temple ever recover...No matter how ill the supplicant or how grave the emergency, the guardians of many temples will not admit a client if he cannot give a rich gift to the custodian ...

From time to time the medicine men come to their clients and jab magically-treated needles into their flesh. The fact that these ceremonies may not cure, and may even kill the neophyte, in no way decreases the people's faith in the medicine men.

So powerful is the belief in the healing temple that tribal members will even go there in order to die, even though they know they have an incurable illness for which care by an untrained family member would provide a more soothing ending to their life.

The American medicine man practices a powerful form of voodoo that can either cure or kill. It is among the most powerful in the world. I met a woman whose husband had been the victim of voodoo death by the medicine men. This poor lady's husband, who was in his seventies, went to visit the medicine man and was told he had a fatal disease that would kill him in 30 days. This man had been active up until the day he visited the medicine man. He returned from the visit, lay down on his bed for the next 30 days, and died.

The power to heal by the medicine man is also immense. The mere sight of a medicine man can inspire healing on the spot. So great is this awe and power that a client often recovers before he has taken the herbs and potions.

The healing and spiritual practices of our own and other cultures are only strange and bizarre when seen out of context of the spiritual belief system in which they work.

One reason I've gone into such detail about Belief Medicine and so-called "strange" healing practices of other cultures is to expand our awareness until we realize that our "judgments" of those other cultural beliefs and practices are just that—judgments, and not facts or realities.

In addition to judging anything and anyone we don't understand, many of us are judging others and ourselves all day long. "That person is stupid. What a dumb thing he just said." "It's her fault. She's always messing things up for everyone else." "That guy is so fat." "Wow, is she skinny." "African-Americans are dumb." "White people can never understand." "The Mexicans are ruining our economy." "The Japanese are ruining our economy." "Ibo healing practices are insane."

Judging serves one purpose. It temporarily removes us from our own pain. However, it harms each of us profoundly, stunting our psychological and spiritual development, keeping us isolated, separated, and walled off to love. Here is a simple way to become aware of your judgments and then begin to let go of them. Practice this just before going to sleep at night:

Judgment Review
Mental Fitness Technique #10

Imagine that you are with a Divine Being, a Higher Consciousness, a being who embodies love, compassion, wisdom and strength. Scan this being from head to toe (or top to bottom if this Presence is a glowing light without form). Let yourself relax into being in his or her presence.

Now begin to get in touch with the judgments you've experienced today. Review in your mind each and every person, place, or event that you judged. Remember each incident as completely as possible, recalling the thoughts, feelings, sensations, and images. Then imagine that each judgment flows out of you, as if it were liquid. Offer each judgment to God. Imagine that, as you mentally see the judgment, it flows out into your hands. You then offer the judgment to God, knowing that he/she is not standing in judgment of you. I'm sure he or she will gladly take the burden from you.

Remember not to judge yourself over your judgments. Rather, try to adopt a meditative, witnessing attitude in which you allow yourself to see how your mind has been working. Release the judgments one at a time. Practice this technique for a year and you'll probably come close to completely stopping the flow of judgments. When that happens, the heart begins to expand and open up. Love begins to flow so that we can both give and receive it.

I was working with a patient, Joe, around the need to look at his judgments. After practicing the above "Judgment Review," he said to me," I know why I do that. I need the distance, the separation, the space that judgments provide. This reminds me of my mother. She's 65 and still doing, doing, doing for others. She can never say, 'No.' And I'm like that. I can't say, 'No.' Being judgmental allows me to keep my distance from people and is kind of a way of indirectly saying, 'No.' I'm afraid if I'm more available to people, they'll want more of me, more of my time and energy. I'll be sucked dry."

I asked Joe to practice the judgment review each night. This technique helped peel away one layer of the onion so that deeper issues in his life could be examined. Love cannot coexist in the heart of man along with greed, anger, jealousy, and envy. By practicing the Judgment Review, we can begin to remove obstacles to love.

Mixed Messages About Healing

It is often asserted during medical school and psychiatry residencies that religious commitment is harmful to health. Yet scientific studies have proven that the opposite is true, that religious commitment is beneficial to both mental and physical health. 72% of Americans agree with the statement, "My religious faith is the most important influence in my life." (Princeton Religion Research Center, 1994).[8] It is not surprising why so many people feel uncomfortable with their doctors. Although most Americans believe that religious faith is the single most important influence in their lives, medicine has largely ignored this set of beliefs, and instead has been slow to let go of Freud's belief that "Religiosity is in many aspects equivalent to irrational thinking and emotional disturbance." "Religious beliefs are illusions." In Freud's personal and private correspondence, he confided in Reverend Oskar Pfister, "I am a completely godless Jew."[9]

Not one of Freud's major clinical cases, which formed the foundation for his theories, were believing Christians or Jews. In his attempt to remain "rational," Freud did quite a disservice to the future of psychiatry. Freud not only disliked religion, he did not like to listen to music because he didn't want to be powerfully moved by something that he couldn't understand rationally.

Modern medicine has come a long way since Freud, but the long-term effects of his pseudo-scientific rationalism remain to be overcome. A recent review of four major psychiatry journals revealed that religion was evaluated in less than 3% of all quantitative studies.[10] When religion was evaluated, by far the most common variable studied was religious denomination, a variable which solid science has proven to be worthless to study. What is vital to health is religious commitment, a variable examined in less than 1% of all psychiatric studies.

We'll get into some of the research on religious commitment in a minute, but first I'd like you to consider this question: "If psychiatry and medicine have given so little attention to studying religious commitment, what is the scientific basis for the disregard of religion, and the persistent view of religious commitment and experience as a health risk?" There is no basis, other than a gut-level, irrational reflex. Scientific medicine is, in fact, out of step with the beliefs of the average American, as well as the scientific studies that are now verifying the beliefs of the average American. A review of all quantitative psychiatric articles during a 12-year period found that 72% of the religious commitment variables were beneficial to mental health. Psychiatrist David Larson, M.D. has been studying specific components of religious commitment— ceremony, prayer, social support, relationship with God, meaning and purpose—and has found that commitment is the most important religious variable.[11] Commitment is a powerful predictor of health and recovery. Among these "commitment variables," relationship with God, ceremony, and social support have been proven to be an overwhelmingly positive influence on health. According to Dr. Larson, "Religious commitment, when measured appropriately, is associated with mental health benefit at least 80 percent of the time." The simple effect of regular church attendance is tremendous. One large study found that people who did not attend church were four times more likely to kill themselves than were people who attended church frequently (Comstock and Partridge, 1972).[12] Another study, by Stack, showed that church attendance predicted suicide rates more effectively than did any other factor, including unemployment.[13]

No matter what the problem or illness, religious commitment has been shown to have a protective influence. Drug and alcohol abuse is a particularly interesting subject, when examined in terms of religion. Drug abuse is related to an absence of religious commitment, and in particular, to a decline in faith during the teen years. 89% of alcoholics had lost interest in religion during their teen years, compared to 20% of a control group.[14] It is no wonder that Alcoholics Anonymous and other 12-step programs, have been so successful in treating addictions. A crisis in faith may, in fact, be one of the main causes of addiction. So, a program like AA that requires acknowledgment of a Higher Power is the appropriate "cure."

Religion is also good for marriage. Not only do religiously committed couples report a higher rate of marital satisfaction, they also report more satisfying sex lives, which is perhaps a surprising finding, since many of us, especially psychiatrists, consider religion to be a repressive force. Women who state they are very religious report greater satisfaction and happiness with marital sex than do either moderately religious or non-religious women.[15]

Religious commitment, as measured by church attendance, not only decreases stress and improves quality of life, it also may extend life. One study (Comstock and Partridge, 1972)[16] found that the risk for men dying from atherosclerotic heart disease was much less for those who attended church at least weekly. A two-year study of the elderly in New Haven, Connecticut (Zuckerman, Kasl, and Ostfeld, 1984) showed that the less religious had a mortality rate twice that of the more religious.[17]

Other studies have shown that religious commitment reduces delinquency, psychological stress, and depression. Even hypertension is significantly alleviated by religious commitment.[18] The studies you've just read about were carefully designed. For example, studies that found that religious commitment decreased hypertension and death by heart disease, controlled for a variety of other factors. Good mental and physical health could have just been a by-product of religion. It could have been that the religiously-committed smoked less, drank less, ate better and exercised regularly. In fact, they did, but with those factors controlled for, the results remain significant. This data holds true for people who are not practicing a healthy life style. Among smokers, those who consider religion to be very important were seven times less likely to have an elevated diastolic blood pressure than were those smokers who did not value religion in the same way.

The bottom line is that religious attendance, along with a host of religious commitment factors, should be a major consideration in evaluating health. Lack of religious commitment is a reliable risk factor for illness and death, and should be evaluated by physicians along with smoking, cholesterol levels, and exercise.

Religious belief has been studied for 50 years in America, with a consistent finding. 95% of the U.S. population believes in

God. There is a huge gap between what the average American believes, what is known about the positive effects of religion, and how medicine practices. This discrepancy is part of the American belief system. We're ignoring the facts, and can't afford to do so anymore.

Psycho-Spiritual Assessment can be applied to any medical problem, any experience, and any life challenge. It is not enough for a doctor to say to a patient, "You have bone cancer, and I recommend a course of chemotherapy immediately." We physicians must find out what the cancer means to our patients, and why they think they have cancer. Once we know what our patients believe, we can work as a team, making shared decisions based upon shared, or at least mutually respected, beliefs.

We must begin to close the gap, so that what you believe is similar to what your doctor believes and how he practices medicine. One of the most exciting results of the new religious studies is that one can easily teach doctors how to incorporate religion into their work. In one particular study, psychiatrists were taught how to take a religious history and how to treat depression with a cognitive approach that included religious content. Patients did better with this approach, but the doctors who considered themselves atheists had an even greater success rate using this "religious" technique than did believing doctors.[19]

What you believe should be similar to what your doctor believes. How can your doctor help you at the deepest level if he thinks you're "hiding" behind your religiosity, or if he thinks your visions are the results of imagination or a nervous breakdown? If you've had a strange experience, such as a vision, you want someone to whom you confide it to help you keep your head together, and reinforce the importance of the event. You want someone who can reassure you that your vision is special and not abnormal.

1.   Bobette Perrone, Henrietta Stockel, and Victoria Krueger, *Medicine Women, Curanderas, and Women Doctors* (Norman and London: University of Oklahoma Press, 1989) and Ari Kiev, M.D., *Curanderismo: Mexican-American Folk Psychiatry* (New York: The Free Press, 1968).
2.   Personal communication regarding Chinese Medicine with Raymond Woo, M.D., D.O.M. (1996).

3. Deepak Chopra, M.D., *Quantum Healing: Exploring the Frontiers of Mind/ Body Medicine* (New York: Bantam Books, 1989).

4. Dr. Vasant Lad, *Ayurveda: The Science of Self-Healing* (Santa Fe: Lotus Press, 1984).

5. Frank Lawlis, Ph.D., *Unity in Diversity: Cross-Cultural Perspectives* (San Diego: Atlantis the Imagery Newsletter, June, 1989).

6. David Reilly, "Is Evidence of Homeopathy Reproducible?," *The Lancet,* 344: 8937 (Oct. 1994), 1601-1606," and in *Brain-Mind Bulletin* (Los Angeles: Feb. 1995).

7. Horace Miner. "Body Ritual of the Nacirema," *American Anthropologist,* 58: 3 (1956), published by the American Anthropological Association.

8. Princeton Religion Research Center, *Religion in America* (Princeton University Press, 1994)

9. Oskar Pfister, *Psychoanalysis and Faith: The Letters of Sigmund Freud and Oskar Pfister* (New York: Basic Books, 1963).

10. David Larson, M.D., M.S.P.H., and Susan Larson, M.A.T., *The Forgotten Factor in Physical and Mental Health: What Does the Research Show?* (Rockville, MD: National Institutes for Healthcare Research, 1994).

11. *Ibid.*

12. G.W. Comstock and K. B. Partridge, "Church Attendance and Health," *Journal of Chronic Disease,* 25 (1972): 665-672.

13. S. Stack, "The Effect of Religious Commitment on Suicide: A Cross-National Analysis," *Journal of Health and Social Behavior,* 24 (1983): 362-74.

14. D. Larson, M.D. and W. Wilson, "Religious Life of Alcoholics," *Southern Medical Journal,* 73: 6 (1980), 723-727.

15. Carol Tavris and Susan Sadd, *The Redbook Report on Female Sexuality: 100,000 Married Women Disclose the Good News About Sex* (New York: Delacorte Press, 1977).

16. Comstock and Partridge, "Church Attendance," *Journal of Chronic Disease,* 25 (1972): 665-672.

17. D. Zuckerman, S. Kasl, and A. Ostfeld, "Psychosocial Predictors of Mortality among the Elderly Poor," *Americal Journal of Epidemiology,* 118 (1984), 410-423.

18. Jeffrey Levin, Ph.D., and H. Vanderpool, "Is Religion Therapeutically Significant for Hypertension?," *Social Science Medicine,* 29: 1 (1989): 69-78.

19. L. Propst et al., "Religious Values in Psychotherapy and Mental Health: Empirical Findings and Issues," *Journal of Consulting and Clinical Psychology,* 60 (1992): 94-103.

Chapter 7

Getting Conscious About Consciousness

Quarterback great Joe Montana (retired) "steps back into the pocket. He's not the fastest quarterback and he's not the strongest, but he is arguably the best ever. Montana looks down-field, calmly looking left, then right. Joe acts like he has all the time in the world to throw the ball—even with several 300-pound linemen charging him. Montana throws deep, just as he's smashed to the ground—and Jerry Rice grabs the ball in the end zone to clinch a third Super Bowl victory for the Forty-Niners." (Imaginary sportscast.)

Montana was just the best, and that's partly because he often played football in an altered state of consciousness that athletes call "the zone." The zone is where Michael Jordan "lived" on the basketball court and is part of the magic of Tiger Woods. When Montana was in the zone, he saw all the receivers, and defenders, and felt as if he had all the time in the world. His mind was very steady and calm, not filled with thoughts, doubts, questions, and desires. When Montana was in the zone, he felt as if the game were being played "through him." He had a sense of almost divine perfection, as if nothing could go wrong. And when he was in the zone, not much did go wrong. He "saw everybody on the field." And he "knew" that the football would arrive exactly where it was supposed to. Sometimes, athletes who have had great success while playing in the zone feel that the game was played through them.

The zone is one of many altered states of consciousness. Most of us live in the consciousness of four dimensions: three dimensions in space, and a fourth dimension of time. Of course, those four dimensions are the parameters of so-called "normal" consciousness. Some of the top physicists in the world have speculated that there are as many as ten dimensions. Consciousness is difficult to define, but easier to describe in terms of its qualities, which are time, space, level of alertness, and awareness. Like the words "God," "spirituality," and "love," "consciousness" is a word which medicine has chosen to ignore as much as possible.

Time is one of the most extraordinary aspects of consciousness. When we're bored, time seems to move slowly, and when we're really enjoying ourselves, time seems to move all too quickly. Under certain dramatic circumstances, our perception of time is radically altered. Racecar driver Dennis Adams raced in the NASCAR circuit for three years and was in a few dramatic wrecks. Adams noticed that time slowed down as an accident unfolded and slowed down more and more as his consciousness of the imminence of the accident increased. As time slowed down, Adam's thoughts and actions dramatically speeded up, as if he had much more time than he should have had to prepare himself.

Pepe Romero, the world-renowned classical guitarist, can consciously alter time to suit his own needs. If he needs to play 16 notes in one second, he simply expands the second...rather than trying to play faster. Thus, whereas that blazing speed can be a real stress for many musicians, for Pepe it's quite simple. He has as much time as he needs. He simply makes the time and changes it as he needs to. In certain altered states of consciousness, states of merging, being at one with all, time ceases to exist at all. That is difficult for people who have not had altered states to comprehend, although most people have had some kind of experience of this slowing, whether it's after receiving some bad news, while "crashing" from hypoglycemia, or after driving on an interstate highway for ten hours. When time stops, one simply "is." One experiences a sense of unity with Life, God, and Nature and feels free from the laws of time.

"Space" is the second major quality of consciousness. Several years ago, as I was driving my car out of the driveway, my 12-year-old gorgeous and sweet cat, Daisy, ran under the front right wheel of the car and was struck. I dashed out of the car, saw Daisy covered with blood and having massive convulsions. I did a quick "medical check," to see if I should take her to a veterinarian. But I quickly discovered that her heart was in ventricular fibrillation and that she would die quickly. I held her, stroked her, and talked to her. She quickly died and the grief that I felt was so huge that it had no boundaries. I had never experienced such "pure pain." Pure, raw, pain. Such pain that the borders and boundaries of my own mind melted away. Time stood still and space took on new proportions. There was no past, present or future, and my mind was not bound by space. There was no shame or blame or mental activity. I was pain. I realized that grief was an altered state of consciousness.

Imagine what a distorted view a psychiatrist would have if he didn't understand consciousness. Here's a hypothetical case. Imagine that a patient (we'll call him M.J.) tells his shrink that he can jump so high and so far that people who have seen him jump say it looks as if M.J. is walking on air. M.J. tells his psychiatrist, "It's as if gravity doesn't affect me, like I can defy the laws of space. I've even seen videotapes of myself in the air and I can't even believe it's me. Sounds crazy, huh, Doc?" The doctor might reply, "Yes, this certainly sounds like a terrific fantasy, a deep narcissistic dream, a child-like magical wish that reality could be other than it is. This wish must be hiding a deep-seated depression." I do not mean to imply for a second that M.J. see a psychiatrist. But if he did, the psychiatrist would have to acknowledge that when Jordan was in the zone, he was in such an altered state of consciousness that he actually thought he could fly. And, of course, he could, and still can, even though retired! Basketball great, Larry Byrd, has said, "Michael Jordan is God incarnated as a basketball player." Jordan's feats of magic are not only an example of extraordinary physical skills but also of extraordinary mental skills. He can handle states of consciousness as well as he can a basketball, and his genius lies in his ability to be skilled in both.

Consciousness also involves levels of alertness. Are we sharp and focused, intensely aware, or feeling dull, or in a coma? All these are levels of conscious awareness. How we process this sensory input depends upon our state of consciousness. Are we being receptive, or are we being active? Are we being aware through one sense, such as vision, or are we experiencing a multimedia show, experiencing the world through sight, sound, touch, smell, taste, and movement, all at once?

Awareness is the most significant component of consciousness and also the most elusive. By awareness I mean our sense of being, our sense of existence, our sense of "I-ness." And as we'll see later, our sense of awareness depends on which level of our being we are focused on: body-awareness, mind-awareness, soul-awareness. Your core and mine is "I am." When we were five years old, we said, "I am playing in the grass." At age thirty, perhaps you said, "I am getting married today." Perhaps at sixty-five, you might say, "I am struggling with arthritis, but I am just so happy to greet each new day." Who or what is the only constant in all the changes in life? "I am" is the constant, and "I am" really means "pure consciousness, the essence of divinity within our human forms. Through all states of consciousness, no matter how altered that state, what persists without change is "I am," our core identity.

The "Who Am I" Meditation
Mental Fitness Technique #11

If what you believe is not in synch with your thoughts, words, and deeds, you will have a "human value deficiency." When thoughts, words, and deeds are one, and are in complete harmony with one's beliefs, all of the five human values will flourish. There are few people in the world today whose thoughts, words, and deeds are one and the same, but they do exist and serve as great inspirations for the rest of humankind.

A spiritual quest requires personal effort and deep inquiry. In order to know where you're going, you'll want to know where you are right now. Where you are is "who and what you believe you are." So let's take a minute to review some of life's most fundamental questions.

Before addressing each question, close your eyes, take a few deep breaths and relax. Allow your mind to let go of all thoughts, worries, and concerns for just a minute. Ask yourself the first question, "Who am I?" Meditate on that question, and allow answers to present themselves from your conscious, unconscious and higher conscious minds. Your answer may come in the form of images, thoughts, sensations, or words. One way to approach the question, "Who am I?" is to ask, "Who am I not? What am I not?" Maintain the same kind of non-judgmental, meditative, reflective attitude toward each question. Witness the answers that present themselves, and don't immediately dismiss the first answer that arises.

1.   *Who am I? (not just my name!)*
2.   *Where did I come from before I was born?*
3.   *What is the meaning of life, if any?*
4.   *What is the mission in my life, if any?*
5.   *Where will I go when I die?*

Now that you have taken a moment to meditate on "who you are," or "who you believe you are," you have had an experience of an altered state of consciousness, no matter how small that shift in consciousness may have been. If you deeply entered into the question, "Who am I?" it may take you a moment or so to return to "normal" consciousness. Now—you're back!

Have you ever walked into a room in your house or at work and suddenly completely forgotten what you're looking for, or why you went into that room? We all do that. That's an altered state. Most of us don't know how to handle altered states and most of us don't like that feeling of walking into a room and totally forgetting what we're doing there. Several years ago I decided to turn the tables on this state. Rather than struggle mentally to remember why I had gone into a certain room, I "surrender" to this lost feeling and allow myself to go into a meditation for a minute or two. I've even done this when I've opened the refrigerator, had no idea what I had been looking for, and I would proceed to go into this "lost" meditation for a minute or two.

Consciousness is not a fixed quality that is the same around the world. It differs from culture to culture. Culture shock is really "consciousness-shock." We go to a foreign country and just feel stunned or shocked. One reason for the shock is the change in scenery, the differences in language, architecture, dress, vehicles, etc. But part of the reason for culture shock is that the other culture exists at a different level of consciousness. Many people have written about India as a "hypnotic state," and I have certainly experienced that. The people have a different language and clothing. They have a different rhythm and spirit. When you enter a country of a half a billion people in a certain cultural consciousness, your own individual consciousness gets a jolt.

Women and men live in different worlds. Jeanne Achterberg, Ph.D., author of *Woman As Healer*, says, "men and women may not communicate much of anything at all to each other since we live in such different states of consciousness and being."[1]

Besides a different consciousness for men and women, there's also group consciousness: the consciousness of a football team, choir, or orchestra in which people must think and act with one mind. Anyone who's watched competitive sports has witnessed the rise and demise of a team's momentum. The "force" goes this way and that. It's with you or it's not. Suddenly, the other team coalesces into a tight unit and that one-mind force becomes unstoppable. One mind is also essential for an orchestra to play a beautiful symphony without the single instrument standing out inappropriately.

In contrast, mob consciousness, another kind of group mind, often has no conscious direction or goal. In a mob, the individual relinquishes his own personal awareness and conscience and surrenders to the movement of the mass. In the late sixties at the University of Colorado, a group of students was trying to take over the administration building and thousands were being swept this way and that. From my standpoint at the periphery of the mob observing, the energy was frightening, like a tornado that could rip through town with no warning whatsoever and go in any direction. The mob was an unpredictable, angry group that was surrendered into one-mind.

Social consciousness, another kind of group mind, changes over time. Sometimes we are raising our consciousness and sometimes we surrender it. Our society's views of women's roles, African-American identity, national purpose and pride, and human evolution, for instance, have changed dramatically over the past half-century.

All the various components of consciousness—time, space, sex, societal orientation, level of alertness, and awareness—are determined by the direction in which our mind is focused. If we are focused on the future, our consciousness is narrow. Whereas, when our mind is immersed in the moment, as it is while playing in the zone, our consciousness seems to expand. When we're fully in the moment, time seems more flexible and we feel as if we have more room within which to work, even though the physical playing field is the same size.

In the West, we have a notion of "normal" consciousness: individualistic, goal-directed, linear, sequential, outer-oriented, task-oriented, and objective. We like it that way. We like to think that we have one state of consciousness, or maybe two. We're awake or asleep. This "normal" consciousness I've just described is a kind of American male consciousness. What we have believed to be normal consciousness is a kind of binary world: good-bad, black-white, hot-cold, fat-skinny, Democrat-Republican, etc. In normal awareness we judge, separate, and classify. We dissect experience. We hold fast to what we consider good and push away (or hate) the opposite. This kind of thinking is why the world is so polarized. This kind of thinking is what we call "normal." Yet psychiatrist R. D. Laing, in his book *The Politics of Experience*, states, "Normal men have killed perhaps 100,000,000 of their fellow normal men in the last 50 years."[2] Laing said that in 1967. If he's remotely correct, then approximately two percent of the world population was murdered during the 1900s. We call it war and consider it more or less to be normal. War is not the creation of schizophrenics or other psychotic people. It's a product or a result of our normal consciousness!

Most of us live at the level of the body, mind, and personality, and we identify ourselves, for example, as a "forty-year-old American male high-achiever." The person who is experiencing mystical union with the divine or with nature is no longer identifying with his or her physical body, or even his or her personality. His awareness has risen to the level of soul, whose boundaries are limitless.

According to Eastern thought, consciousness can be fixed at any of the levels of human being: the physical body, the energy body, the mind, the intellect, the layer of bliss, and the soul. The more we identify with the "outer" layers, the more "normal" consciousness seems to be. The more we identify ourselves as spiritual beings, or beings full of spirit, the more our consciousness expands, until time and space no longer hold any significance.

In the final analysis, our state of consciousness is determined by our level of spirituality, or sacred awareness. The great ones, the saints, sages, and mahatmas, are the true masters of consciousness. They are the masters of time, and live in a state of consciousness in which "normal" time does not even exist. They live in "God's" time, which is not bound by ideas of past, present, and future. They're like Michael Jordan when he's in the zone, except that they can enter higher states without a basketball in their hands and can stay there as long as they choose.

The Language of Consciousness

Eskimos have more than 50 words for snow. Americans have more than 30 words for money, and fewer than 10 words for consciousness. There are over 400 words in the Sanskrit language for consciousness. Just for the letter "A," there are 56 Sanskrit words for consciousness.[3]

It becomes obvious, simply by examining language, that if you want to know a lot about snow, ask an Eskimo, for they live in "snow consciousness." If you want to know about money, ask an American, for they live in "money consciousness." And if you want to know about consciousness, study the Sanskrit language for the Indians live in "consciousness," having made it their business for thousands of years to study the "inner landscape."

In English, the few words we do have to describe the different states of mind and consciousness, especially those related to mysticism, have a negative connotation, such as: unreal, bizarre, ominous, spooky, weird! Because to Western culture, "normal" consciousness is considered to be the state in which most of us live—and should live—most of the time, altered states of consciousness are considered abnormal.

Why should it be that Eastern and Western thought is so different? Why should it be that Eastern religions strive for liberation and have mapped out the territory of altered states of consciousness? One hypothesis regarding these differences involves language itself. Western language is linear. We read one letter, one syllable, and one word. We read one word after another until a thought, a sentence is complete. Eastern languages (Sanskrit, Chinese, Japanese) is written in symbols, not in sequential, linear structure. It is the very nature of symbols, of images, to lead us deeper into meaning and into experience beyond language. Put another way, the West uses left-brain language: logical, linear, object-oriented, goal-oriented, analytical terms that help us separate one thing from another. Through our left-brain we see differences. The right brain, however, does not obey the laws of time and space. The right brain synthesizes and finds similarities rather than differences. This brief summary of brain function is an over-simplification, but it is important to understand some of the general differences between right and left-brain. We are learning to use the incredible left-brain problem-solving capacity of the West with the synthetic, right-brain, mystical experience of the East. Neither is better. "Inspiration" and "perspiration," "intuition" and "intellect" when combined, bring greater understanding and skill in all endeavors. Both intuition and intellect are needed to understand consciousness and to experience different states of consciousness.

The Sanskrit language describes a range of consciousness that all of us go through to some extent every day. We move through the obvious ones: full alertness, to dreaming, to deep sleep, to waking up, to falling back asleep. Throughout the day, we also go through phases of being sharp or dull, alert or out-of-focus. We shift our sensory awareness from inner- to outer-directed. We take a little break to relax and close our eyes. Even the physical changes our bodies go through affect consciousness, so that a dip in your blood sugar will make you foggy, and caffeine will jack you back up. We have television consciousness, in which, after a long day at the office, we just kind of "zone out." We're not sharply focused and not tired enough to go to sleep. We're on consciousness's version of autopilot.

Delivering a baby is another altered state of consciousness, one that I won't pretend for a second to have experienced. There's even bowel-movement consciousness! Aren't you in an altered state sitting on the toilet?

Making love is definitely a highly altered state of consciousness, a state in which many people feel their own individual barriers and boundaries drop, a state in which many people feel themselves merge with the other. Of course, the guys in the gym or at the bar won't talk about it that way, but it's not just the orgasm that's the charge. It's the love and the union of consciousness.

In America and other Western societies we have "holiday" consciousness. That's the time of year when we're allowed to feel happy all the time. It's a feeling in the air. But we're not supposed to feel great all the time. We're not even allowed to. We wouldn't even know how to.

Mental illnesses involve split, shattered, or contracted consciousness. It can narrow to a fine point, as in hypnosis; shatter as in schizophrenia; contract as in depression and anxiety. And consciousness can expand taking us to realms beyond space and time, beyond the limits of the physical body. Yogis, shamans, and other spiritual seekers are intentionally trying to expand their consciousness, striving to attain a state of perpetual joy and love.

By looking first at different kinds of mental illness and then at higher states of consciousness, we'll begin to see just how different mental illness is from mystical states. But we must avoid the pitfall of glorifying these higher states. A brief story illustrates this: A Buddhist monk in training enthusiastically runs to his Roshi, or teacher, to tell him that he has just experienced Nirvana, or unity consciousness. The Roshi replies, "Don't worry. It will pass." We need to remain balanced about all of our experiences, not attaching too much or too little significance to any of them, appreciating that we eventually will see them in their proper perspective, in spite of the tendency of medicine and psychiatry to dismiss, devalue, or denigrate them.

I have spent decades pondering consciousness and wondering who "I am," and have had several experiences of samadhi or nirvana. While I have more and more moments in which time stands still and I fall into the beautiful experience of just being in the moment, my knowledge, experience, and wisdom are still like the bud of a rose that is slowly opening. Only a great spiritual master can judge just how far this bud has opened.

A friend of mine, Kate, a sixth generation healer from the U.K., has broadened my understanding of consciousness. I first met her in 2003 after failed corneal transplant operations in 2000 and 2002. Before Kate began her healing work on me, all she knew was that I had some kind of eye problem. At the time I was taking Prednisone, a powerful drug that helps prevent transplant rejection.

A wave of Prednisone hit Kate twenty feet before I shook her hand and actually met her.

After a couple of hours of healing work, we sat down to talk about what each of us had experienced. Kate knew more about me than any person in my life had ever known, including an ex-wife and a former fiancée. She just knew everything, even my mother's frame of mind while raising me and when she was pregnant with me.

I met with Kate many times, and I began to realize that she lived with one foot in the world of physical reality, and one foot "on the other side." Talking to dead people was quite natural to her. She can fill in "psychic details" in a conversation without making any effort, and without preparing to tune in.

While Americans are primarily visual, Kate processes the world through sound and consciousness. Living in San Diego is a challenge for her, as "beach consciousness" permeates this area. Everyone has to have the perfect body. We are very visual here on the West Coast, and for most women there is a constant, unconscious pounding from the pressure to have the perfect body. It is difficult for many men also, but I think it is worse for women.

After several healing sessions, Kate said to me, "I can't explain to you right now what happened. I have to digest the experience and in a few days I will try to find the words to translate what happened into something you can understand. I don't even understand it yet."

I've met and worked with many healers and shamans. Kate has an unusual blend of an extraordinary gift for healing and for receiving information in non-ordinary ways. She also has a keen intellect. She believes that the healers of the world need a totally new vocabulary. Really all that happens in a healing session is that Kate opens her heart to divine love, and as the recipient of the healing, one feels bathed in that same love. Her job is to direct that powerful energy of love, or rather her job is to allow the love, or God, to direct her.

My point in talking about Kate is that consciousness is difficult to talk about. A fully realized saint or avatar would have to translate some of her experience to Kate. Kate has to translate her experience of consciousness into words I can understand. And I am attempting to translate what I know into words that the reader can understand. I am also assuming that many people reading this book are far more advanced than I in their journeys through consciousness.

Kundalini: a Great Masquerader

Medicine has always been faced with illnesses that are difficult to diagnosis and that masquerade as other illnesses. Syphilis is one such disease that has fooled many doctors. AIDS was the same. Chronic fatigue syndrome is still a great masquerader and can look like depression, arthritis, lupus, AIDS, or cancer. As medicine becomes more enlightened about spiritual experience, we are much better equipped to assist people in finding out what is wrong in the body, mind, and spirit. The emergence of kundalini energy is one of the greatest masquerade acts of all time. Kundalini, a sudden release of intense energy throughout the body, may look like mental illness—like mania, depression, or anxiety. It may look like physical illness—like gout, arthritis, muscle spasm, or "an acute abdomen," a true medical emergency. It may sound like encephalitis, a brain infection. But kundalini is a prolonged altered state of consciousness. It is not a disease. A physician may be puzzled by a patient's complaint of a darkened, painful, throbbing, big toe and will pursue a diagnosis of gout or arthritis. Complaints of back pain will lead to a complete orthopedic, or chiropractic, workup. Strange visual and energy surges will lead a psychiatrist to explore mania, anxiety, or schizophrenia. Kundalini demonstrates the powerful body-mind-spirit connection.

The average person needs to know that kundalini exists within all of us, that certain spiritual practices that stir up kundalini generally should be avoided, especially kriya yoga, which should only be practiced under the guidance of a master teacher, and that what feels like a crisis is an opportunity for extraordinary mental and spiritual growth. Like other states of consciousness, kundalini is viewed differently in different cultures.

Gopi Krishna, an influential teacher of Eastern philosophy wrote the classic *Kundalini: The Evolutionary Energy in Man* in 1967 about his experiences with kundalini energy, which began as he was meditating one day and noticed a pleasing sensation at the base of his spine. Suddenly, like the "roar of a waterfall," a stream of "light" rushed up his spine into his head and he became immersed in a "sea of light." For decades, Gopi Krishna would experience these rushes of energy as well as great mental and physical anguish and tremendous physical pain. Through the process of dealing with kundalini energy, however, Gopi Krishna was forever changed and ultimately was the embodiment of peacefulness and enlightenment.[4]

Lee Sannella, M.D., has published the most exhaustive research on kundalini in the West in *The Kundalini Experience: Psychosis or Transcendence*.[5] Dr. Sannella describes kundalini as the progression of energy that ascends from the legs to trunk and back and then to the head. This energy is said to move through so-called "chakras" or energy centers, of which there are seven.[6, 7]

Some of the chakras correspond to major nerve plexuses in the abdomen and thorax. Each chakra not only represents a center of energy and nervous system function, but also represents and embodies states of consciousness and a variety of qualities. For example, the lower three chakras correspond to our lower, more animal nature, instincts and feelings. The chakra at the level of our heart is related to love. The chakra at the top of our head is related to transcendent consciousness. These energies lie within us, usually dormant.

For the Chinese physician, the chakras are part of the invisible network of chi. The chakras are seven major "wheels of energy" through which all of our energy flows. For most of us these chakras are merely concepts, but for some people the chakras' energy is actually visible. Buddhist and Hindu masters from ancient times to the present have drawn pictures of the chakras.

When the sleeping, dormant kundalini energy awakens, as the very real, but usually unconscious, prana or life-force becomes more conscious to us, it rises through these energy centers and takes us through a process of evolution of our consciousness. A variety of mental and physical "symptoms" arise, change, and dissolve as the energy moves through us. I hesitate to use the word "symptom" because that means "sickness" or "pathology." There is no pathology in kundalini, although there may be discomfort.

When the kundalini process has run its course, the so-called "symptoms" stop and the individual finds that he is much better integrated, mentally and physically, than he was before.

The person who has progressed through all the stages of kundalini is full of love, so full that others are attracted to him as if he were magnetic. A great internationally-renowned yoga teacher, Indra Devi, who recently passed, had this kind of magnetism. People who had never heard of her would walk up to her on the street, hug her, cry on her shoulder, and then suddenly step back and say, "Oh, my. I'm sorry. Who are you?"

Symptoms of kundalini range from mental to physical experience: cramps in the toes, darkening of toenails (especially of the big toe), vibration, tingling, feelings of heat, and spontaneous body movements. Pain and a feeling of pressure may develop at any point where the kundalini is blocked. Aside from body movements, rushes of energy, and pain, there are still more physical changes. The abdomen may contract and be drawn flat. One can have diarrhea or constipation, decreased or increased salivation.

The individual may hear a variety of sounds: bells, flutes, roaring. In Chinese Taoist and medical philosophies, other symptoms are identified, including itching, coldness, warmth, and feelings of weightlessness or heaviness.

People experience a wide range of emotions—powerful, ecstatic feelings of joy, or panic, fear, and anxiety. They may fall into deep states of meditation spontaneously, or have extraordinary visions of light, deities, and unearthly realms filled with great love and joy. They may feel themselves surrounded by divine light with an indescribable luster.

Sometimes the kundalini energy causes people to assume yoga postures, postures that they may never have learned or they may dance ecstatically. Often people feel no control over these body movements, which can be fluid, dancing movements or wild jumps and gesticulations.

As you can imagine, this can be a pretty terrifying state. Many people going through the kundalini process wonder if they're going crazy and certainly most psychiatrists would say they are and would treat these people with anti-psychotic medications.

Even the greatest of saints have wondered about their own sanity. Paramahansa Ramakrishna, one of the great Indian saints of the nineteenth century, went through this process and asked some spiritual teachers if he was losing his mind.[8]

Mark A., age 36, had an experience similar to those of Gopi Krishna and Paramahansa Ramakrishna, and was referred to me by a psychologist who had been working with him. They had not had much progress in therapy so my colleague asked for my opinion. Mark was anxious, panicky, and wondering if he was losing his mind. Although he had once been a very social person, full of love for just about everyone, he had become afraid to be around people and preferred just to stay home. But he was a restaurant owner, married with two young children, and couldn't afford to stay home. Mark was particularly afraid and upset about tremendous energy "surges" inside him. The energy was moving into his head and causing lots of pressure. The intensity of the energy made him shake at night, which made it harder for him to sleep.

These surges had started with a chi fast, a diet of Chinese herbal teas that are intended to increase chi, prana, or life-force energy. The fast worked and Mark began to have so much energy it frightened him. Although he had practiced kung fu for a decade, loved physical activity, and was very powerful physically, Mark began having a hard time with kung fu because it stirs up this energy so much that he just couldn't stand it.

Once all this energy was activated, it became harder for Mark to focus on his work in the restaurant. He "saw" energy streaming out of other people's heads and felt that people just looked different. "People look brighter and more defined." All of his senses were heightened. The world almost looked psychedelic to him. When he listened to music, he would break down and cry because he would start "merging" with the music. He didn't just listen to the music; he became the music. "Music sounds like it's from heaven," he said.

Mark seemed like a regular guy. He was very sweet and expressed a range of emotions and thoughts. Mark had a very angry, dominating father, however, who had put a lot of fear into him in his early years that had carried over into his adult life. When this new energy got stirred up, Mark's fear also became much greater. He was full of fear. He was afraid of this energy and afraid that the energy was making him more distant from his wife. He loved his wife dearly and was afraid of hurting her emotionally, or losing her and the children.

His medical doctor couldn't find anything wrong, but in order to be thorough, I asked Mark questions about his health and ordered some lab tests. I believed that Mark was suffering through a kundalini process but I had to make sure he didn't have a serious physical illness which could have accounted for the anxiety and energy surges.

I evaluated Mark's thyroid. If his thyroid gland had been hyperactive, it would have given Mark lots and lots of energy, and he'd probably feel euphoric as opposed to depressed. However, his thyroid tests were normal. And he didn't have the usual problems you see with hyperthyroidism, such as tremors, weight loss, or intolerance to heat, so I was able to rule that out as a cause of the energy surges.

Much less likely a possibility was a pheochromocytoma, a tumor usually associated with the adrenal gland. It produces either epinephrine or norepinephrine, also known as adrenaline. These are the hormones of the fight-or-flight response, so a person with a pheochromocytoma will have lots of energy, his heart may be racing, even pounding; and his palms will be sweating. He may be anxious or fearful. But Mark didn't have a pheochromocytoma.

I also checked to see if Mark had a drug problem. Use of stimulants, such as amphetamines, could make Mark feel overly-energized. But he didn't use any drugs whatsoever—except for the ones I had prescribed to help calm him down, and he didn't drink a lot of coffee.

After I was confident that we were not dealing with a physical problem, I went through a process that all psychiatrists go through. I examined all the mental illnesses from which Mark might have been suffering.

At the top of my "diagnostic list" was mania. Mark had enormous energy, as does the manic person. But he lacked all the other key symptoms of mania. His thoughts didn't race. He was not staying up all night. He was not spending a lot of money, money that he didn't have. He wasn't traveling a lot. He wasn't on the phone constantly or writing letters to everybody he knew. He was not psychotic or paranoid and he hadn't lost touch with reality.

Although I had ruled out serious physical or mental illness as a cause of Mark's problem, I needed to carefully look at the possibility of an anxiety disorder, a condition much less severe than the other possibilities I had been considering. Mark had all the symptoms of social anxiety disorder (SAD). He had "a persistent, irrational fear of and compelling desire to avoid a situation in which the individual is exposed to possible scrutiny by others, and fears that he or she may act in a way that will be humiliating or embarrassing." (From DSM-IV, the psychiatric guide to diagnosis).[9]

I further had to consider that he had "significant distress because of the disturbance and recognition by the individual that his or her fear is excessive or unreasonable." And his problem was "not due to another mental disorder, such as Major Depression or Avoidant Personality Disorder."

Mark clearly met all the standard criteria for SAD, but I was not satisfied that the diagnosis completely dealt with all of his problems, for it did not explain the energy surges and the paranormal phenomena. His main problem was a kundalini process, which did explain the paranormal phenomena, such as seeing light pouring out of people, and the altered states of consciousness, such as "merging with music." None of these spiritual experiences are caused by social phobia. Rather, the kundalini process was producing the social phobia.

Kundalini energy can act like a magnifying glass. Whatever emotional problems we have become exaggerated during a kundalini process, so the fear that had been part of Mark's personality since childhood became greatly magnified, as did the issues with his father. The energy was so intense that he was afraid he was losing his mind.

I wanted to avoid using any medications that would wipe out the kundalini process. Because his suffering was so great, I did prescribe Xanax, a minor tranquilizer, for Mark to take when he was too anxious. When I was on vacation, Mark called the doctor covering for me and was started on low doses of Mellaril, a major tranquilizer. Mellaril really "snowed" Mark, so he used it only on rare occasions.

In therapy, I helped Mark identify his fears and work through the issues with his father. I also taught him breath techniques that helped bring the energy down when he felt it to be too intense or threatening. I also referred Mark to an acupuncturist who helped him gain more emotional control, and helped re-direct the overwhelming and often chaotic flow of the kundalini energy. The acupuncturist (who is a surgeon) confirmed the diagnosis of a kundalini process.

Mark kept wanting to return to the old Mark, the way he used to be. He had a hard time accepting that the kundalini energy wouldn't quickly disappear. Several things made the process easier for him. I taught him a technique to help him embrace fear, rather than run from it, and I led him through imagery techniques in which he pictured and felt the presence of God right next to him. This was a critical and important part of therapy. To go through the kundalini process without a clear spiritual focus is quite difficult. Mark imagined that God was with him through his suffering, guiding and protecting him. By making a deeper spiritual connection, through the imagery technique, Mark's fears diminished.

I directed Mark in some imagery and meditation exercises to let go of the energy surging within him, instead of trying to contain it. I asked him to "hold" God's hand and just let the energy flow out of his head. This imagery helped him feel much better.

Mark also responded particularly well to "mindfulness meditation," which helped him focus more on the moment, the here-and-now—to get into the moment of cutting the meat, rolling the tortillas, serving the customers in his restaurant—to experience the present, live the moment, and not focus so much on the kundalini energy.

Through using these mental techniques, Mark became better able to allow the kundalini energy to unfold. Because he was able to bring a spiritual perspective to his problem, Mark has been able to get past the initial traditional medical diagnosis of SAD and deal with the deep-seated emotional and psychological issues in his life. Had he accepted that first diagnosis and the usual medications prescribed for it, he would not have confronted and grown past his fears. Although this spiritual work of self-reflection and analysis is difficult and slow, Mark is glad that he is following this approach rather than medicating away his anxiety. Although he will never be the old Mark, he is becoming a better, happier person. He is regaining his equanimity, has begun to get closer to his family again, and is overcoming his fears. He is getting stronger, healthier, and happier as the kundalini process works itself out. When the kundalini energy has completely run its course, the probability is that Mark will be a transformed person, more full of love and peace than the old Mark.

The kundalini experience can be a one- or two-time altered state of consciousness or a process that unfolds over time, as it did with Gopi Krishna, Paramahansa Ramakrishna, and Mark A. Kundalini does pass. The uncomfortable symptoms do go away, and are replaced by qualities that had previously been missing, such as serenity, love, and forbearance.

Once the kundalini process has started, people should be encouraged to go through the process, look at the fear, allow the energy to flow, and move into higher states of consciousness. Once the experience has passed, one generally has an improved perspective on self, life, and spirit.

Managing Kundalini
Guideline #2

Here are some general Guidelines for Managing Kundalini Energy, once it has surged, or begun to stir:

1.   Practice the one-minute-imagery ritual for anxiety four times a day. Pick one of the five stress-reducing imagery techniques from "Learning to Relax" (Chapter 13, Guideline #12).

2.   Practice breathing deeply and slowly throughout the day. This will help stabilize your energy without stirring it up more. Practice the breath technique which lowers energy and is calming: inhale to the count of 4, hold your breath to the count of 4, exhale to the count of 8.

3.   Avoid fasting.

4.   Get plenty of rest. Avoid sleep deprivation. Fasting and sleep deprivation are likely to cause kundalini energy to surge even more.

5.   Avoid any martial art that stirs up chi, prana, or energy.

6.   Balance your energy with therapeutic, touch, reiki, huna, acupuncture, or yoga. Make sure you find a good practitioner. Yoga postures can increase or decrease kundalini energy, so you'll want to find a yoga instructor who comes highly recommended.

7.   Make dietary changes. If your diet has been "light vegetarian," consider adding cheese, other dairy products, then poultry, fish, and beef—in that order. Honey can also lower energy.

8.   Find ways to "ground" the energy. Physical exercise, especially when one is in direct contact with the earth, is helpful. Gardening is a good way to "ground" the energy.

9.   Use the following imagery technique to see where the energy may be obstructed:

Redirecting Obstructed Energy
Mental Fitness Technique #12

Close your eyes and relax. Slowly become aware of the flow of energy within your body. The energy may be a powerful current. At other times, it may be almost imperceptible. The energy may seem to flow from toe to head, head to toe, or from the center on out.

Identify the flow of energy. Let's say, for example, that you feel energy moving from your toes up to your head. In your mind, follow the flow of energy. If you perceive any blockage in the energy, imagine that there is a door at that point. Open the door and explore the room that lies behind it. Make whatever adjustments that are necessary in order to allow the energy to flow through the room, and then allow it to continue on its upward course.

An infinite array of images may appear in the blocked rooms. People from the past, who have been our tormentors, often appear in the blocked rooms. Perhaps a room will be filled with memories. If you don't know how to handle the people, places, things, or symbols that appear in the blocked room, invite your chosen form of God to appear in that room with you. Ask God for advice as to how to deal with the obstruction.

10.   Assume the attitude of "going with the flow." While you don't want to try to stir up kundalini, if it is stirred up, don't fight

it. Rather, realize that the kundalini process is an incredible opportunity for transformation. See where the energy is blocked. Practice "surrender" in whatever way works for you, remembering that "surrendering" is an active process, and does not mean "giving up."

Assume the attitude of "going with the flow." While you don't want to try to stir up kundalini, if it is stirred up, don't fight it. Rather, realize that the kundalini process is an incredible opportunity for transformation. See where the energy is blocked. Practice "surrender" in whatever way works for you, remembering that "surrendering" is an active process, and does not mean "giving up." Surrender is "fully embracing and accepting what exists in this moment." The first step in dealing with anything is "awareness."

What's the truth of the situations? Become of aware of your thoughts, feelings, and bodily sensations...and then just "be" with what is. Imagine "being with what is" for just 15 minutes. How about an hour, or a day? This process is about non-striving. Move into action after you've spent some time in awareness of what the moment brings without trying to change things.

1. Interview with Jeanne Achterberg, Ph.D., "Woman As Healer," *Atlantis, the Imagery Newsletter* (Dec. 1990).
2. R.D. Laing, *The Politics of Experience* (New York: Pantheon Books, 1967).
3. Homer Youngs, *Translations by Baba,* A Sanskrit-English dictionary (Tustin, CA: Sri Sathya Sai Book Center of America, 1975).
4. Gopi Krishna, *Kundalini: The Evolutionary Energy in Man* (Berkeley: Shambala, 1971).
5. Lee Sannella, M.D., *The Kundalini Experience: Psychosis or Transcendence* (Lower Lake, CA: Integral Publishing, 1992).
6. Ajit Mookerjee, *Kundalini: The Arousal of the Inner Energy* (New York: Destiny Books, 1982).
7. John White, *Kundalini: Evolution and Enlightenment* (New York: Paragon House, 1990).
8. *The Gospel of Paramahamsa Ramakrishna.* Originally recorded in Bengali by M., a disciple of Ramakrishna; translated into English by Swami Nikhilananda (New York: Ramakrishna-Vivekananda Center, 1942).
9. *Diagnostic and Statistical Manual of Mental Disorders: DSM-IV* (Washington, D.C.: American Psychiatric Association, 1994).

PART II

GETTING ENLIGHTENED

Chapter 8

Higher States of Consciousness

Part II, which begins with this chapter, is filled with amazing stories of spiritual and paranormal phenomena such as: angels, ghosts, auras, miraculous cures, as well as stories of higher states of consciousness. By understanding "phenomena" and altered states of consciousness, we will be better able to answer the first question of Psycho-Spiritual Assessment, namely, "What is your main concern?" Once we have named, examined, embraced, and integrated these experiences into medicine and psychiatry, and into our own lives, we will be prepared to look even further beyond the current horizon. We won't have to push mystical experience back into the shadows. Rather we can follow the advice of the Roshi quoted above: "Don't worry. It will pass."

Spirit or Soul is beyond words, ineffable. All the saints, sages, and holy men and women throughout history who have directly experienced the light of the soul or who have had overpowering spiritual experiences report that these experiences cannot be adequately described in words. Words can only be like signposts that say, "There is a light in the distance." Beyond the last signpost, the last word is the light. The Love, the Peace, the Awe of Spiritual Experience cannot be done justice through words.

As we open the door to the light and explore higher states of consciousness, keep in mind a few key principles: 1) Altered states of consciousness can arise spontaneously or they may be the result of a conscious spiritual discipline. 2) Higher states of consciousness are not a sign of mental illness, but rather are a great gift, an opportunity for self-discovery and spiritual growth. 3) With years of practice one can go in and out of higher states at will. 4) Higher states almost always transform the individual in a positive way.

Once we find the door to the Light (or it finds us), we can learn to walk in and out of the Light or stay in the Light forever. Throughout recorded history, men and women have been capable of voluntarily entering the highest states of consciousness. Some of these great souls, such as Jesus and the Buddha, will be forever remembered, while others remain unknown. Even today such great souls exist. These enlightened ones feel a sense of oneness with everything at all times, and are able to go about their work in the world without retreating to a cave. The enlightened ones live in a state of perpetual peace and happiness.

In the following pages, you'll read about specific altered states of consciousness. Keep in mind that these "enlightening" experiences are not reserved for the few, but are available to all.

Out-of-Body Experience

There are two major classes of out-of-body experiences (OBEs) to look at: simple and complex. In one, we simply drift out of our bodies. There are no flashing lights, no feelings of divine bliss, no angels, no dark tunnels or celestial kingdoms that are characteristic of complex OBEs. I had one of these "simple" experiences while lying in bed. I suddenly drifted out of my body, right up to the ceiling. I could touch the ceiling with my hand...or so it seemed, even though my body was still lying in bed. And that was that. After my short flight into space, I simply drifted back into my body. Mind you, I was fully awake. There was absolutely no reason, no event, no stress, and no drugs to trigger this event. And it's only happened once to me. I stay in my body the rest of the time. Other people who have had simple OBEs may soar far out of their bodies. They may feel as if they are connected to their body by a cord, often felt to be of "silver."

The most humorous out-of-body experience (a complex OBE) I've heard of happened to the late Doctor Benito Reyes. When he was 16 years old, he suddenly flew out of his body. He was quite exhilarated and frightened as he "flew around." When he re-entered his body, he landed upside down, with his head in his feet. I can't comprehend what that means, but that was his experience. At that moment, he heard a voice, a voice that would become his spiritual teacher, his guru. The voice said, "Now do that again, but land right-side-up." Doctor Reyes spent the rest of his life (when he wasn't working, teaching, driving a car, etc.) taking astral journeys. In fact he and his wife "traveled together." These journeys were not just for fun, pleasure, or escape. They had work to do. Both Doctor Reyes and his wife were able to go to realms of consciousness in which they could see disembodied souls. In particular, they met countless souls killed in World War I, souls who had died so suddenly and so violently that they had become lost on their journey from this plane of existence to the next. The Reyes spent their lifetime of astral traveling to help these lost souls make their excursion to a higher plane, to take them to the other side.

If this sounds crazy, I can vouch that I met Doctor Reyes, heard him give a two-hour lecture (without notes), and found him to be of solid character—an absolutely brilliant, loving, and grounded human being. His credentials were most impressive: he was the founder of two highly regarded universities, World University in Ojai, California, and the University of the City of Manila, in the Philippines. His degrees included Ph.D., Ll.D., Litt.D., L.H.D. He lectured at Harvard and Brown Universities, was a Fulbright-Smith-Mundt Professor at Boston University, and authored seven books.

In my clinical practice I hear about out-of-body experiences frequently and the most frequently-reported OBEs occur in people who have been severely abused. Amanda, about whom you'll read more in "The Lost Mind" (Part III of this book), suffers from borderline personality disorder. She was the victim of mental, physical, and sexual abuse. Her father, an alcoholic, began sexually molesting her when she was eight and continued for six years. An older brother also molested her. Her father was violent when drunk, would beat her for the slightest "error" on her part, the slightest deviation from perfection. Her mother was cold and aloof. Amanda learned to cope with the agony by "leaving her body." In traditional psychiatry we would say that Amanda was "dissociating." The question that psychiatry has failed to address is "where does consciousness go when it dissociates?" I believe that what we call dissociation may often be an out-of-body experience. Amanda's consciousness has dissociated, or separated, from her physical body. Her mind and consciousness have temporarily vacated the confines of her body. Amanda was not personally experiencing the emotional and physical ravages. In fact, she learned to "leave her body" at will and would often go into states of ecstatic bliss while out of her body.

I have since questioned dozens of other people who survived extreme abuse and more than half of them report that they had left their bodies during the abuse. Of course, "leaving the body" does not make one immune from the effects of abuse. The pain, the memory, the thoughts, and the feelings are deeply registered in one's heart and mind, and years of inner work are required to recover emotionally.

Out-of-body experiences often lead people onto a spiritual path, onto a quest for God—a search for meaning, a hunger for truth and peace. Amanda is a case in point. The pain of her abuse was out-weighed by the ecstasy of her out-of-body experience. That joy kept her going through depressions, suicidal feelings, and physical exhaustion and pain. Eventually, she no longer required frequent psychiatric hospitalizations to stabilize her, and she moved into a Buddhist mountain retreat. Amanda, who long ago decided that spiritual reality was more valid than material reality, wrote me from her Buddhist retreat: "Spirituality usually begins with an earnest grasping directed towards the outside world in what too often proves to be a vain attempt to locate sacredness, a sound sense of connection, value and meaning in our lives. Encouraged by a culture that trains us to be good consumers, we search for ways to purchase and possess something ineffable, formless and vast that can't be acquired with any amount of external exchange." Amanda's experience of the light helps her remember what is most important to her—her spiritual quest.

"Leaving the body" can either cause mental illness or alleviate it. Even people with no evidence of mental instability may leave their bodies. Some people with cancer are beginning to report that they leave their bodies when the physical pain is too great. In this instance, the OBE serves a dual purpose; first it alleviates severe pain, and secondly, expands our awareness.

NDE – Near-Death Experience

Another kind of out-of-body experience, the near-death experience (NDE) has been extensively researched by Raymond Moody, M.D., author of *Life After Life*, and by Melvin Morse, M.D., author of *Closer to the Light*.[1] NDEs are common occurrences in emergency rooms. People who have suffered near-fatal heart attacks and became unconscious, upon awakening often report leaving their body and drifting above their body or into a corner of the E.R. They observe the doctors and nurses frantically working on "the body" and they feel a sense of detachment and tranquility. From their vantage point they have a full 360 degrees of vision. Normally, we can see only what's in front of us. However, the person in the NDE can often later report exact details of what was done and what was said while he was "unconscious." He may even know the exact amount of time that has passed.

During an out-of-body experience the patient may find himself flying through a tunnel and emerging into a realm of light where he may be met by deceased relatives and friends, divine personages, God, or beings of light. He or she often feels an indescribable sense of peace. Before returning to their body, some people in an NDE will have a "life review" in which their life flashes before them. Upon returning to the body, people may feel or hear a "click" as consciousness re-connects with the body. Most people are dramatically changed by having a near-death experience. They have less fear of death than before, or no fear. They feel full of love and peace and may have an urge to serve others, to share that love and make the world a better place. Above all, they report that the NDE is super-real, more intensely real than any other life experience.

In his second book, *Transformed by the Light*, Dr. Melvin Morse showed, through extensive and careful research, that children who had a near-death experience were also transformed.[2] As adults, compared to people who had never experienced an NDE, these people showed: significantly less fear of death, more zest for life, and increased psychic powers. They scored better on a whole host of personality profiles, including: less drug use, better income management, fewer psychosomatic complaints, better nutrition and more exercise, personal growth, social activity, and spiritual awareness. 25% of adults who had NDE's are unable to wear watches. Watches simply won't work for them, inexplicably working in fits and starts, or stopping altogether. The NDE has permanently changed their electromagnetic field. Yet the same watch works for someone else. Dr. Morse found that their psychic abilities were four times greater than normal people's and twice as great as the psychic abilities of those who call themselves "psychic." Dr. Morse's study showed that people are indeed "Transformed by the Light," but the experience of light during an NDE is essential for the transformation. Simply being out of your body does not provide the impetus for life transformation.

While most people who've experienced an NDE have been transformed for the better, they face some challenges. Many find it difficult to fit back into their old life; it's not easy sharing the experience with loved ones, so the individual may feel a sense of isolation. A common challenge is "feeling homesick." These people have experienced life after life, and they do not fear death. Instead, many really miss what it felt like to have come home.

Death-Bed Experience

The San Diego Hospice has reported OBEs and DBEs by other patients as well. DBEs have not been studied as thoroughly as the NDE, but tend to be characterized by a sense of peace and tranquility, a divine light, visitation of angels or God in some form, visitation of deceased relatives.

It is a testament to the San Diego Hospice that they take these experiences seriously and factor them into the equation of total patient care. Patients are given pain medication to ease terminal suffering but consideration is given to the possibility that too much medication might prevent someone from having a profound spiritual experience in their hours or days before passing. In the spirit of true medicine, Hospice physicians seek to know if a terminal patient who is displaying unusual symptoms is having a delirium (an organic brain syndrome) that might be caused by a metabolic disorder, the illness itself, medication, or other purely organic cause—or a death-bed experience.

Celedonio Romero, classical guitar great and founder of the Romero Guitar Quartet, suffered a painful, lung cancer death. Yet, despite his physical suffering, he exuded love and peace as death approached. He remained so in love with life, his family, and music that even on his deathbed he continued to give instruction to guitar students and to his three sons, who are all classical guitarists.

During those final days, in which Celedonio found it increasingly difficult to breathe and in which he encountered extreme physical pain every time he moved at all, he laughed and smiled through the ordeal. Because of his difficulties with breathing and because of blood tests which showed poor "oxygen perfusion", Celedonio was asked to wear an oxygen mask at all times during those final days. Periodically, however, he would take off the oxygen mask and smile at his children. Pepe, one of his sons, naturally panicked and told his father to put the oxygen mask back on. Celedonio, with sparkling eyes, replied, "Don't you see. I don't need this. I am doing this for you, not for me." Then Celedonio would put the oxygen back on, but only to make his children happy. He remained in a state of mental and spiritual bliss in spite of his physical agony.

He remained so in love with life and with music that minutes before he took his final breath, he said, "La guitarra, la guitarra." According to Pepe, "At the moment my father died, his love became so vast that it felt as if his love blew through me. Never in my life have I experienced such a profound love. My father was a saint. He lived like a saint and died like a saint." As a good friend of Celedonio's, I agree with his son, Pepe.

After Celedonio died, his mouth stayed wide open for four hours in a fixed position. His wife, Angelita, who had not been present at the moment of his death, began to open the door to his hospital room while his mouth was still open. Before she had fully entered the room, his mouth suddenly closed and turned into a smile. Angelita was greeted by a sweet smile rather than a cold, rigid expression.

I am sure there is a good explanation for how this change occurred physiologically. Electrical activity remains in the body after the spirit departs. It is possible that a sudden electrical discharge in his nervous system caused his mouth to close. The physiology may have been human, but the timing was divine. Of course, this experience was a bit terrifying for Celedonio's children and grandchildren who were present and observed his mouth suddenly close.

Celedonio didn't actually die. Let me explain. I often make reference to Celedonio and his three sons, Celin, Pepe, and Angel. They are extraordinary examples of peak performance, of spirituality in everyday life, and familial love. On one occasion, I was talking about Celedonio with a patient of mine, Robert, a retired cop with amazing paranormal abilities combined with the toughest street smarts you want to see in a homicide, combat-ready policeman.

After sharing a pertinent story about Celedonio, Robert asked, "Was Celedonio a very distinguished man, with elegant silver hair, a bit balding, about five-foot-seven?" I replied that he was. Robert continued, "Well, I've been seeing this man standing next to you the entire time you've been talking about Celedonio." I asked for a more detailed description to make sure it was Celedonio.

I shared my visitation by Celedonio Romero with his son Pepe. Weeks later Pepe called and said, "By the way, that was not my father who visited you in the office."

I asked, "How do you know that?"

And Pepe replied, "Because Papa came to me last night in a clear vision and told me to tell you that it was not he who visited you in your office. It was your own father who visited you." I quickly realized the physical resemblance between the two and was grateful to hear about my father's visit. How often he assists and watches over me, I do not know.

So, did Celedonio and my father die? In physical body, of course they died. But their souls and personalities live on in very clear, tangible ways on the other side of the veil, participating in our lives without the advantages and disadvantages of a body.

Death is often a time of great, conscious spiritual opening. The person departing this world, like Celedonio, may be having profound spiritual experiences, as may those around him. The period after death remains a "psychic opening," in which the dead can make contact with the living. However, the great lesson in watching a loved one die is in observing that how they die is directly related to how they lived. Celedonio was a modern-day Zorba who lived and died with gusto.

We, in the West, need to learn more about the art of living and the art of dying, for one does not exist without the other.

Healing Trance

Lenora, who works as an office manager for a large surgical group, can enter higher states of consciousness at will and has done so for years. Sometimes, however, she just slips into this state. Sometimes she feels she is able to connect or be with other people while in a higher state of consciousness, and heal at a distance. Her healing trance is a kind of out-of-body experience, a genuine spiritual experience. Here is one of Lenora's remarkable experiences in that state:

Monica, a 20-year-old niece of a friend of mine, had been in a serious automobile accident. She had a serious brain injury that the doctors in the hospital were not able to cure. Monica was semi-comatose. She could talk but nothing she said made any sense at all. When she spoke, it was nonsense. She wasn't aware of her surroundings and couldn't recognize or respond to anybody. After a couple of weeks in the hospital without progress, Monica's doctors felt she was not going to recover, at least not very soon, so they were making plans to transfer her to a long-term rehabilitation center. In the meantime, the doctors had decided that they would soon have to put in a feeding tube (a nasogastric tube) because Monica wasn't able to eat or drink.

I spoke with Jamie, her mother, on the phone, and she was quite distraught about the situation. I had met Monica a couple of times because her husband was a patient of one of the doctors I work for and Monica had come into the office a few times. So I could picture Monica in my mind as Jamie spoke about her.

After I spoke with Jamie, I lay down to go to sleep and I slipped into a state that I've entered many times. I've been told that this state is called "chidakash." All of a sudden I was visualizing the area in Monica's head where I was perceiving the damage to be. I was not in my physical body nor was the area I was looking at a physical body. And Monica didn't have a physical body during this experience. I wasn't seeing her in the hospital. There were no surroundings.

But I knew exactly where I was going and I knew exactly what my intention was. I scanned her very well and focused in on the back part of her head and suddenly found myself saying to myself, "She has a hole there. How can she heal herself when she has a hole there?" My perception was that there was damage in a particular part of her brain.

As I was focused in on that part of her head, I suddenly became aware of Monica's consciousness, not her physical body, but her consciousness. Her consciousness wasn't focusing in on me being there, but she started to focus in on the area I was looking at in her physical body. At that point I said to myself, "I wonder if she can heal herself now." Because neither of us were in our bodies, but were rather consciousness meeting consciousness, I didn't need to speak with her in words as we ordinarily do. I simply needed to help her become aware of herself and of the hole in her brain that I was seeing. That was all I felt I needed to do. From there it was her choice to go back into her body, or not. So that was my experience. And then I fell asleep.

The very next day I got a call from Jamie saying that Monica had woken up and was completely normal and healed. Shortly thereafter, Monica came into our office to pick up some medication for her husband. I was so happy to see her and I said, "Monica, how are you?" She responded, "Oh, I'm fine." Initially we had a normal, friendly interaction until I said, "Do you remember anything at all about when you were in a coma?" At that point she kind of shook her head, stopped talking, took a step backwards and her face got red, and she sat down in a chair. I again said, "You don't remember anything at all?" And she said, "No, I don't."But I could tell that the whole cadence of her voice was changing.

Now I don't really know what was happening. I don't know if she was remembering the interaction we had had on some level, or if it was my feeling toward her that seemed to be throwing her off. I was feeling an incredible love for her. When you connect with someone in an altered state as I did, you develop an incredible bond with that person. Once you connect on such a deep level with another human being, you're not limited to just the physical senses. You've connected completely. So I felt such love for her, a kind of deep love you usually don't feel for another human being. But from my experience with her, I touched something deep inside both of us. I don't know if Monica was aware of that connection. As I spoke with her in the doctor's office, I was trying to stay balanced and not get absorbed into my own feelings. I was amazed at the consuming love I felt for her—a very spiritual love, probably the way we should love one another all the time.

I didn't want to press her. It really didn't matter to me whether she remembered it or not because I felt that I should stay detached from something like that. I couldn't feel like I could take credit for doing anything anymore than I would have taken the blame if she had died. I believe that when you have an injury of her severity, consciousness can literally get knocked out of the body. I simply pointed it out to her.

In this remarkable story of love, compassion, and inspiration, Lenora is very matter-of-fact about her abilities, and shows no pride or ego: She makes no claims about being a psychic or a healer, and does not view this experience as special or extraordinary. Lenora often "travels" to realms unseen by physical eyes. On one occasion, she was out of her body, perusing the scenery, when she came face-to-face with a man hang-gliding. Needless to say the man was shocked to be soaring through the air and suddenly be greeted by a woman, who was soaring without a hang-glider.

Now imagine how Lenora would have felt is she had no understanding of consciousness. She may have felt as if she were losing her mind and could not have even entertained the notion of "consciousness meeting consciousness" or "out-of-body" flyer meeting hang-glider.

Identity Switching

In "healing trance" Lenora was deeply aware of another person and able to interact with her in some realm of consciousness that is quite out of the ordinary. In the state called "identity switching" one goes even further. Not only is one person deeply aware of another, he believes that he temporarily becomes that other person or being. Identity switching is almost the opposite of possession in which a "foreign entity" takes over the personality. In identity switching the individual feels as if he has become someone or something else. He has taken on a new identity but does not feel the terror of having lost his personality.

Most American Indian shamans can assume the form and identity of animals and convey messages through the form of the animal. This shamanic practice is widespread among the Kwakiutl and Nootka of the Northwest, the La Cota, Crow and Blackfoot of the Plains, and the Maidu of Southern California. Identity switching is least common among the Southwest Pueblo Indians—the Navajo, Hopi, and Acoma. Aztec and Mayan cultures also relied on shamans who could assume the identity of an animal. A good friend of mine, Shama Smith, an internationally-recognized psychic, has had countless experiences that involve altered states of consciousness, including identity switching. Shama tells me that on one occasion she left her body and literally became a friend of hers. We'll call her friend "Jane." In that state of "being Jane," she had a fight with Jane's husband. Several days later Jane spoke with Shama and told her she had just had a terrible fight with her husband. The argument she told Shama about was exactly the same, word for word, as the fight Shama had had with him when she "became Jane."

A restaurant and hotel owner in Oregon, a woman of incredible good cheer, told me that she once stopped her car because a mountain lion was sitting very near the edge of the road. She gazed into the mountain lion's eyes and temporarily "switched places" with the animal and experienced "mountain lion consciousness." She had the same experience again with another mountain lion and then with a bobcat.

Now how is this different from a schizophrenic who tells me that he is John the Baptist, Jesus Christ, Napoleon, or Elvis Presley? "Shama becoming Jane" might sound as if Shama and I are both crazy—she for reporting the experience and I for believing her. You have to look at experiences in context. A schizophrenic has a destroyed personality, is usually unable to work, sustain relationships, or enjoy life. They are full of fear and may be quite frightening. When one has worked with hundreds or thousands of schizophrenics, as I have, you come to know "what they feel like." Their whole world is a fiction of their psychotic imagination.

I don't want to imply that there are certain states of consciousness that "normal" people have and that sick people can't have. Borderlines, as you'll read later on, can be very psychic and go into mystical ecstasies. Their consciousness is what I would call "fluid." They can leave their bodies. I'm sure they can experience identity switching. They also can become psychotic, hear voices, and become so depressed that they're frequently attempting suicide. Their extreme fluidity of consciousness allows them to experience a broad range of states of consciousness.

Identity switching illustrates not only that consciousness can temporarily expand beyond the physical body, but also that it can merge or become one with the consciousness of others, whether human or animal. As we have already seen with other spiritual and paranormal phenomena, such experiences often transform the individual for the better. People who have experienced identity switching usually find deep spiritual significance in the experience. Let's review Shama's experience in "becoming Jane." Months after Shama shared her story with me, she called to make a further point. "You know," she said, "I know why I had that experience. It wasn't just for the fun of it. You see, Jane had really been bugging me. She had been clingy and demanding and I had to put some distance between us. She was driving me crazy. For a while, most of my thoughts about her were negative. However, after I became her, I developed tremendous compassion for her. I knew what it was like to be like her and to be her. I didn't suddenly just let her begin walking all over me again, but I felt incredible love for her. I really knew what made her act the way she did."

Identity switching, although a profound state of expanded consciousness, is just a glimpse of what is considered by saints and holy men to be the goal of spiritual practice, the "highest" of spiritual states, the mystical states of ecstasy, unity consciousness, nirvana or samadhi.[3]

Nirvana

When a person is in a healing trance, they are experiencing an altered state in which their consciousness is detached from the physical body, and, equally, they feel immense compassion for another being. In identity switching, the individual is not only "out of his body," he has temporarily "become" the other. In nirvana, also called "samadhi," or "unity consciousness," one's entire consciousness merges with God, Nature, or Universal Spirit. This is a state of supreme bliss, of unspeakable joy, of complete peace and tranquility. One loses all identification with the physical body and with all sense of separateness. In nirvana, consciousness expands to its ultimate limit, merging with everything. There is no "other" to feel compassion for or even to merge with. There only is—one. All is One. Nirvana is not falling into a trance or some state of unconsciousness. These states may be caused by hysteria or imagination. Nirvana is not hysteria. It is the ultimate experience, a heaven on earth that one can experience without dying. Only the ego dies in the state of nirvana.

Here is an example of a mystical experience, nirvana, reported to me by Joy Thomas, author of four books: (1) *Life Is a Game, Play It*, (2) *Life Is a Dream, Realize It*, (3) *Life Is a Challenge, Meet It*, and (4) *Life Is Love, Share It*. She writes:

> One morning I was sitting on my bed meditating. After reaching a place of deep stillness, I began to see small pinpoints of light. They were of different colors and seemed to be whirling in and around each other within a boundary. That boundary, I realized, was my body. I seemed to be seeing my own body as a form made of

moving atoms, and I was also aware of the feeling of a limited body mass.

As I watched, the little specks of light began to move faster and spread wider. Looking beyond them, I saw the sliding doors of the closet begin to dissolve into similar dots of light. Gradually the atoms of my body began to merge with the atoms of the doors, and it felt to me as if the boundaries of my body had expanded. The expansion continued through the closet to the outside wall, and as the specks of light blended into each other, the front yard became visible to me.

There in the front yard was a large boulder I had recently purchased to beautify our yard. It began to break down into beautiful varicolored lights, each whirling and turning until the boulder and I were one. The expansion continued slowly down the street, with trees, houses, and cars all becoming a part of my body. Sun, moon, stars, and galaxies finally joined in, and I felt the boundaries of my body expand until I included the entire universe.

Then the vision of the whirling lights began to fade, the sense of my body gradually completely dissolved, and I was aware only of being infinite bliss. How long this sense of boundless being continued, I don't know. The moment I began to think, "Isn't this wonderful," I began to return to normal consciousness.

Experiencing a feeling of being at one with nature is nirvana. The state of oneness that Pepe Romero experiences when he is performing is a form of nirvana. During many of his concerts, he loses all sense of personal identity, all sense that he is playing the guitar. There is no Pepe and there is no audience. In his words, "There is only the music—and really there is only love." This is a state of oneness with everything, a state where the sense of "I" has vanished. Pepe says, "It is as if I have one foot in this world and one in the other. Except the normal, ordinary world becomes just a memory. It's not real for me anymore." Pepe is more than "in the zone." He "is" the zone.

Call it "nirvana," "samadhi," or "unity consciousness"— they all mean the same thing here. These states of perfect peace, boundless love, and indescribable joy are not a "high" in the usual way one thinks of a "high." The mind is absolutely still. It is as if the individual spirit or soul has merged with the vast ocean of Infinite Wisdom or God. In these high states of consciousness, the soul is no longer yearning to find God, yearning to be with God, yearning to merge with God. In this nirvana or samadhi, one's consciousness has expanded so completely that there is only the experience of One. There is only peace, only love only joy, only One.

Because this experience of nirvana may sound like a "high," we need to contrast it with drug use and mania. The euphoria of mania is caused by a flood of norepinephrine throughout the nervous system—a massive adrenaline rush. It's a fragile "high," an unstable state that rapidly gives way to anger, fear, and depression. The manic, as you will read later on, is speeded up. He's talking fast, walking fast. His thoughts are racing. He is so irrational that he is making terrible business decisions and may be destroying his marriage. That certainly is not the case with Joy. Her thoughts weren't racing. There were no thoughts at all. In nirvana, one's thoughts do not race.

Nirvana is an experience completely unrelated to the physical world. It is not the happiness we experience when "things go right" or when we get what we've been desiring. Nirvana arises out of fulfillment of the soul, not fulfillment of material desires.

---

1.   Melvin Morse, M.D., *Closer to the Light: Learning from the Near-Death Experiences of Children* (New York: Villard Books, 1990).
2.   Melvin Morse, M.D., *Transformed by the Light: The Powerful Effect of Near-Death Experiences on People's Lives* (New York: Ivy Book, 1992).
3.   William James, *The Varieties of Religious Experience* (New York: Collier Books: Macmillan, 1961).

Chapter 9

Visual Paranormal Experiences

One sure way to get the attention of your loved ones and make them wonder if you've lost your mind is to tell them that you just had a vision of an angel, heard the voice of God, or had a "certain" knowledge of a calamity about to occur. These strange experiences are a large part of what make people wonder if they're "losing their minds or experiencing a miracle." Spiritual experiences, in general, are common and visions are particularly common.

In writing about visual paranormal experiences, I am in a real bind in determining what terms I should use. The term "hallucination" implies psychosis or insanity; "vision" implies a positive, beneficial experience of a spiritual or mystical nature—a revelation; "apparition" and "ghost" seem occult or paranormal; "perception" has a neutral connotation.

Some visions are spiritual, some paranormal, some due to a brain delirium, and some psychotic. I've coined the term "Extra-Sensory Vision" (ESV) to refer to a wide range of visual experiences. There are two main categories of ESV, namely "hallucinations" and "visions." A hallucination is the experience of a sight, sound, smell, or taste in a situation in which there is no verifiable physical cause or evidence of that experience. In other words, a vision is a hallucination, seen with the eyes, of something or someone outside of oneself. It is not the same as an image or a fantasy, in which one "sees" something in one's "mind's eye," mentally. Visions are seen outside oneself.

Because there are so many strange experiences related to vision, I have devoted an entire section of the book to this subject, in which we'll look at angels, ghosts, visions of the departed, psychic attack, possession, thought-forms, artistic hallucinations, past-life memories, and the human aura. With the first three, it is obvious why I have included them in this chapter, Visual Paranormal Experiences. While few of us can see psychic attack, possession, and thought-forms, these experiences are visible to those with advanced psychic sensitivities and power.

Visions Versus Hallucinations

A spiritual vision is usually a very pleasant, uplifting experience. People may "see" God, angels, saints, or indescribable light. Such a vision usually brings a new direction to life and leaves the individual with a "lighter" countenance, a greater joy in life, and more love to share with others. Visions may occur spontaneously, in a normal state of consciousness, or they may occur as part of an altered state, a mystical state of union, or during a kundalini experience.

Visions of deceased loved ones, mother, father, husband, or wife, happen all the time and it is the "normal" experience in some cultures. Whether or not it is "objectively" true that people are visited by the departed on a regular basis, the experience is common, especially in non-Western societies, where the visitations are considered normal. In Western society, grief counselors regularly reassure bereaved people that seeing and talking with departed loved ones is part of the grieving process.

People who are approaching death often experience visions of deceased relatives who have appeared to them to help them in their transition. Karlis Osis and Erlunder Haraldsson studied this phenomenon in a variety of cultures and found that "death-bed visions" are nearly identical from one culture to another.[1]

Schizophrenics tend to hear voices much more frequently than they have visions, which are almost never pleasant when they do have them. Their visions are part of a psychotic thought process. They feel controlled by the vision. This may sound odd, but they have a psychotic relationship with their hallucination. Most psychiatrists would say, "A hallucination is psychotic itself," and, of course, I disagree. The "normal" person doesn't have a psychotic reaction to a vision. He may be frightened by a ghost—or even by the sight of the Virgin Mary—but he is not likely to feel as if his mind is being controlled by the vision. In all my years in clinical practice, I have heard a schizophrenic describe a vision as spiritual on only one occasion. She hears voices as other schizophrenics do, but also has glorious visions of saints and holy men—visions that bring her great peace. Yet, she is quite the exception to the rule.

People with borderline personality disorder can have any experience and "rotate" through all states of consciousness. They can have wonderful spiritual experiences and they can be floridly "crazy," which, of course, makes a psychiatrist's job very difficult. I have found that borderlines can have "split images." They may see an angel and the devil at the same time. It's a function of the split—the inability to integrate "good" and "bad"—inside their personality. The image is as split as their heart and soul is split. Borderlines, who may have purely spiritual visions or purely psychotic visions, experience visual hallucinations much more frequently than do schizophrenics.

A psychotic hallucination is a projection from one's unconscious mind into the outside world. For example, a borderline may be filled with conscious and unconscious murderous impulses. Those impulses can be projected outside himself or herself. One borderline patient of mine hallucinated Godzilla. Godzilla joined her in the shower, ran around her house, and even ran across the highway while she was driving. Not a very safe situation for anyone concerned. Godzilla was a projection of her own murderous and angry impulses.

On rare occasions, borderlines will also see "creepy crawly" things: bugs, ants, snakes, or small birds. But it's very rare. The more fragmented the vision, the more likely it's part of a psychotic process for someone who feels very fragmented inside. Someone who sees a single benevolent angel is better integrated mentally than someone who sees and feels hundreds of bugs crawling all over him.

Someone having a hallucination of bugs crawling all over his skin may be in a state of delirium—a disorder of brain chemistry. People in DTs (delirium tremens) withdrawing from alcohol often have this kind of hallucination, which should be checked out right away by a doctor. Delirium is fatal ten percent of the time. In delirium, not only does one have visual hallucinations but the entire visual field is distorted—the foreground and the background. In contrast, a schizophrenic hallucination is not accompanied by a distorted background.

In order to know for certain if we are experiencing a vision or a hallucination, we first must be sure we're not having an illusion or a fantasy. Illusions are not hallucinations. An illusion is a distortion (almost always visual) of something that is already there. For example, at dusk, we may see a rope lying on the road and think that it's a snake. We're not hallucinating. It's an illusion. A mirage of a lake in the desert is an illusion. Our brain and mind are misinterpreting sensory information, because we're not being provided all the information we need to make an accurate assessment.

In a sense, magic is a form of illusion. By sleight of hand, the magician pulls a rabbit out of his hat. There's nothing paranormal going on here. It's just that the magician's hands are so much faster than our eyes, and he fools us by directing our attention away from the "real action," the place where the deception is going on. We're not hallucinating. Again, we're just misinterpreting the sensory input.

Visions are common in the stories of the lives of many saints and great mystics and for others who are spiritually advanced. Artist and poet, William Blake, wrote of his visions, "A vision is not a cloudy vapor or a nothing. It is organized and minutely articulated beyond all that the mortal and perishing nature can produce. I assert that all my visions appear to me infinitely more perfect and more organized than anything seen by the mortal eye."

One of the only things that a saint has in common with a schizophrenic is the fear of being ridiculed and called "crazy" for their voices and visions. St. Hildegard of Bingen experienced so many visions, she felt overwhelmed at the task of trying to remain silent about them.[2] A vision of divine light instructed her to speak about her visions, however, saying to her, "You shall proclaim it as you have heard and seen it in the miracles of God." St. Theresa of Ávila also was troubled by her voices and visions. She saw angels, cherubim, bright lights, Jesus, and many other visions, but had few people in whom to confide at first, afraid she would be called "crazy." Later on, after she became regarded by her contemporaries as a saint, she came to dislike the special attention showered on her, and especially disliked people looking upon her and talking about her, as a saint. Theresa's visions were between her and God, yet, because she was unable to conceal her "raptures," it was impossible for her to conceal her spiritual experiences from the world.

Although people came to know about her visions, Theresa had no interest in sharing them with the world. She felt no pride, no greatness because of them. To her, her visions were not the point of her spirituality. Her contact with the spiritual world made her better prepared to work in the "real" material world.[3] In contrast, the schizophrenic becomes isolated from society, and often very attached to his hallucinations and ruled by them. The saints, however, have all learned how to live with one foot in each world.

In this age in which many believe that a deeply spiritual life is synonymous with mental and physical health, it is important to remember that many saints suffered physically, sometimes throughout their entire lives. Such was the case with St. Theresa. The nineteenth century Indian saint, Paramahansa Ramakrishna, also had tremendous physical suffering. Ramakrishna worshipped many forms of God, although he was of Hindu origin. He worshipped each form of God so intensely that each one of them appeared to him. When he worshipped Jesus, he forgot about everything else in the world, and was visited by Jesus. When worshipping Shiva, only Shiva was in his mind and Shiva too would appear to him. Ramakrishna's main love was Kali, the Hindu Divine Mother. Ramakrishna "saw" Kali and spoke with her often. Toward the end of his life, Ramakrishna developed cancer of the throat, which made it difficult for him to eat or drink. His devotees couldn't bear to see their guru in such pain and begged him to ask Kali for help. Ramakrishna did not feel that it was appropriate for him to ask Kali for help with a problem as "mundane" as his physical health. This attitude of detachment from the body is common among saints and sages.

As Suzuki Roshi, the great teacher who brought Zen to the West early in the 20th century, was dying of throat cancer, he said to his students who were worrying about his comfort, "This is only suffering Buddha." There are more aspects to us than our bodies.

The visions and voices of the great ones are part and parcel of their lives, and their great works. Because of their love, compassion, courage, and great works the saints have gone down in history. The visions of the saints remind us to examine all visions and hallucinations with an open mind. When we keep an open, but critical, mind we can embrace our own visions.

If you've had an unusual visual perception, by the time you've finished reading this section on visual paranormal phenomena, you'll know what to call the experience. Here are some basic guidelines for Sorting Out and Dealing with your visual perceptions:

Sorting Out and Dealing with Visual Perceptions
Guideline #3

1.   First decide if your visual perception was a paranormal or spiritual experience or not.
2.   If your vision clearly sounds like a drug-related hallucination, go to a doctor and get treated for the condition.
3.   If your vision was a genuine spiritual experience, you need do nothing further. Be grateful for the divine gift you have received. Take the inspiration from the vision and try to live a more noble life. Follow the advice of your angel.

Ghost-Busting
Mental Fitness Technique #13

If you are troubled by a visitation and aren't sure what to call it, but know you don't like it, here is a technique I developed between 1978 and 1985.[4] The beauty of this technique is that it doesn't matter what you call your experience. If the spirit of your deceased uncle is visiting you more often than you'd like, you can quickly turn the situation around.

Here is the three-step process:

1.   If you are being visited on a regular basis, figure out what the pattern is. Let's say your deceased uncle visits you in the evening shortly before you go to sleep, let's say at 9:00 p.m. Rather than being frightened about your "uncle's" random appearances, you can turn the tables by waiting for him from 9:00—9:15 p.m. every night. That's all you have to do. Whether or not the vision appears, you now control that 15-minute block of time. If your "uncle" visits you, he will be coming on your terms.

For most people, this first step will radically cut down on visitations, and will frequently eliminate the "intruder" completely.

2.   Starting the second week, when the spirit of your uncle visits, begin to communicate with him. Ask him why he's visiting. Simply chat with him. By so doing, your fear will continue to drop, and your relationship with the vision will change.

3.   If your "uncle" is still visiting you, and you still don't like having him visit, beginning the third week, say the following words to him if and when he visits: "Why are you late?"

Don't be fooled by the simplicity and the humor in this technique. The theory and technique here evolved out of intensive study of the great American psychiatrist, Milton Erickson.[5] Not only does this technique work, it works 100% of the time given three particular conditions.

These three conditions are:

1.   Your vision is a single figure. In other words, your uncle visits you over and over again. This technique does not work as well if there is a changing cast of characters in the vision or if multiple people "visit" at the same time.

2.   Your vision is whole and intact. In other words, the vision of your uncle is fairly complete, and not just an apparition from the waist up.

3.   Your vision is not ghastly or overwhelming.

There are few guarantees I can make as a doctor, but this technique, given the right conditions, has nearly a 100% success rate. Of course, you may not want your deceased uncle to stop visiting. That's a different story.

The reason this technique works is simple. No matter what name you give your vision, you're having some kind of relationship with it, a relationship in which you may feel out of control. This technique turns that relationship around by 180 degrees, so that you move from fear of the vision to actually wondering why it's late. When you can ask, "Why are you late?" there simply is no more fear.

Now, here is the fourth, and final, step:

d.   You may begin to miss the visitations by your uncle. If that is the case, grieve the loss as you would any other loss.

Now that you know how to deal with an unwanted "visitor," you can more happily embrace all of your visions, especially the ones in the next section—angels.

Angels

Don P., a likable, soft-spoken, outwardly tough fireman of few words, was referred to me by his oncologist who thought it would be good for him to learn some imagery skills to help him cope with the lung cancer that had spread to his brain. He had six inoperable tumors in his brain and wanted to fight the cancer with every technique he could find. In our first session, I asked Don the 25 spiritual questions psychiatrists are afraid to ask, and Don volunteered, "I don't know if you'll believe this, but as I was coming out of surgery after the first cancer operation, I had a real vision. I saw this giant eagle that swooped down and picked me up in its claws. It carried me over hills and valleys finally landing at the top of a great cliff. It dropped me into its nest. I wasn't scared at all, even when the eagle began 'tearing out my guts.' I knew it meant he was eating the cancer. Suddenly a beautiful angel appeared over me, hovering in the air."

At this point Don broke down and began sobbing. "Why me?" he asked.

"What do you mean?" I replied.

"Why would I deserve an angel? I've never done anything special." He sobbed, trying to get control of himself.

"Don," I said. "You're asking the wrong question. The question is not 'Why me?' The question is 'Why not me?'"

"Why do I deserve an angel?"

"That's exactly my point, Don. Everybody deserves an angel. To think you are not worthy of the love this angel brought you is incorrect thinking. Now I don't know if we can save your life through imagery, but I can tell you that to be open to healing your cancer, you're going to have to open yourself completely to love. You're going to need to let go of old ideas that you're not good enough, not worthy, or that God doesn't love you. The angel came to you. That's proof in itself that you deserve the experience. The human heart has one seat. Either fear or love can sit in your heart, but not both. And if fear rules your heart, there is no room for love. Each of us can make a conscious choice each day between fear and love. Choose love. Love heals body, mind, and spirit. Love is expansion. Fear is contraction of the heart." This is how I speak to my patients.

This was a new way of thinking for Don, one that he needed. I told Don, "Whether you live or die soon, connecting with this deep love is the real healing. We're going to be working with your angel a lot from now on." Psycho-Spiritual Assessment was quite helpful for Don:

First, we helped Don clarify his main concern. He had experienced an angel, a genuine spiritual experience, which occurred while he was in an altered state of consciousness called "twilight state."

Second, I encouraged Don to express his feelings about the experience. He felt happy, ecstatic, tearful, doubtful, and confused all at the same time.

Third, we explored the meaning of the experience. Don's realization that he had been visited by an angel made him rethink his entire spiritual belief system. God and the angels were no longer far away or reserved for the few. Don began to believe that every one of us, including himself, can have a direct experience of God. He's right!

Psycho-Spiritual Assessment allowed us to move quickly in therapy. In this first session, I encouraged Don to deepen his spiritual practice by giving himself permission to accept the gift he had already received—the gift of the angel. Over the course of several weeks, I had him imagine himself with the angel over and over again, allowing himself to connect more and more deeply with love, with the angel, with God, and with the deepest levels of healing.

Sixty percent of Americans believe in angels. According to Sophy Burnham, author of *A Book of Angels* and *Angel Letters*, every culture and every major religion in the world, with the single exception of Shintoism, describes angels. It is my belief that "helpful angels" are real—and that they are significantly different from psychotic visual hallucinations.[6]

Although some believe that it is very difficult to tell an angel from a "fallen angel," or from a visual hallucination, it's really not very difficult. Angels come with a simple and universal message. They teach people to love and forgive. They teach people to love everyone, friend and foe alike. Angels inspire great hope and almost invariably cause a positive and permanent transformation in a person's life. Angels may look like "regular folk" or may be divine beings of light with wings. They may be solid or translucent. They may even appear as orbs of light. If your apparition is telling you to hate, to kill someone else or yourself, it's not an angel.

According to Ms. Burnham, angels do not relate to terms like "angel" and in fact may be confused if you ask them if they're an angel. They are beings from another realm who are beyond labels. We have the need to label. Angels don't. Angels don't necessarily appear to "religious" people and are probably more likely to appear to "regular," not strongly religious people. They either appear at times of great stress and rescue us or their appearance serves as a source of strength throughout life to help people through hard times. Their appearance and actions may or may not be apparent to more than one person. Here are a couple of examples, reported to me by good friends:

Mary, age 80, was driving her old Buick, when it got stuck on railroad tracks. She and her two friends in the car were terrified as a train was bearing down on them. Mary could not get the car off the tracks. Suddenly, she saw two brown, powerful arms grab the steering wheel, turning it powerfully and dislodging the tires from the railroad tracks. A moment later the car lurched forward, out of danger of the train. Her friends were startled beyond belief and they asked her how the car was able to move. They saw the miracle. They didn't see the angel.

Sometimes, people have experiences or visions that they attribute to angels, but they really haven't seen an angel. That was the case for Jack, age 35, a U.S. Navy man with 16 years experience on the high seas. What he saw during Operation Desert Storm he had never experienced in all his years at sea. As his ship was passing into the Persian Gulf, he and all on deck saw a rainbow of pure white light arch across the waters and the Gulf in the distance, like a rainbow, but an archway of pure white, glowing light. The ship passed under the arch of light and gave Jack and all the others on board the feeling that they would be in God's hands during the ensuing battles. Jack felt that an angel was showing the way and saying, "Don't worry. Everything is going to be O.K."

I have heard the following story from two people who do not know each other and, as far as I know, have never spoken with each other.

Carla Jones was driving on one of L.A.'s freeways when she was startled by the presence of a "non-human being" in her back seat. This casually-dressed being, whom she felt was an angel, told her that there was going to be an earthquake the next day in Los Angeles. Carla looked back to the highway to re-gain her bearings and then looked again to the back seat. Her "angel" was gone. This apparition rattled Carla and, as a result, her driving became quite erratic—enough so that she was pulled over by the police. When the officer asked her what was wrong, Carla replied, "Officer, I don't think you're going to believe me."

He said, "Go ahead. Try me. I'll listen."

After Carla told her story, the officer replied, "You are the seventh person today who has told me the same story."

Another woman told me the same story with one minor difference. The officer who pulled her over told her that she was, "the ninth person today who has told me the exact same story."

That night the murders of Nicole Simpson and Ronald Goldman took place. The following afternoon Americans were glued to their televisions as they watched the famous chase of O.J. Simpson, the accused (and subsequently acquitted) murderer. Perhaps Los Angeles, the city of angels, is so much the city of earthquakes that even angels refer to imminent social upheavals as earthquakes.

History is full of angel-sightings. The Prophet Mohammed's vision of the angel Gabriel provided the inspiration for an entire new religion—Islam. The best known such experience in the West are visions of Mary, mother of Jesus, who first made her appearance to James the Apostle in Spain in 40 A.D. She appeared to James as she has generally appeared during her frequent visitations over a 2,000-year period—dressed in a long dress, wearing a head cover and surrounded in a globe of light. A mist often surrounds her feet. Her most famous appearances include: Our Lady of Guadalupe, Lourdes, Fatima, and Medjugorje.[7]

In 1531, Juan Diego, an Aztec Indian, had a vision of Mary, who said to him, "Are you not under my shadow and protection?" While initially frightened by the vision, Juan Diego, felt immense love and comfort in her words. His vision became known as Our Lady of Guadalupe."

In 1858 Mary appeared to a 14-year-old girl, Bernadette Soubirous, her sister and a friend, living in the French Pyrenees. Over a six-month period, Bernadette was visited by Mary 18 times. In 1862, the visions were declared authentic, and the site of those visions, Lourdes, became world renowned as a pilgrimage site, a site of hope for mental, physical, and spiritual healing.

Thirteen Irishmen standing near the Church of Knock, in 1879, experienced a vision of Mary, wearing a large radiant crown. On her right stood St. Joseph and on her left, St. John the Evangelist. Although the remainder of the citizens of Knock did not see Mary, many reported a bright light illuminating the church and its surroundings.

The 20th century has had ever-increasing visits from Mary. The miracle of Fatima, Portugal, occurred in 1915, when she appeared to three children and said, "Don't be afraid. I will not hurt you. I am from heaven. I come to ask you to come here for six months in succession, on the 13th day at this same hour." Mary's final visit was "set" for October 13, 1917. Seventy thousand people stood in the rain awaiting her final appearance and were not disappointed.

In 1920, a vision of Mary hovering in the sky apparently stopped Russian soldiers "dead in their tracks." Instead of crossing the Vistula River and then invading Warsaw, the Russian soldiers withdrew.

In 1981, Mary first appeared to six children in Medjugorje, in the former Yugoslavia, promising to give each child ten secrets, ten prophecies. Her vision and her words have been consistent with the legendary sightings at Fatima and Lourdes. The children report her having said, "Children, darkness reigns over the whole world.

People are attracted by many things and they forget about the more important," and "By means of the messages, I wish to make a beautiful mosaic in your hearts."

What is apparent to me is that divine visitations are nothing new, nor are miracles. Rather, there has been an unending flow of the miraculous into every day life through recorded history. What may be of special import regarding the visions of Mary is the rise in worship of the goddess. In *Woman as Healer*, Jeanne Achterberg, Ph.D. speculates that historically the decline in worship of female forms of God has gone hand-in-hand with decline in care and respect for the environment, as well as the decline in civilization as a whole.[8] When worship of the pre-Christian goddesses, such as Diana and Ishtar, became banned by the church, in favor of an "all-male" cast of Gods, society soon plunged into the Dark Ages.

Worship of Goddess is not better than worship of God. The re-emergence of Mary and other forms of Goddess worship indicates a restoration of balance. In Chinese philosophy, life is a balance of yin (female energies) and yang (male energies). We, in the West have been out of balance for a long time. Body, mind, and spirit have been split apart, as have God and Goddess.

Whether or not we choose to believe that "Mary sightings," and angel sightings in general, are real, it is a grave mistake to write off these experiences as hallucinations, imagination, or the attempts of psychologically-unstable people to get attention. Although we may never be able to put every angel and every vision into a neat box, with the same ease that we can sort out pneumococcal pneumonia, viral pneumonia, coccidiomycosis pneumonia or the flu, we can receive messages from many altered states of consciousness, and can allow angels to alter our consciousness.

We can grow in hope and faith if we remember that we are not alone in our "angel-sightings." Angels have been reported for thousands of years by people from a great variety of cultures. The spiritual masters, gurus, saints, and shamans from every religion and every culture all agree on the existence of angels. We each must decide if we believe angels exist, and then, if the situation presents itself, decide if we have had a genuine vision of an angel or not. Here's how to deal with your "angel."

Embracing Angelic Visitations
Guideline #4

1.   Decide if you saw an angel or if you were hallucinating. If your "angel" left you feeling inspired, full of tears of joy, more full of love, you most likely really did see an angel. Congratulations!

2.   There's nothing more you need to do about it, other than feel grateful for the experience, and do as the song advises, "Fall on your knees. Oh, hear the angel voices." Rejoice if you've seen an angel. Express your gratitude to God and the angel.

3.   If you believe there was a message the angel was trying to convey, but aren't sure what it was, write down the words the angel spoke, if any. Meditate on those words. Angels never present themselves for no reason, nor do they speak for no reason. If no words were spoken, meditate on what the angel was doing, how he or she was dressed, and the feeling the angel inspired in you. Continue meditating on the meaning of the visit until the message is clear.

4.   Do not lose hold of the power of an angelic visit. Write down the experience in all its detail, and then re-visit the angel in your imagination on a regular basis, so that you can continue to receive the inspiration the angel intended to bring you.

Visions of the Departed

Approximately 105 million Americans believe they have had messages from dead people or visions of them, and in many cultures, visitations from the dead are an expected and normal part of the grieving process. All Hopi Indian widows receive visitations from their deceased husbands, who return in order to complete unfinished business. If the marriage was peaceful and well adjusted, the husband visits a few times and then leaves for good. If the marriage was conflicted, the spirit of the husband visits frequently and the experience is emotionally upsetting.

A patient of mine, who is a Lutheran Minister, tells me the following story. Reverend Paul Thomas routinely consoles grief-stricken parishioners. On one occasion he was consoling the mother of a young man who had suffered an epileptic seizure. As they sat on a couch outside the emergency room where her son was being treated, the young man's mother suddenly gasped and said to Paul, "Did you see that?"

"Did I see what?"

"Did you see my son? His spirit just walked out of the operating room, hand-in-hand with the spirit of his deceased father (Steve's father had died six years previously). They both looked so happy, so content, and so full of light. Steve and his father smiled at me and then walked away together." Reverend Thomas hadn't seen it, but he certainly believed she had. Moments later, the emergency room doors swung open, and the surgeon sadly told them that her son had just died.

Stephanie, a travel agent and friend of mine, had a vision of her departed Grandmother Helen, who appeared six months after her death:

I came out of a deep sleep and was startled to see that the room was incredibly bright. At first I thought it must be morning and the sun was streaming in through the window. Then I saw my deceased Grandmother Helen. She looked absolutely beautiful. She was just glowing. I was so happy to see her and in my usual gregarious manner I said, "Grandma, it's so good to see you." She was very happy to see me and replied, "Something wonderful is about to happen!" "Really!" I said. We communicated for a while non-verbally. I could see her only from the waist up. She was completely engulfed in light. Although she died in her 90s, she appeared to be about 50, although her hair was still white. She was dressed in a white tunic or robe.

I fell back asleep and when I woke up again, the sun was just beginning to rise. It was then that I realized that Grandma had visited me in the middle of the night when it was pitch black. It wasn't the sun that was illuminating the room. It was Grandma.

I was so excited and curious about her saying, "Something wonderful is about to happen." I expected some dramatic thing in the family, but maybe the news was on God's plane or about something of a spiritual nature.

When the family was at the breakfast table, I shared my vision and my son said that he had been visited by Grandma in a dream that same night.

Spirits of the dead can visit us in a variety of ways, not just in the usual way in which they appear, standing in front of us. My friend Pepe had an unusual visitation from his departed father, Celedonio. Shortly, after Celedonio died, Pepe saw his father lying on a "sheet of light" with his head pointing toward Pepe and his feet pointed away. Pepe saw that his father was not only lying on a sheet, or plain, of light, but was part of the light.

One day, Pepe told me he was heading to the cemetery to visit his father's grave. I was puzzled. "Pepe, you are in nearly constant contact now with your father. He is as real and present to you as he was while in his body. You can have ongoing conversations with him. Why do you go to the cemetery?" Pepe replied, "I love my father's soul and can see his spirit, or close my eyes and meditate and be with him. But I also loved my father's physical form, and when I miss his physical form, I go to the cemetery, where his physical form is buried."

It made sense to me.

As physicians, we would be seriously harming people if we told them, "You're just seeing things. I'm going to put you on some Xanax for a few days until you're feeling better." Being visited by the dead does not mean someone is denying reality or avoiding the pain of grief. Visitations from the dead do not interfere with the grief process. They're part of the grief process and they help us find meaning and purpose in life. Like angels, visions of the departed usually bring hope and inspiration. They help us awaken to our higher nature, offering comfort in times of pain and suffering and direction when we are confused. Such visitations help us face our own mortality, for those who have had such experiences develop a firm belief in the continuity of life after physical death. Those who have fully embraced their mortality are the ones who can best give themselves to the moment, to life and living. Experiences like these should be shared with one's physician, and physicians should be asking patients about them. In so doing, the doctor-patient relationship will grow stronger, and we will all be better able to face both life and death.

Ghosts and Hauntings

Some people's sixth sense is more highly developed than others, and can peer into other dimensions in a way that escapes the grip of time and space. Shama Smith is one such person, an extraordinary professional psychic and a friend of mine. As a psychiatrist I can vouch for her sanity. As a friend I can attest to her solid character, her loving, compassionate nature, her sense of humor, her solid business sense, her strong desire to be of service to others and her deep love for God.

Shama has solid credentials. She has worked with a team of psychics, who were part of the UCLA Parapsychology Department, in conjunction with the Metropolitan Los Angeles Police Department, the California Highway Patrol, the Santa Barbara Sheriff's Department, the Westminster Police Department, and other California municipal police departments, as well as the FBI and Interpol. Shama was researched, examined, and trained in the UCLA Parapsychology Department of the Neuropsychiatric Institute (NPI) before becoming part of their team of consultants. She also has advised and consulted for three heads of state and the governor of a foreign country. Because psychics are not part of a recognized profession in the United States, she has always worked for free for the government. Although the FBI may call her for an assignment, taxpayers would throw a fit if their tax dollars were going to a psychic.

It took Shama between five and six years to begin to differentiate clearly between a bona fide psychic impression and an imaginative image. A psychic impression to her is clear without being dramatic, not accompanied by thunder or lightning.

With Shama's assistance, I have gained some understanding about the differences among ghosts, non-human entities, and other "weird" phenomena. On several occasions, Shama and I have gone "ghost-busting" together, each of us bringing our particular outlook and skills to our dealings with people who think they are "haunted."

Before we dive into the story, you'll want to know the differences among ghosts, angels, and entities.

First, ghosts, according to Shama, and the vast literature on the subject, are souls of the dead who remain attached to a physical place, often a house. Ghosts may also be attached to a place that existed long before a house was built on a particular site. "Hauntings," unlike entities, are very long lasting, some of them persisting for hundreds or even thousands of years. Ghosts don't really care who's in the house. It's "their house!" Metaphysically-speaking, a ghost is a spirit that still believes he or she lives in a certain house. A ghost is really a lost soul that has gotten stuck on its way out of death's door and has not found its way to the light.

An entity, which is attached to a specific person, is a non-human being, usually the soul of a dead person. It is a very "low" kind of consciousness, the mental and spiritual remnant of an individual who was quite violent, abusive, promiscuous, or addicted. It is not attached to a particular place. Fortunately, entities don't "hang around" for very long, almost always disappearing within a few years. Entities require "two to tango," and are usually attracted to an individual who has intense sexual or aggressive desires. Entities are only attracted by our strong impulses and cannot co-exist with us unless we are feeding them with the energy of our desires. When a person afflicted by an entity has overcome his addiction to anger, sex, power, or drugs, the entity automatically leaves. Exorcism is of little value in these cases unless the "victim" is given tools to let go of his/her subconscious attachments that keep the entity around. If an entity is periodically attacking someone, it's called psychic attack. If the entity has entered the individual's life so completely that the mind and behavior of the living person are completely co-mingled with the entity, we call it spirit possession. More about that later.

A word of caution: The next two sections—"Ghosts" and "Psychic Attack and Spirit Possession"—contain some potentially frightening stories. If you do not want to delve into this somewhat dark, strange, and scary territory, feel free to go straight to the next section, on the human aura (which begins on p. 194).

Here is an extraordinary story Shama shared with me about how she dealt with a ghost that was haunting her house: "When my husband, Cass, and I moved into a house in Southern California, I was standing in the kitchen the first day and said to him, 'Honey, the house is haunted.' He said, 'Oh no, please don't tell me that.' I replied, 'It is and I know it is.' 'Well how do you know it is?' he asked. 'Well, number one, I can smell it and number two, I can feel a presence around me here.' He asked, 'Why didn't you realize it was living here when we first looked at the house?' I answered, 'Because, Cass, I wasn't tuned into it and it wasn't making its presence felt. Besides that, we needed to find a new place to live quickly and I was feeling pressured. Now that we're settled in and the stress of finding a new place and moving in is over, I'm relaxed and can feel this presence."

According to Shama, sometimes if there's been a grotesque death on the premises, the house will smell, no matter how much cleaning you do. She knew she was smelling or perceiving an odor from another realm, something that would definitely be called "crazy" by most psychiatrists.

Once I had the house in order and had things put away, I made myself an office. I was finally settled down in my office, doing my work when I began perceiving the presence more clearly. I was perceiving a "woman" who would walk into the office and stay close to the door. The vision, the ghost, would stand there and watch me work. The ghost appeared to be in her late twenties and of medium height. I knew she was the presence I had felt the first day.

The ghost started following me around the house everywhere. This went on for weeks. I wasn't frightened because I've had a lot of experience with this kind of thing—although most people feel a sense that their territory has been invaded. I began talking about the ghost with my husband. After we were in the house for a few weeks, Cass came down with bronchitis. He was coughing so badly, I couldn't sleep in the same room with him because he was keeping me awake all night. So

I made up a bed in the office, the room where the ghost most frequently visited me.

I went to sleep and woke up to the sound of violent screaming of a child. And the child was struck dead— struck dead by surprise. I knew the child was a young girl and had been killed without any warning. And then I saw blood in the rugs and I saw myself with blood up to my ankles.

For any of you who think being a psychic is fun, this story may make you re-consider. Shama again:

I came out of a deep sleep by the scream but then entered an altered state that was neither asleep nor awake. In this other state I was able to perceive the story of what had happened in the house.

The information I receive in that state is received in a unit. It's not linear and sequential like the information exchanged in day-to-day conversation. So I experienced the whole story in one instant.

Certainly Shama was not in a normal state of consciousness; she was not in linear, time-and-space-bound consciousness. Shama feels that she wasn't just an observer in this experience but that she also played a part as a participant in the experience by actually feeling the blood coming up to her ankles. As she said:

When I became fully awake, I knew that whatever had happened there was so gory that there was tremendous bloodshed. Psychiatrists perceive an object from the outside, walking around it, making notations, recording data, and making decisions. In a psychic's line of work, the idea is not to walk around the object but to enter into it, so it's a co-existence. And that's the only way a psychic can ever experience how another person really feels. Even though I was fully experiencing what was going on, there was part of me that knew that it was O.K. I was not terrified, upset, or feeling victimized. I was in the experience but also witnessing it.

At that point, I ran into the bedroom, woke up my husband and told him, "Now I know someone was murdered in this house—a child. It must have been a savage murder because the child lost all of her blood. Tomorrow I'm going to speak to the landlord and tell him that I know." Cass said, "Please, honey, don't go tell the landlord that."

The next morning she did go to the landlord's house and said, "You can be honest with me. I'm not going to move out. I'm not upset but I want to tell you what I saw in the house and then I want you to tell me what happened." She told him the story and he said, "By law I don't have to tell you anything about the house— but I will. Here is the landlord's story: "A woman named Kendra had lived there with her daughter. It was Monday. Kendra's daughter didn't feel well and stayed home from school. That morning while her daughter was watching television, Kendra struck her daughter over the head with a baseball bat and then stabbed her countless times with a butcher knife. Then Kendra stabbed herself to death. They both lost all the blood in their bodies. The carpet was literally soaked with their blood. We couldn't hire anybody to take out the carpets so my wife and I had to take the rugs out ourselves. My wife has never returned to the house."

As Shama tells the story:

> After I heard the actual history, the presence of Kendra continued to follow me around the house. It was as if Kendra wanted to talk to me and was reaching out to me. I told Kendra that she was dead, because she didn't know that she was, in fact, dead. Many psychics, myself included, believe that if you die suddenly, you are so disoriented that your spirit may remain around the premises where you last lived or worked.
>
> I sat down in a chair and began talking to Kendra like you would talk to a friend. I thought that if Kendra had any religious background, she probably had been exposed to Christianity, so I spoke to her about Jesus and told her that Jesus does forgive and that she had to forgive herself and ask God to take her into the Light. She needed to head to the Light to go on to a new life. Kendra understood me. She understood her own confusion and her death.

Consider how frightened most of us are to even think about death. It takes great courage, in my opinion, to actually try to face death and talk to the dead. Shama again:

I told Kendra that she was dead and did not live in this house anymore. I told her that she had committed the murder while she was not in her right mind and she needed to see it in that light and forgive herself. I spoke with her very compassionately as opposed to screaming at her, "Get out!" Most people, of course, would scream at a being like Kendra if they could sense her, because they experience the presence as an invasion of their privacy and they're terrified.

Their conversation continued for about an hour and then Shama burned frankincense, lit candles, and prayed for Kendra for several hours, to "purify body, mind and spirit—including spirits of the dead."

That night, after Shama had gone to bed, she was awakened by a candle that began burning spontaneously on its own. It was a brand new candle, which she claims she had never lit—"But it lit itself. I woke up to the illumination of the entire room. It was so beautiful and the illumination was so strong that it felt like more than the light of that one candle. That intense spontaneous lighting of the candle made me feel that Kendra had finally gone into the Light. And she never came around our house again."

Shama is able to enter a realm that exists outside of time and space, a "place" that is actually no place, but from which she can obtain information. Many people see ghosts, and how they choose to deal with them is important. By realizing that a ghost, unlike an entity, is only attached to a physical location, any of us can be better prepared to cope with the situation. When we're dealing with an entity, it is essential that we discover the part of ourselves that is attracting it. However, when we're dealing with a ghost, the love and compassion that Shama displayed is the key to defusing this potentially-frightening situation.

Ghosts have probably been around as long as has the human race, and have been researched and written about for centuries. The Brown Lady of Raynham Hall is one of the most reliably photographed ghosts in history, usually seen dressed in a long brown dress or cape and carrying a lantern. The ghost was first seen in 1835 and last seen in 1936. During the early period of her visitations, a Captain Frederick Maryat intentionally slept in the room where the "Brown Lady" was most often seen. The Captain was awakened by the ghost and was so startled that he pulled out his pistol and fired at point-blank range. The bullet had no effect on the ghost, which continued its haunting for another 100 years.

The Borley Rectory is considered to be one of the most haunted houses in England. The rectory was initially inhabited by Benedictine monks. In the late 1800s, Reverend H.D.D. Bull tore down the old rectory and built a new one on the same site, at which point in time, the hauntings commenced. One of the ghosts frequently seen at the Borley Rectory was that of a 13th century nun, who according to legend, had fallen in love with one of the monks. The monk and the nun tried to escape in a horse and carriage, but failed. The monk was hung, and the nun was imprisoned, and later died, in the rectory.

The Tower of London has a long history of hauntings. In 1483, two princes were murdered in the tower. Subsequently, their ghosts were repeatedly seen until 1674, when their bones were removed from the tower and were given a proper burial. Anne Boleyn, who was beheaded by her husband, King Henry VIII, in 1536, is the most frequently seen ghost of the tower.

Hauntings are not limited to Western cultures. The trampled burial sites of indigenous peoples are another source of ghostly visions. In Hawaii, native burial sites that have been moved or destroyed by the booming tourist industry, have become fertile ground for ghost-sightings.

Regardless of the time, place, or culture, the reason for hauntings appears to be the same. The spirit of the dead remains attached to a physical place, such as a house, a tower, or a burial ground, instead of leaving the material world behind and moving on to higher planes of consciousness.

Psychic Attack and Spirit Possession

A great many of you will have visions of departed loved ones, which you should experience as a gift, a blessing. A few of you will see or feel ghosts, and should not be bothered by them. And a very, very small number of people will experience psychic attack, or its more severe manifestation, "spirit possession." These latter two phenomena are included for the sake of completeness. The average person need have no concern whatsoever about being possessed. However, it is a good idea for medicine and psychiatry to be familiar with these phenomena, so that they can be of assistance in these rare situations.

In 1974, Barry Taff, Ph.D. (Doctorate in Psychophysiology), part of the UCLA Parapsychology Department came in contact with Mrs. B., a 35-year-old woman who claimed that her house was haunted.[9] Dr. Taff, who has examined over 3300 cases of ghosts, hauntings, and poltergeists, visited Mrs. B. in her home. She reported that she recently had been raped by a ghost. In speaking with Dr. Taff, he told me his initial reaction. "I felt like rolling my eyes. I thought she was hysterical and had an over-active libido. I was convinced that she was psychotic, and that was that."

Ten days later, Mrs. B. called him again, asking him to please come see her again, and he agreed to do so. When Dr. Taff arrived, he was surprised to find that the house was icy cold inside. The house had no air-conditioning and it was a hot, California, August afternoon. The house smelled of a foul, rotting odor, the source of which Dr. Taff could never ascertain scientifically. Dr. Taff reported: "I saw a lot of strange things. I saw the fuse box violently ripped out of the wall, candelabras shaking and falling. My team and I began to see little balls of blue-green light. We sealed the house of all sources of light and electricity. The balls of light grew brighter. They zoomed around the house and flew around us. We photographed a great deal but the results were paradoxical. When we saw something, such as a ball of light, it never showed up on film. But many things we didn't see with our eyes did show up on film. One photo revealed an arc of light over Mrs. B.'s head. I took the photos to the Editor of *Popular Photography*. He could find no evidence of fakery or trickery, nor any scientific explanation for the phenomena recorded on film.

"On one occasion something physically pushed me back. On another occasion, I had taped black poster board on the ceiling with duct tape in order to seal out light. The poster board had been violently ripped off the ceiling, along with some of the dry wall. I witnessed this myself and saw some poster board violently rip off the ceiling and hit Mrs. B. in the head. All of this activity would come and go. The stench would come and go. The incredible cold would come and go. Finally, after several years, things finally quieted down for her."

Dr. Taff calls this kind of phenomenon "poltergeist activity." Poltergeist means "noisy ghost," a definition that doesn't really clarify anything for me, so I have chosen the term "psychic attack." Mrs. B. is a classic case of psychic attack. Spirit possession, in my opinion, is caused by the same "entities" that cause psychic attack, the only difference being that in spirit possession, one's mind, and not just one's body, seems to come under control of some outside force. Not only are strange events occurring around one, such as fires spontaneously igniting, or fuses blowing, one's mind becomes the target of attack.

Here's a case of spirit possession, reported to me by one of my patient's, Amanda, whom you will read about in the chapter on borderline personality disorder. During her twenties, she "fell" under the tutelage of a so-called spiritual teacher whom I would have to call "evil." Amanda's teacher taught her how to let "entities" enter her with the stated goal of helping Amanda tap into a higher consciousness. Amanda learned a method of "making herself (her Self) very small." When her sense of self was as small as the tip of a pin, the entities would enter her body and mind. In her own words, "I invited them in and they would actually jump into me. I could see and feel them, and did whatever they told me to do. My body would spontaneously develop weird movements. My voice radically changed and became that of a man. And my voice had an echo to it as if I were speaking in a large room with marble floors. There were a lot of people around me during this period, dozens of people, including a famous parapsychology researcher from a prestigious Ivy-League university. People said that my face was like a chameleon. My face, my eyes would change shape and color. At first I couldn't clearly see the entities. They just had an undefined form and color. But later I could clearly see them. They were so ugly...and scary.

"Through the entities I gained certain paranormal powers. I could put ideas into other people's heads and make them think that the idea actually was their own. This turned really evil when my teacher asked me to use these new powers to help her get the man she wanted. She wanted me to use this power to break up the man's marriage—which I did. The process left me so sick I nearly died. I was so naive at the time. I trusted my teacher and she led me down a very dark and evil path. Once I realized that what I was doing was truly evil, I never did it again. I left my teacher and never invited entities inside again."

Before I concluded that Amanda had been possessed, I had to wonder if she was crazy—and she wasn't. She doesn't hear voices. She does not suffer from hysteria, hysterical fits of blindness, amnesia, deafness, or seizures. She doesn't feel that her mind is being controlled by radio or television. She's a survivor of abuse and suffers from those problems: mood swings, panic, chaotic relationships, and self-sabotage. But she is not just "fantasizing." I do a great deal of guided imagery work with Amanda, which she works with easily. As a specialist in imagery, I can say with little doubt that the entities she sees are not fantasy or imagination.

People who suffer from either psychic attack or spirit possession, fit a particular personality profile. According to Dr. Taff, Mrs. B., "fits a typical personality profile of people who experience these phenomena. She was abused as a child by her father. She was very angry, very impulsive, and had a lot of repressed anger. It's like she was wound up and had nowhere to go with her feelings. She also drank a lot, which is very common with this phenomena. The more unstable she was emotionally, the more poltergeist activity."

To me, Mrs. B. sounds like she suffers from child abuse with subsequent borderline personality. This personality type combined with drinking makes one "psychically open." These people are a "paranormal accident waiting to happen." When you add to this dangerous concoction a lifestyle that includes drugs, alcohol, addiction to sex, and addiction to rage, one's consciousness is lowered to such an extent that "lower forms of consciousness," such as "entities," have an open door through which they can launch psychic attack.

Spirit possession may sound like mumbo-jumbo to a Western-trained scientist, but we have to acknowledge that possession is recognized in every culture around the world. It would be foolish to ignore the possibility that possession may be present in all cultures, including our own. In spirit possession psychiatry has the ultimate challenge of trying to understand the underlying biology, the defects in brain metabolism, the psychopathology, the results of child abuse, low self-esteem, as well as the cultural, paranormal, and spiritual components.

It is conceivable that our mental hospitals are filled with people who suffer from possession, or a combination of possession and mental illness. Perhaps psychiatry needs to find a way to make psychiatric hospitals more sacred, to make them less inviting for the entities that possess people. Perhaps we need to incorporate devotional singing, meditation, and prayer, and also the burning of frankincense, along with appropriate medication. By making our environments more sacred, we become less prone to possession. We need to discover what is polluting our mental environment and our physical environment, and then begin the job of cleaning up.

The further I have gone in trying to clarify the different mental states, mental illnesses, spiritual states, spiritual illnesses, and strange phenomena—the more subtle and difficult the questions become. There are no easy answers and I do not intend to enable people to say to themselves, "I really am not responsible for what happens to me. I'm under psychic attack from an outside force." This book aims to help people take more responsibility for their lives, not less.

Now let's take a minute to see the relevance of entities, psychic attack, and spirit possession for you, the reader. Here are the key points to remember:

Coping with Psychic Attack
Guideline #5

1.   The chances that you are possessed or suffering psychic attack are incredibly low.

2.   Psychic attack, when it does occur, is relatively short-lived.

3.   Psychic attack is not truly random. I do not mean to imply that people who suffer from psychic attack are evil or bad or that they somehow deserve the fate they receive; nor would I accuse the patient with lung cancer of causing his own demise by smoking all of his life, or the person with colon cancer for eating too much red meat. Yet the way we live has a profound influence on all aspects of our lives—body, mind, and spirit.

4.   Each of us can do our part in eliminating the essential precursor to psychic attack and possession—namely a childhood filled with abuse and/or neglect. As parents, or future parents, it is our duty to raise our children with the utmost love, respect, honesty, consistency, and non-violence. These are the real preventive medicines. Abuse and neglect cause a "tear" in the mind-body fabric, causing a low grade depression and an immune system that begins to fall apart decades later. Abuse also causes a separation of the soul or spirit from the mind-body, so splits occur on all levels, leaving a child feeling empty and not whole. This "crack" in body, mind, and spirit is a set-up for psychic attack and possession.

5.   Parent by example. Don't expect your children to avoid drugs and alcohol if you're abusing them yourself.

Thought Forms

Lisa, a 30-year-old Lieutenant in the Navy, was frightened by a vision that appeared to her in a condominium into which she had recently moved. She saw a "two-foot wide, hideous, black cloud with 10 sharp hooks around the middle" floating around her bedroom. After the initial shock, Lisa, who had studied metaphysics, realized she had just seen a thought form. She recognized the cloud with hooks, for she had seen a picture of one in a metaphysics class. From her class she had learned that the color black, when present in a thought form, represents resentment or malice. The hooks represented a strong sensual craving. Lisa did not feel that her own mind had given rise to the thought form and was quite sure it "belonged" to someone else.

After collecting herself, Lisa told her landlord, Bill, that she had had a strange experience in her new home and wanted to know who had lived there before she had moved in. Her landlord, Frank, replied, "My girlfriend, Janet, used to live with me. I asked her to leave three weeks ago. She's an angry alcoholic and was incredibly sexual most of the time. She still calls, leaves messages and is desperate to get back together with me."

The thought form that Lisa saw was one of many described by Madame Blavatsky, one of the founders of the Theosophical Society (a group of "adepts" and spiritual seekers with well-developed siddhi powers). According to Madam Blavatsky thoughts and prayers have power, real consequences, and are visible.[10] The difference between a thought and a prayer may be subtler than we currently believe. The difference may only be one of intention and direction of the thought.

Year-by-year I am coming to appreciate the power of thought and prayer at deeper and deeper levels. Last year I was at a party where a film about Ram Das, now in a wheelchair, was being shown. It was an inspiring film. Ram Das, a wonderful teacher for decades, suffered a stroke, which compromised a good deal of his cognitive functions, but he continues to wear a smile. After watching the film, people shared their feelings and thoughts about the film as well as anything that the film stirred up in us. One woman told an amazing story:

"I used to live in New York City, where I attended synagogue religiously. The rabbi's wife suffered a brain infection and was in a coma for weeks. We all prayed for her. When the rabbi's wife came out of the coma, the first thing she said to her husband was, 'I want you to please thank all the members of the congregation for praying for me. Their prayers are what pulled me through. But why didn't Mimi Goldberg pray for me?' Her rabbi husband responded, 'Mimi didn't know you were sick. She was in Israel when you became ill and didn't know. Otherwise, she certainly would have prayed for you."

I have believed in the power of prayer for a long time, and Larry Dossey's ground-breaking book, *Healing Words: the Power of Prayer*, filled with scientific, well-controlled studies on the effects of prayer, took my own faith to a higher level. Hearing that a person in a coma was aware of each and every prayer that was sent her way took my understanding to another level. Now, when I pass the scene of a car accident, I will "throw" a prayer to the victims of the accident, feeling confident that even one prayer from a total stranger has a positive effect.

The Theosophists, including Madam Blavatsky, were able to see thought-forms, and decided to study and classify them carefully.[11] The group observed people under a variety of conditions: joy, anger, grief, jealousy, etc. They observed people praying, worrying, and laughing. Each member then drew a picture of the thought-form that hovered over, or nearby, the individual in question. And the results were startling. They all saw the same thing for a given condition and were able to draw over 50 pictures that correspond to a specific human condition.

The Theosophists identified and explored three qualities of thought forms: color, shape, and clarity. The color arises out of the nature of the emotion a person is experiencing. The black color of Lisa's vision was due to Janet's anger and intense desire. The shape, which included hooks, reflected Janet's attachment to Bill. She still had her "mental hooks" in him. The intense clarity of the thought form, the sharpness of the edges was produced by the intensity, the power, of Janet's thought. The more definite the shape of a thought-form, the more time, attention, and power is being given to it.

Because Lisa was educated about thought forms, she was not affected by the hooked cloud. She could not make it go away, but only had to wait it out. The cloud appeared a couple of more times, although fainter in intensity, and then disappeared for good.

Of course, not all thought-forms are nasty-looking. A purring cat, for example, generates "fuzzy, pink puffs." Most of us cannot see thought forms, yet we know how it feels to enter someone's house when there's been a big argument going on. We can "feel" the bad vibes, the anger, even if we can't see it. It hangs in the air. If you take the effect of the "anger that fills the air after a fight" and multiply it by a million, you can imagine a very powerful thought. And a very powerful thought is what psychics and others with siddhi powers saw hanging over the European Balkan States and the former Soviet Union.

Thought-forms arise out of the energy we give to them. The more energy we pour into the thought-form, the greater its power becomes. Centuries of negativity gave rise to the former Soviet Union's "dark cloud." When a thought-form has sufficient energy, it begins to affect our lives. The principle "like attracts like" governs thought-forms. An alcoholic person generates a powerful alcoholic thought form, and other alcoholic thought-forms are attracted to it.

Some experts on alcoholism believe it to be a disease, a physical illness, and in fact alcoholism has been proven to have an inherited component. I believe it also has psychological and spiritual causes, and I agree with the philosophy of AA, which brings a powerful spiritual dimension to healing. Yet, alcoholism can give rise to a certain type of thought form.

The world is filled with thought-forms, both positive and negative. After some time, thought-forms develop a life of their own. They feed off of us, and are created by us, and we feed off them. It's a vicious, unconscious cycle. So even when an alcoholic stops drinking, he still has to contend with something that 12-step programs are not familiar with—the alcoholic thought-form. If the thought-form is given no further energy, it will wither and disappear. Here are guidelines to help you make sure you don't give a negative thought-form energy:

Pulling the Energy Out of Negative Thought Forms
Guideline #6

1.   Practice mantra meditation. By so doing, your mind will be filled with thoughts of God, thereby weakening the influence of negative thoughts.
2.   Practice the ABCs of Anger Control. (Avoid loud speech. Breath slowly and deeply. Curtail swearing.) Because unbridled anger psychically attracts more negative thought-forms, you'll want to eliminate anger as an energy source.
3.   Practice watching your thoughts. When a repetitive negative thought arises, begin by noticing it, without trying to push it away. By simply observing the thought, it already will begin to lose its power. After observing the negative thought, turn (or return) your

mind to your mantra, or picture your chosen form of God beside you.

4.   Avoid drugs and alcohol. Their use dramatically increases the power of negative thought-forms.

5.   Consciously lift your thoughts to a higher level. If all you think about, all day long, is drugs, sex, and violence, you will attract those into your life. Instead think of ways to be of service, ways to be more peaceful, loving, honest, and non-violent. The power of these positive thoughts will automatically make negative thought-forms vanish.

6.   Avoid the company of those who bring you down, those who are addicted to negativity. Surround yourself with good people, moral people.

Artistic Hallucinations

An artist enters such an altered state of consciousness that he may have all kinds of extraordinary experiences, and may "hallucinate," or have extra-sensory perceptions, in any sensory modality.

Richard Del Maestro, producer and composer of several albums, including *Language of the Heart*, had a fascinating experience while he was composing the score for a film at the Reuben Fleet Space Theater in San Diego. He was given seven days to score the entire film, which was about a half-hour long. He either had to give up the project or work for several days with zero sleep (constant work). Having already been working 22-23 hours a day, he needed to work 24 hours a day non-stop until he had finished. At the end of that period he could "see the music pouring out of his hands in a spiral formation," and phoned me to share his experience. Yet, Richard was in such an altered state of consciousness while he was composing that he had no recall of the vision. It was only after I reminded him about what he had told me that he began to remember.

Writing music or creating a painting is almost a visionary experience in itself. The composer is hearing music that isn't there. Sometimes the power of that perception can be extraordinary. I have composed more than 2,200 songs—each with different melody, lyrics and style (rock-and-roll, country-western, reggae, rhythm-and-blues, chants, devotional-spiritual, and children's music). During one Christmas season, I began to write a spiritual oratorio. Or, rather, I should say it began to write me. When the music would hit me, it would be so loud and powerfully emotional, that I would have to pull over to the side of the road, if I was driving, for I would be reduced to tears by the music.

I heard the music as if an entire symphony orchestra were inside of me. Violins, cellos, trumpets, timpani, clarinets, flutes— the whole orchestra was playing inside me and a choir was singing the words. I had no choice but to write down the words whenever I heard them. Unfortunately, I don't write down musical notation very well, so the entire orchestral arrangement is now long forgotten. However, in 2009, I returned to the basic inspiration to write and record an oratorio, a composition for orchestra and choir. The artistic task is nearly complete.

Unusual experiences, including artistic hallucinations, are common among artists because they get into a "flow" state while working. The artist often loses all sense of separation between himself, the paintbrush, the canvas, the paint, and the subject that he is painting. He may enter a kind of samadhi, or unity consciousness, in which he is one with the art. It's like a great athlete being in the zone. In these "flow" states, the artist may "become" the work of art or "become" the entire process of painting. During such states, time ceases to exist for the artist, boundaries blur between self and others, and a host of paranormal phenomena may arise.

In the case of great composers like Mozart, one may wonder if he wrote the music or if "the music wrote him." Mozart was able to see and hear an entire symphony in a single moment, and would then proceed to write down what he had already seen and heard. The situation with Johann Sebastian Bach is even more mysterious. Musicologists of the 20th century have calculated that if the world's greatest music transcriber made it his life's work to simply copy Bach's work, note for note, working 24 hours a day, it would take over 100 years to accomplish the task. Not only did Bach accomplish the impossible, he wrote at the level of perfection. Surely, this super-human feat could only have been accomplished if

Bach were living and writing in a state of unity consciousness most of the time. Perhaps Bach was "hallucinating" music all the time.

So close was Bach's music to perfection that for many people, Bach has become the link to God, the first step that told them that there was something greater than our lower selves. To quote the late guitarist and composer, Celedonio Romero, "Bach is the link between man and God."

Of course, the lives of artists are not always blissful. Salvador Dali's paintings were greatly influenced and inspired by tormenting visions that he had experienced as a child. Although those hallucinations were not artistic hallucinations in the strict sense of the word, they shaped his artistic vision. For many people, Dali's ghastly, rotting visions would have caused a life of suffering and insanity. It is the great challenge of the artist to take all experiences, even terrifying hallucinations, and turn them into creative works.

There is great suffering and great joy amongst artists. Although all of us are born with creative gifts, most of us choose not to be artists, but should be grateful to those who have walked the often-frightening path of artist, for without art, without sculpture, poetry, dance, and music, life would lose its beauty and meaning.

The Human Aura

The human aura is a complex visual experience that many psychiatrists would call a hallucination. Everybody has an aura, which changes according to one's mood, physical health, and state of consciousness.[12] The physical body, the energy body, the mental body, the intellect, and the soul each has a different kind of aura.

The human aura can be any color and is visible from head to toe. Do angels really have circular halos over their heads as depicted in Byzantine frescoes, or do they really have magnificent bright auras surrounding their heads? I vote for the latter.

No other visual phenomenon is equivalent to the human aura, which is as real as the person from which it emanates. The aura can be extraordinarily beautiful, composed of the most intense, deep blues, or, again, the most exquisite delicate violet that no artist can paint. The aura is not a fixed "light show" that follows us around. When we're angry, red streaks of light permeate our aura. When we're deeply in love, our aura is pink. On two occasions, I have seen the most extraordinary one-inch-thick indigo aura that hugged the head of a brilliant physicist.

Auras are not only seen surrounding our heads but also around the surface of our body. Each internal organ also has its own aura. Nurse-teacher Janet Quinn, R.N., Ph.D., first began to explore the auras and spiritual experiences after attending a workshop on therapeutic touch.[13] The instructor was discussing different aspects of the human aura, when one of the students in the class asked her, "How does the aura of cancer differ from the aura of an infection?" The class was seated in a circle. The instructor looked around the circle, got out of her chair, walked over to Dr. Quinn and placed her hand over her bladder. The instructor said, "This is the aura of a bladder infection." Indeed Dr. Quinn did have a painful acute bladder infection that day.

There is nothing new about auras. They have been described as far back as ancient India, Egypt, and Greece. The word "aura," comes from the Greek word for "air" and refers to that "airy" energetic field surrounding all living beings. In Indian and Chinese philosophy, auras are directly connected to the idea of chi or prana. The invisible chi, which flows through channels, or meridians, which is highly concentrated in the chakras (wheels of energy) and which may erupt violently as kundalini, manifests as the force field surrounding our physical body—as the human aura.

Ancient Egyptian art depicted the human aura. Pre-Christian artists, especially in ancient Persia, drew people with luminous clouds around them. And many paintings of saints show a halo around their heads, clearly depicting the radiant aura of an enlightened being. Modern day shamans from all cultures are familiar with auras, and those shamans with the most highly-developed siddhi powers see them easily. In a sense, it is understandable why so many artists have painted auras. Painters are people who have highly developed their sense of sight, both inner and outer sight. It is not surprising that people who have devoted their lives to studying the human form, people whose primary way of perceiving the world is through sight, would have developed their sight to the point where seeing auras is a natural extension of their already highly-developed visual acuity.

According to Rosalyn Bruyere, author of *Wheels of Light: A Study of the Chakras*, the meaning and the colors in the aura varies from one culture to another.[14] Ms. Bruyere, who has highly-developed the ability to see auras, says that people in the West display a yellow aura when thinking and a blue aura while daydreaming. During a 600-mile journey up the Nile River, she never observed blue or yellow in the aura of Islamic people. When she traveled through Israel, she again saw yellow auras, which she associates with Western modes of thought.

In reviewing Ms. Bruyere's findings, it strikes me, not that people in the East have a different color in their aura than do people in the West when they are thinking. I think it more likely that each state of mind, each mood state, and each state of consciousness is associated with a specific auric color. Because people from different cultures exist at different levels of consciousness, I believe it is more likely that she was observing the aura associated with a particular culture. People in deep meditation display the same characteristic aura, no matter where they live; and people who are in a fit of rage show the same kind of aura, no matter what their native land or cultural belief. Enlightened masters from all traditions have huge, bright auras, not tightly fitting their heads, but oftentimes extending many feet from them. Sometimes the aura of an enlightened master will be so vast that one cannot see the end or the edge of it, as if it were merging with the sky.

The main thing to remember, if you're seeing auras, is that it's really no big deal. There's nothing to be afraid of, and seeing auras definitely is not a sign of mental instability. Seeing auras is a perfectly acceptable and normal mode of perception and is commonly seen in all cultures. Some people have a more highly developed sense of hearing. Seeing auras is a kind of highly developed sight.

Working with Auras
Guideline #7

1.   If you see auras, simply regard them as another normal way of perceiving.

2.   Remember that, if you're seeing auras, it probably shows that you're taking the time to relax into perceiving the world in ways that are more intuitive and spiritually-oriented.

3.   The great spiritual masters all tell us to avoid the trap of becoming "attached" to siddhi powers, of which seeing auras is one of the most common. They advise us to avoid letting our ego get inflated about seeing auras, nor to make a public display of these powers. One should make as little to do about auras as possible, not because they are dangerous, but because over-emphasis on siddhi powers leads one away from the spiritual path, from the ultimate spiritual goal, namely liberation itself.

4.   Avoid the pitfall of thinking there is something special about you if you can see auras. Don't fall into the ego's trap of feeling "better" than others if you can see auras.

5.   Some people can't help seeing auras. If that is the case, be discreet about your knowledge and abilities. I still don't advise that you actively train yourself to see auras.

6.   If you insist on developing this specific siddhi power, study the color and shape of auras and notice how a particular aura corresponds to a particular mood. This ability has practical applications. Once you've learned what the aura of an enraged person, who is about to blow, looks like, you can keep your distance. On the other hand, when you see a shimmering, golden, luminous aura, with tinges of pink, you can learn to approach that person, knowing he or she is a loving, moral person.

7.   Remember that, in some cultures, trying to see someone's aura is considered an invasion of their personal space. This is the case among some Native American tribes. Therefore, you'll want to ask permission to look at their aura. This is a good rule to follow with everyone, not just Native Americans.

8.   The ability to see auras can be developed. If you want to develop that ability, first ask yourself why you want that ability? Do you just want to show off? Would seeing auras be the equivalent of the "Spiritual Olympics" for you? If so, forget it. Don't try to see auras. If, on the other hand, you want to see auras because you think that ability would make you a better person, and would allow you to serve people at a deeper level, then, by all means, develop the ability.

9.   You can find books that will teach you how to see auras, but here's a way to begin. Look at people in "soft focus." Act as if you're looking through them without allowing your eyes to be in sharp focus. Try to sense the energy around a person's head. Then try to see a white light surrounding the head. After a while, you'll be able to sense a general aura of light around everyone. In time, you'll be able to see specific colors.

10.   Remember the caution of the Roshi's word to his disciple who had just experienced nirvana. Don't worry. Your excitement about auras will pass. Stick to the path of love, truth, and dharma.

The Divine Weaver:
Integrating Unusual Experiences
Mental Fitness Technique #14

For some people, having an unusual experience, such as seeing auras or angels is no big deal. For others, such experiences require a quantum shift in one's belief system in order to integrate the experience into the fabric of one's life. One must not make too much of such experiences, nor too little. Here is an imagery technique to help you integrate any experience, whether "unusual," "mystical," or "ordinary."

Imagine yourself entering a cave. This is a dark place of great mystery. You go deeper and deeper into the cave, making your way by the light of a candle which you are holding. After navigating several twists and turns in the cave, after squeezing through narrow tunnels and hallways, you suddenly enter a vast opening, a giant room within the cave. In one corner of this vast room is a divine, radiant being, sitting at a loom, weaving a variety of beautiful fabrics and tapestries. After you observe him weaving these tapestries, you begin to recognize some of them. He is weaving tapestries from your own life, pictures from your childhood, pockets of pain, memories of happy experiences. He has been weaving this tapestry of your life for a long time—forever.

You approach this divine being and talk to him or her about the experience that you want to have better integrated into your life, for your experience does not yet feel as if it is completely part of you. It still feels separate from you. As you tell this divine being about your experience, all of the feelings, thoughts, sensations, perceptions, images, and states of consciousness flow out of you as if they are a current or a stream. That stream of experience ends up at the feet of this divine weaver. No matter what form that stream of experience takes, the divine weaver quickly picks up part of the stream and continues his weaving. He is now weaving a cloak or coat out of the colors and impressions of your experience. Old experiences, old memories, are also woven into this new creation, until finally your new experience becomes a finished work.

The divine being stands up, holding up your new multi-colored cloak. Your new experience is symbolically woven into the cloak. The divine being places the cloak around your shoulders. Notice how it fits. Is it too tight? Too loose? If so, ask the divine weaver to make the proper adjustments.

Finally, you place your cloak of experience around your shoulders, and you begin to make your way back out of the cave. With each step you take, you notice that your experience no longer seems so separate from you. It has begun to become part of the fabric of your life. As you step out of the cave into the sunlight, you notice that your cloak is even more beautiful and radiant that you had first noticed in the dimly-lit cave. Wear this cloak. Walk in the sunlight. Feel the safety and protection that it provides you.

Past-Life Memory

Victoria was ten years old when we met. Since the age of five she had been re-living a past-life. Because this past-life was quite a famous person, it may make this story less believable. Nonetheless, I am writing about her because the details of her past-life memory are extraordinary.

When Victoria was five years old, she "knew" that she was the wife of Abraham Lincoln. She frequently dreamt about Lincoln. Then when she was nine years old, the dreams of his assassination became more frequent and more intense. Before I proceed, I want to explain that Victoria comes from a Catholic family in which there is no discussion of reincarnation, paranormal phenomena and the like, and there are no books about these subjects in the house.

The whole story blew wide open when Victoria's mother asked psychic Shama Smith to do some relaxation work with Victoria to help with anxiety and depression. As soon as Victoria relaxed, she began sobbing uncontrollably. Because Victoria's parents were having a lot of difficulties, Shama assumed that

Victoria was upset about the family distress, which did eventually end in divorce. Shama asked her why she was crying. The answer was one that totally shocked Shama.

Victoria began speaking with a voice not heard in the 20th century, but one that came from the distant past. Victoria, sobbing in a 19th century voice and dialect said, "They killed him."

"Who did they kill?" Shama asked.

"They killed my husband, President Lincoln." She went on to describe in great detail how the assassination took place. Mary Todd Lincoln was wearing a dress, cinched at the waist, with five petticoats underneath. She wore a broach around her neck. Victoria said that she and the President were at the theater with the mayor and his wife. It turns out that Lincoln's companion was a major in the military, not the mayor.

She continued. "Then this man came from behind and stabbed the mayor. And then he shot my husband." Victoria was in excruciating pain as she recounted all of this, crying her heart out as if she had suffered the terrible loss that morning. After Lincoln was shot, Victoria saw James Wilkes Booth (whose name she did not know) jump from the balcony onto the stage. It was a long jump that injured one of his ankles. Booth briefly buckled from the pain, then quickly regained his strength and raised his right hand, which held a knife or a gun. Victoria wasn't sure which. And then, "He said something in German." Actually, Booth said something in Latin. After that, Booth ran from the theatre.

Shama and Victoria shared the experience with her mother, who purchased some books on Mary Todd Lincoln. Victoria was the spitting image of Mary Todd Lincoln, so much so that when a visitor saw a book on their coffee table, she asked, "Why does that book cover have a photograph of Victoria?" The woman looked closer, read the title, and was shocked. Victoria could have been the identical twin of Mary Todd Lincoln.

As a result of deeply re-experiencing the assassination, Victoria's nightmares and depression began to lift. In order to gain closure, Victoria and her mother flew from California to Washington, D.C. to return to the scene of the crime. They entered Ford's Theatre where Lincoln had been shot. As they approached the area where Mary Todd and Abraham Lincoln had been seated,

Victoria became profoundly weak, as if the life force was being drained out of her. Her mother quickly picked her up and carried her outside where she returned to normal after a few minutes.

From there, they went across the street to the hotel where Lincoln spent the night as he lay dying. On the first floor of the hotel was a couch where Mary Todd had slept that night. Victoria took one look at the couch and said, "They've changed it all around. That is not the couch that the President's wife slept on." And then Victoria again became profoundly weak, and was carried outside to recover. The experience helped Victoria in her healing process, although it was painful and draining for her.

After returning from Washington, Victoria wanted to put the whole past-life behind her. Because her story was so extraordinary, I asked Victoria if she would be willing to spend some time with me, recounting her story. She did not come to me for psychotherapy or for help with any problem.

Before she began to tell me about all of her experiences, she said, "Do I have to do this again? I am so sick of this." What was striking was that Victoria had no ego attachment to her past-life experiences. She felt no pride at having been married to President Lincoln. She felt nothing special about her memories. She was a regular teenager who was just sick of re-telling and re-living her past-life memory. She was sick of the attention and just wanted to get to the business of being a teenager.

If Victoria's experience was not a past-life memory, what could it have been—imagination, psychosis, delirium, or a manipulation for attention? Because I have worked at the crossroads of miracles and madness for decades, this is not a difficult "differential diagnosis" to figure out. She did not suffer from five years of delirium, a brain condition in which one is quite disoriented, does not know the time or date, and may be quite emotional unstable and irrational. When you have a high fever, you experience a brief delirium. You are confused, disoriented, can hardly move, and don't know what day it is. Victoria did not have a chronic brain disorder. Was she psychotic, which includes conditions like schizophrenia, mania, extreme depression, or someone with borderline personality disorder (BPD)? Rarely, people with BPD can become psychotic, which means, "loss of contact with reality." The psychotic person may be hallucinating or having delusions, which are fixed, usually bizarre ideas involving either paranoia or grandiosity. Victoria was quite in control of all her faculties. Except for her unusual experience, she was like any other ten-year old American girl. She showed no trace of psychosis. Was she fabricating the whole story in order to get attention? Could she have done that because of family stress? Quite the contrary, Victoria was sick of her own story. She didn't want to talk about it. She kept it under wraps for five years, telling no one until she fully re-experienced the past-life while working with Shama. And family stress was not unusual in the Western World.

Was she just imagining that she was married to Abraham Lincoln? Some people who talk about their past lives do so because they are on an ego trip. They may or may not have been Queen Victoria, Napoleon, St. Thomas, or some other well-known figure in history. But they tell their story as if that is who they are now, recounting simply to boost their ego and false self-esteem. This notion of "imagination" came up when former First Lady, and current Secretary of State, Hillary Rodham Clinton, had consulted with Jean Houston to help her be the best First Lady she could be. Rodham Clinton was instructed to close her eyes and imagine that she was having a conversation with Eleanor Roosevelt. As someone who has worked with mental imagery for more than thirty years, I can say that conscious mental imagery is not the same as imagination, or "making things up." Hillary Rodham Clinton faced quite a bit of ridicule for her progressive thinking in using mental imagery. Some accused her of being crazy and others of being lost in imagination. She was using "creative imagination," but was certainly not confusing reality with imagination.

Small children often "imagine" that they have an imaginary friend, either a person or animal. They almost always outgrow the experience. After reading this book, you may wonder if your childhood imaginary friend was just imagination or if it was a visitor in non-physical form who faded out at the age when society tells us all to "grow up," which is by first grade. Imagination is defined as, "the action of forming mental images or concepts of what is not actually present to the senses, a conception of mental creation, often a baseless or fanciful one." Victoria was having experiences that were not based on the usual information gained from the five senses. The extraordinary emotional pain, depression, and grief are not part of imagination; an imagery experience is quite fleeting. The average person while daydreaming might spend a minute or two in "imagination." Imagination never lasts for five years. The other details of Victoria's story mitigate heavily against imagination. She knew details of the assassination that no one else knew. Even her errors were characteristic of past-life memory. For example, she thought she was sitting next to the "mayor" when, in fact, he was a "major." She heard John Wilkes Booth shout out something in "German," when in fact he was speaking in Latin. How many highly educated people know that Booth said some words in a foreign language? Not I, I confess. Her own experiences in Ford's Theatre, in which she became profoundly weak, add further support that hers was a powerful paranormal experience.

In a sense, Victoria's experiences were post-traumatic stress disorder (PTSD). She was reliving the assassination of Lincoln the way a military veteran remembers the war—with terrifying flashbacks, problems sleeping, feeling jumpy, and anxious. Truly God only knows why Victoria's past life bled through so powerfully that she was re-living it as a PTSD experience. God did something very smart when she created human beings. God made us almost entirely amnesic for our past lives. We have all been saints and sinners, and have all committed terrible crimes, over the course of tens of thousands of years. It is a good thing that when we are born, we are not burdened with conscious memories of the past. We are born anew, given one more chance to raise our consciousness, and to learn to be more happy and complete. In rare cases, that mechanism breaks down, and I cannot offer a theory that explains why Victoria, and others like her, have such powerful "bleed-throughs" from a past life.

It is not uncommon for people to reincarnate with physical features that are quite similar to a past-life and to have identical, or nearly identical, birthdays. What can we learn from Victoria's story and what is there to analyze? First, we can identify that she had an experience that included paranormal phenomena and that occurred in an altered state of consciousness. The duration of the overall remembering was very long, at least five years. The experience with

Shama lasted about one hour, which is very long for such an experience. It is very important that Victoria received support, understanding, and validation. It would have been easy for such a young person to feel as if she were going insane. Fortunately, she had an understanding mother and someone like Shama to help her work through and release from the Mary Todd Lincoln past-life.

Time will tell how this past-life memory will impact Victoria as an adult. Generally, powerful paranormal and spiritual experiences open a doorway or gateway to "the other side," the unseen world. A point will come when Victoria will start asking questions like, "Why me? Why did I have such an unusual, powerful, and painful experience? Is there any spiritual meaning that I am to learn from the experience?" For now, the tough job of being a teenager is enough work. But one day, I suspect that her Mary Todd Lincoln life will become the launching pad for a deeper spiritual quest, a journey into the meaning of life, the existence of God, and her purpose in this life. I think she already is quite clear that the soul continues on from lifetime to lifetime. She has earned the "knowing" within her the hard way, but that experience is hers and can never be taken away. Regardless of how the rest of her life unfolds, her past-life memory will always stand as one of the bright lampposts along life's long and winding highway.

It's important for psychotherapists to have an understanding of past-life memory, and not just to avoid mis-diagnosing. When a patient is about to experience a past-life memory or is in the throes of one, I have a very powerful emotional reaction. One patient of mine, Katrina, during our first meeting, was describing the details of a horrendous personal crisis, in which family members were truly plotting against her. They were intent on establishing a major psychiatric diagnosis, and in gathering proof through illegal means to try to nail down the diagnosis. There is always a part of me that is the skeptic. I want to believe my patients and it is my inclination to believe. But my left-brain must observe what is going on to make sure I am not missing something. In this case, it was important that I looked carefully for signs of mental illness. I concluded that her story was true and she was quite sane. Katrina became very emotional, frightened, and tearful as she described the details of how she was being set up. Before she began to say the words, "I felt like I was being burned at the stake—again!" I saw the past-life and watched her burning to death as a "witch." I am quite empathic and compassionate with my patients, but have the kind of objectivity that allows me to help without completely identifying with my patient's suffering. But this was different.

As I saw her burning to death on a stake, I felt so much emotional pain welling up in my chest, I nearly burst into tears. I literally could not speak, so I let her continue to do the talking. She did share her conscious memory of the past-life in which she burned as a witch, and then she burst into tears in my office. She saw that her current situation was a replay of the past-life. Several months later she spoke about the set-up again, and once again I saw the past-life and I had the same overwhelming emotional reaction.

A doctor's best barometer is his own internal reactions to patients. Over decades of working with thousands of patients, I have learned how I respond to a host of different problems and illnesses. I'll discuss this process in "The Lost Mind." I know that when I feel a certain way, I am probably dealing with a manic. When I feel sucked in, drained, confused, idealized then put down, I am probably dealing with someone with borderline personality disorder. What I felt with Katrina was completely beyond any reference point I had. I made a mental note: "So this is how I feel when someone is re-living a painful past-life while in my office." That information will help me the next time a patient walks in with the same kind of crisis. Of course, there are other important issues. On one level I had merged with Katrina. My "inner witness" remained quite intact, but my heart had become one with Katrina's and I was sharing her pain. She could see it in my eyes. She knew I was feeling what she was feeling and with the same intensity. I wasn't just thinking about her nightmare. I was right there with her, and in that profoundly shared pain, I believe there was great relief for Katrina. In temporarily taking on some of the pain, I may have helped her release some of the pain she was carrying. And not unimportantly, I validated her sanity, her understanding of her current crisis, and the reality of the past-life that was triggered by her current crisis.

Should all of us know our past-life memories? Should we intentionally try to gain information from our past lives? I think that some people make too much ado about such experiences, embellishing the re-telling of the memory with layers of ego. Most people who have had past-life memories have only had fleeting glimpses into a past-life. If that glimpse provides useful information, then it is worth pursuing. If that life helps establish a sense of connection, of continuity of the soul, then the experience is worth putting energy into. Most of us are afraid of death. If we have an experience that we know was from a past-life, it provides a knowing that the soul does go on and on, dressed in different clothing and different characters on each stage that we are thrust upon to play our roles. It is a good thing if a past-life memory solidifies one's sense of the eternity of one's soul.

---

1.   Hilary Evans, *Alternate States of Consciousness: Unself, Otherself, and Superself* (Wellingborough, U.K.: The Aquarian Press, 1989).
2.   Anne Gordon, *A Book of Saints: True Stories of How They Touch Our Lives* (New York: Bantam Books, 1994).
3.   René Fulop-Miller, *The Saints That Moved The World* (Salem: Ayer Company Publishers, 1945).
4.   David Gersten, M.D., "Psychotherapy of Visual Hallucinations: A Paradoxical Intervention," *Journal of Strategic and Systemic Therapies* (JSST), Volume 7, Number 4, Winter 1988, London, Ontario, Canada.
5.   Jay Haley, *Uncommon Therapy: The Psychiatric Techniques of Milton H. Erickson, M.D.* (New York: Norton and Company, 1973). See also Jay Haley, *Strategies of Psychotherapy* (New York: Grune and Stratton, 1963).
6.   Sophy Burnham, *A Book of Angels* (New York: Ballantine Books, 1995).
7.   Scott Sparrow, Ed.D., *Blessed Among Women: Encounters with Mary and Her Message* (New York: Harmony Books, 1997).
8.   Jeanne Achterberg, Ph.D., *Woman as Healer: A Panoramic Survey of the Healing Activities of Women from Prehistoric Times to the Present* (Boston: Shambala, 1991).
9.   Barry Taff, Ph.D., Personal communication, 1996.
10.   *The Collected Works of Madam Blavatsky*, 14 vols., Compiled by Boris de Zirkoff and Dara Eklund. (Pasadena: Theosophical University Press, 1981).
11.   Annie Besant and C.W. Leadbeater, *Thought Forms* (Madras: Theosophical Publishing House, 1901).
12.   Lanetta Gregory and Geoffrey Treissman, *Handbook of the Aura* (Norwich, England: Pilgrims Book Services, 1985).
13.   Janet Quinn, R.N., Ph.D., "Aids, Hope, and Healing," *Atlantis, the Imagery Newsletter (Dec. 1991).*
14.   Rosalyn Bruyere, *Wheels of Light: A Study of the Chakras* (Sierra Madre, CA: Bon Productions, 1989).

Chapter 10

ExtraSensory Perception

Extrasensory perceptions may involve any of our five senses. In addition to visual phenomena, ESP may be heard, smelled, tasted, touched, or sensed.

Voices and other paranormal phenomena, like visions, cannot be measured through blood and urine tests, x-rays, CT scans, photographs, radiation detectors, electrical field detectors, direct examination, or by physical observation. Nonetheless, we should not dismiss them or pretend that because something can't be measured in such ways that it does not exist.

It's not terribly difficult to distinguish an angelic voice from a psychotic hallucination. The effect of the miraculous in our lives is predictable. Miracles, like angels, make our lives more meaningful. Love is the sign of the miraculous. Miracles lead us to become more loving, more honest, more humble, more dedicated. They build character and help us develop a sense of unity and community. If some strange phenomenon does not produce this kind of effect, it most likely is not a miracle. If a voice or hallucinated smell does not help build character, does not help us become more loving, it most likely is not a genuine spiritual experience.

ESP of Sound

During psychotic episodes, people hear voices that are loud and usually menacing. The voices are very real to them but are entirely a projection from their inner subconscious world into the outside world. Yet they experience the voices as coming from outside themselves.

Voices of a spiritual nature are referred to as "clairaudience." I've personally had this experience twice, and here is one of those experiences. When I was Chief Resident in Psychiatry at UCSD, I had an appointment one morning with one of the staff members named Joe. We were supposed to meet at eight a.m. Just prior to eight, I was in the back office of the psychiatric ward chatting with the unit secretary, Nancy. At eight o'clock, I heard Joe's very loud voice calling my name and a few seconds later, one of the staff members, Ron, walked into the room where Nancy and I were, looked at me and prepared to say something. I said to Ron, "Go ahead and send Joe back here." Ron turned rather pale and said, "Joe's not here. He's on the phone. He just called to say he's sick and can't come in today."

Now, I'm not schizophrenic. First of all, having heard one or two voices doesn't make you or me "crazy." Secondly, the voice I heard directly related to a real event that was taking place in the outer world. It was a psychic experience in a real context.

Let me offer here another story of ESP of voices: Hank, who is now in his forties, had a life-saving experience of hearing voices when he was in his early twenties. He was in quite a highly dysfunctional marriage with a disturbed woman. One morning, after spending the night sleeping on a couch, Hank was awakened by a loud voice that gave him these instructions: "Wake Up! Do not open your eyes. Now slowly roll over. Now open your eyes just a very tiny bit." Hank had never heard this voice or anything like it before, but he obeyed. Through his barely opened eyes, he saw his wife coming across the room with a rifle aimed at him. She was walking slowly and quietly. Hank continued to pretend to be asleep. When the rifle was within reach, he suddenly grabbed it and took it away from his wife.

Hank was young and needed one or two more miracles before he got out of the marriage. On a second occasion, the same voice loudly woke him. He got out of bed and went into the kitchen where he found his wife boiling oil that she was about to pour all over him.

He finally got the message, loud and clear after he came home, walked through the door, to see his wife waiting with a loaded rifle, which she proceeded to fire. The bullet grazed Hank's shirt without harming him, but he fell to the ground as if he were dead. His wife approached him slowly, getting ready to put a couple of more bullets in him to make sure he was dead, but Hank surprised her and pulled the rifle out of her hands. He then left the marriage.

He has worked as an acupuncturist, massage therapist, and teacher, and has found his life calling as a storyteller. He doesn't need "voices" to save his life anymore. Now, if we really wanted to get into splitting hairs, we could ask, "who was that voice?" Was it the voice of an angel? Was it a dead loved one, voicing a warning from "beyond"? Was it his own telepathy expressing itself as a voice? Neither a schizophrenic nor borderline will hear a voice once or twice in their life and then function at a totally normal level for the rest of their lives. His experience was "clairaudience."

Meera hears voices on a regular basis, but she is not crazy. When her husband, Gary, returns from work, she frequently hears him arrive five minutes before he actually does. She hears his car pull up, hears him closing the car door, and then hears him whistling. Meera cannot tell the difference between Gary's "real" arrival and the "perceived" arrival. Because Meera and Gary are so connected to each other, even during a period of separation early on in their marriage, Meera was having the same kind of experience. On one occasion, Gary had moved out of their shared house and moved to another city. One night, during their separation, Meera was awakened by hearing Gary screaming her voice. They worked out their marital conflict, and after getting back together, Meera learned that Gary had been so upset during their separation that he had screamed out her name in the middle of the night, the same night during which she heard his voice. As you can see, genuine voices of a spiritual or paranormal nature, can be pretty mundane.

The schizophrenic often hears voices that give destructive instructions, such as "Jump off a bridge," or "Throw yourself in front of a car." The paranoid schizophrenic often hears voices that confirm his paranoia, such as "Watch out, they're reading your mind!" These voices are mundane, but psychotic and potentially dangerous. Meera once heard a voice that illustrates just how practical a genuine spiritual or paranormal voice may be. A female voice said to her, "Coffee is the root of all of your problems." Prior to that experience, Meera had been drinking four or five cups of coffee in the morning, which put her on an emotional roller coaster. She was shaky from hypoglycemia, couldn't think straight, and was exhausted most of the time. After she heard the voice, she gave up coffee and her symptoms disappeared. "I realized," Meera said, "that coffee is poison for me."

"Hearing the voice of God" has become associated with insanity in the West. Yet, history is replete with spiritual masters who spoke to God and heard back. St. Hildegard was so reluctant to speak about her voices and visions that the voice of God said to her, "Oh human weakness. Ashes of ashes. Frailty of frailty. Speak and write what you see and hear. And write it not as it pleases you, but write it after the will of Him who knows all and orders all in the hidden depths of His secret council."[1] These certainly are not the kind of words schizophrenics relate.

St. Francis of Assisi's life was also radically transformed by voices. Francis was a wealthy man of the world as he headed off to war, proudly announcing to his family and friends that he would return a knight. On the road toward Spoleto, Italy, he fell ill with fever and delirium. While in that feverish state, a voice said to him, "Go back to your native town. There it will be made known to you what you shall do." St. Francis' fever opened a doorway for a spiritual experience.

Francis obeyed the voice without knowing why. Instead of returning as an honored knight, he returned as the defeated laughing stock of the town. Within a short period of time, Francis renounced everything that prior to that time had been important to him. He took a vow of poverty, gave away all his money and possessions, and proceeded into the hills of Assisi wearing only the clothes on his back. While he initially became looked upon as a pitiful, pathetic creature who had ruined his own life, later on he was recognized by the Pope, and the world, as a saint.[2]

A second set of voices gave Francis another life-changing jolt. "Francis, do you not see that my house is in ruins? Go and restore it for me." That message stirred Francis' imagination and led him to found a new religious order within the Catholic Church. Francis, along with a small band of men, approached the Pope for approval in beginning this venture of "restoring the church." At first, the Pope laughed at Francis, but soon changed his mind, realizing that he was a sincere, devout person. Francis organized the religious order of the Franciscan brothers and helped re-instill the heart of Christianity, love, service, and sacrifice, into the church.

A "true" voice of guidance can be either the inner voice of conscience or the outer voice of God, and following its directives usually guides one in the direction of our hearts, in the direction of love, peace, and right action. If you've heard the genuine voice of God, fall on your knees and listen. Pray for more guidance to understand the meaning of what was said. When you are clear about the meaning, do everything in your power to follow the "divine directives."

ESP of Smell

The first thing you want to determine about a hallucinated smell is whether it can be smelled out of both nostrils. If the odor is in only one nostril, a neurological problem might be indicated, possibly a tumor growing along the olfactory tract, the nerve pathway leading from smell sensors in the nose into the brain. If the hallucinated smell is related to a neurological problem, it will usually be a bad smell.

Millions of normal people hallucinate smell. A psychologist I know perceives coffee periodically when there is absolutely no way for that odor to be there. Odors of a spiritual nature are often fragrant like jasmine flowers.

Death too has a smell beyond that of physical decay. I don't know how to describe it but anyone who has been around death knows the smell. It's not related to the physical body. It's a smell related to a non-physical plane of existence.

On some occasions, however, death has a sweet fragrance that feels intoxicating. Guitarist Pepe Romero told me that when his father, Celedonio, died, a sweet fragrance, like jasmine or gardenias, poured out of Celedonio's body and filled the air. I believe that the sweet fragrance of his death is directly related to the sweetness with which he lived and died.

According to psychic Shama Smith, a violent death leaves an odor or an energy that lingers months and years after the death and, is a terrible smell. Shama on some occasions has smelled death hours before the time of death. Yet, on other occasions, she smells death after it has occurred.

As with any sense, psychic experience can be associated with the sense of smell. During the '70s, because I was meditating a lot, and had plunged headfirst in my chosen spiritual path, my extra-sensory perceptions were heightened, and I was using those heightened abilities to assist in medical diagnosis. In the late '70s, I worked as a G.P. in the Urgent Area Clinic at Kaiser Permanente Hospital in San Diego. The doctors had a heavy caseload, seeing 20 to 35 patients in four hours. I'd pick up the chart, which would be sitting in a slot on the patient's door, and I'd try to sense what problem the patient was having—without opening his chart to read it. When I picked up one chart and closed my eyes, I began to experience a terrible smell. I walked in the room and asked the patient how I could help him. He told me that he was experiencing a terrible odor in one nostril. He had a hallucinated odor caused by a brain tumor and I had smelled the same thing psychically.

Another way to look at the "psychic odor" is simply as "deep empathy and intuition." You just open yourself up to the other's experience. As a result you feel what they feel, see what they see and, sometimes, smell what they smell.

Among devotees of Sathya Sai Baba, the perceived odor of jasmine is common. The fragrance can arise anywhere and when it does so, one feels almost intoxicated by the smell. On many occasions these perceptions of jasmine have been experienced by many people at the same time. Five people were driving in a car, while an elderly Sai devotee was smoking a cigarette. Suddenly, the car filled with the scent of jasmine. Everyone smelled it and marveled at both the sweetness of the smell, as well as the sense of peace it brought. In addition, the jasmine brought a message to the smoker. He said to the others in the car, "I think Baba is telling me it's time to stop smoking." He never smoked again.

I experienced a "hallucinated odor" after my first session with Kate, the healer from the U.K. When I returned home, there was an intense odor of incense burning at the foot of the steps that leads to my front door. It was so strong, it seemed as if six or seven sticks of incense were burning. The aroma was heavenly. I knew that the incense was a paranormal experience, and a confirmation of the powerful and positive work that had begun with Kate. But, I walked next door just to appease my scientific mind, to see if my neighbor was burning incense. She wasn't. I walked the short distance back home and walked through what seemed like a wall of incense. It was quite wonderful and uplifting.

Probably the best-known ESP of smell is that of roses, which accompanies a vision of Mary, the Mother of Jesus, or indicates her spiritual presence. The bodies of saints are also reported to give off this sweet, uncorrupted smell of roses. If one has had the extrasensory perception of roses or jasmine, you might want to approach it this way:

ESP of Smell—What to Do
Guideline #8

1. Pray—immediately.
2. Express gratitude for the experience.
3. Stay in the moment and remain with the feeling of awe. Let the experience carry you further in the direction in which it is taking you. Don't think about it. Just "be" with the experience.

Extra-Sensory Perception of Empathy

We can perceive in an extra-sensory manner, through any or all of our senses. We may "know" something is about to happen, or feel someone else's emotional or physical suffering—without really knowing how we know. Every mother has had the experience of knowing when her child was in serious danger or had been injured, whether her child was still in school, or if he were in his 50s. The ESP of empathy is simply very deep empathy, an understanding that does not rely on the five senses. It arises out of compassion, love, and empathy for others, and a desire and willingness to lessen others' pain and suffering.

Mary, a nurse who became quite psychic after getting off drugs and alcohol, "perceives" other people's pain. She might be in an elevator and suddenly be seized with a terrible pain in her leg. She'll look around the elevator and see a man with a leg cast on and will know she's experiencing his pain. Or she'll be walking down the street and feel a terrible facial pain. She'll look around, up and down the street, and will see someone with a face that has been severely traumatized from an automobile accident. Mary has the experience called "sympathetic suffering," a kind of "ESP of empathy."

The most extraordinary example of perceived pain is so-called "phantom limb" pain. This is a pain in an amputated limb. Someone who has had his left leg amputated may continue to experience pain in his left foot, a foot that no longer exists. This is a neurological problem that is poorly understood.

Phantom pain is quite different from so-called imaginary pain. Many people have pain for which their doctors cannot find a physical explanation. They're often told their pain is imaginary, because the doctor can find no reason that explains why the pain persists. If you're in pain, you know it's not imaginary. Technically, so-called imaginary pain is neither imaginary nor hallucinated, and is often debilitating.

Phantom pain has proven to be a puzzle to modern medicine, for they have found no theory that explains the pain, nor any treatment that works. No one knows how it works, but I would like to propose a theory, and then a treatment. Before trying to explain phantom limb pain, I'll take a moment to describe Kirlian photography, a technique for photographing the aura. I have seen Kirlian photographs of leaves in which one sees a colorful halo around the leaf. In cases where a piece of the leaf has been cut off, the Kirlian photograph continues to show a complete leaf. The missing part of the leaf still exists in the "auric field." Perhaps the missing limb of a person still exists in the auric field. If it does, perhaps it is this "second body," the aura, which is transmitting information about its still existing limb to the "first body," which is responding with the message, "The limb is no longer here." The mind may be generating pain based on a conflict between information in the two bodies. This theory is but one of many possibilities, and I am suggesting this theory more to raise issues rather than to settle them.

What I can say with certainty is that mental imagery, in combination with energetic medicine (acupuncture, therapeutic touch, huna, reiki) has the potential to re-integrate a person's "multiple bodies," so that all of one's bodies are "in agreement."

Before I tell you how I work with amputees, I'd like to broaden the topic to include not only Vietnam, Afghanistan, and Persian Gulf Veterans and other military men and women who have lost a limb in the line of fire, but also the millions of women who have lost a breast due to cancer. While working with one woman who had had a mastectomy, I asked her, "What did they do with your breast once they removed it?"

"Oh, I don't know. I have no idea."

"Of course, you have an idea," I replied.

"Well. All right. I think they probably just tossed it in the dumpster."

"Yes, they may have, or they may have put it in a jar in formaldehyde. Who knows? It may be sitting on a shelf somewhere. But how do you feel about it?"

"Actually, I think about it a lot. I dream about it. I miss it. I don't feel whole or complete anymore."

"What you need to do," I told her, "is to give your breast a proper burial. We can do that using mental imagery, to begin with."

There has been a kind of secrecy about the whole issue of "missing body parts." Women don't know what happened to their lost breast, so, at first they imagine the worst, and then they repress that image, and forget that they ever imagined anything in the first place. But they do remember, and they suffer. Simply by visualizing the lost breast or leg and "giving it a proper burial," one can finally grieve and then regain a sense of wholeness.

By using a combination of imagery techniques and energetic techniques, body, mind, and spirit can be healed. When you consciously grieve the lost part, I believe that your mind, body, and auric body will finally come back into alignment. The physical pain will be less as will the emotional pain.

Grieving a Body Part
Mental Fitness Technique #15

Let's start with a mental imagery technique.

Picture that missing body part and see it "whole" and perfect. Now, you need to bury or cremate this part the same way you'd bury a loved one. Perhaps you'll want to place the body part in the soft, fertile ground of a mountain forest, or on the calm bottom of the Pacific Ocean.

Add rituals to your ceremony. If you are burying the body part, imagine that you are lighting candles. Say a prayer. Perhaps, you'll want a rabbi, minister, or priest to assist. Invite your loved ones to the funeral.

Before the actual burial, say "good-bye" to the body part and thank it for all the years in which it served you well. Now, proceed to the conclusion of this memorial service.

Letting Go—Grieving Body Parts
Guideline #9

Here is a simple program, which will radically help you with a phantom limb, or any other body part that has been permanently removed:

1.   Close your eyes. Become aware of your current belief about the missing body part. Where is it? How was it disposed of?
2.   How do you feel about how you think it was disposed of?
3.   Next, you'll want to create a ceremonial burial for the body part. Start by using the imagery technique you just read.
4.   Once you've held a memorial service in your mind, your healing can be even deeper if you carry out the same ritual in the "real" world. Mold a symbol of the missing body part—the arm, the leg, the breast—out of clay, or whatever substance appeals to you. Take this molded, sculpted representation of the missing body part and perform an actual memorial service. Actually go to the woods, the beach, the jungle, or the desert, and repeat the ritual you first created in the above imagery. Of course, you may modify the "actual" burial, depending on how you are feeling, thinking, and imagining at the time. Remember to be bold and creative. Throw your heart and soul into the exercise. You won't recover your breast, but you will recover your soul.
5.   Because there is a very good possibility that the human aura "remembers" the missing body part, seek out a practitioner of energetic medicine. See an acupuncturist, an expert in therapeutic touch, or a practitioner of Huna (Hawaiian healing).

By using a combination of imagery techniques and energetic techniques, body, mind, and spirit can be healed. When you consciously grieve the lost part, I believe that your mind, body, and auric body will finally come back into alignment. The physical pain will be less as will the emotional pain.

1. René Fulop-Miller, *The Saints That Moved The World* (Salem: Ayer Company Publishers, 1945).

2. *Ibid.*

Chapter 11

Miracles

The Random House Dictionary defines a "miracle" as: "1) an effect or extraordinary event in the physical world which surpasses all known human or natural powers and is ascribed to a supernatural cause. 2) Such an effect or event manifesting or considered as a work of God. 3) A wonder; marvel." I believe that the key words in that definition are "known human powers." If an experience cannot be explained by known human powers, we call the experience miraculous. Because our understanding of "known human powers" changes from year to year, so does our idea of what is miraculous.

Not too long ago, the mind and body were considered to be separate and unrelated aspects of man. Science did not begin to grasp the power of the mind and the ability of the mind to cure the physical body. Now, however, an entire field of science exists, psychoneuroimmunology, which has proven not only that the mind can dramatically affect the body, but also even how those changes take place. Hope can cure cancer. Prayer can cure cancer. These cures were once called "miracles," or else they were called "spontaneous remissions."[1] Now science is coming to understand that such healing is part and parcel of normal human powers. What was once believed to be a miracle is now understood through science. Until full human potential is totally understood, there will be a large gap between what actually happens in the world and what we think is possible. When we experience that gap, we call it a miracle. Really, a miracle is an indication of our incomplete knowledge, an indication that we don't have all the answers to explain all the data and all the phenomena. We will always be ignorant about something, and therefore, will continue to need to use the word "miracle".

Many of the stories in this book seem miraculous—the visions of a saint, the healings at a distance, the premonitions of the future, but the experiences in this next section are even more miraculous. Yet, I wonder if these experiences would feel miraculous to a saint or shaman, or if they would just be part of reality as they see it.

We'll explore the miraculous by starting with those experiences which science is beginning to understand, namely mind-body miracles.

Mind-Body Miracles

Much of my practice of integrative psychiatry is devoted to the use of mental fitness techniques, such as meditation, use of the breath, and guided imagery, tools that help us access the mind-body connection. An entire series of books can be written about mind-body miracles, but we will cover only a few examples here, just to give you the flavor.

I once treated a 60-year-old man who had suffered from life-threatening asthma for 55 years. Using guided imagery techniques, we were able to cure him in two sessions! Fifty-five years of asthma cured with two sessions using guided imagery. That sounds like a miracle, perhaps spiritual healing, but it's not a "real" miracle. It's evidence of the immense power of the mind to heal the physical body.

Marci is a 20-year-old friend of mine who was in a head-on collision on a San Diego freeway. The combined speed on impact was 140 miles per hour. When I got to the hospital to see her, she was in a lot of pain from fractured vertebrae in her neck—pain that even morphine wasn't helping very much. In five minutes, using guided imagery, her pain dropped to "zero" and stayed at "zero" for four or five hours.

Many scientific studies now document the power of meditation and guided imagery. In fact, Blue Shield of California offers payment for guided imagery therapy. Using guided imagery, people can raise or lower the platelet count in their blood, or their white blood cell count.[2] In fact, there are many different kinds of white blood cells and through guided imagery, people can raise the number of a specific kind of white blood cell. The power of the mind is so great that it holds sway over life and death. Many cancer patients have died on time to satisfy their doctors who have told them, "You will be dead in three months." Women tend to die after major life events, such as birthdays, Christmas, or anniversaries. Men, on the other hand, tend to die just before such events. This is a kind of miracle—the miracle of the power of the mind.

One of the most remarkable mind-body miracles with which I am familiar took place in the early 1900s. A surgeon was treating a young man who had small bumps all over his body, and was planning to surgically remove them. A friend of the surgeon, a psychiatrist and hypnotherapist, suggested that the surgery be put off because "hypnosis is very successful at eliminating warts." The surgeon agreed to the experiment, but was flabbergasted to discover that all of the small tumors had disappeared. The psychiatrist did not know that the boy had not, in fact, been suffering from a case of warts, but rather had a serious genetic disease, which produced skin cancers. Because the psychiatrist was so hopeful, he probably was able to over-ride the boy's genetic code, his DNA. There are only two explanations for this cure: 1) hypnosis changed the DNA itself, or what is called the "genotype," or 2) hypnosis changed the "phenotype," the expression of the DNA. I think the latter is the more likely explanation.

These "miraculous" events are only miraculous because we don't fully understand the power of the mind. In time the mind-body connection will not seem so miraculous.

The Power of Prayer

Larry Dossey, M.D. in *Healing Words: the Power of Prayer and the Practice of Medicine*, writes about the power of prayer.[3] He reports on a study done at San Francisco General Hospital by a cardiologist, Dr. Randolph Byrd. The research involved a group of four hundred hospitalized cardiac patients. Half of the patients were prayed for and half were not. This was a true controlled double-blind study. Neither the patient, the doctor, nor hospital staff knew who was being prayed for. Prayer groups around the country prayed for individual patients.

The results of the study were so dramatic that if it had been a study of a new drug, it would have been heralded as a major medical breakthrough—a new miracle drug. What was so dramatic? The "prayed-for" patients were discharged from the hospital sooner, had fewer complications, required less antibiotic treatment, and had less pulmonary edema. The "prayed-for" group had fewer deaths, fewer instances of CPR (cardiopulmonary resuscitation), less need for mechanical ventilation (attachment to breathing machines), and less need for diuretic medication.

Dr. Dossey is not specifically and solely interested in prayer. He is interested in scientifically demonstrating what he calls the "non-local" nature of the mind. The mind is not just confined to the brain. The mind does not just emerge out of the brain.

Dr. Dossey, through the prayer study and other studies, believes that the mind is truly not local. The mind is not confined to the body. If prayer can have profound, documented results—over great distances—then it is clear that the mind is not confined to the narrow space between our ears. The prayer studies have begun to demonstrate what every culture has believed since the beginning of time—that one can reach out with love and caring, and touch and heal in a way that is beyond the tyrannical grip of time and space.

What is the difference between the "miracle of prayer" and the "miracle of mind-body healing"? Clearly, the latter can be explained by the power of the mind acting within the body. The power of prayer requires deep reflection. Have we connected with the Absolute, with God, who acts as an intermediary? Does God hear our prayers and then carry out miracles? Or is the power of prayer related to the power of thought? Our thoughts are not confined to the body and can have an impact at great distances. I pose this as a question without an answer. I can only guess that the "miracle of prayer" sometimes works through the power of our own thought, acting at a distance, and sometimes works because God has truly been touched by our yearning and responds in miraculous ways.

But next we'll see that there are miracles—and there are miracles, the grand, absolutely inexplicable wonders that are the signature of God.

God's Invisible Hand

There is no limit to the range, type, or quality of miraculous events. The only rule is that these miracles defy the laws of cause and effect, the laws of physics, the laws of time and space, and our general concept of how things normally work in the world. These are what I call the "true miracles." These are the events that cannot be explained by mind-body medicine or the power of the mind to act at great distances. These miracles are the handiwork of a Greater Intelligence.

Miracles often come into our lives at times of birth, death, and major crisis. I experienced one such miracle before my daughter, Rachel, was born. I was driving about 35 miles per hour in Denver several weeks before Rachel's birth. Suddenly, a white dove flew in front of the windshield of the car, and just hovered in front of me for almost one full block. The dove hovered motionlessly as I continued to drive the car without slowing down. In other words, somehow the dove was not only hovering in front of my eyes, but was also flying at 30 or 40 miles per hour keeping perfect pace with the car. I knew instantly that the dove was sending an omen, a sign that everything would be fine with the upcoming birth of my child. And so it was! After a hectic labor, the obstetrician discovered that the umbilical cord had wrapped itself around Rachel's neck three times. Suddenly, she was going into a distressed condition. But with the quick, if not somewhat terrified actions of the medical team, Rachel was born some 60 seconds after she went into distress, in "mint condition," and for me remains as one of the great miracles in my life.

Isaac Tigrett, founder of the Hard Rock Cafe and The House of Blues, has had his life divinely spared on several occasions. On one occasion he fell asleep at the wheel while driving his Porsche at night. He woke up as he flew off a cliff. As he and his car hurtled through space, tumbling, spinning and slamming into the ground over and over again, his car was torn to pieces. The roll bar was ripped off. Both doors were completely ripped off. There was practically no front or back of the car left and there was no windshield. Just to add to the dangerousness of the situation, Isaac didn't have a seat belt. Certain death was averted by the sudden presence of a divine being who wrapped his arms around Isaac and exerted powerful pressure on his shoulders as if to keep Isaac firmly in place in the car; strong, gentle, incredibly powerful hands cradled him. Those divine arms held Isaac so tightly that he couldn't fall out of his convertible. Isaac walked away from the accident untouched, from a car that was totally and completely destroyed.

Sometimes miracles bring bad news, and may come as an omen of impending death. Linda Chavez, former White House Aide to President Reagan (and my sister-in-law), had an unusual experience when she was 12 years old. Her sister Wendy, who was six, suddenly developed a severe kidney ailment. In fact, she got sick on Linda's birthday. Several weeks later, Linda was outside in the front yard of her family's apartment. Linda noticed a yellow bird, perhaps a finch or canary, flying around in a somewhat sickly manner. Linda put her hands out and caught the bird in mid-air.

She brought it into the house, put it in a shoebox with grass, and poked holes in the box. She thought it might be injured because it wasn't very active. The bird lived for only a day or two and then died. According to Linda, her father was very "superstitious" and believed that a bird dying was a sign of someone about to die. Such, in fact, was the case. A few hours after the bird died, Wendy died of pneumonia and heart failure secondary to her kidney disease. Linda did not make a big deal of these events. However, her father experienced the bird as an omen that came true, a sign from God that something "bad" was about to happen. Nonetheless, if we consider that the bird's death was a miracle, it may mean that God's invisible signature was present in the family's life, showing the connectedness of life, and the presence of God even in death.

Animals, and pets in particular, have long been associated with the miraculous. My black cat, Leo, who lived 18 years (and stepped on my computer keyboard far too many times while I've been writing this book), was quite a magical fellow in his "youth." On one occasion, Stanley, an out-of-town friend was visiting. I semi-jokingly warned him, "By the way, watch out for Leo. He can do some very strange things, like walk through walls and closed doors." The evening of July 4th, Stan and I and my daughter Rachel headed out to watch the local fire-works display. I like to keep Leo inside on July 4th, because there are people who consider black cats evil and have been known to attack them on July 4th (and on Halloween). As the three of us stood on the front porch, I held Leo with one hand, and the front door knob with the other. I then tossed Leo inside the house, and quickly slammed the door shut. The three of us turned to leave and were stunned to see Leo "pop" into existence right in front of us. He didn't run in front of us. He spontaneously appeared. Stanley's eyes grew wide as saucers. I said, "See, I warned you." Rachel was speechless.

Of course, stories abound of cats and dogs traveling thousands of miles over entire mountain ranges, finally finding their lost owner in a new home. No one knows how these animals find their way to an old home, nor to a location to which they've never been. One can theorize about powerful extra-sensory perceptions of animals, but I think it all boils down to love. Our pets love us so much that they follow their hearts until they find us.

From time to time, people schedule an appointment with me because they're looking for a real miracle, especially cancer patients. I've never promised a miracle, nor performed one, but miraculous events have occurred in the lives of patients under my care. The most amazing of these miracles came into the life of Sheryl, a long-time friend of mine whose sister, Anita, had died of ovarian cancer four years before Sheryl's first official visit with me. Anita had been given six months to live from the time she was diagnosed, but lived for four years by using a host of traditional and complementary techniques.

Sheryl was not worried about her lung cancer, which was so advanced by the time I met with her that her doctor had given her only one month to live. She was not afraid to die, but couldn't bear the thought of her mother losing her two daughters to cancer, so Sheryl was interested in fighting the cancer for her mother's sake.

I taught Sheryl mantra meditation and some imagery techniques in which I had her imagine that she was filling up with healing golden light. Sheryl imagined the cancer dissolving in the heat of the light. I also suggested that she take a variety of nutritional supplements. During that session, we spoke about Sai Baba and I gave her a bottle of "holy water." I had been the recipient of some very rare lingam water, which had been produced by pouring water over a lingam, an egg-shaped stone, which Sai Baba had materialized, or manifested, and which he had created expressly for the purpose of healing. Even though the water is rare, stories like the one that follows are common when it comes to the miracles surrounding Sathya Sai Baba. I told Sheryl that I would stand by her whether she lived or died, and it seemed almost a foregone conclusion that she would soon die.

Sheryl was scheduled to have surgery a couple of days after our first appointment. Her surgeon had planned on removing her entire right lung, which was full of cancer, but when he "opened her chest" during surgery, he discovered that the cancer had spread across into her left lung and was wrapped around the great blood vessels—the aorta and the pulmonary artery and veins. They "closed" Sheryl, gave her a single radiation treatment and sent her home to die.

I didn't hear from Sheryl for a few weeks after our session and I feared the worst, but was stunned to hear her sweet, energetic voice one day. "David," she said, "I have had the weirdest, most amazing experience with Sai Baba. I was meditating a few weeks ago, right after our session. Suddenly I had a vision of Sai Baba. It was as if he were standing right in front of me. He began reaching into my chest pulling cancer out. I didn't actually see cancer coming out of my body, but I experienced it in this vision. And all day long, even with my eyes open, I could feel him putting his hand inside of me, pulling out the cancer. And you won't believe this. Or maybe you actually will believe this. My cancer has shrunk by 75%. My surgeon simply cannot believe it. I believe it but I don't understand at all why Sai Baba is doing this for me. I don't even know him, and hardly know anything about him. I was raised a Christian and I'm still a Christian. Why would he help me? Why would he save my life?"

Because I've known of so many miracles surrounding Sathya Sai Baba and the people and circumstances around those miracles, I've learned not to try to explain the miracles. "Sheryl, there is simply no way of knowing why this has happened to you. Perhaps, it was your good karma. Perhaps, it was because your motivation to live arose from completely unselfish motives. I have no idea. But I am so happy for you." Sheryl called me a few months later to tell me she was continuing to improve. And then she called a year later to say that the cancer had entirely disappeared.

Although most of us believe in miracles, many of us do not realize just how miraculous a miracle can be. We set limits, believing that certain events can take place miraculously and that other events are totally impossible even through a miracle. Like millions of other devotees of Sathya Sai Baba, I have personally witnessed and experienced some of the most inexplicable, yet common, miracles, that of materialization or manifestation. Sai Baba manifests objects out of thin air. His most common materialization is sacred ash, or "vibhuti." With a wave of his hand, ash pours out of his hand. Sai Baba says that ash is the most sacred of physical objects for it cannot be further reduced. Everything eventually ends up as ash. Vibhuti is a symbol of our mortality and a reminder of that which is immortal and permanent.

As a child of five or six, Sai Baba would sit underneath a tree during his school lunch break, would reach up into the tree and materialize a variety of fruits from all over the world—a mango for one friend, a pineapple for another, an orange for another. He would also materialize pencils for his classmates if they had none. Miracles never go unchallenged. Sai Baba's teachers knew about his miraculous powers even when he was in third or fourth grade. On one occasion, his teacher instructed him to slap another student in the face to punish that child for some minor infraction. Sai Baba refused and was told by the teacher that he had to stand on his chair, which Baba proceeded to do. The teacher, who had been sitting on a chair, began to get out of his chair, only to find that he could not separate himself from the chair. He was stuck to it. Another teacher walked by, saw the predicament and said, "I guess you haven't heard about Sai Baba and his miracles. I suggest you tell him he doesn't have to stand on the chair anymore." The teacher followed those instructions and immediately discovered that he was no longer stuck to his chair.

During one trip to India, I met a South-African fellow named Bharata who shared this incredible story with me:

> After my young wife died of cancer, I was so distraught. The pain, anguish, depression, and despair would not disappear. After six months of this mental torture, I loaded my pistol, held it up to the right side of my head, pressing it against my flesh. I looked at a photo of Sai Baba and, with tears in my eyes, prayed, "Please forgive me for what I am about to do. I can no longer go

on living. After I kill myself, please take care of my two young children."

After I finished my prayer, I pressed the barrel of the gun deeper into my skin, and then pulled the trigger. There was an enormous bang when the gun fired. Suddenly, my children knocked on by bedroom door, shouting, "Daddy, daddy, what was that sound?" I thought I was dead and in heaven. Still, there I was holding the pistol, which was smoking, so I quickly hid the gun under the bed, and replied to my kids, "What sound? I didn't hear anything!" My kids entered the room, and something immediately caught their eye. "Daddy, look. There is a hole in the wall right over Sai Baba's picture. What is that?"

Bharata couldn't explain to himself or to me how the bullet could not have gone through his own head. "It was impossible." Bharata subsequently returned to India, where he had visited before, this time to express his gratitude, for he believed that Sai Baba had somehow prevented him from killing himself.

Bharata continues, "When Baba approached me, he materialized some vibhuti, the sacred ash. But rather than the usual way in which the ash gently pours out of his hands, this time vibhuti 'fired' out of his hands and the ash exploded in my hands."

I cannot begin to explain miracles. All I can say for certain is that there is a reason for every miracle. Sai Baba does not perform miracles for the sake of entertainment, nor for power, fame, or money. Each miracle that I have experienced has taught me a spiritual lesson, a lesson in love, faith, or hope. Each miracle has answered some question that I had not yet spoken to Sai Baba.

Although I, and millions of others, are inspired by Sai Baba's love and are guided to a higher life through his miracles, I have no desire that the reader follow my chosen path, only that you follow your own path. Every religious tradition is filled with a rich history of miracles. Let's quickly review some of the greatest miracles, which devotees of a particular religion usually regard as fact, and others regard as fiction.

Jesus was said to have raised the dead, and materialized large quantities of bread and fish, not to mention restoring sight to the blind. Moses was reported to have parted the Red Sea during the exodus from Egypt. In Hinduism, Krishna is believed to have lifted an entire mountain with one hand, in order to protect his devotees from a monsoon. All these claims are preposterous in the light of "scientific" thought. One can easily dismiss all of these miracles associated with three major world religions. It certainly is easiest to dismiss miracles from someone else's religion.

The Sphinx poses a problem that cannot be so easily swept away. Considered perhaps the greatest statue on earth, no one can figure out how it was made. Up until 1985, the Sphinx was believed to be 5,000 to 7,000 years old. Recent research indicates that a more accurate figure may be 10,000 years. In either case, here is the dilemma, and the miracle. The Sphinx was made out of individual slabs of limestone (with approximate dimensions of 30 feet by 12 feet by 10 feet), each one weighing 200 tons (400,000 pounds). In the late 1980s a research team attempted to duplicate the feat of lifting a single 200-ton block. The experiment took six months to plan and required 20 men and two of the largest cranes in the world. The boom of the larger crane stood 220 feet high and required a 160-ton weight to counterbalance it. They finally succeeded in lifting the one piece 50 feet off the ground, the distance equal to the top of the Sphinx. After succeeding in lifting one 200-ton block, the engineers and scientists concluded, "We have no way of explaining how the Sphinx was made." Egyptologists have long claimed that a sophisticated system of ropes, pulleys and a lot of manpower made construction of the Sphinx possible. The conclusion of the more recent research project was that the Egyptians simply did not have anything close to the technology required to build the Sphinx. Not only that, the research team concluded that, even with modern technology, modern hydraulic cranes, the task might still be impossible. I have no idea how the Sphinx was created, but I suspect that spiritual powers were required, in addition to serious manpower.

Some of modern miracles remain more secluded than the Sphinx. The so-called Shiva caves near Rishikesh in the Himalayas are not easy to reach, but are said to contain an ongoing miracle. Milk has dripped from the cave ceiling for millennia and continues to this day. This liquid is not the usual water that drips from stalactites in caves all over the world. This is milk.

Miracles are happening every day and to a lot of people. Perhaps sometimes they are a manifestation of our own thoughts, our own spiritual and psychic powers. And perhaps some of them are God's silent signature on our lives. Perhaps some of these great miracles are the handiwork of both man and God—man's human and siddhi powers, and God's divine power. These events indicate to us that there is more in our universe than is dreamt of by most of us, most of the time. These extraordinary divine miracles restore faith, bring peace and consolation during adversity, and give us the courage to keep walking toward the Light. They cause us to ponder what we call "reality."

Most of all, miracles show us that God loves us. Sai Baba says, "Miracles are so natural to me that I am amused when you label them miracles." "Love is my highest miracle." "All the ostensible miracles are only droplets of that Ocean of Love. Do not be dazzled by the droplets." Regarding the limitations of science, Sai Baba says, "Normally the scientist of the mind looks outside to what can be perceived by the senses in the world. The scientist of consciousness, on the other hand, always looks inside to that which is beyond the senses or the grasp of the mind."

"One has, therefore, to rise beyond the mind to consciousness to achieve self-realization. To gain the infinite, universal atma (soul), the embodied self must break out of the puny, finite little prison of individuality."

"How can science, which is bound to a physical and materialistic outlook, investigate transcendental phenomena beyond its scope, reach, or comprehension? This is a fallacy on the face of it. One belongs to the material and the other to a spiritual plane. Science must confine its inquiry only to things belonging to the human senses, while spiritualism transcends the senses. If you want to understand the nature of spiritual power, you can do so only through the path of spirituality and not science."

"That which transcends time and space, cannot be explained or understood by modern scientific methods, tools or thought discipline born of the five senses, which are themselves conditioned by the limitations of natural laws governing time and space."

Spiritual inquiry requires an open mind and intellectual courage. Humankind needs to try to comprehend God, miracles, life-after-death, and the meaning of life. Without this spiritual hunger, this spiritual quest, life lacks purpose. I have seen and experienced miracles beyond a shadow of a doubt, and I hope you too will patiently embrace all of your miracles until your own spiritual path is clear. After you have done your own research and lived your own life, you must be the judge of your own experience. Please do not wait for science to prove to you that miracles exist or that God exists.

Science cannot even begin to explain the experience of love, which is more common than miracles. We can search for the next thousand years to find "love in a bottle," but we will never isolate love, or find it in a part of the brain. We may find neuropeptides that increase in the brain and in the blood when we experience love—but we must not confuse those neuropeptides with love itself. This most universal of experiences, love, cannot be explained, confined, limited, defined, or put in a bottle, so how can we begin to intellectually understand the infinite, the miraculous? The intellect can only point us in the direction of the infinite, of God. But the infinite cannot be grasped by the finite. The indescribable cannot be put into words.

Good medicine can be described with one word— "Practical." Combining science and spirituality is the practical thing to do. Simply put, it's what works. It's what relieves suffering. It's what preserves health. It's what helps prevent illness. It's what gives meaning, purpose, understanding, and hope to suffering and to life.

Being practical means giving a hungry person lunch. They don't need preaching. They need food. And being practical means providing the "spiritually-hungry" with soul food. Being practical means that a doctor needs to be able to say, "I don't know the answer but I have some strong hunches. I think part of your long-term depression can be directly attributed to your childhood, to your parents giving your brothers more attention, to your teachers telling you that girls aren't smart enough to excel at math or science. I am almost certain that your brain chemistry is out-of-balance.

But I also believe that your sense of distance, fear, and estrangement from God is at least as important as the mental, physical, and social factors." I have arrived at this conclusion through 35 years as a physician—through trial and error, through reason and intuition, through consultation with specialists in psychopharmacology—through consultation with priests, rabbis, and holy men—from my patients who have been Christians, Jews, Muslims, Hindus, Buddhists, non-Christian Native Americans— and from my friends who are all of the above religions as well as Sikhs and Zoroastrians.

Having explored the world of paranormal phenomena, altered states of consciousness and miracles, let's take a linear approach to this most non-linear phenomena—miracles.

How to Embrace Miracles
Guideline #10

1.   When you've had an experience that may seem miraculous, begin by suspending judgment. Don't come to any immediate conclusion. The power of saying, "I don't know the answer, but I am willing to tolerate the uncertainty of the situation" is powerful.

2.   Compare your miracle with those reported by the world's major religions. If your miracle is in keeping with ancient wisdom, you are on safe ground in considering the possibility of a legitimate miracle.

3.   If you decide the experience was not miraculous, try to find another explanation, but do not try to quickly pigeonhole the experience, so that you can bury it in the recesses of your mind.

4.   If you decide it was a genuine miracle, pray and meditate that you can fully benefit from the experience. The possibility that God showers miracles does not mean that all of us make the best use of them. If we know we've experienced a miracle, yet do not allow the experience to change us, the miracle will have been wasted on us.

5.   Seek to know the deeper meaning of the miracle. What is the lesson in it for you? How are you supposed to change? Does the experience of the miracle call on you to be more loving, honest, peaceful, non-violent, or moral?

6.   Here is a potentially frightening suggestion. If you are sure you've witnessed a miracle, allow your current reality to be shattered. That's what miracles do. They shatter the mind's tight grip on our "reality." We can dismiss the miracle and say to ourselves, "The miracle actually did not happen. Reality is the same as I've always believed it to be," or we can say, "My current understanding of life is incomplete. I am going to tolerate this shaky uncertainty and keep soul-searching until I understand what the saints and sages have been teaching. I know the experience was real. I just have no way of explaining it."

7.   After you have "diagnosed" your miracle and integrated the experience into your belief system, remember the words of the Roshi, "Don't worry, the experience will pass." In other words, don't get hung up on miracles. Don't get hung up on angels, auras, or prophetic dreams. Experience them. Learn from them, and then move on.

8.   In order to look for the miracle behind the miracle, you may want to make a conscious effort to make direct contact with the Source. Here is a simple, yet powerful technique called "Practicing the Presence," also called "Visualizing the Divine Form" that helps us feel closer to God, and to experience his presence more frequently. This technique draws you closer to God, to Higher Consciousness, and fosters the feeling of devotion, the highest, purest kind of love.

Practicing the Presence
Mental Fitness Technique #16

Each day, upon arising from bed, think of your chosen form of God, and then "carve" him out of thin air as if you were a sculptor. Fill in the details from head to toe.

Imagine you reach out and hold his hand as he lifts you out of bed. Continue to picture him beside you throughout the day, sitting in the car with you, walking with you, sitting beside you at business meetings.

If you like, "ask" God to wait outside the bathroom when you need to use the facilities.

These steps are the way I approach the miraculous in my practice of psychiatry. If I don't understand a patient's miraculous story, I'll say, "I don't know right off the top of my head what to call this experience. Let's look at this together." Out of that pregnant unknowing, that willingness to tolerate uncertainty, that hunger to know the truth, both doctor and patient can set aside the "supposed-to-be's" the "what-looks-normal"—and can have a deep, honest, profoundly healing discussion. People are afraid and embarrassed that someone might say, "You're crazy for talking about entities, nirvana, possession, clairvoyance, past-life memories, and life after death."

Let us remember that what was once held as pure nonsense, unreality, and superstition often becomes scientific fact. Old scientific explanations are only partial truths. And to that I must add that this book is only another small partial truth.

Just as Lincoln, Gandhi, and Martin Luther King fought the delusion of racial superiority and the immorality of racism and oppression, the times now are asking us to fight the delusion of scientific superiority/spiritual inferiority. We must over-turn the false idea that spirit doesn't matter. And the times are desperately calling us now to take a new look at psychiatry and medicine, because, despite extraordinary technological advances, something is desperately wrong. It's time to shed false beliefs, look at new realities, and take courageous steps into the future.

By incorporating the wisdom of the ages with modern science, psychiatry can actually help the manic, and the mystic. Doctors must treat all patients with knowledge, wisdom, and compassion. We must not glorify psychotic experience. We must treat psychotic people with great compassion and with appropriate medication. But we should not treat the mystic with Zyprexa. And we should not treat the schizophrenic with a strong dose of yoga and meditation.

It's time to admit that Spirit counts, that angels fly (or walk), and that some people can read minds. It's time to try to figure out the difference between schizophrenic hallucinations and spirit possession—between ghostly hauntings and the visions of alcohol withdrawal—between mania and kundalini. It's time for medicine to fully embrace the idea that spiritual experience is—real!

The next Part of this book, The Lost Mind, will lead us through the darker nights of the soul.

My main purpose in writing The Lost Mind is to help you to embrace your miracles, your pre-cognition, your Vision. You will read descriptions of the main mental illnesses and will say, "Nope. I don't have that. I really did see my late Aunt Sadie."

There is another purpose to The Lost Mind. All of us know someone who is struggling emotionally, and The Lost Mind will shed light on problems you don't understand. Understanding leads to compassion.

If you do have a bona fide mental disorder, the next section will help you love and accept yourself more. And my hope is that it brings greater compassion in how you deal with family and friends who are experiencing extreme mental suffering.

Lastly, you will learn that I do not advocate an "either-or" way of explaining behavior. That approach says, "Either you've experienced a miracle or you're crazy." The Lost Mind will open you up to the possibility, and likelihood, that all of us get depressed, anxious, and even a bit crazy, but we still experience the grace of God and have mystical experiences.

The Lost Mind strives to show that each mental disorder has a spiritual challenge, and some mental disorders actually increase the likelihood of paranormal and mystical experience while other disorders make those experiences less likely.

After 911, most New Yorkers suffered from post-traumatic stress disorder (PTSD) and 40% of those living in New York City were treated with SSRI anti-depressants like Zoloft and Paxil. While they have all been given a formal psychiatric diagnosis, they are no less prone to paranormal and spiritual experience. In fact, stories abound about miraculous experiences for New Yorkers. One of the most touching involved a group of men sifting through the rubble and ashes at ground zero. A burst of dust flew into the air, and then, out of nowhere, a huge number of monarch butterflies arrived and flew within that pillar of smoke and debris. One man looked up at the butterflies and simply said, "Souls."

Do not think that mental suffering excludes the miraculous. It is often the miraculous that is the cure, and it is often out of suffering that miracles arise.

1. Andrew Weil, M.D., *Spontaneous Healing* (New York: Alfred Knopf, 1995).
2. Quinn, R.N., Ph.D., "The Effect of Imagery on Platelets," *Atlantis, the Imagery Newsletter* (Dec. 1991).
3. Larry Dossey, M.D., *Healing Words: the Power of Prayer and the Practice of Medicine* (San Francisco: Harper San Francisco, 1993).

PART III

THE LOST MIND

Chapter 12

What Is the Mind?

As we've seen, one's own culture and beliefs have a profound effect on how one views illness and consciousness. To differentiate a case of miracles or kundalini, from madness or brain disease, you need a rudimentary understanding of mental illness.

Before you learn about real mental illness, however, it's important to know that there is "craziness" and there is "CRAZINESS!" Many medical doctors and lay people use the word "crazy" very loosely. A sweet, intelligent, kind, fifteen-year-old girl who suffers from severe chronic fatigue syndrome/myalgic encephalopathy (CFS/ME) was told by doctors at Kaiser Permanente that she was crazy—that there was nothing wrong with her physically, because the traditional medical system does not perform laboratory tests for CFS/ME. After eight months, they had found only one abnormal lab result, an elevation in the level of protein in her urine, even though for eight months she had been running a fever between 102 and 104 degrees. "Just pull yourself together. You're just depressed," she was told over and over again.

After Kaiser had given up on Tess as a "loony," her mother, a long-term patient of mine, asked me to evaluate Tess. Amino acid testing and specialized immunological testing showed a severe metabolic impairment, and an immune system quite similar to that seen in AIDS patients. Tess definitely was not crazy, definitely was very sick physically, and I almost certainly could help her. After three weeks on a nutritional supplementation program, she began to feel better.

Psychiatry has been deaf and blind to spiritual issues. Oddly enough psychiatry is nearly blind to the physical aspects of mental/emotional problems. While psychiatrists go to medical school, just like surgeons, internists, and OB-GYNs, most psychiatrists treat a person from the neck up. They consider thyroid problems (in the neck) to see if thyroid hormones are contributing to the mental illness, but that is where they stop.

While the focus of this book is on differentiating spiritual and paranormal experience from mental illnesses, in reality I function as a holistic physician. More than half of my practice involves the treatment of chronic physical problems such as CFS/ME, fibromyalgia, irritable bowel syndrome, asthma, allergy, skin disorders, and cardiovascular disease.

I work from the premise that the nervous system, immune system, digestive tract, and endocrine/hormone system are four closely-related systems. I may be able to cure one patient's depression by treating parasites or generalized candidiasis (a yeast infection). Sometimes anxiety is caused by food allergies, mercury toxicity, or infection with HHV6 (human herpes virus 6).

It is beyond the scope of this book to delve into nutritional medicine. I do want to share with you that, whether my patient "suffers" with angels, diarrhea, or depression, I take a very comprehensive look at the total person.

Now, back to Tess, who was misdiagnosed and consequently was not correctly treated for CFS/ME accompanied by high fevers. Medical practitioners had taken away her hope. Tess started to get better the moment she began to feel hopeful. One year after my treatment prescription of "hope," counseling, and amino acids, Tess fully recovered and returned to a normal life. Tess healed not just because of the amino acids, but also because of our doctor-patient relationship. The deep sense of trust that Tess felt with me, the hope I was able to inspire in her, and the validation of her illness I provided helped her turn on her own inner healing resources.

The medical profession is, and always will be, limited by current technologies, and it does not have the right to dismiss mysterious symptoms as fabricated or crazy. But all too often medicine does mislabel as crazy any illness it can't easily explain. "You're just pre-menstrual, or depressed, or hysterical, or crazy." This lack of understanding and empathy can actually be life-threatening. Tess was dying when I first met her, and I believe that if she hadn't died, she would have become a chronically sick person if she continued to receive the message from medical authorities that she was just a little crazy. The power of our words, as doctors, is enormous. According to Bernie Siegel, M.D., author of *Love, Medicine, and Miracles*, we can kill with our words, and we can heal with our words.[1] We can even make someone feel crazy by telling them they are crazy—even if they're not.

Until recently, every paranormal phenomenon, every vision, every miracle, every mystical experience has been neatly jammed into the system of traditional psychiatric diagnosis, as a hallucination; every accurate premonition has been called magical or wishful thinking. In the next pages you'll encounter a variety of symptoms seen in mental illness, including: depression, anxiety, hallucinations, confusion, manic euphoria, suicidal thoughts. You will realize that your vision, your clairvoyance or kundalini is not a symptom of insanity, and will learn what your experience "is not."

Even if you or someone you know were to fall into one of the categories of mental illness that you will read about, I want you to know that mental illness can be treated. Powerful medications are available to treat most of the major kinds of mental illness. Medication, in conjunction with psychotherapy, saves lives. For instance, 50% of all Americans will experience a clinical depression at least once in their lives, and there are many ways to work with depression. The main message I want to get across, however, is that it's O.K. to be depressed and it's O.K. to be treated for it. There is no spiritual victory in refusing proper medical treatment. It is not "unspiritual" to treat your depression with medication. It's the practical and spiritual thing to do.

Likewise, if you've just been in a serious car accident, it's not time for aromatherapy. It's time to get to the nearest emergency room to have a well-trained, conventional medical doctor stop the bleeding and fix your broken bones.

I want to help lift the veil of fear that stops people from getting help, whether they need help for depression, schizophrenia, or a mystical experience. We, as physicians, are here to help you no matter what is wrong. We're here to treat depression and psychosis and, in my opinion, we're here to accept the angels and mystical experiences and help you to be inspired by those experiences. Whether it's a case of "angels," "depressive blues," "manic highs," or "mystical union," know that an honest diagnosis will help enormously in alleviating any fear or doubts you may have about your sanity. Knowing the truth will allow you to get help no matter what the diagnosis is. Knowing the truth can even help you find meaning in illness, just as you'll read in the section on depression in which Paul discovered that his "dreaded" depression was actually a gift, a direct answer to his own prayers.

As we explore the various kinds of mental illness, we'll proceed from those in which real spiritual experience is least likely, such as severe disorders of brain chemistry (organic brain syndrome and schizophrenia), to those in which spiritual experience can occur frequently, such as borderline personality, depression, and anxiety. For people with schizophrenia, spiritual experience is unlikely, but still possible. People with multiple personality disorder and borderline personality disorder, have experiences that are a mixture of imagination, psychosis, and real spiritual influence.

From the standpoint of traditional psychiatry, the human mind is our greatest possession. However, in Eastern thought, the intellect is seen as "higher" than the mind, and the soul is seen as the "highest." The soul is never lost, although it may be difficult for many of us to make contact with it or understand it, and it may be "covered" with layers of mind. In Eastern philosophy, our mind is a bundle of hopes, wishes, thoughts, and desires, separate from the intellect, which guides the mind to discern with "wisdom and discrimination." Through the intellect, we find our purpose, meaning, and goal in life. The mind carries out the instructions our intellect gives it.

When the mind becomes lost, the real "we," the soul, seems far away. The mind can become lost in many ways. The schizophrenic's mind is so lost that he cannot tell himself apart from others. The manic mind runs so fast that lives are ruined. The depressed mind may run so slowly and negatively that we may think of taking our lives. The anxious mind is so worried about the future that we forget about living in the present. We are run by fear, forgetting our higher nature. The borderline mind feels as if it has nothing to hang on to, and so the borderline feels as if he lives at the edge of a great void.

Most of us have some of the qualities I've just mentioned. We have a little bit of mania, a bit of depression, a bit of anxiety, a bit of the void. Most of us even have had brief periods during which we wondered if we were really going crazy. The fact is that we all lose our minds to some extent, even in a simple display of anger or a sudden attack of fear. Everyone has lost his mind, if only for a few minutes. It's O.K. to lose your mind. We all do it. What is not O.K. is to suffer over our suffering, to become anxious about being anxious. The fact that all of us "lose our minds" from time to time gives us the empathy and compassion to live with one another and help one another. The big difference between most of us and the people you'll read about in these pages is that your "loss of mind" is fleeting and temporary, whereas during an acute psychotic episode, the person with schizophrenia has nearly completely lost his mind, and the borderline lives at the edge of the void, frequently experiencing a condition of profound empty depressions, addictions, extreme mood swings, multiple moods a day, and a sense that one lives without a solid foundation, a condition of intense suffering.

The various mental illnesses appear distinctly different at first. The schizophrenic and the borderline begin their course of suffering in very different ways. However, a person who has been schizophrenic for 30 years may be difficult to distinguish from a manic or borderline who has been ill for 30 years. The severe mental illnesses generally start with a bang and then progress to a state of chronic dullness, a state of sameness with other mental illnesses. After 30 years of mental illness, people appear "burned out" whether due to schizophrenia, mania, or borderline personality. The spiritual person, on the other hand, develops his or her uniqueness more and more, and is moving in the opposite direction of the person with mental illness. Spiritual practice brings out the best in us, the best in our hearts, minds, personalities, and intellects.

There are people on the spiritual path, however, who become stuck at a certain level of insight and develop a kind of pseudo-spirituality. They appear spiritual, but don't act it. The "pseudo-spiritual" start to look alike, just as the chronically mentally-ill do. But the "truly-spiritual," the great spiritual adepts, the saints, and the sages have all developed their uniqueness. Their personalities are loving, humorous, powerful, and quite distinctive. Like the average American, the average saint has lost his mind from time to time and has seriously wondered if he were going crazy.

But the average saint differs from the average insane person in one very important way. He doesn't get "stuck" in his insanity; he witnesses it and then lets go of it.

In exploring The Lost Mind, remember the universal message of saints and sages throughout history, who have said that only one thing is eternal—the soul. In this understanding, the soul is never lost. It cannot be lost. It always was and always will be. It is eternal, constant, and never-changing. We are not our minds and we are not our "lost minds." We are the witness of these changes, all these phenomena, and all these so-called states of mind. We treasure our minds and glorify them without realizing that it is the light of the soul that gives the mind any light at all. To quote Sathya Sai Baba, "The soul is infinitely more beautiful than its surroundings."

OBS: When the Chemistry Isn't Right

There are so many ways for the brain to go out of whack: stroke, drug intoxication, fever, medication side-effects, drug withdrawal, alcohol intoxication, alcohol withdrawal (DTs), cancer, all kinds of metabolic disorders, infections of the brain, trauma (getting hit on the head), inflammation of the brain tissue or of the blood vessels in the brain, environmental toxins, heavy metal poisoning, hypothyroidism, and degenerative diseases (such as Alzheimer's disease or AIDS).[2] In all of these conditions, which doctors call "organic brain syndromes," brain chemistry is extremely abnormal. There are two main ways in which brain chemistry may go awry. Either the brain is under direct attack by trauma, cancer, or stroke—or there is a metabolic problem, in which case we are suffering from an imbalance that affects our entire body, as well as our brains. When we get the flu, for example, we are suffering from a minor abnormality of brain chemistry. We can't think straight and our minds are fuzzy.

Unlike schizophrenia, in which a small part of our brain has abnormal metabolism of the neurotransmitter dopamine, in organic brain syndromes (OBSs), most of the brain is functioning abnormally, and most of the neurotransmitters are out of balance. Even in the mildest of OBSs, "diffuse slowing" is evident on the

EEG (electroencephalogram). Some kinds of OBS, especially those associated with approaching coma, show epileptic-type bursts on EEG.

When our brains aren't working right, we get disoriented. We can't remember the day of the week, the date, the month, and, if we're in really bad shape—the year. Our ability to form new memories begins to fail. All of our higher cognitive functions are "shot." We can't think straight or figure out the simplest of problems. Our ability to do simple mathematic calculations falls apart. But people with abnormal brain chemistry can fool us into thinking something else is going on.

Fritz, a delightful 80-year old professional musician, is a good example. His sister was concerned about his ability to continue living alone in a mobile home in New Mexico. She had visited him and was upset to find him leaving on the gas stove when he wasn't cooking, and leaving the house a complete mess. Fritz also was finding it more difficult to manage his daily affairs, and was developing some strange ideas, believing that his neighbors were plotting against him, for instance.

He was an easy man to speak to, cheerful and gregarious. He had played more than a dozen musical instruments, all professionally. I asked him about his favorite violin pieces—the Beethoven Violin Concerto, and the Mendelssohn Violin Concerto. Fritz could tell me details about his first 70 years of life, but when I asked him about his mobile home, he couldn't even tell me in which state he had been living. His short-term memory was rapidly vanishing. He didn't know where he was, what year it was. He couldn't remember my name from day to day, but we had wonderful chats about the various orchestras in which he had played.

The paranoia, the confusion, the disorientation could all be part of a schizophrenic episode, or even a psychotic borderline break, but Fritz was suffering from advanced Alzheimer's Disease, a case of dementia, or organic brain syndrome. There is no known medical treatment, although there are nutritional supplements that can boost one's brain power. The best I could do for Fritz was to help find him a nice, safe home, a place with medical supervision, a place that would prepare his meals and take care of his basic needs.

People with organic brain disorders aren't all as sweet as Fritz. They also can behave impulsively, and lose control of their sexual and aggressive feelings. To illustrate this: 80% of the violent crime in my city, San Diego, is caused by people who are on drugs, people who are suffering from an acute drug-induced OBS called "delirium." Patients with OBS develop perceptual difficulties and experience either illusions or hallucinations. Illusions mean, "misinterpreting what you see or hear." So a patient might see a pattern on the wallpaper and think that animals are crawling over the walls. They may also hallucinate—see or hear things that are not there at all, although they have visual hallucinations more often than auditory. Schizophrenics, on the other hand, have many more auditory hallucinations than visual.

People with OBS "wax and wane." Throughout the day they go through periods of being much better, then much worse. Schizophrenics or manics don't do that. People with OBS, including those suffering from Alzheimer's disease, tend to get much worse at night. When darkness falls and things become harder to see, their brains go even more out of control. It's what doctors call "sun-downing."

These people are really ill physically. They may have fevers, and a whole host of other medical problems depending on what is causing the brain to get sick. To a psychiatrist who has worked with many people with "functional" or purely mental illness, it is easy to recognize people with OBS. Although they may have some of the same symptoms as schizophrenia, such as hallucinations, they "feel" entirely different to the psychiatrist. Of course, schizophrenics, manics, and borderlines can develop organic brain syndromes, in which case it becomes difficult to determine how much of the problem is mental and how much is the organic brain syndrome.

Not much about organic brain syndrome can be called "spiritual". Probably the most spiritual state associated with OBS comes in the last days of life. A dying person can be in a delirium, an extreme confusional state—and can be "visited" by relatives from the other side. In this case, the OBS may actually facilitate the spiritual experience. Such was the case with one terminal AIDS patient who died at the San Diego Hospice. In his final days of

AIDS delirium he went into an ecstatic rapture for almost a day. According to his internist, the patient's eyes were full of light. Even the room appeared radiant to the doctor. One day after that spiritual rapture, he passed away.

However, with OBS the real spiritual challenge lies with the health care professionals and the patients' families who treat and live with people who suffer from this illness, since spiritual practice requires conscious, disciplined effort, and people with OBS can't control their minds because of the nature of their illness. The family caregivers have the greatest challenge, for they not only face the loss of their loved one as they once knew them, but also must cope with an exhausting and often depressing job—often a 24-hour-a-day job. The family needs hope, faith, and encouragement to carry out this difficult task, a task that often ends only when the person with OBS dies. The healthcare professional must pay special attention to the emotional and spiritual needs of the family, making sure they have sufficient support, alleviating guilt that often arises in the family, and providing comfort to those who spend their days providing comfort.

Although it is most unlikely that you, the reader are currently suffering from Alzheimer's Disease or some other kind of dementia, here are some guidelines to help ease the suffering of loved ones with OBS.

Help for Alzheimer's
Guideline #11

1.   Because these people are so confused, and because their higher mental functioning is so impaired, they cannot easily understand complex ideas and complex conversations. Make your points short, concise, and to the point.
2.   Do not give them more than one "bit" of information at a time to deal with.
3.   Remember that they get worse at night, because, when they lose the sensory input of light, they get more confused. Keep a night-light on, or a brighter light if they'll tolerate it.

4.   Keep a clock by their bedside. This helps orient them, which is helpful because they become confused about the day, the time, and their location.

5.   Keep a large calendar by their bed.

6.   Frequently tell them the date and time in order to keep them oriented. For example, "Hi, dear, it's six o'clock in the evening. It's time for dinner." Don't be afraid to say repeatedly, "It's Friday, November 23rd. And it's 2012."

7.   Keep something familiar to them, such as an old mug, a teddy bear, or photographs of the family, by their bedside, especially if they're in the hospital.

8.   Don't baby them. On the other hand, provide as much safety and protection as is necessary.

9.   If they reach the point where they no longer recognize you, it can be very painful, especially if you've been married to this person for 50 years. At this point, you'll want to remember their deepest reality, their spiritual nature. Their bodies may no longer be the same. Their minds and personalities may have totally changed. The soul is the only part of us that is eternal and unchanging, and it is that part with which you can still connect, and which you should strive to see as their real identity. Speak heart-to-heart and soul-to-soul rather than mind-to-mind with the patient with Alzheimer's Disease. You will find it more and more difficult to communicate mind-to-mind, in a logical way, but you can deepen your ability to communicate soul-to-soul.

Schizophrenia:
When the Brain and Mind Drive Each Other Crazy

Nick was 36 years old and didn't look out of the ordinary. But his out-patient psychiatrist was afraid that Nick was about to murder someone. Nick believed that his next-door neighbor had sophisticated computer equipment that was linked to satellites. The satellites were "controlling Nick's mind," and he wasn't the slightest bit happy about it. In fact, he had tried to run down his neighbor with his car. Nick's psychiatrist, Doctor Freeze, was not able to get Nick to take medication, and fearing that Nick was too dangerous to be left to his own devices, had him committed to a mental hospital—where it became my job to accurately diagnose the situation, and get Nick to take medication, if that was my recommendation.

Nick was hearing voices. "They're real." "I have illegal access to a United States spy satellite. They follow me, and track me. They can make me sick and affect my brain. I am furious with Doctor Freeze, my psychiatrist. He says it's all a chemical imbalance. My neighbor really has the equipment. I've seen it, but nobody believes me or even bothers to check up on him. I've made lots of phone calls to the police and FBI but nobody will check it out.

"There are satellite beams that come down into my head. They're talking to me right now. They're threatening to kill me. If they try to kill me, I'll kill them."

I wanted to re-direct the conversation for a moment, away from the delusions, so I asked him about his baseball cap. Nick took off his baseball cap and showed me the metallic "chromium" shields he had installed on the inside of his cap. "The baseball cap shields me from the microwaves from polarized molecules from the satellites. The satellites are 400 miles above the Earth." Everything in Nick's life revolved around his delusion, which there was no breaking through. It was solid as a rock, and no matter what question I might ask, his answer would fill in another piece of the delusional puzzle.

How did Nick know all of this technical terminology? He was in the heating and air-conditioning business and knew the field of electronics quite well. I asked him why the government would be so interested in controlling his entire life. "Because I know too much! I'm also very psychic. I know when people are lying. I know when someone is trying to drive me nuts."

Much as I trust the diagnostic skills of most psychiatrists, I always resist the temptation to simply go along with the labels and diagnoses that people "carry" with them. I always like to come to my own conclusion regarding diagnosis because I take into consideration the spiritual side of diagnosis and treatment, a dimension that is almost always lacking in traditional psychiatric diagnosis.

Nick could have been suffering from a number of problems. He could have been suffering from an "LSD" psychosis or the long-term effect of chronic amphetamine abuse—but he wasn't. Nick wasn't a drug user. I have seen people who have used amphetamines for years however, who do think, feel, and act like Nick. He was not sleep-deprived. He had not gone overboard on spiritual practices, meditating for hours a day. Another patient of mine, Chuck, I once admitted to a mental hospital because he had been fasting for three weeks, meditating almost incessantly, and was depriving himself of sleep—intentionally. He "cracked"! Chuck became extremely paranoid, was hearing voices, and was delusional. His spiritual practice had actually triggered an acute psychotic episode, a schizophrenic episode, from which Chuck recovered quickly, with the help of Haldol, an anti-psychotic medication. Nick, on the other hand, was not suffering from any type of spiritual illness, nor from an illness triggered by spiritual practice.

Nick suffers from paranoid schizophrenia. Most people think that schizophrenia means "split personality" but that is not the case at all. "Split personality" means borderline personality disorder. We'll get to that later. Of all the mental disorders (not counting organic brain disorders), schizophrenia is the most biological. Real and permanent physiological changes happen to the schizophrenic's brain, especially problems with dopamine metabolism.

When I was a first year resident in psychiatry, I dreamt of curing schizophrenics through compassion, wisdom, and intensive psychotherapy. I had been strongly influenced by some success stories I had read about in college, stories of the successful treatment of schizophrenics through psychotherapy alone. The book *I Never Promised You A Rose Garden*, was one such inspiration for me, as was the work of R.D. Laing, British psychiatrist and author, who claimed to have cured many schizophrenics through psychotherapy conducted in a therapeutic community. I was in for a big shock when I discovered that love was not enough. I have now come to believe that the dramatic cures I had previously read about probably involved psychotic borderlines and not schizophrenics. People with borderline personality can be cured, even if they're psychotic. Only over the past 30 years has psychiatry been able to distinguish the schizophrenic from the borderline.

Although research into the role that the family plays in triggering and perpetuating schizophrenia has been fruitful, the greatest contribution, in my opinion, to the treatment of schizophrenia was the development of anti-psychotic medications, such as Haldol and Zyprexa.

Nick needed anti-psychotic medication. I could either work to gain his trust and get him to take medication voluntarily (no small feat!), or I could take an adversarial approach, file the necessary legal papers, take him to court, and let the judge decide if we had the right to force Nick to take medication—against his will. I always prefer the former choice, although neither approach is better or more "spiritual" than the other. The use of medication was the best, the only effective treatment, a treatment that would help Nick overcome his insanity, and would protect his community from his real homicidal potential.

In order to gain Nick's trust, I did my best to center myself. As I sat with him, I silently recited my mantra so that I would be as calm and non-reactive as possible. I mustered as much love as I could. I prayed. "Dear Lord, help me do what I can to give Nick relief." I listened without judging. Confronting a paranoid schizophrenic about their delusions is a complete waste of time. I've learned simply to side-step the delusions and find a way to appeal to a "higher" part of the individual. "Nick, I know your mind is being bombarded by a lot of influences. I know you feel the satellites are controlling your mind. You need to make your mind stronger, and the medication, Haldol, will help your mind grow stronger, so that it's easier for you to combat all of those influences." Because he felt accepted and understood, at least to some extent, he took the medicine, and within two weeks was sane enough to go home. His voices had gone away, as had his desire to kill his neighbor.

Schizophrenia is a biological mental illness, a disorder in which "the brain and mind drive each other crazy," which usually starts during adolescence or early adulthood. Suddenly someone who might have been pretty normal has his first psychotic break. Because of a cascade of neurological changes, it seems as if a bomb goes off in their brain, their mind, and their consciousness, literally destroying the fabric of their personality. They are almost never the same afterward. They suffer from severe psychotic symptoms: auditory hallucinations (hearing voices), bizarre delusions ("crazy" ideas), dramatically disordered thinking, and incoherent, loose, illogical, rambling speech. During the psychotic episode the patient may be terrified and paranoid. After the episode ends, the patient's mood is flattened or dulled. In fact, this last symptom may be the most important. Nick, like other schizophrenics, had developed such an enormous imaginary world that he had become separated from the real world. Unlike most of us who act and react to the world around us, the schizophrenic reacts more to his inner world than to the people and things in the outer world. So Nick had a facial expression that was flat. He was very hard to "read." There was a kind of emotional deadness about him, a feeling that nobody was home.

Schizophrenia is a disorder of thinking, thinking that becomes delusional. Schizophrenics may have religious delusions and believe that they are Jesus, Mary, or John the Baptist, or John Lennon, or Marilyn Monroe, or any person other than themselves. Or they may believe that somebody whom they've never met is in love with them. They often believe that they are getting special messages designed just for them from the radio and television, or that the FBI had their dentist implant powerful transmitters into their teeth and is monitoring their every move.

Schizophrenic delusions can take on just about any name and form. People may develop body image delusions and may feel they look like or that they have become an animal, or that they are a member of the opposite sex. Schizophrenics almost always hear voices but rarely have visions or visual hallucinations. They may become violent during a psychotic episode, although that is not the rule. Generally, they are completely out of touch with what we call "reality."

Schizophrenics have psychotic episodes that have a beginning and an end. Nick isn't "crazy" all the time. Like other schizophrenics, his episodes usually are brought under pretty good control with medication. After and between psychotic episodes, the schizophrenic goes home, maybe works, maybe has relationships, but the psychotic episodes continue to come back and the person's personality gets more and more eroded through the years.

Schizophrenics get burned out. The voices, which initially occurred just during a psychotic episode, often increase in frequency until they are present all of the time. Over the years, the voices usually become fainter. They become whispers or background noise, but the individual retreats more and more from society. The world becomes too frightening and too hard to fit into.

The progression of schizophrenia is from an acute disturbance of the norm to a chronic dullness. Eventually the "abnormal" state becomes the norm. Although the schizophrenic's first psychotic episode is characterized by loud and clear voices, or auditory hallucinations, in time the voices become distant, muffled, and unclear. The person on the spiritual path, in contrast, is moving in the opposite direction and is learning to listen to the one "voice" and not the many. The spiritual person's "voices" become louder and more distinct as he quiets down the mental noise and can listen to the voice of conscience. The aspirant has learned how to distinguish the real voice from the mumbles of the noisy mind and uses that knowing as an anchor and a powerful positive force in life. The schizophrenic, on the other hand, is overwhelmed by the voices.

Not only does the schizophrenic lose his emotional center and his sense of self, he usually struggles to regain that which is forever lost, namely "who he was." The schizophrenic may have been a talented straight-A student in high school with a number of hobbies. After his illness has progressed, he probably is no longer even able to attend school, and has lost interest in most of his hobbies. Still he remembers who he was and holds onto that image as a false safety-net. This difficulty in "letting go of who they were" is a big problem for schizophrenics, as it is for others whose mental illness has severely compromised their functioning in the world. The fact is that 99.9% of schizophrenics are worse off than they were before their illness and it's very hard to come to terms with this reality. For the average person, however, the memory of our past successes can serve to inspire us to even greater achievements. And memories of spiritual experiences remind us that if we keep putting one foot in front of the other and continue with our spiritual practice, we will reap the rewards of more spiritual experiences and a richer, more meaningful life.

Schizophrenia is very different from mystical experience, and the schizophrenic is very different from the mystic. However, on paper they come very close to looking the same. A schizophrenic patient who tells you he is psychic usually is not. To be clairvoyant or have extra-sensory perception requires that an individual be open to his environment and to the people around him. Schizophrenics, especially those who are suspicious or paranoid, may be aware of their environment, but only in regard to where they believe danger lies. They are not open to the feelings and thoughts of others in general. They are buried in their own inner world. In contrast, the mystic lives in a state of union, of a conscious oneness with all of life. The schizophrenic lives in a tragic, lonely state of fearful separateness.

After decades of working with schizophrenic patients, I noticed something that turned into an interesting theory. Schizophrenics are quite distractible. They turn their heads and look fearful when someone coughs, a car backfires, or when they notice someone new working at the local market.

I began to ask questions and discovered that the schizophrenic tends to incorporate all stimuli into his delusion. When he hears someone sneeze, he can quickly conclude that the sneeze was a cue from the FBI. In other words, it is as if the schizophrenic swallows the world, devouring all information to confirm his fearful delusion. Everything in his life is connected (and inter-connected)—through fear.

The mystic also believes that everything is meaningful and connected, but each new person, each unusual sneeze is seen as part of a giant web of love. The mystic swallows the world and all stimuli and becomes more deeply connected to everything— through love. A psychiatrist who does not make this clear distinction between connecting through fear versus love, can mistakenly diagnose the mystic as a psychotic person.

Nick connects through fear. He is very unlike the vast majority of us in terms of the severity of his confusion. However, if we consider that all of us lose our minds temporarily when we lose our temper, we can find something in common with Nick. I find it useful to remember, when working with the Nicks of the world that I too can be confused, and that my mind full of thoughts can often impair my ability to connect deeply with others and with God. I cannot "be" Nick, but by identifying my own confusion, I can glimpse the terror in which he lives, and can be of more assistance to him.

This severe confusional state called "schizophrenia" is primarily caused by a chemical imbalance. It is not a mystical state. But can schizophrenia be explained entirely by abnormal brain chemistry, or is there something unseen, something as-yet immeasurable that contributes to the chemical cascade in the schizophrenic's brain? That, I believe, is a question that will challenge psychiatrists of the future. Is it possible that something physical and paranormal actually is going on with schizophrenics? Is it possible that their brains are chemically so out-of-balance that they become tuned to a different frequency? Are they sensitive to different vibrations of thought and energy? And if so, do they misinterpret those vibrations, those energies in a frightened, delusional way? Could part of the schizophrenic's abnormal brain chemistry be attributed to invisible demons that can possess one's mind? The doctor of the future will have to face these questions in order to understand not only the schizophrenic's brain chemistry, but also the possible influence of unseen forces.

From a genetic-evolutionary-cultural perspective, schizophrenia may have been a healthy adaptation at one point in human history. Schizophrenics, especially paranoid types, tend to be "night owls" and loners. In early indigenous cultures, the paranoid schizophrenic may have made a good night watchman. He would have been the perfect candidate. He liked the night, preferred to be alone, and was "hyper-vigilant." As you already read in Belief Medicine (Chapter 6), the schizophrenic, does in fact, do much better in indigenous cultures, but deteriorates when he moves from the small village to the large modern city. From this perspective, it could be that schizophrenia is an evolutionary step that humankind has outgrown.

However, there may be yet another reason why the schizophrenic gene remains in existence, other than due to the rules of biological laws. After I had worked with mental patients for many years, I began to be able to sense schizophrenia in a patient even before I knew about his voices and delusions. I began to feel more deeply and appreciate the extraordinary emotional distance, the aloofness of the schizophrenic. Eventually, I developed the ability to diagnosis schizophrenia almost instantly. A few years later, on several occasions, I began to notice that some of the relatives of schizophrenics had a bit of the same "schizophrenic feeling." On one occasion, I mentioned to a friend, Sandy, that I believed her cousin, Lee, carried the schizophrenic gene. "That's ridiculous," she responded. "He is so gregarious and funny. He loves people, has hundreds of friends, is brilliant, and works hard."

"I still think he carries the gene," I replied.

Several months later, Sandy casually mentioned that Lee's brother, Maynard, wasn't doing so well. Not knowing anything at all about Maynard, I asked what was wrong with him. "Oh, I thought you knew," Sandy replied. "He's schizophrenic and has been in and out of mental hospitals."

Lee has never had any mental problems, yet I still believe he may carry the schizophrenic gene. If my theory is correct, the schizophrenic gene is being expressed only to a minor degree, not enough to cause problems. Perhaps, a small "dose" of the schizophrenic gene can even do something good for us. That may be the case with Nathan, one other person I know, whose brother is schizophrenic. Nathan has that dreamy far-away look, similar to what I perceived in Lee. But Nathan, in my opinion, is highly advanced spiritually. He is loving, courageous, a powerful "dharmic" leader, and has frequent mystical experiences.

I have no proof for my theories, but would propose that a strong dose of the schizophrenic gene creates the brain biology that causes schizophrenia, which is a spiritual confusional state. Perhaps, a very small dose of the gene opens us up to spiritual awareness and mystical experience.

Mania

I met Alexia during my first year of psychiatric training. Alexia's brain had too much of the neurotransmitter, norepinephrine, which caused her to have too much energy, too much aggression, too much sexuality. She entered the mental hospital dressed in black silky pants and a heavy black cotton cape.

Her Grecian black hair and blue eye shadow were dramatic but her pink lipstick was subtle. As I first approached her, she was rifling through her purse, sorting out pills and handing the nurse a $500 bill for safekeeping. Alexia believed she was being poisoned by her former husband, and she needed everything, including her $500, kept in a safe place, away from her husband.

After a brief introduction, our first interaction was the obligatory physical examination. In between looking in her eyes, ears, nose, and throat, I asked her what problem necessitated her hospitalization. "Well, doctor, nothing necessitated my hospitalization. You see, my husband, that is, my former husband, has been poisoning me and tearing my house apart. I'm in the hospital to run up a big hospital bill that he'll have to pay. That bastard will have to pay for it. Anyway, I don't have to be here. There's nothing wrong with me and you know it. You and I know the real reason for my being here."

Alexia made total sense about 75% of the time, and the other 25% I wasn't sure. At any rate, I did not know the same "real" reason she thought I knew, but I did know that she had been racing all over town in a taxi. She had been buying vast numbers of expensive art objects. She had been staying up around the clock, making phone calls around the world, and writing letters to anyone and everyone. Did she look like a "mentally-ill" person? No. On the surface she was warm and engaging, a young 45-year-old. She was a bit extreme but a lot suspicious. She spoke a mile a minute, gushing a barrage of upper-middle-class educated coherent phrases. She seemed to have boundless, but frenetic, energy, and felt high as a kite. She wasn't the least bit upset about her mania; everyone else in her life was upset with her.

As I continued with the complete physical exam, Alexia asked, "Doctor, what kind of vagina do I have?"

"Female type, Alexia. Female." She laughed uproariously.

"You're fabulous, Doctor. Is it large, medium, or small?"

"I stick to my original statement—female type." I struggled to maintain my "perfect medical objectivity," no small task for a first-year resident in psychiatry. "Your physical exam is entirely normal."

"Great physical, Doctor!"

I checked out Alexia's story, reviewed it with her family, and discussed the case with the Medical Director of the hospital. She was clearly manic, a most unfortunate condition, in my experience, because they usually don't want to be treated, although they respond well to treatment with lithium (and other "mood stabilizers") combined with anti-psychotic medication, like Zyprexa or Haldol. They like being "naturally high," even if the high is destroying their life, as it was with Alexia's. Everything moved too fast for Alexia. She became grandiose and began to lose touch with reality. She stayed up night after night, writing long letters to everybody she knew. She traveled around the country, blew most of her money, and ran up her credit cards in a hurry. A manic can blow through a lifetime of savings in a month, while destroying a marriage and friendships at the same time. Through the history of psychiatry diagnoses have come and gone. Alexia would now be called "bipolar." For now I want to focus on the manic side.

I tested Alexia for a number of other problems that have mania as a symptom, including: an over-active thyroid gland, a pheochromocytoma (a tumor that produces adrenaline), Cushing's Disease (an excess of cortisol, a steroid hormone), and an amphetamine addiction. She did not suffer from any of them. In retrospect, Alexia did not have any of the psycho-physiological or spiritual prerequisites for a kundalini process. She did not have a conscious spiritual practice, was not meditating, or fasting. And she was not experiencing the huge surges of light and energy that pour up the spine of the person in a kundalini crisis.

With the diagnosis clear, the treatment seemed clear. Get Alexia to take lithium. I wrote the orders for her medication on a Friday, explained their actions and potential side effects—and headed home for the weekend. Upon arriving back at work on Monday, I learned that Alexia was taking her lithium religiously, but took her Thorazine only when she wanted to. She felt that it made her too tired (which it probably did), adding, "and besides, I don't need medication anyway." I didn't worry about the situation, figuring that once the lithium took hold, all would be well. I tried to forget that lithium can take several weeks to take effect.

As the days progressed, Alexia became more and more paranoid (she felt that she was being mistreated and lied to by me, and I thought the opposite!). She couldn't find her contact lenses or her underwear; she kicked a nurse who tried to give her medication.

Working with Alexia became more and more frustrating and confusing. Manics have an ability, which may be psychic, to zero in on others' weaknesses, their Achilles' heals, with deadly accuracy. They can usually do it instantaneously. They can size you up the moment they meet you and somehow, sorting through the millions of impressions, know the one item that is sure to throw you off guard. They take one look at you, shake your hand—and they know your weak point, your most vulnerable characteristic. The more I talked with her, the more she understood my weaknesses and the better she was able to "play the manic game."

My Achilles heal is that I was a late bloomer. When I was 18, I looked 13. When I was a medical student, some patients wouldn't let me touch them because I looked like a high school student. As a psychiatrist in training, I was still sensitive about my maturity. Manics had a way of getting to that issue immediately...by calling me "David." I would introduce myself as "Doctor Gersten," but they would look at my nametag and say, "Nice to meet you, David!" Alexia quickly began calling me by my first name, which at first drove me nuts. Here I was finally beginning to practice psychiatry, wanting the ego-gratification and respect of being a "real doctor," and being called by my first name hit me really hard.

For years every single manic patient would call me "David." It was so predictable that I was able to stop responding defensively and began to use this information to help me diagnose mania. That may sound like a strange way to diagnose or to assist in diagnosis, but, in fact, the "feel" of the patient is critical to diagnosis.

I succeeded in getting Alexia to take the lithium, but not for very long. She decided to leave A.M.A. (against medical advice), and she prepared to say her good-byes at the community meeting on the ward. As Alexia prepared to say farewell, I was impressed with how serenely she had sat through the entire meeting and how she couldn't sit still for longer than 30 seconds during her first community meeting. Clad entirely in white, in stark contrast to her black entry outfit, she arose from her chair and took a position in the center of the room, assessing the peasants below her, glancing from one face to another. She looked no less regal than when she entered the hospital cloaked in black.

"I would like to say good-bye to this fine establishment. My care has been (with a pause here), extraordinary." She whirled around to Pat, a pleasant and shy nurse whom I had never heard utter an unkind word. "You have been the perfect bitch. No, I take it back, the imperfect bitch." She hovered over Pat like a great bird. Pat turned various shades of red and remained speechless. Alexia proceeded around the room. I anxiously awaited my coronation/ crucifixion and listened to the loud grumbles my stomach was making, intermixed with the knotting and twisting inside me that nobody could see. As she approached me, she smiled and glared at the same time.

"Doctor Gersten, you could make a fine physician someday. In my 45 years I have never had such a thorough physical exam as the one you gave me, but you have a long way to go. You've been a perfect ass and an expert at mistreating me." She continued to berate me, but the impact of her words began to pass over me. I felt like I had survived, fully expecting to be slaughtered by something, some exposé, some public revelation of my weaknesses. Alexia must have known how much I disliked having to perform complete physical exams on patients admitted to a psychiatric hospital. It was the law. I had to do it. But it made me uncomfortable.

After the community meeting I approached Alexia one last time. "Alexia, I think that coming from you, I've just been paid a back-handed compliment."

"You have. I told you, you give a damn good physical, but that's all you do well." By the time Alexia left the hospital, I wasn't angry with her. She had frustrated me. She had beaten me at her game. She had exposed some of my weaknesses, but still I respected her. I respected the fight in her, even if she took it out on me. I had used all the psychiatric skills available to me as a first-year resident. And I was happy that she had made significant improvement in her mania.

I even respected her need for control, her need to fight the dark depression that had sent her to the depths for five months back in New York City. Certainly 20 years later I would deal with Alexia much differently, but I would have no illusions about how hard it is to treat a manic. At the extreme of mania, the Alexias of the world becomes psychotic, paranoid, and grandiose. In fact, when she is acutely psychotic, it may be hard or impossible to tell her apart from a schizophrenic. However, apart from the personal history, the story, there are a couple of ways to tell schizophrenic psychosis from manic psychosis. The manic almost always has a grain of truth, a grain of reality in her story. He or she may, in fact, be a millionaire businessperson who just went off the deep end. And her grandiose ideas may have started from a place of logic, fact, or truth.

Unlike the manic, the schizophrenic, who says, "satellites are controlling my mind" seems totally crazy to his physician. The manic, however, made me question not only her sanity—but my own! She feels half crazy and half sane, yet can be very psychotic. When manics are too high, they can look just like a paranoid schizophrenic. They can hear voices and have paranoid delusions. While the schizophrenic mentally "arms" himself against you in order to protect himself, the manic "disarms" you in order to protect himself, in order to maintain a sense of control, in order to keep his fragile ego from breaking into pieces. The feeling he gives his physician and the people around him is very different from the feeling one experiences with a schizophrenic.

The manic is a perfect teacher of spiritual lessons for the psychiatrist because the spiritual path requires a conscious effort and desire to detach from one's ego. When I was able to stop feeling defensive with Alexia, she became a terrific teacher, zeroing in on my weaknesses, my ego defenses, and exposing them to the world. This kind of painful experience can accelerate one's psychological and spiritual growth, if one can keep an open mind about it. Alexia revealed my over-attachment to my identity as a doctor, for which I am grateful to her. I am also thankful that she revealed to me my discomfort in performing physical exams, and my disappointment at not dealing with the "perfect" open-minded patient with malleable attitudes. The ego-destruction Alexia blessed me with prepared me to be a better doctor, a more humble doctor, for every patient I met after her.

The ego blows which I received while working with Alexia arose out of her ego hyper-inflation, a state which is the opposite of the ego-deflation which a depressed person experiences. The manic's ego is huge and unrealistic. The manic believes he or she is the greatest, the best, the richest. Her ego feels harder and harder and less available to constructive criticism. In fact, if one actually gets through to the manic and forces her to realize her true state, she may immediately plunge from a manic high to a depressed low.

Alexia, and mania in general, sounds pretty crazy, but we can understand the psychology of mania by remembering the nature of the mind. In A Day in the Life of a Spiritual Psychiatrist (Chapter 3), you read that the average person has ten thoughts every minute. The average manic, on the other hand, probably has 30 thoughts every minute. The manic mind behaves the same way as the normal mind but is racing, full of desires, quests, and dreams. But the manic's mind is racing so fast that she can't implement any of those thoughts.

Whereas, the spiritual person's mind becomes more and more quiet through spiritual practice and more one-pointed in focus, the manic becomes less peaceful and more scattered. In many ways, the manic and the spiritual aspirant are "traveling" in opposite directions. Whereas, the normal person and the spiritual aspirant make plans that are appropriate to their dreams and talents, the manic's dreams are much greater than their talents. As a result, the manic fails in both secular and sacred pursuits. In order to reverse this downward spiral, the manic requires mood-stabilizing medication, like lithium, to stabilize brain chemistry, and meditation to slow down the mind.

In my opinion, rigidity of the ego is the psychological basis of both mania and depression. Metaphorically, each individual's personality is like a particular kind of stone. Let's say you take a hammer and chisel to a stone. Some stones will break in half along one clear fracture line. Manics and depressives fracture along one such internal line. Some stones break into 5 or 10 pieces, similar to how a borderline responds to stress. Some stones break into dozens of pieces like someone with multiple personality, and some stones break into far more pieces, similar to the acute psychotic episode of a schizophrenic. But, what is the personality? It's the totality of the ego, mind, intelligence, and will.

In this light, the primary task of the psychiatrist working with the manic or with the schizophrenic is the same, namely, bringing compassionate understanding to their treatment. Sometimes the spiritual growth in the doctor-patient relationship may actually be greater for the doctor than for the patient, as was with the case with Alexia. And this is not a bad thing. So long as the doctor is doing everything in his power to aid in the healing process, he has done his job, and done it well. But we physicians must admit to ourselves the limitations of what we can do. We can aid in miracles, and we can do our best, yet still see little in the way of patient's improvement. Whether we deal with success or failure, the spiritual approach asks us to accept both success and failure equally, not to be elated with success nor defeated by failure. It is through this kind of sacred awareness that both doctor and patient heal and proceed in their mental, physical, and spiritual growth.

One thing psychiatry has done wrong over the past fifteen years is misusing the diagnosis of mania and bipolar illness. Huge numbers of people with borderline personality disorder, depression, or anxiety are being misdiagnosed as bipolar. I have seen many glaring examples in my practice, many people who came to me already diagnosed as bipolar, when, to me, they clearly were suffering from something else. If I am right, why is this going on? First of all, bipolar is a diagnosis that sounds good. Would you rather suffer from bipolar illness or have borderline personality disorder? The choice is clear, even thought the misdiagnosis verges on psychiatric mass hysteria and malpractice.

The diagnosis of bipolar illness opens the pharmaceutical door for the psychiatrist. If you are bipolar, we can treat with anti-psychotic medication (Zyprexa), mood stabilizers (lithium), and anti-depressants (Paxil). If you're not sleeping well, you might need a benzodiazepine like Dalmane or Restoril. Even anti-convulsant drugs like Dilantin and Tegretol are used to treat bipolar illness. Psychiatrists have quite an armamentarium for treating bipolar illness, and there is a sense of comfort in having so many drugs to work with. But many people with borderline personality disorder are diagnosed as bipolars, and over the course of decades are tried on virtually every category of medication available to psychiatrists. The sad truth is that borderlines respond poorly and erratically to medications. Medications rarely work and when they do, it is hit-and-miss.

So extensive is the bipolar infatuation that even people with CFS/ME have received the bipolar diagnosis. When I first met Robert, for evaluation of CFS/ME, he told me he was on lithium and an anti-psychotic medication. I took a thorough history to make the diagnosis. I concluded that the diagnosis of bipolar was not only wrong, it was ludicrous. I asked Robert, "Why did the psychiatrist think you are bipolar?" He replied, "Because I talk so fast."

Robert really did speak fast, and I told him it was perplexing to me. I had not met a person with CFS/ME who had the energy to speak so fast, and I shared that bit of information with him. He looked just a bit startled, and then said, "Doc, I am so frightened about this illness. I've lost my job. I can't exercise. My memory and concentration are gone. I have a really long and complicated history and I was speaking fast to make sure I told you everything." I thanked Robert for clarifying the issue and re-assured him that now he could speak at a normal rate and not worry about telling me virtually everything that had gone on. I told him that we had lots of time and that, quite frankly, speaking at the speed he did is an energy drain for people with CFS/ME. I also told him to taper off the lithium and the anti-psychotic medication, which he did, without having any change in his mental state.

I am writing this to send a loud alert to the world. The bipolar diagnosis is being badly misused. Bipolar illness is real. It has a strong genetic component, as does schizophrenia. But many people being medicated for bipolar illness are suffering from borderline personality disorder. The bipolar diagnosis replaced the term "manic-depressive." With the term "bipolar," I don't know if someone is talking about mania, depression, or both. The reason for the change from "manic-depressive" to "bipolar" is not clear, but I have not found it useful.

Borderline Personality Disorder: When Spirit and Mind Collide

If there is a hell on earth, other than war, those suffering with borderline personality disorder (BPD) have lived there. As an example of BPD, I will share the history of a woman, now in her fifties, who has spent her life battling the demons of abuse. I'll call her Amanda. The history that follows is a composite of several people. I worked intensively with people with BPD for eighteen years, both in in-patient and out-patient settings. I no longer work in psychiatric hospitals, but I do work in an office setting with survivors of abuse who have a passion for truth, and a hunger for recovery that cannot be quenched. I worked with Amanda for several years, through 1997.

As a child, Amanda was the victim of mental, physical, and sexual abuse. Her father, an alcoholic, began sexually molesting her when she was eight and continued for six years. An older brother also molested her. Her father was violent when drunk, would beat her for the slightest "error" on her part, the slightest deviation from perfection. Her mother was cold and aloof. She knew about the abuse, did nothing about it, denied that it ever happened, and insisted on keeping the family secret unspoken. Finally, Amanda pressed for the truth when she was 40 years old.

At age 17, she ran away from home, and retreated into the woods for 20 years, living in deserted cabins, walking miles a day to fetch water from the river, living off the land. Her mountain friends were also refugees from society. At last, she had some peace of mind.

When she moved back to the city, she couldn't cope very well. She fell apart emotionally and sometimes would go through 20 different moods in one day—from elation to suicidal depression, from rage to serenity. She went from one chaotic relationship to another, often ending up with men who beat her. She could not stop herself from repeating the abuse with which she had grown up. She attempted to kill herself many times. Yet Amanda is immensely gifted, a talented singer, painter, yoga instructor, and has held many jobs. She is also tremendously intuitive.

Amanda gets so overwhelmed by her emotions, that she is regularly "acting-out," constantly engaging in behaviors that temporarily relieve her anguish, but undermine her safety and security. She comforts herself with alcohol, speed, or men. She can never seem to get the basics of her life handled—food, clothing, and shelter. Her emotions, finances, housing, and relationships are always in a state of flux.

Amanda suffers from borderline personality disorder. I regret having to use such an awful label, which doesn't sound as if it conveys a real diagnosis, but I'm afraid we're stuck with it for now. Many patients, who are neither neurotic nor psychotic, but fall somewhere in between, are labeled "borderline."

The first impression one has of a borderline personality may be that they are very depressed. A common mistake in psychiatry is to treat this depression with anti-depressant medication, which rarely works. An important question to ask is, "How long have you been depressed?" Borderlines usually say they've been depressed their entire life. In other words, their depression is not something they can compare to a time or a feeling of happiness. Depression is not a change for them. It is the baseline.

Amanda's inner world is filled with all shades of emotion. She feels torn to pieces inside, as if she is always standing at the edge of a great void and terrified of falling into the void. Her void is "wider than the Grand Canyon, a bottomless pit." Amanda has many unpleasant mood states that simply don't have words or names, so patient and doctor begin to call all of that intense emotion "depression" for convenience's sake.

Although Amanda does not get psychotic, other borderlines can get just as psychotic as schizophrenics. The predominant feature of their psychosis is confusion and auditory and visual hallucinations. They tend to have visual hallucinations much more often than schizophrenics do, and also tend more readily to get frightened and paranoid.

Unlike almost all schizophrenics, borderlines can appear quite normal and often can function quite normally. They may have terrifying episodes of depression, despair, suicide attempts, or psychosis, but when they are well, they may be able to feel well, look well, and perform adequately both in the working world and in relationships. They may sustain long-term relationships, but there is almost always a lot of chaos in those relationships.

These people have "sliding states of consciousness." They readily go in and out of different mental states and different states of consciousness. They can be depressed in the morning and elated in the evening. They can attempt suicide the next day. Borderlines can "slide" in many directions. They may slide into a state of psychosis that is similar to schizophrenia, and they may slide into the "spectrum of mood" and develop something that looks like mania. Or they can develop what looks like a panic disorder. There simply is no foundation to their personality, so they live as if they are in quicksand, constantly struggling to get out, and constantly being dragged back into the mud.

Borderlines are the real "split personalities." They are fire and ice—Jekyll and Hyde. When they are good, they are very, very good and when they are bad, they are horrid. The source of their problem originates in childhood. Their parents would not love and accept them unconditionally, through good times and through bad times. When Amanda was angry as a child, her parents despised her, so she "disowned" her anger, split it off, tucked it into some corner of her mind until it broke loose decades later. She didn't receive a healthy message, "I love you even when you're angry." As a result of child abuse/neglect, and the tear in the mind-body-spirit "fabric," four persisting inner states develop: 1) the wounded inner child, 2) the battlefield, having arguments in their minds as adults when they are alone, 3) the void, and 4) the inner abuser. The inner abuser is the part that embodies the rage that was hurled at them as children. Whether a child chooses to fight back or become the quiet, passive opposite of the abusive parent, this inner abuser part develops. It carries a huge charge. It is like dynamite. For some, the inner abuser is that part that leads to homicide and suicide. For others, the inner abuser shows itself by sabotaging that individual's life. The inner abuser is so powerful that, even if I have cured a person of CFS/ME, and completely balanced their body chemistry, the inner abuser can undo all of the good overnight. While the void is always very easy to see, the inner abuser is difficult to find. You don't want to mess with the inner abuser until you have spent six to twelve months of deep, consistent work with a skilled psychotherapist, working through the first three inner states listed just above. Only after the void is healed, will I begin working with the inner abuser. In Native American terms, the inner abuser is coyote. It is a shape-shifter and changes forms, so even when you have found it, it can turn into something else. The inner abuser lives in the vicinity of the void, so that is where I go "hunting." These metaphors are everyday reality for me, but I realize that for the reader, it may seem strange to speak of these four inner states as realities. But their impact on the adult survivor of abuse is very real, very agonizing, and very difficult to treat. However, the condition is treatable.

Unlike most schizophrenics and manics, borderlines can be very psychic and can experience a wide range of super-normal states. Why is this? They have "permeable" ego boundaries. They don't seem to know where "they" stop and "other" people begin. So they are often "open to the universe" and receive information easily. Many of my borderline patients have had psychic experiences while I was with them, knowing the phone was about to ring, or having a precognitive dream. They may have experiences of divine light into which they blissfully merge. The downside to their openness, however, is that they are also terribly open to their own unconscious minds and can't seem to stop the flood from the unconscious that can pour over them. When Amanda tells me that she sees auras around me and around many people, I believe her. When she tells me that she sees "entities" and "negative thought forms" hanging out in the mental hospital, or "stuck on the walls," I believe her. And when she tells me that for two years as a mountain woman she was frequently in a state of samadhi or nirvana—I believe her.

Borderlines can be extremely difficult to work with because their anguish is so severe and they are so desperate and needy. The mental health professional usually perceives the borderline in one of two ways: 1) the patient is like a "black hole." No matter how much you give, they want more. In fact, if you don't set very clear limits with them, you will feel sucked dry. I don't mean this in any kind of disparaging way. 2) the patient is like "tar" or "taffy." While working with them, you feel as if you are stuck to them, and it doesn't usually feel good. If psychiatrists are not aware of their own internal reactions, they are likely to be manipulated by the patient, or get angry, or reject them. However, as I have tried to illustrate in this section, if the psychiatrist can simply be aware of how he feels in the presence of the patient, and simply observe that feeling, he is in a position to diagnose accurately and be of service.

I last worked with Amanda 13 years ago. I enjoyed working with her. I liked her as a person, and I am not easily pulled into the borderline's "split." Amanda's inner battlefield is projected out into the world. For her there are "good guys" and "bad guys." Frequently a borderline in a mental hospital will be adored by one nursing shift (let's say morning shift) and will be highly frustrating to the evening nursing shift. A borderline will idealize one person and denigrate the next. The Amandas of the world can drive their psychiatrist and everybody else crazy—in a hurry. But you can work with them by being very open, loving, compassionate, and non-judgmental, but, at the same time, by setting very strict limits and boundaries, you can help them stabilize themselves. Borderlines test limits like a three-year-old trying to see what she can get away with—and the adult borderline can't help it any more than the three-year-old can.

Amanda's complete diagnosis is extremely complex. Before I give you a quick diagnostic run-down, let me add one piece to her puzzle. Amanda is absolutely exhausted. She's been exhausted for so long, she's forgotten that she's exhausted. She's so tired she can't always concentrate or think straight. Not all borderlines are exhausted, but many suffer from a compromised immune system, which can lead to exhaustion. Her immune system is shot. Her muscles ache. She runs a low-grade fever. Her exhaustion makes it that much more difficult for her to maintain any mental or spiritual balance. She has a severe case of chronic fatigue syndrome. Her physical suffering is so great that when I referred her for treatment with a chiropractor, Dr. Glenn Frieder, he told me that she "carried the suffering of at least ten people put together." Dr. Frieder also said to me, "There is something very special about this woman's energy. While working with her, I felt as if I were in some kind of energy field. It was really a good feeling. I worked on her for three hours, and, at one point, her psychic energy seemed to explode. It was as if the room lit up with her energy. Pretty weird for someone who is that sick and exhausted, don't you think?" I told Dr. Frieder that Amanda has more psychic power than any professional psychic I know of and that I too have experienced dramatic energy shifts around her, as well as within myself, while working with her.

Amanda is a book in herself. What does this complex person look like? She usually dresses all in black with loosely-fitting clothes. Her hair is cut close to the scalp and is dyed white. She has an uneasy smile, but a good sense of humor. Because she has been so violated by people, she dresses and acts in a way that is intended to keep people away. For quite some time she wore a huge nose ring, three-quarters of an inch in diameter. Despite her striking, attractive appearance, she is completely out of touch with how she looks. When she observed a videotape of herself that was taken as part of in-patient psychotherapy, she was stunned. "I truly had no idea that was me when I saw that person speaking on the video. I simply could not recognize myself."

In spite of her stark and dramatic appearance, people are drawn to her. They sense something unique about her. People approach her out of the clear blue and ask, "Are you a psychic or something? Can you give me a reading?" Even in the mental hospital Amanda is approached in this way. One of the nuns at Mercy hospital sat down with Amanda every single day during her hospitalization and asked Amanda for spiritual advice. Sister Ann would say, "Please, Amanda, tell me what you know. You're the only person I can talk to about spirituality." Amanda was happy to share her wisdom with Sister Ann, but I advised her to protect herself from the general public. "When someone asks you if you're a psychic, tell them 'No. I'm an artist.' And that's not a lie, because you are an artist."

Every year or two in her life is so full of change and drama that it is as if she has lived 20 lifetimes already. Not all borderlines share Amanda's complexity, but they do share her basic emotional make-up and her inner turmoil.

Amanda is an extreme example of something that is common—childhood abuse. Almost all of us suffered from a degree of abuse or neglect, either physical or psychological, while we were growing up. We all experience an inner void from time to time, the depth of which depends on the severity of our abuse. Our addictions, our compulsions, our workaholic life-styles often arise out of the void. By asking ourselves if we experience a void inside, we all can begin or continue the process of self-healing. We can all explore the void in our imaginations, although we should do so only with the assistance of a mental health professional who can assist us in "jumping" into it or "climbing" down the sides. But take God or a Higher Power down the void with you, because the void cannot be healed without faith and surrender to something greater than ourselves. There are not many black-and-white statements I make as a psychiatrist, but in my 20 years working with the void, with abuse, I have come to know that the void can never be healed without a spiritual focus being central to the healing process. I have also learned that 100% of adult survivors of abuse have a deep inner void.

Amanda may sound as if she has little in common with the average person, but we can empathize with her better if we realize that the core of her problem is a lack of deep trust in herself and in others. Almost all of us know what it feels like to be betrayed by someone we love. A powerful emotional bond is severed, and may never be reparable. The borderline first experienced such a dramatic rupture in trust as a small child. Continued episodes of abuse or neglect deepened the lack of trust until the void became a permanent internal state. It is very important for the reader to know that the teenage years are also critical to human development. An individual who enters the teen years on emotionally-shaky ground can become emotionally strong if the teen years are filled with loving and trusting relationships. However, if that shaky individual encounters a series of betrayals during the teen years, he or she may grow up to be a borderline. Therefore, it is critical that we, as a society, pay special attention to our teenagers.

On rare occasions, a "normal" adult, who had a normal childhood, can develop a profound lack of trust in the world, similar to that of the borderline. That is the case with many Vietnam Veterans. The death, destruction, dismemberment, and seeming meaninglessness of the war broke the spirit of many of our fighting men and women. Almost anybody can be broken emotionally, and that is the experience of many surviving prisoners of war who were tortured until they broke. At the breaking point, we lose faith in ourselves, in others, and in God. Most of us, however, can deal with breeches of trust we experience as adults. We can choose to avoid our betrayers or maintain a healthy physical and psychological distance.

Perhaps, the saints exemplify the exception to the rule that torture breaks us. Saint Joan of Arc, driven by the voice of God, became a valiant soldier for the French, handing the British one defeat after another at the end of the hundred-year war.[3] Joan was to be put to death if she did not renounce her visions and voices. When asked about her "alleged" religious experiences by the British courts, Joan replied, "The angels? Why, they often come among us. Others may not see them, but I do." Joan claimed that she took her directions directly from God and was not willing to retract her statements even if it cost her life. Joan was found guilty of being a "heretic and idolater," and was sentenced to burn at the stake. On May 29, 1431, at the age of 19, Joan proceeded toward the stake and was burned to death. As she went up in flames, she prayed that God would forgive her tormentors. Five hundred years later, in 1920, Joan was canonized as Saint Joan of Arc.

Almost all of us would have been emotionally broken by the experiences that Joan had to endure, but she died with a smile on her face, and the name of Jesus on her lips. Like other great saints, Joan was moved by a profound trust in God and in her spiritual experience, a trust so great that renouncing her beliefs would have been more agonizing than was the physical pain she actually endured. A great spiritual adept, like Saint Joan, has followed the path of trust to the extreme, whereas the borderline cannot find a way to avoid feeling betrayed over and over again. This is not to say that a borderline cannot become a saint. However, the borderline must overcome enormous doubts, fears, and feelings of mistrust in order to follow his or heart.

It is appropriate to examine Saint Joan in the same context as Amanda, for Amanda shows how one person can be emotionally challenged and saintly at the same time. In order to make better sense out of this complex individual, I have used the Psycho-Spiritual Assessment (PSA) on numerous occasions. I'll illustrate two PSAs, one which dealt with Amanda's visions, and a second one which dealt with more profound challenges:

1.   Amanda's "main concern" of visions was a genuine spiritual experience. She was seeing angels. She also displayed a host of paranormal abilities, including clairvoyance, clairaudience, telepathy, and the ability to see auras and thought forms.

When someone's main concern is a spiritual experience, it is helpful to clarify the concern in greater detail than if the concern were a symptom or problem. When someone reports an angel, I need to know if they experienced the angel while in normal consciousness or while in an altered state of consciousness. In fact, many of Amanda's paranormal phenomena did occur while she was in an altered state of consciousness—samadhi, healing trance, and out-of-body experiences.

2.　　Next we assessed how she felt about her main concern, the spiritual and paranormal experiences. She felt a mixture of peace, love, even ecstasy, along with fear. She was afraid of her abilities because so many people could sense that she had psychic powers, and as a result would bombard her with questions. Amanda found it difficult to manage her own life, and could not handle the demands others placed on her for "psychic help."

3.　　What did Amanda's main concern (paranormal experiences and altered states of consciousness) mean to her? At a profound level, Amanda felt an ongoing sense of divine connectedness, as if she were being guided through her mental and physical suffering. In fact, shortly after we met, and after I had begun teaching her meditation techniques and a variety of guided imagery techniques, Amanda confided that she had prayed intensely one week prior to our first meeting that she would find someone who could help her along her spiritual path. She felt that her random discovery of a spiritual psychiatrist was a direct answer to her prayers. Of course, I only served as a guide, and not a guru. Through the course of psychotherapy, however, she found her true spiritual guru.

4.　　Once we acknowledged the validity of her spiritual and paranormal experiences, we had several dharmic action steps to take. The main task was in assisting Amanda in setting limits on others so that they would not drain her. While in the psychiatric hospital, patients and staff alike frequently asked Amanda for spiritual and psychic advice. Amanda gave too much of herself and found herself depleted rather than energized by her hospital stays. So I taught her how to "create a force-field" around her. To her amazement, as soon as Amanda created a ten-foot force field, people would approach her and would seem to bump into a wall about ten feet away from her, and they'd walk away. I also asked her to practice an imagery technique called "the figure eight," in which she pictured others with a golden circle around them. This technique helped Amanda clarify her own boundaries and dramatically slowed down the energy drain she had previously been experiencing.

Far more significant than the paranormal phenomena were Amanda's many problems, of which her mood swings, mental confusion, physical exhaustion, and pain were primary. Here's how that Psycho-Spiritual Assessment looks:

1.   Amanda's main concerns were serious mental and physical problems, which were caused by childhood abuse and chronic fatigue syndrome with fibromyalgia. We "named" these main concerns "fatigue," "pain," and "mood swings."

2.   She felt terrified and overwhelmed by the great number of problems she had to bear as well as the intensity of those problems. The pain alone devastated her life. The extent of her mental and physical suffering was enough to provoke many others into suicide. Lack of money added to her problems, for it is almost impossible to recover from chronic fatigue syndrome without spending hundreds of dollars a month on nutritional supplements. We had to cope with her financial realities, and Amanda was on welfare.

3.   What did the fatigue, pain, and mood swings mean to her? One of the great spiritual lessons for Amanda was learning to simply hang on for dear life. However, she was able to find meaning in each catastrophe and managed to keep going because she felt that life had a purpose. Even in her darkest hours, she remembered God and prayed that she could better surrender. She believed that one of the great lessons in her illness was learning forgiveness, for much of her suffering was due to the mental and physical torture she experienced at the hands of her kidnapper. Amanda was actually able to find meaning in those years of torture. She believed that even if she didn't fully understand why she had to suffer so greatly, God knew why.

4.   I mapped out a treatment plan, a series of action steps, which involved physical, mental, and spiritual exercises. Physical steps included: nutritional supplementation, medication, chiropractic treatment, and breath techniques to help quiet down the anxiety. Strategies aimed at alleviating mental suffering

included finding a structured spiritual living arrangement, continuing psychotherapy, practicing imagery and meditation techniques, chanting a variety of mantras. She also began to read sacred texts, attend religious services, and pray fervently.

One of the main action steps we have undertaken is a thorough exploration of the void, a guided imagery technique in which one "jumps into the abyss" while "holding the hand of God." We worked on the void for months, with the result that her inner emptiness began to be filled by feelings of peace and love.

Multiple Personality Disorder

This section on multiple personality disorder (MPD) follows the section on borderline personality because MPD is a severe form of borderline personality. If severe abuse and neglect in childhood give rise to the horror and pain of borderline personality, then the trauma that gives rise to MPD is nothing short of true torture.

Like borderlines, multiples often experience a host of mystical and paranormal states—depending upon which sub-personality is the active one. When Ann was crazy, she was very, very crazy. But some of her 45 personalities were balanced, intuitive, creative, and psychic. Yes, some of these personalities could even experience mystical bliss.

Multiples experience another amazing phenomenon. The different sub-personalities can have different physiologies. One personality can have full-blown diabetes. Another personality is completely free of diabetes. This is an incredible example, and proof, of the reality of the mind-body. Sub-personalities are not only different mental states, they are truly separate mind-body states.

This is not a story of successful therapy. It's a tale of one woman's incredible ability to survive psychological and physical torture. The price she paid, and the only way she knew how to survive was by creating multiple personalities—over 45 personalities. MPD is incredibly rare. The only reason I am including it in this book is because so many people ask, "What's wrong with me? Is this just a memory of abuse? Do I have multiple personalities? Am I possessed? What is this awful thing in me that keeps sabotaging my life?" I want to show you that, whatever is going on in your life, the chances that you suffer from MPD are almost zero.

Some don't believe that multiple personality disorder (MPD) even exists. I have worked with only two true MPDs in my life, but there was no question in my mind from the first time I met with Ann. She was admitted to a psychiatric hospital after having shown up at another hospital. She had been instructed by one of her multiples that she was going to the hospital for a union of the multiples. During our initial session and during the half year that I worked with her, I saw her sub-personalities come and go in a flash. She could be coherent one minute, furious the next. She would get very angry one moment and ask, "Why did you call me Ann. My name is Mary." Suddenly, she would plop herself on the floor and become five-year-old Jenny—cute, smiling, and innocent.

Ann, now in her fifties, didn't realize she was a "multiple" until about ten years ago. Slowly, the memories of trauma had begun to come back to her and she had identified one personality after another. She began to keep and still keeps a three-ring binder with a section for each of her 45 personalities. Each section includes a diary of that personality, a personal history. Each personality has relationships with different people. One personality acts "normal" in public. One personality has a boyfriend. Each personality has a different voice, different gait, different posture, and different handwriting.

What stunned me most was my discovery of Ann's inner landscape. Ann "lives in a 3-dimensional world" of her own making, a world inside her own head. I learned this when I first began to use guided imagery with Ann. I tried a variety of techniques that I believed could facilitate both expression of each personality, as well as an ultimate integration into one solid person. I asked Ann to select a mantra that would have meaning for her and then I asked her to close her eyes and imagine that she was sitting at the center of a large circle. I asked her to invite her sub-personalities into the circle one at a time and teach each one the mantra. My hope was to have all the personalities chanting the same mantra at the same time. In fact, about ten "multiples" entered the circle and joined in the process.

Then Ann stunned me by saying, "Oh, Beater-Killer is stuck in the pipes." Further discussion revealed that Ann "lived" in an imaginary inner world with a well-structured inner landscape. Different personalities lived in different parts of the landscape.

I asked Ann to draw me a picture of this inner landscape, which she did. As Ann "gazed into the distance," she first described a barren area, a no-man's land—that stretched for two or three miles. Beyond that were huge panes of glass—"flexible, organic glass, almost like skin"—that some of the multiples could penetrate. A huge desert stretched for miles—and then there was the Wall, which was "high as a castle." Giant ropes were part of the Wall— and some of the "alters" could emerge through the ropes. Then another desert. And then began a complex system of underground pipes. One pipe led to the forest, a place where the friendlier multiples "live." Another pipe led to a series of buildings. There were blocks of land, interspersed with rivers and lakes. The far reaches of Ann's landscape include: the Jungle, Quick Sand, Hades River, Mirror Walk, the Labyrinth, the Dormitory, and the Mausoleum. When I asked Ann what lay beyond all of that, she would always grow silent and depressed and would not say more.

It was astonishing for me to learn that anyone lived within the confines of such a well-developed inner landscape. It was as if she lived in a guided imagery experience in which she was led through deserts, over walls, and across rivers. Her imagery never went away and it was completely real to her. Equally fascinating was the fact that within her pre-set landscape, she could still practice imagery techniques that I introduced. Most of us see images we bring up on a blank, inner screen, but Ann briefly incorporated guided imagery into her existing landscape. One could not alter her inner landscape any easier than one could make a real lake appear or disappear.

When Ann was in the hospital (which she was many times while under my care), she was extremely lucid about her inner world. She was able to remember the real torture that caused her agonized existence, and was able to tell me which of her multiples was active at a particular moment. However, outside of the hospital and in my office, she was always terribly frightened and I had little access to the multiples, except by observing the extraordinary personality changes. The structure and safety of the hospital allowed her to feel secure enough to share her inner world. Without the safety of the hospital, Ann fought for survival on a daily basis, driven by her multiples, but unaware of their activity, hardly aware of her sudden and dramatic personality changes.

Here's one example of such a change. One day she came into the office in her usual fashion—looking depressed, hunched over, anxious. After talking for a few minutes, she noticed that I had "Kermit the Frog" on my desk. She went over and picked up Kermit and then sat on the floor. She instantly became one of her five-year-old personalities. She was laughing, giggling, and having a good time with Kermit. Slowly, she "traveled" through several other personalities, until she was more adult-like. She began to wonder how a frog ended up in her hands. At the end of the session, I asked Ann to put Kermit back where she had found him. She looked around the room with a bewildered look and then put Kermit on the floor beside her. She had virtually no recall of how, when, or where she got Kermit. Many of her multiples simply had no communication with other parts of herself.

Ann could do some astonishing things for someone so fragmented. One day she arrived at my office after having absolutely no idea who she'd been or where she'd been for the past 48 hours. She had taken a long bus ride to get to my office. It was only when she got off the bus in San Diego that she realized that she was coming to her appointment with me. On another day, she brought in a tape recording of a song she had written and recorded in a small home recording studio. One personality wrote the lyrics, another the melody. She recorded the song by playing a keyboard and singing at the same time. One personality played the keyboard, one handled the engineering of the equipment. When I asked her who sang, she said, "Oh I guess I do the singing—except I can't hear myself sing at all. I have to play back the tape to hear what it sounds like." Her songs are amazing. She also draws and paints, creating astonishing works of art. However, most of the time, Ann just gets by in life. She has attempted suicide many times. She often gets lost in the small community in which she lives. The police know her and will pick her up and take her back home.

What keeps her going? "If I kill myself it will be a victory for those horrible people." Who were those horrible people? Father, grandfather, brothers, and friends of her brothers. And what was done to Ann I will not write about—and that is for the protection of you, the reader. I will share only one recurring theme. Ann and others with MPD usually had a pet of theirs murdered during childhood, by a close relative, and the child almost always had to watch the murder. When she first told me the gruesome details of the years of torture, the images were emblazoned into my mind. The pain I felt in listening to her was almost unbearable. I can't imagine what it must be like to have to live with those images every day of your life. I could only extrapolate from the pain I felt in hearing her story.

An image has to be pretty powerful for the therapist himself to become traumatized by listening to a story. Those same images are an awesome and terrible force for Ann. A world of multiples arose very early in life to help her keep some sanity—multiples that hold the memory, that do battle with each other, that hold the rage, the guilt, as well as the joy and creativity.

I am no longer seeing Ann. When I made the commitment to work with her, I knew I was making at least a ten-year commitment. I don't know why she stopped coming. She did not kill herself and I hope and pray that she took something from the work we did that will help ease her pain. Life is indeed strange. It is inexplicable why terrible things happen to good people. Ann is a good person, a kind and absolutely brilliant person. A person who once held jobs, sang in bands, even while the multiples were splitting her apart.

Although I had said this story does not have a happy ending, that's not entirely true. From my own perspective, I would have liked to have seen Ann improve more, but she did have one joyous and momentous experience shortly before she left therapy. She visited New Mexico for her son's wedding, an event that was very scary for her because her childhood tormentors were going to be there. Not only did she handle the situation well, but she had some very good fortune. Her daughter-in-law is Native American so there were two weddings, one Western style and one Native American style. After the Indian wedding there was a special ceremony to which Ann was invited, a rarity for a white man or woman. In fact, it was the first time it had happened with this tribe. A lot of attention was focused on Ann at this ceremony, enough so that it began to make her quite uncomfortable. To her astonishment she learned that this ceremony was in her honor, as the mother of the groom. A number of rituals were performed and Ann was made a formal member of the tribe and a full member of the family into which her son had married. She was over-joyed and came back to California literally with a new family—a functional, loving family.

Shortly after her return, she asked to be hospitalized again because she was becoming suicidal. But her new family remains for her. She has been drawn into a circle, a tribe, of people who love and accept her.

I wish her well on her journey and I hope that this beautiful new outer landscape that has embraced her will help slowly to dissolve the inner landscape that has been her protection and her prison.

Many of us "normal" folk have a variety of sides to our personality and it's important for you to know that normal people can be happy, sad, angry, jealous, compassionate, greedy, and joyous all in one day. Now you know that this normal variety of mood changes is nothing like multiple personality. What the average person experiences is much less severe than what the borderline experiences, and what the borderline experiences is much less severe than what the multiple experiences.

---

1. Bernard Siegel, M.D., *Love, Medicine and Miracles* (New York: Harper and Row, 1986).
2. Fred Plum, M.D. and Jerome Posner, M.D., *The Diagnosis of Stupor and Coma* (Philadelphia: F.A. Davis, 1972).
3. Anne Gordon, *A Book of Saints: True Stories of Now They Touch Our Lives* (New York: Bantam Books, 1994).

Chapter 13

When the Spirit Can Help the Mind

It is unlikely that you suffer from the mental illnesses that you've just read about. It is far more likely that you, like most of us in the West, are depressed or anxious from time to time, stressed-out, over-worked, or are in emotional pain about some real-life loss, such as divorce, loss of a job, or death.

For many of us, the small depressions can give way to a big, incapacitating depression. And the everyday wear-and-tear, the stress of modern life, can lead to a more severe anxiety disorder if not handled properly. While psychiatry can treat both depression and anxiety with a variety of medications, you should know that mind-body techniques and spiritual approaches can alleviate or eliminate depression and anxiety. By asking the deeper spiritual questions and seeking spiritual solutions, the real heart of the matter, the source of the problem can be discovered and healed.

Depression

Paul is an extremely successful priest, well respected in his community, a "spiritual power-house." But his energy fizzled out and, at the suggestion of the Mercy Hospital chaplaincy service, Paul came to see me in my office. Affable, lovable, brilliant Paul had plunged into a depression on the anniversary of his father's death, which was also the anniversary of his own diagnosis of osteosarcoma (bone cancer) from which he had fully recovered. He had just completed an important and lengthy job assignment and now felt a big letdown. This wasn't the first time he had been depressed; it had happened twice before.

Paul felt like a slug: slow moving, tired, exhausted, and listless. He shuffled his feet across the floor as he came into my office. He spoke slowly. Paul felt an "emotional heaviness," a huge weight on his shoulders. He was despairing, felt helpless and hopeless. He had begun to doubt everything—even his worth as a priest. "Maybe I'm just not cut out to be a priest anymore. I'm no good. I can't concentrate. I can't make decisions. I'm all washed up.

I'm worthless. I don't want to disgrace my church, my parish." Because he was very depressed he could no longer work eighteen-hour days, giving mass, communion, performing weddings and funerals, visiting his parishioners in their homes, and taking care of emergencies in the lives of literally thousands of people.

I could tell, even from our first meeting, that Paul had nothing to be ashamed of. Although it was hard for him to tell his story, I was convinced that he was a very good man, and a superb priest. I wanted to make two things very clear to Paul at the end of our first session. I assured him he could be helped—and I told him point-blank, "Paul, you are a priest. And you're a good one. Being a priest is your life. You're not at all confused about that. You have never had any other desire than to serve your community as a priest, and you still have no other desire. You are a priest." We shook hands. Paul smiled, looked me in the eyes, mustered a smile, and said, "Yeah, I am a priest. Thanks, Doc. I really needed to hear that."

50% of Americans will experience at least one very serious clinical depression in their life, similar to Paul's episode. Depression is caused by inner and outer stresses, by genetics, brain chemistry, even by the amount of sunlight we get. Paul had the genes for depression. It ran in his family. He was not a victim of a "bad childhood," or bad mothering or fathering. He loved and respected his parents. They were the salt-of-the-earth and, like their son, brilliant. Some of the stresses in Paul's life needed to be fully worked through. Unresolved, those stresses combined to make for some bad brain chemistry.

The biological basis of clinical depression is our neurotransmitters, the chemicals in our brain that allow one nerve cell to communicate with the next nerve cell. There are numerous neurotransmitters, the most common of which are serotonin, dopamine, norepinephrine, acetylcholine, and GABA. When there are not enough of these chemicals in our brain, we become depressed.

I prefer to balance brain chemistry using the least drastic means possible. I performed amino acid testing on Paul and found him to be deficient in tyrosine and phenylalanine, amino acids that turn into norepinephrine in the brain. But sometimes amino acids work slowly. Paul grew impatient with the amino acids—so I started him on Prozac. He continued to get more deeply depressed however, and so at his request, I hospitalized him. For this kind of clinical depression, it's important to break the descent as early as possible, because once the depression "sets," a person believes his situation is absolutely hopeless, and the risk of suicide must be treated as aggressively as the risk of heart failure after a heart attack.

Upon admission, Paul requested treatment with ECT (electro-convulsive therapy), a therapy much maligned by Hollywood. I am not a big fan of ECT, but it does have its place. In the past, Paul had received acupuncture treatment for pain, and he responded well. In his mind he found a connection between ECT and acupuncture, and felt both "boosted" his electricity. After only two treatments with ECT, Paul began to recover. After six treatments, he left the hospital, and continued to steadily improve.

Paul is a "normal" American, with a normal, but severe, depression. After his release, Paul began to feel whole again rather quickly. His thinking cleared up. He regained his hopeful, cheerful, and inspiring attitude. I taught him to use a mantra, "Jesus Christ."

Although I never shared with him anything about my personal spiritual path, we talked about God a great deal, and about the spiritual meaning of his illness. There were, in fact, deep spiritual lessons that Paul learned through his recovery. He became much more balanced after his depression than he was before he got sick. We talked about love, service, forgiveness, and I did my best to help Paul grow closer and closer to Jesus. Paul's illness seemed more than a biochemical abnormality: the confluence of environmental, psychological, and biological factors.

We took a broad look at his life, from the moment he woke up until he fell asleep. And I got a picture of a man who had not set proper boundaries in his life. He had been available 24-hours a day. I convinced him that even with his normal huge levels of energy, he still needed to learn his limitations. So he stopped taking phone calls after 9:00 p.m. He stopped doing things at work that he could delegate. He gave up doing things that drained him and that he did not find meaningful. I also discovered that he had not been eating breakfast, but began eating heavily around lunchtime, ate through the afternoon, and then ate double and triple portions for dinner. I suggested that he eat breakfast, and cut down on the huge dinners. "You need to fuel your engine on a more steady and regular basis. This is part of the problem you've been having. You're plunging into a full schedule with no fuel in your system." Paul corrected all that, and his energy grew stronger.

Some eight months after he had been hospitalized, we uncovered a spiritual cause of his depression. Paul had gone to a mountain retreat for a week, during which period he contemplated the pain and anguish of two of his parishioners, a couple who was about to give birth to an anencephalic baby, a baby with no brain. Because their emotional pain was so great, Paul prayed intensely during his week of contemplation, "Oh, Lord, their pain is so great. Please let me take on some of their pain." When Paul returned from the retreat, he went to visit the couple who, by now, had given birth to the child who mercifully died after six hours. Before he left their house, Paul began to feel the first wave of depression, which grew into a tidal wave.

When he told me this part of the story, I replied, "Well, you see your depression does go much further than just an imbalance of neurotransmitters. You actually got what you prayed for. You took on some of their pain, some of their illness. You'd better be more careful what you pray for."

Paul pondered my words for a minute. "You're right. I did take on their pain—and their baby's pain." The insight sank deep into Paul. He began to see the bigger picture. His illness wasn't just an illness. It was part of his spiritual journey—and it actually was the answer to his deepest prayers. Paul had traveled from darkness back into the light. A few weeks after Paul and I began to understand the spiritual roots of his depression, he received a card from the couple he had prayed for. The card, which was mailed on the anniversary of their child's birth —and death —, expressed their gratitude to Paul. They thanked him not only for his loving care during their time of grief, but also because they believed that he had taken on their suffering.

Although Paul's depression may have been caused, at least in part, by a loving and meaningful act of taking on another's suffering, his depression took him further and further away from meaning. In fact, things seemed to become utterly futile and meaningless the further his disorder progressed. The person making slow, steady spiritual progress, on the other hand, gains more and more meaning in life. In fact, even those things that previously had seemed meaningless or irrelevant, such as stopping to smell a rose, or watching the sunset, become more precious and meaningful. The little things in life become treasures and joys to the person who is evolving spiritually, whereas they lose all meaning to the depressed person and feel like a burden to him.

After I had helped correct Paul's brain chemistry and his depression began to lift, I began to zero in on the little things in life, such as how he ate his meals, how he went for walks, how he dealt with previously "boring" meetings at work. A complete body-mind-spirit diagnosis gave us the tools to transform Paul's life radically. Realizing that his physical diagnosis was History of bone cancer, and his mental diagnosis Major Depression, gave us the information we needed to get started. It took some time to flesh out the details of his spiritual diagnosis and to complete his Psycho-Spiritual Assessment.

Paul and I worked with the four questions in the Psycho-Spiritual Assessment (PSA), and as a result, his recovery was dramatically accelerated. Let's review his PSA.

1.   Paul's main concern, at the time I met him, was a profound, painful feeling of depression. Although Paul was clairvoyant and could go into healing trances to help his parishioners, these phenomena were never a main concern, at least during the time I worked with him.

2.   How did Paul feel about his depression? He was terrified. He was afraid that his life was ruined and that he would remain depressed forever. He felt hopeless and helpless.

3.   What did the depression mean to Paul? His "sympathetic suffering" (taking on the pain of his parishioners) gave us a more complete picture of his life, and helped him realize that his depression was more than a biological disorder. He felt that his depression was triggered, at least in part, by prayers that actually were answered. He prayed that he could take on the suffering of his parishioners, and he did. Paul also suffered from what I call "ego deflation." Although traditional psychiatry believes that abnormal

brain chemistry can explain every aspect of Major Depression, I disagree. I believe that each kind of personality is prone to a particular kind of suffering and a particular kind of mental illness. Some of us are prone to depression, others to anxiety. The combination of brain chemistry and the "depression-prone personality" is the cause of depression. From a spiritual standpoint, the depressed person's ego is being harshly confronted by real world reality and is being "chiseled away." The good news about this "ego deflation" is that each time we pass through the chiseling process, we have less ego, and, as a result, we become better able to resist depression. We then have the opportunity to become more enlightened.

4.   Dharma. Paul's initial action steps included anti-depressant medication (which did not work), and electroconvulsive therapy (which did work). After he had come out of the deep, dark pit of depression, we explored many other action steps, which we will discover over the next few pages.

Psycho-spiritual counseling has many facets. With Paul, I explored how the spiritual process of ego deflation can be painful, but it should be openly embraced. Every one of us is faced with ego deflation on a regular basis and so it behooves us to develop our own personal strategy for dealing with it. Like everyone else, I have experienced innumerable instances of ego deflation, and these experiences help me identify what my patient is going through so I may better help him or her. I experienced one powerful lesson in ego deflation in 1976 when I auditioned with classical guitarist, Celin Romero. I had called him, asking if he would instruct me on guitar. Celin asked me to prepare some music, and then play it for him. When I first met Celin, and after we spent a few minutes getting to know each other, he asked me to play for him. I played "Romanza," a classical guitar piece, which I had practiced for ten years. I had played no more than 15 seconds when Celin interrupted me, leaned back in his chair, puffed on his Cuban cigar, and said, "I will teach you under two conditions. First, you must give up everything you ever knew about how to play the guitar, and second, you'll have to practice a half hour a day. The second request was an easy one for me. Giving up everything I knew about guitar was shocking, but I knew I was dealing with a world-class master of guitar. I thought for only a few seconds and agreed to his terms. Over the following few years, I was privileged to be taught by one of the greatest music instructors in the world. The ego deflation was swift in this case. Rather than being proud about my guitar playing, I totally surrendered to Celin.

I have seen many people become depressed after receiving constructive criticism. Many of us prefer to be praised most, or all, of the time, but those who offer genuine criticism are our real friends and helpers.

By understanding ego deflation, I was able to make a more "complete" diagnosis of Paul's depression and could see that his abnormal brain chemistry had a spiritual cause, a spiritual component, spiritual meaning, and a cure that involved spiritual practices. He has weathered the storm, his ego has been chiseled down, and he is much happier than he was before he became severely depressed.

Finally, Paul and I focused on action steps. Now that he believed that his depression was caused, in part, by sympathetic suffering, he needed to take some action. He decided never again to pray to take on another's suffering. In terms of the "ego deflation," Paul made a conscious switch in attitude, from fearing ego deflation to welcoming the blows of constructive criticism.

After his depression was worked through, Paul wanted help with both secular and sacred issues. I asked him to picture God with him in the room and to connect with God at the deepest level he could imagine, and then connect at an even deeper level. We did guided imagery work in which I asked him to imagine himself walking up to a cathedral which had five pillars in front. Each pillar had the name of one of the five core human values (truth, right action, peace, love, non-violence) engraved on it. I asked Paul to meditate on the five pillars and then "walk" into the cathedral. Once he was seeing himself inside the cathedral, I asked him which human value he needed more of in his life. "Non-violence," Paul replied. "Sometimes, I feel a little edge of anger behind my own words, and I'd like to work on that."

"O.K., Paul. Simply allow non-violence to pour into you. Imagine that the cathedral is an embodiment of non-violence.

Imagine that non-violence is a kind of energy, and then allow that energy to fill you up."

On other occasions, I would ask Paul which passage from the Bible was most relevant to his current main concern, be it a symptom, problem, experience, or goal. During one session, in which Paul had been troubled and worried, he replied, "Therefore I say to you, do not worry about your life, what you will eat or what you will drink; nor about your body, what you will put on. Look at the birds of the air, for they neither sow nor reap nor gather into barns; yet your heavenly Father feeds them. Are you not of more value than they? Consider the lilies of the field, how they grow. They neither toil nor spin. Now if God so clothes the grass of the field, which today is, and tomorrow is thrown into the oven, will He not much more clothe you, O you of little faith? Therefore, do not worry."

I asked Paul to allow an image to emerge representing that Biblical passage. "Picture yourself among the lilies of the field, and feel the serenity of that scene. Notice how well cared for the lilies are, how the Lord provides for them. And then allow yourself to feel the same kind of care. Allow yourself to deeply experience a sense of peace. There is no room for worry."

Over and over again, Paul and I used the tools of Psycho-Spiritual Assessment to help him understand what he was experiencing (naming it), how he "felt" about it, and what it "meant," so that we could figure out the "dharma," what to do about it.

Because half of us will suffer from depression at least once in our lives, it would be helpful for you to know a little more about depression, so that you can make the same kind of meaningful changes as Paul. There are many kinds of depression. They all involve abnormal brain chemistry. Paul's brain chemistry was way out of balance. Others with depression may have less of a brain chemistry imbalance, and more of a psychological imbalance.

Science has begun to understand the mind-body connection over the past twenty years. Physical illness affects the mind and mental illness affects the body. Spiritual illness affects both mind and body. Because we are able to diagnose problems of body, mind, energy, and spirit, we are better able to treat our patients with approaches that are physical, mental, energetic, and spiritual.

Here is a powerful spiritual technique, which I have found to be very effective in treating depression:

Smiling Buddha
Mental Fitness Technique #17

Picture your chosen form of God or Divinity (Jesus, the Buddha, Krishna) and imagine that he or she is very happy. He is smiling, radiant, and overjoyed. He is happy with you.

That's all there is to it. Depressed people often experience God as a critical, elderly, guilt-inducing patriarchal figure. By simply imagining that God is happy and smiling, and is with you, all aspects of depression can be alleviated, including the biological and psychological symptoms.

Anxiety Disorders

Caroline's life was being ruined by one powerful emotion—panic. On two separate occasions she had gotten stuck in elevators. Not just stuck. On one occasion an elevator had gone into free fall for several stories. A decade later, she had not recovered, but rather had become more and more terrified of elevators, and other enclosed spaces, such as subways and airplanes. She suffered from the anxiety disorder called "claustrophobia," which, in the early days of psychiatry, would have been called a "neurosis."

The panic Caroline began to experience in elevators was crippling. Her heart would race and pound so hard it felt as if it were going to "jump right out of her skin." She would begin to sweat profusely, shake, tremble, grow short-of-breath, and come close to fainting. She would have a sense of impending doom, feeling that she surely was going to die on the spot. She would feel so overwhelmed she was afraid she was going insane.

For years she had completely avoided elevators, refusing to do business in any building more than one story high. As the owner of a jewelry store, this self-imposed limitation caused her some difficulties—but she was able to work around it. Her physical problems (rheumatoid arthritis with chronic pain, and generalized candidiasis with mood swings) made it harder to cope with her anxiety and added to the intensity of her panic.

Although Caroline weighed about 250 pounds and stood five-foot-four, she was an attractive woman, always stylishly dressed in keeping with her professional image as a successful jeweler. She finally called me for help with her disorder because she required surgery for an umbilical hernia and a large benign tumor, and was terrified of both the surgery and the elevator she would need to take to get her to the operating room. She kept postponing surgery because of her anxiety but knew that she had to deal with this panic because she also had an insurance problem.

Her health insurance was going to be switched to a new company, and fearing that her new company would not approve her elective surgery, she grew more and more panicky. She realized she could no longer delay, and had to schedule the surgery right away while her insurance would still pay for it.

I said to her, "You have two big issues here that you need to look at separately. One issue is your fear of elevators. The other is your fear of surgery." Caroline was very anxious about surgery, terrified of "being put out," afraid that she would die on the table or experience terrible problems with recovery. "Caroline, you need the surgery. Tell your doctor you insist on having your surgery in a hospital that has an operating room on the first floor. That way you can focus on the surgery and we can deal with your fear of elevators at a later date. If your surgeon won't or can't comply with this request, get another surgeon. It's that simple."

That piece of advice was liberating for her. Her surgeon was able to obtain temporary privileges at a suitable hospital. So now I was left with the task of helping her get through surgery. We could deal with her elevator phobia later. I worked with Caroline using a combination of meditation, relaxation, and guided imagery techniques.

"Caroline, your fear of surgery is a spiritual issue. I'll explain that in a minute, but first tell me about your faith." She replied that she loved God deeply, trusted him completely, and that deepening her spiritual life was a prime goal for her.

"This is an issue of trust and surrender. Once you've done everything you can do, you have to surrender and let go. You've decided on the best surgeon. You've decided on the best anesthesiologist, and the best hospital. There's nothing more to decide, and nothing more to do. This is the time when you need to leap into the void and trust God. Trust that God will work through the surgeon. Trust that the situation is now beyond your control and must be surrendered to. You see, I don't believe you fully trust that God is going to be there for you. We could talk about your brain chemistry that makes you anxious. We could continue working on imagery and relaxation, but the bottom line here is much deeper."

Caroline began to cry. "Maybe God is just too busy to listen to me." She paused. "Do you believe in re-incarnation, Doctor Gersten?"

"Yes, I do. Why do you ask?"

"I have an actual memory of being Jewish in a past-life. I was be-headed. God wasn't there for me. Maybe he's not there for me now."

We talked about the past-life memory. I encouraged her to express her fear, her disappointment, her lack of trust, and her anger toward God. I asked her to picture God in whatever form s/he presented himself/herself, and share all her feelings. "Tell God how you feel. If he can't take it, he's not God!"

I told Caroline that her primary spiritual diagnosis was "crisis in faith," and for several weeks we worked on the "faith factor." I taught Caroline a mantra, "God the Father," as well as pre-operative imagery techniques.

Caroline let the hospital staff know about her claustrophobia, and virtually everyone she came in contact with treated her with love, respect, and understanding. After her pre-op visit to the hospital, the director of nursing called her on the phone, asking if they had made her feel comfortable—and "was there anything further they could do to make her surgery go even more smoothly?" Her anesthesiologist was an "angel." "He put my mind completely at ease." She added, "Even when they took me for an EKG (electrocardiogram), the staff was concerned about my claustrophobia. They asked me if they could close the door or not during the EKG. It was just incredible."

Before surgery, Caroline was very jittery so the night before surgery she practiced the pre-op imagery techniques I taught her, and meditated using her mantra. The morning of surgery, she was so calm that she startled her anesthesiologist by her serenity.

The operation was performed with a local anesthetic, so Caroline was awake the entire time. The surgeon offered to play music she liked—Pavarotti. Throughout the operation she silently chanted her mantra, keeping herself calm and centered.

When the surgery was over, it was more than just "over." It was a real success for her. It was a healing experience, a coming together of the best of Western medicine—a good surgeon, a good anesthesiologist, compassionate and competent nurses. "God was really with me all the way—but Doctor Gersten, I couldn't have made it without the mantra."

Caroline's panic disorder had physical, mental, and spiritual components. There are many angles from which a doctor could look at her situation, and each would lead the doctor in a different treatment direction. Here's a brief look through the telescope/ microscope that gave me my view of her "mind-scape." It is possible that her predisposition to anxiety originated in her past life when she was "be-headed," or in childhood in situations where she felt abandoned, betrayed, or trapped. The fear slowly began to rise to the surface in her late teens, when she first noticed a slight discomfort in elevators, and then became fully conscious after she experienced two traumatic events in elevators. Her physical problems (rheumatoid arthritis, chronic pain, and generalized candidiasis) contributed to "anxiety physiology," to a brain pre-disposed to panic. Caroline's system was easily triggered into a massive adrenaline rush, a severe fight-or-flight physiology. The "adrenaline rush" was not the ultimate cause of her suffering, in my opinion, but rather was the chemical pathway that was triggered by a combination of psychological, physical, and spiritual factors. In effect, Caroline's brain and mind were driving each other crazy.

Surgery confronted her with a crisis in faith, a fear that God would abandon her, bringing a spiritual dimension to her fear. I believe that her crisis in faith was the main cause of her anxiety.

The completion of surgery was not just something she survived, from a physical standpoint. It was a healing for her—a healing of body, mind, and spirit, a renewal of faith.

Anxiety, with its spiritual cause, a crisis in faith, is so much a product of Western civilization that many of us take it for granted, and most of us experience anxiety from time to time. Most of us don't need medication for our anxiety. We need meditation. We need to become aware that anxiety arises out of a failure to live in the moment. Anxiety exists because most of us think far too much about the future, and we focus on things over which we have no control. Most of us can alleviate anxiety by becoming aware, by bringing out attention back to the present when it wanders into the future. By practicing meditation, one becomes more firmly anchored in the present. And meditation can be an all-day affair, especially mindfulness meditation in which one pays attention to each bite of food one takes, each step one takes, each breath inhaled.

Anxiety is further alleviated by surrendering to God, as you understand him, and by realizing that anxiety, from a spiritual standpoint, is a crisis in faith. Ask yourself what you don't trust about God and then have a heart-to-heart talk with him. Many of us believe that we must first have spiritual experience before we can have faith, but in many instances the opposite is true. We must make a leap of faith and then spiritual experience will follow. Through a conscious effort to develop faith, anxiety will diminish.

Although a severe mental illness, such as schizophrenia, which arises when the brain and mind drive each other crazy, is extremely unlikely to occur in a highly-advanced spiritual adept, anxiety is experienced by all of us, to one degree or another. Whereas, a person with anxiety disorder may find that one specific type of anxiety is fixed in the mind and returned to over and over again, the mind of the spiritual aspirant passes over experiences that would be annoying even to the average person. The person who suffers with anxiety, or panic disorder, as Caroline did, finds it impossible to stop re-playing the frightening scene in their mind. The anxious person simply doesn't know how to escape the mental prison in which he or she finds himself.

In order to illustrate the difference between how an anxious person and a spiritual aspirant handle stress, I'll use the example of a stressful workplace. Let's say that your workspace is small and cramped, and that there are far too many people walking in and out of your space. If you're claustrophobic like Caroline, that small workspace will drive you crazy. You'll keep saying to yourself, "I wish this were larger. I feel as if I'm going to explode. I wish my boss would do something. I wish people would leave me alone." The spiritual aspirant, on the other hand, would see the cramped workspace as a lesson to be overcome, and might, as a result of that attitude, begin to turn that small workspace into a small temple. Perhaps she would place a flower on her desk, along with a picture of a saint. The aspirant would say to herself, "I know that God wouldn't give me more than I can handle. I'm here, so I must be able to handle it." Given the choice of worrying versus turning the cramped workspace into a temple, it is obvious which choice makes for a happier life, happier work, and even more productive work. The spiritual aspirant rarely feels trapped, for she realizes that obstacles are only lessons. Therapy with Caroline involved helping her act more like a spiritual aspirant and less like a prisoner of her own mind.

From my personal life, I have learned some important lessons about anxiety and fear, and have shared those insights with Caroline and others with panic. Although fear makes us want to run away from whatever is scaring us, fear actually holds a key to our power. Like most Americans, my biggest fear in life was stage fright. Public speaking terrified me. After I completed my training, I thought I'd never be "trapped" into public speaking again. But after several years in private practice, one of the psychiatric hospitals in which I was working asked me to give a lecture to the staff, on any subject I chose. I refused and was told I had no choice. "Give a talk or we'll kick you off the staff!" The six weeks leading up to that presentation were anxious ones for me. When the talk was over, I joined Toastmasters, a public speaking organization, so that I could come to grips with this panic that had begun to limit what I could do in life.

For well over a year, I continued to feel nervous about public speaking, even at Toastmasters. After several years, however, I overcame the fear and grew to love public speaking.

In fact, many synchronous experiences happened to me, either while lecturing or immediately afterwards. In all my years of public speaking, the beeper that I carry with me has never gone off during a presentation, but on at least ten occasions, it has gone off at the exact moment when I've concluded the presentation. It felt like a "divine reward." I knew that after I had faced the fear, I was more deeply connected with a higher reality. I was more in tune. Through stage fright I learned that fear is the gateway to personal power. It is as if our greatest joy and power resides within a special sacred temple that is guarded by two lions. Most of us run as soon as we seen the lions, turning our back on fear. The brave ones pass by the lion, enter the center of this sacred temple where they claim their power, and stand victorious over the lions of fear. Once we have claimed our power, we can share it with others, with those who are terrified of the lions.

Let me share what has happened to me after years of facing my gateway to power, walking past the lions and giving speeches. I am no longer afraid before a speech or presentation. However, energy builds, and it does so in a rather methodical way. About one hour before a presentation, my energy is gathering steam and focus. Ten minutes before I go on, I sit down, close my eyes, and meditate. When I go on stage and begin speaking or performing, the energy explodes. I feel the energy release and my consciousness expand. My personal ego boundaries dissolve to a large extent, and in this state I am very tuned into every one in the audience, or at least, it seems I am one with everyone.

When people come up to me after the presentation, I am operating at a different level of consciousness than I ordinarily do. My psychic abilities are greatly enhanced. After one lecture, about 15 people were all around me, asking questions. The last person in line was a teenage girl with her mother. Her mother said, "My daughter is very depressed." I replied, "She is more than depressed. Your daughter is really angry. She is furious and feels like a caged animal." The girl burst into tears at having her feeling seen and validated. Mom made an appointment, and after she and her daughter sat down in their chairs in my office, I began the conversation, saying, "When I shook your hand, and told you what I did, there was more I saw. I saw that you have been cutting your wrists with razor blades, or if not, you are thinking about it right now." In fact, the teenage girl already had the scars on her wrists from razor cuts, which she concealed with long shirts.

I have shared this experience with many patients, not including the part about the suicidal girl, so that they might appreciate that their fear is actually a window or gateway to their power. By finding a way to face the fear, they can get through it, and by getting through it, they will be transformed for the better.

Lastly, remember that if you are experiencing panic that looks and sounds like what Caroline experiences, you are not going crazy. Panic is not insanity. It is immense suffering, triggered by biological and psychological factors, and it can be healed.

Learning to Relax
Guideline #12

In order to learn to relax, I recommend you practice two kinds of techniques:

A.   Mantra meditation or some other form of meditation.
B.   Follow meditation with one of the following five imagery techniques. If stress is a big problem for you, which it is for most of us, I strongly advise that you practice all five of the following imagery techniques. After you've done that, then select the one that best suits you.

The Feather
Mental Fitness Technique #18

Imagine you are a feather floating in the air high above the earth. You become more and more relaxed as you slowly float downward through the air. You glide to the ground, finally touching down gently and softly. Lying on the ground, you are totally and completely relaxed.

The Wave
Mental Fitness Technique #19

Imagine you are at the beach, lying on the warm sand. The waves are rolling in and each one comes closer and closer to you until the waves are starting to wash over your body before they roll back out. As each wave falls away from you and returns to the sea, tension, anxiety and stress are removed in the process. With each wave you feel a little more relaxed. Just feel the wave gently pulling tension out of you.

Do you get so rushed and so stressed out at work that you don't feel you have the luxury of relaxing, that you don't have the luxury of a break to let go of stress? The Wave Imagery innovated by Phyllis Krystal was designed for you. It is not a long, drawn out process. Once you learn how to "ride" the wave, you can teach yourself to relax in just a minute.

The Clock
Mental Fitness Technique #20

Imagine a clock with only one hand. When the hand is at 12:00 high, it represents the most intense stress you have ever experienced. It's electrocution time with every hair of your body standing on end. When the hand is at 6:00, it represents no stress whatsoever. You're just floating in a tank of jello, or you're a wet, limp noodle lying on the floor.

Now, get in touch with the level of stress you are under right this second, and set the pointer appropriately. Inhale a deep breath, and as you exhale, imagine the pointer moving down toward 6:00. As you continue to exhale, drop your shoulders, and let go.

If necessary, reset the pointer, repeat the breath, and let the pointer sink down even further toward 6:00.

The Clock Imagery was developed by David Bresler, Ph.D.[1]

Peaceful Place
Mental Fitness Technique #21

One of the simplest and most powerful ways to learn to relax is through the "peaceful place" imagery:

Imagine yourself in some setting in nature—perhaps high in the mountains, or on a beach, near a lake, or in a desert. Find yourself walking along a path in this setting. Notice what the sky looks like, how the air smells, what the ground feels like beneath your feet as you walk. With each step along your path allow yourself to grow more and more relaxed.

As you look ahead, you see a little cottage. It's there just for you. Walk up to this cottage. What does it look like and what is it made of? Go inside and walk around your cabin. Decorate your perfect cabin to your own taste, with your own artwork. Everything about this place is peaceful. If you like lots of sunlight, imagine that your cabin has lots of windows with an incredible view.

Sit down in a comfortable chair in your cottage and soak in the relaxation. This is your place, a million miles from nowhere—if that's where you want it to be.

Of course, if the word "cottage" or "cabin" does not suit you, call your dwelling whatever you like.

Footprints of Stress
Mental Fitness Technique #22

Millions of Americans leave work feeling stressed out by the end of the day, and they bring that stress home with them. Here's a simple way to leave stress at the office:

When you've finished your work for the day, before you prepare to leave the building in which you work, take three deep breaths, allowing yourself to let go of tension with each breath. Then, as you walk toward the exit, imagine that tension flows down your body and out of your feet. Imagine that you are leaving behind footprints of stress. Imagine that with each step you are leaving behind one percent of your stress. By the time you reach the front door of work, you can easily have left most of the stress behind.

Now go back over these five relaxation techniques and put a star by those that you liked best. Number them from one to five, in order: Number one being the technique that works best for you and Number five being the one that works the least well for you.

Neurosis and Suffering

We all yearn for the kind of intense love about which poets write and singers sing, and we all want to be standing "inside the fire." Yet, too often, many of us are afraid to enter the fray of life, to give our all with heart and soul, to work with reckless abandon, to give with no thought of return, to dare to fully live our own dreams and not someone else's. We stand outside the fire.[2]

Those who stand the furthest from the fire, who find it the most difficult to live fully in the moment, are often those whose childhoods were missing love, who were abused or neglected. Being fully loved as a child, allows one to become whole, to be at peace with oneself, to have a sense that all is right with the world, and that it is safe to stand inside the fire. Almost anyone can learn to live fully, completely, and happily if their yearning is strong enough. But those who have suffered the most from abuse, neglect, and inadequate parental love have the greatest challenge, the most obstacles to overcome in order to live a fuller life.

When we're "standing outside the fire," from a psychiatric standpoint, we're neurotic. By examining the lives of saints, sages, philosophers, poets, and even country singers, we can begin to see what life is and what living is. In this section, you'll see how emotional suffering interferes with life.

I once understood a great deal more about neurosis than I now do. Strange as it may sound, most of psychiatry doesn't understand neurosis. In fact, we don't use the diagnosis of neurosis anymore. It's not in the DSM IV, our diagnostic manual. Perhaps psychiatry has become so slanted in the direction of biological diagnosis and chemical treatment that it has begun to neglect the true psychological disorders, such as neurosis.

A lot of the people we thought suffered from neurosis we later diagnosed as borderline personality disorders, mood disorders, or phobias. In fact, Sigmund Freud, who wrote 26 volumes of books based on his work with neurotics, was probably working with people suffering from borderline personality disorder.

When neurosis used to exist as a diagnostic reality, we thought of neurotics as people whose sense of self was fundamentally well formed—as we still do. Neurotics have a solid foundation of self-identity, of conscious selfhood. This is in great contrast to people with borderline personality disorder. Because these people suffered severe abuse or neglect as a child, they grow up without a solid foundation. They stand at the edge of a great void. Their sense of self never formed. Neurotics, on the other hand, have a stronger sense of self.

In this era of HMOs, PPOs, and increasingly complicated billing procedures, psychiatrists no longer can bill for "neurosis." But, even if insurance companies won't pay for treatment of your neurosis, let's take a look at what used to be called neurosis and find some new ways of looking at a very old problem.

Freud believed that man was doomed to neurosis because his id (sexual and aggressive impulses) will always be at odd with the superego (society's restriction, limitation, and regulation of our impulses). Freud postulated the "ego" as a mental function that makes compromises between the id and the superego and allows us to function in the world. Freud believed we always live in a mental battlefield where sometimes the id gets its way and sometimes superego gets its way. We survive by taking our impulses and channeling them in productive ways, such as building bridges or having babies.

Neurosis is one of those words, like spirituality, that is difficult to pin down. Although psychiatry has thrown out "neurosis," it hasn't stopped millions of us from neurotic suffering. Suffering is part of the human condition and can be best understood when a spiritual perspective is added to the traditional psychiatric perspective. Neurosis is mental suffering that is self-perpetuating. It is the act of getting stuck in an emotion. We all go through suffering when a parent or loved one dies. We go through grief, which includes sadness, pain, anger, guilt, and confusion. *Neurosis is a failure to move through thoughts and feelings.* So grief is "normal" emotional pain, but if we get stuck in a mental loop in which we can't let go of the anger, the sadness, or the guilt, all of which is a normal part of grief, the pain becomes neurotic. We get stuck in neurosis and continue to repeat the same thoughts, words, feelings, and actions. When each thought and emotion is welcomed, embraced, and examined without judgment, we move through suffering. We grow stronger and don't develop neurotic suffering.

From a spiritual perspective, neurosis is the failure to either recognize what is right action or moral conduct, or a lack of will or courage to carry out right action. The Sanskrit term for right action is "dharma" and it has no adequate translation in English. Nonetheless, it is an important idea. Every living creature has its own dharma. The dharma of the tiger is to hunt and kill; that of the koala bear to eat eucalyptus leaves; that of the monkey to leap from limb to limb in trees. Animals rarely develop neurosis because they live their dharma. Each person has his own personal dharma, as well as the general dharma of a human being. If it is your dharma to be a musician but family and societal pressures have driven you to be an accountant, you are likely to suffer, for you have not followed your dharma, or as Joseph Campbell said, "You have not followed your bliss." Neurosis is living someone else's life, someone else's dream. It is a failure to identify and claim our unique role in the world, to identify how one fits into society, and to carry out that dream to its fullest potential. Neurosis is the failure to "stand inside one's own fire."

Why would anyone choose wrong action over right action? Wrong action arises out of fear, out of a lack of self-confidence, and out of ignorance. The Buddha said that ignorance is the root of all suffering. From the Buddha's perspective we all suffer until we develop sacred awareness, awareness of the unity of creation, and of the divinity that permeates all things, living and inanimate. Neurosis is born out of the belief and identification of our separateness. Neurosis is ignorance, and is a misguided attempt to deny the fact that life is uncertain and unpredictable. None of us knows what life has to offer us one minute from now, whether we will face good news or bad news. Life is a complete mystery, a mystery that most of us don't like. We like to create the illusion of certainty in an uncertain world, and the only way to create false certainty is by clinging to old habit patterns and rigid thought patterns. We all suffer from life's uncertainty until we learn to embrace uncertainty and stop fighting the current. It is as if we are floating downstream on a powerful current and we deny the direction of the flow and try so valiantly to swim upstream.

From this wider spiritual perspective, we can now further expand our definition of neurosis. Neurosis is the inability to live in the present, to surrender to the moment, to live our own personal dharma. And neurosis is the inability to let go of the preoccupation of control, whether conscious or unconscious. It is the need to struggle to maintain the status quo that results in struggling against the flow of life. Because of our difficulties living in the present, we suffer, which leads to another part of the definition of neurosis; neurosis is mental suffering perpetuated by a failure to let go. It differs from pain, grief, and "normal" suffering which we allow to runs its course. We lock suffering in place by ruminating on questions such as: "What if ...," "If only such-and-such had happened ...," or "if only things were different."

As you can see, a spiritual perspective to neurosis is quite different from the psychoanalytic view. According to Freud, religious belief is a sign of neurosis, a way to deal with conflict and the unresolvable differences between our impulses and society's needs and restrictions. In fact, Freud labeled mystical experience as "infantile helplessness" and a "regression to primary narcissism." However, from the spiritual standpoint, neurosis is ignorance of spiritual truth.

From this spiritual definition of neurosis, it is obvious that all of us suffer and most of us suffer neurotically. When we stop clinging, when we stop controlling, we move from neurotic suffering to "normal" suffering, and in the process, our suffering decreases.

Now let's take a look at a few examples of neurosis. Renée is a psychologist who is conflicted about money. It's hard for her to tell her clients how much she charges, hard for her to know how much a particular patient can afford. It's hard for her to ask for payment. Renée's neurosis is caused by confusing her urge to serve and help with her need to be paid for her work. Many psychotherapists feel uneasy with money and feel unworthy of charging the "going rate." That's a very simple example of neurosis. Renée has a repetitive pattern of suffering over money.

Understanding dharma was quite helpful to a patient of mine, a cop, who had killed a man in the line of action. Robert had prided himself in never having fired his gun once in 15 years of police work, despite the fact that he works in one of the most dangerous parts of San Diego County. But that finally changed. As is usually the case, Robert was the first to arrive at the dangerous scene. Robert is so intuitive that he often arrives at a major crime scene before the dispatcher has put out the call. And the dispatchers ask him, "Are you psychic or something? I mean you're always the first one there, and half the time you're there before we call you?" "Just doing my job," Robert replied. Robert's life is full of synchronicity, and he knows it.

One night Robert had to arrest a fellow named Billy. As Robert approached, Billy reached into his pocket and put his hand on a weapon. Robert coolly said, "You really don't want to do that. Right now I have to arrest you for a very minor charge. Don't make it worse." Billy continued to pull the shiny weapon out of his pocket and for the first time in his professional life, Robert pulled his gun and fired one shot at Billy's shoulder. But Billy spun and the bullet severed his spinal cord and killed him. Robert's actions were not those of a cop-gone-mad. "I was in the zone. It was as if it all happened in slow motion. I was perfectly still inside. In fact, I'm at my best when things get really dangerous. A lot of cops get a real adrenaline rush as they're going into battle. That's not what I feel. As the moment of truth approaches, as the deal goes down, I become incredibly still inside. I'm in the zone. I'm not high on adrenaline and I'm not scared. I just know what has to be done. And that's the way I felt when I shot Billy." Still, Robert felt bad about the shooting. He knew he had carried out his duties carefully and properly, but he had wanted to complete his career as a cop without ever having shot anyone. I had to work on that one with him.

"You know, Robert, you did what you had to do. Your ego is attached to the idea of never having to pull the trigger, but that just wasn't in the cards for you." I talked to Robert about dharma, and about how there are no jobs that are better or worse than any other jobs. Every society has a warrior class. Robert's dharma was that of being a good cop, a good warrior, and sometimes the dharma of being a cop calls for the use of overwhelming force. Robert felt reassured when he understood that he had upheld dharma and had not violated it. By applying an understanding of dharma in a psychiatric setting, I was able to help Robert overcome the doubts, sadness, and confusion that the shooting had caused in his own life.

Robert was experiencing a kind of neurosis, and was "suffering over his suffering." The symptoms of neurosis are broad and include: anxiety, depression, insomnia, obsessive thoughts, compulsive behaviors, and irrational fears. The obsessive-compulsive neurotic, who has a lot of unresolved feelings of anger, may "have to" wash his hands 40 times a day. He doesn't know why he has to do it, but if he doesn't, he becomes anxious. Millions of people have minor compulsions, such as forgetting if they've locked the front door after leaving, and returning to check to see if the house is locked. Just to put to rest any stereotypes you might have about policemen, let me share a bit more about Robert. He was very good at what he did, and handled emergencies with great authority. At least that is what people see when they watch him in action. But they don't see him dialoguing with the dead. On one occasion, when Robert arrived at the scene of a murder, he was giving orders, organizing the other officers, making arrangements with the coroner's office, etc. But Robert was also seeing the recently departed soul in a tree watching his dead body below. Robert mentally talked to the man's spirit and told him that he was dead. He no longer belonged with that body, and it was okay for him to leave and head toward God or the Light. Robert had great composure working on both sides of the veil at the same time.

Elizabeth is a 25-year old graduate student in mathematics who has neurotic conflicts about her spiritual teacher, Sathya Sai Baba. "I used to see Baba in a different way than I now do and I try to make my mind see him the way I used to. I want to let my mind go but I'm making it do something it doesn't want to do. I force myself to see Baba the way others see him. Sometimes I'll feel so happy when I'm thinking about him and then I'll wreck the feeling by obsessing. Deep down I want my ego to die and I know that love allows the ego to die, but the ego says, 'I don't want to die,' so my ego fights for survival. I'm afraid to give up this game I know I'm playing. Even though my ego fights so hard to stay in control, when it's gone, I feel so comfortable and don't feel I have to try to control things."

Spiritual pursuit does not make one free from neurosis as Elizabeth's story shows. She has an obsessional neurosis in which the focus of the obsession is her spiritual teacher. However, anything or anyone can be the focus of an obsession. Elizabeth suffered from a spiritual neurosis. She was locked into a fixed view of God and of her spiritual teacher and was afraid to abandon her preconceived ideas and just let things be, let things develop naturally.

In my own practice of psychiatry, I have run across a situation many times which has caused me some suffering, but that suffering was transformed once I understood what was going on at a spiritual level. Because I once had severe chronic fatigue syndrome, periodically I had to cancel sessions with my patients when I was too ill to work. Naturally, I felt bad about letting my patients down when I felt they needed to see me. However, over the years, I began to see a pattern developing. When I would go into a CFS/ME "crash," and would be too exhausted to work, most of my patients would call to cancel their session, before I called them. Something "came up" for them. Either they had to go out of town, had relatives in town, had an emergency, or were sick with the flu. When my energy would go up, I'd be barraged with phone calls and requests to see new patients. On several occasions, I received calls from patients who "absolutely had to see me immediately," and I had no time available for them. Immediately after I had spoken with the person in crisis, another patient would call to cancel their appointment, and, as a result, I was almost always able to make room for those who needed my help the most.

My initial suffering was due to ignorance. I was initially unaware that there was a "divine scheduler" in my life who made sure that there was always time for those in greatest need. Although I never developed neurosis or severe anxiety about this problem, I did worry and suffer over it. I felt guilty. Multiply that feeling by ten and you have neurosis.

This brief description of neurosis may seem at odds with what traditional psychiatry believes, but it's not. I believe the root cause of neurosis is ignorance, the failure to see the truth of a situation, the failure to recognize and follow right action, and the struggle to make life appear certain instead of going with the flow.

Freud answered the question, "What mechanisms in the mind produce neurosis?" He showed us that powerful mental conflict leads to suffering.

When internal conflict arises in our minds that we cannot satisfactorily resolve, we develop "symptoms." Let's say your boss has made you so angry that you want to strangle him. At the same time, this is a boss who is not open to communication, so you swallow your anger because you can't afford to lose your job. You're not going to walk around angry indefinitely, so eventually you may develop a symptom, such as depression, anxiety, or headaches because the anger is still inside you but has gotten "buried." The anger is still there, but has been converted into a symptom. Now, if as a child, you were taught never to express your anger or even to feel your anger, you are likely to suffer more in a situation like the one just described. You're not even aware that you were ever angry with your boss. The anger never even reached your conscious mind. You don't even have a chance to go home, talk out the anger with someone else, scream, ventilate, or exercise as a way of burning off the anger because you're not aware that you're feeling angry at all. So you develop neurotic symptoms, you can't sleep, you're irritable with your husband or wife.

If spirituality is sacred awareness, neurosis is sacred ignorance. Neurosis is at the heart of suffering. Whether psychiatry chooses to use the label "neurosis" or not does not diminish the fact that all of us suffer, and some of us suffer neurotically. To suffer is part of the human condition until we become enlightened. To suffer is normal. All of us have hang-ups, conflicts, and struggles which we handle well...or poorly. Sometimes we handle life better than we do at other times. No one is free of conflict. If we are conscious of our feelings and the situations in which we find ourselves, we are better prepared to deal with life's ups and downs. If we can find a way out of the "box of conflict," we will grow and not develop symptoms. If we can't find a door out of that box, we'll suffer more.

Now that you know the cause of neurosis, you also know the cure. If ignorance is the cause, awareness is the cure. Become aware of your suffering and stop pushing it away. Embrace the suffering as you embrace joy. Welcome victory and defeat equally. Practice service or volunteer work, for it helps dissolve the illusion of separateness, the neurosis of separateness. Awareness that all are our brothers and sisters will awaken our hearts to immediately respond to others' suffering. By opening our hearts to our own and others' suffering, we are healed.

Become mindful of each waking moment. Be aware that you are eating when you're eating, walking when you're walking. With practice you'll become anchored in the present moment, which is the place, the time, where suffering does not exist. It is only when the mind dwells on the past or is pulled into the future that we begin to suffer. Re-enter the moment, realize the unity of all living beings, and your burden will lighten.

ABCs of Anger Control
Mental Fitness Technique #23

You don't have to suffer from neurosis to benefit from practicing the ABCs of Anger Control. Most of us have a problem with anger, to one degree or another. By overcoming anger, everyone benefits. We become more peaceful and loving, and those around us benefit from our serenity.

Perhaps the greatest plague of humankind, greater than the black plague and greater than AIDS, is the plague of rage. America is one of the most violent countries in the world. Murder, rape, spousal abuse, and child abuse have become so ordinary we merely watch the body counts, as we grow numb to the reality that each man has but one life to live—and one life to die.

Without subjecting the entire population to years of therapy, how can we begin to help the masses deal with anger? We'll take a look at some very general principles as well as some simple techniques.

The very first question that must be asked, regarding a given person, is: "Do we have to work at taking the lid off of his anger, help him express his anger, or do we need to put the lid on, and keep it on?" For those of us who carry repressed anger, we need to practice taking the lid off, blowing off steam, expressing anger in appropriate ways. Other patients I work with can explode on a moment's notice. They may tell me that they "need to feel their feelings and express their anger," but they're wrong. At a certain point, anger feeds on itself and the explosive, "always angry" type just gets angrier and more out of control with time. So first figure out if you need your lid taken off, or put back on and screwed on tight.

For those who can't seem to keep the lid on, whose rage is at a dangerous level, I advise the ABCs of Anger Control.

A.   Avoid loud speech.

B.   Breathe.

C.   Curtail swearing.

The logic here is simple. Loud speech and swearing are like gasoline thrown on the fire of anger. They cause an explosion rather than resolution. And by taking a series of deep breaths, you'll begin to cool down. These ABCs are so simple, one might think they couldn't work, but imagine what would happen if everybody in the world practiced their ABCs of Anger Control? Now let's continue with our alphabetical treatment:

D.   Drink a glass of cold water. It actually will help cool you down.

E.   Exercise. Burn off the anger. Run, walk, swim, bike, dance.

F.   Find a Friend and talk it out.

Roots of Rage

The ABCs of Anger Control are designed to prevent real physical violence. But remember: a violent slip of the tongue can last a lifetime (or lifetimes!). These techniques are defensive: for the defense of others and of yourself. These are emergency procedures and are not meant as a substitute for individual or group psychotherapy, which are settings where one can learn to safely look at one's anger, release anger in a safe way, and resolve conflict. That's longer-term work. What you've been reading so far is about putting out fires and helping people stop from even striking the first match.

Why do we get mad? It is clear to me that anger is a product of both heredity and environment. I've seen young children who came into the world with a chip on their shoulder. It's hard to believe, but I've seen rage in a baby's eyes and I know it's in the DNA, not in the milk.

But, given this nature/nurture cause of personality, let me explain the Vedanta theory about anger. According to Vedanta, within the lower self, we are driven by desire. Once we have acquired our object of desire, we want to multiply it. When the desire is not fulfilled, is diminished or taken away, we get angry. It's that simple. So how do we deal with desire? If the desire that arises in our mind will not harm others or ourselves, proceed toward that desire. But remember the lessons of the Temple of Delphi: 1) Know thyself and 2) Nothing in excess.

Realize that your anger is YOUR responsibility. Your partner doesn't make you angry. Your partner does something and your reaction is anger. Give up any idea of ownership. Nobody owns anybody. Examine the root of the anger. Examine the desire and realize that the anger comes from fear of losing the desired person.

Taking Responsibility for Anger
Guideline #13

Taking responsibility for one's anger is easier than most of us think. Rather than saying, "You really infuriate me when you gossip for hours on the phone," try this approach instead: "I'd like to talk to you about the hours you're spending on the phone. I feel angry when you do that. I know I have a problem with anger. I'm not blaming you, but I'd like to tell you how I feel so I can get it off my chest. Then, after I've calmed down, I'd like for us to sit and talk about this problem and come to a better understanding."

Taking the Lid off Anger
Mental Fitness Technique #24

If your problem with anger is that you need to learn to "take the lid off," this technique may help you learn to express, release and overcome anger:

Imagine yourself sitting on the ground facing the person with whom you are angry. He or she is also sitting on the ground. From the bottom of your heart tell this person how you are feeling and share all the nasty details. You don't need to be polite. You can yell and scream. Notice if you're speaking in soft controlled tones. If you are, let go of that style and really blow off some steam.

Now imagine that you have three buckets next to you. One is filled with water, one with honey and one with rice. Which one would you like to pour over the other person? Go ahead. Pick up that bucket and pour it all over him. Doesn't that feel good?

Has he learned his lesson or do you need to pour one of the other buckets? Pick up one of the other buckets and empty that one on him. You may have something special in mind that you'll want in that bucket. It's your bucket. Fill it with whatever you like, pour it over him and feel yourself releasing anger as you do.

You can probably easily guess which bucket people love the most—the honey. People just love to imagine pouring a bucket of honey over the person they're mad at. And they almost always like pouring something else over the honey, such as rice, confetti, feathers, pebbles, or leaves.

Nip Anger in the Bud

If you can identify the precursors of your anger, you can put out the fire before it even gets lit. Every day stress shortens our fuse. Identify your stress and deal with it. Don't get too tired or too hungry. Protect your own personal space. Find a way to have time alone every day, if you need it. Become aware of how much physical space you require, and then mentally claim that space. Failure to deal with these precursors to anger will lead to loss of control.

Spiritual Approaches to Anger
Guideline #14

1.   Just as we have "Dark Archetypes," we also have "Angelic Archetypes." Call on your angels, your angelic side, your connection with the Absolute, when you are filled with anger. Picture that Divine, Angelic form standing by you.

2.   Read one passage of spiritual or inspirational text and reflect upon it.

3.   Silently chant the holy name that resonates within your heart.

4.   Practice forgiveness.

5.   Try to love your enemies.

With this arsenal of techniques anyone can gain better control over their anger. They can learn to express it if they tend to repress or suppress it. And they can learn to pour water on the fire if they're fire-setters.

Caution for Survivors of Trauma

It is beyond the scope of this book to delve deep into PTSD (post traumatic stress disorder) whether the trauma occurred during childhood or war. Peter Levine PhD, author of *Waking the Tiger: Healing Trauma — The Innate Capacity to Transform Overwhelming Experiences*,[3] discovered a 3rd survival mechanism— beyond fight-or-flight. It's called the "freeze response." It's the deer-in-the-headlights. An impala being chased down by a cheetah can sense when it is about to be killed. Running 50 miles per hour the impala can fall over, like it hit a brick wall. It falls over, lying on its back, and looks dead. Its consciousness has checked out and if you were to stand in front of the impala in freeze mode, it would not see you. A predator won't attack a dead animal, and in freeze mode, the animal looks dead, so the cheetah will either shake its head and leave, or grab the impala by the ankle, drag it back to its den, and tuck it under a bush. The freeze response lasts 5 minutes, so if the cheetah has some cubs to take care of, the impala has some borrowed time. In 5 minutes the "lights will go back on" in the impala. It will then shiver, then shake, then thrash like a long-haired dog getting out of water. And then, it's back on its feet, back in fight-or-flight physiology, and able to run for its life.

The next day the impala is not telling itself stories about how awful cheetahs are. And here is where people are different. When a person is traumatized, the mind kicks in and creates a story line, such as, "It must be my fault. Daddy would never hurt me like this. I must be bad." Once the mind kicks, the freeze response gets locked in place and usually stays there for life.

Many therapists working with someone with PTSD will have them re-experience the trauma, dive into their anger or fear and express it loudly. Unfortunately, this strategy is worse than nothing for it re-traumatizes the individual and re-activates the freeze response. If this is you, your experience was perhaps that you felt relief after the counseling session, but two or three days later you felt frozen, numb, immobilized, unable to take action, and cut off or dissociated.

Decision-Making—The Scales Imagery
Mental Fitness Technique #25

If you're like most of us, periodically you face decisions that leave you straddling the fence. Indecision, or inability to act on right action, will leave you anxious, angry and/or afraid. You weigh one choice against another and discover that they seem equally weighted. We face such dilemmas in our work as well as throughout the rest of our lives. For some, indecisiveness is such a severe problem that it becomes a neurosis. This technique will help the neurotic sufferer, as well as the rest of us, who need assistance, from time to time, in making decisions.

Here is a powerful technique developed by Don Crawford, Ph.D., psychologist and contributing editor to *Atlantis, the Imagery Newsletter*.

Picture in your mind a scale. This scale is calibrated from 0 to 10. Now imagine that this scale has a needle or arrow that can point at any number on the scale.

Think of something, someone, or some experience that you absolutely love or loved. That's a 10, so picture the needle on the scale going directly to 10. Now, let the scale return to a neutral position. Think of the worst experience in your life—the most painful experience. That's a 0, so picture the needle on the scale going to 0.

Now that you've practiced using the scales, think of one of the choices you are contemplating. Then allow the needle to settle wherever IT chooses. If it lands on 10, that means you are 100% in favor of that choice. If it lands right in the middle on 5, you are 50% in favor of that choice; and if it ends up on zero, you do not want this choice at all.

This exercise is so simple one may wonder how it can work. The scales directly access your unconscious mind providing information that your rational mind couldn't find.

I have seen this tool used successfully for business executives making difficult corporate decisions. My daughter has also found it very helpful in buying presents for her friends. On one occasion, when she was a teenager, she was torn between buying one present versus another. I asked her to picture the scales. One of the presents "came in at 9" and the other at 6. She immediately felt comfortable buying the "9."

Don't forget to brainstorm, think, plan, reason, and research when you're trying to make a decision. By using the "scale" imagery, your decision-making abilities dramatically increase because you are using both right- and left-brain function.

Body Rocking—Let Your Body Decide
Mental Fitness Technique #26

Our intelligence is involved in determining truth vs. untruth and right action vs. wrong action. The mind, a bundle of thoughts and desires, is not a useful tool in making decisions. But your body doesn't lie. Make a list of your five favorite fruits and your five least favorite fruits (or foods). Make another list of your favorite and least favorite places on Earth. Let's say that papaya is your favorite food and spinach is your least favorite.

Stand up and close your eyes. Take a couple of deep breaths, and then picture papaya. Within 30 seconds your body will rock forward or backward, often very slightly. Let's say you rocked forward to the image of papaya, and that you rocked backward to the image of spinach. That means that, for you, rocking forward is a "yes" and rocking backward is a "no." Test out various fruits, people and places to confirm that rocking forward is a "yes." You've used these experiments to define how your body tells you yes and no. Now, you can tackle more important questions, such as, "Do I want to move to Peru?" You don't need to ask the question. You just need to picture Peru or the word "Peru." If you rock backwards, your body is telling you that you don't want to move to Peru right now.

The more you are in tune with what you want, the more you listen to your body, the easier it will be for you to make decisions, which will help you in many aspects of life, and will leave you less angry or fearful.

Using Symbols to Help You Make Decisions
Mental Fitness Technique #27

Imagery is instantaneous. You can get feedback from your symbolic unconscious mind in seconds. Imagery isn't relegated to the use of doctors, nurses, business executives, and Olympic athletes. Anybody can tap into imagery on a moment's notice to help solve any dilemma or make any decision more easily. Imagery does not have to be a process that requires 30 to 60 minutes of deep work. If you're stuck, and don't know whether to turn right or left, so to speak, and you still need more clarification after practicing the "scales" imagery and the "body rocking," just close your eyes for a minute. Now:

Ask your unconscious mind to provide an image that clarifies the situation and shows what is best for the highest good of all concerned.

Here's an example. A friend of mine and his 12-year-old son were asked to be part of a family gathering, a gathering that the son had mixed feelings about. They both did this exercise and here's what they "saw." The son saw himself comfortably being part of the gathering. The father told his son, "I saw a five-pointed star and it means I'm supposed to be the sheriff. I'm the protector. I'll make sure it's safe for you." The decision was easy and a good time was had by all at the gathering.

---

1.   David Bresler, Ph.D., "The Clock Imagery," *Atlantis the Imagery Newsletter* (Feb. 1992).
2.   Garth Brooks, *Standing Outside the Fire* (Words and Music by Jenny Yates and Garth Brooks, 2007).
3.   Peter Levine, Ph.D., *Waking the Tiger: the Innate Capacity to Transform Overwhelming Experiences* (Berkeley: North Atlantic Books, 1997).

Chapter 14

Miracles or Madness

In this section, The Lost Mind, you've been reading about the inner workings of the minds of people with each major mental illness. A person with borderline personality disorder "feels" entirely different than someone with is acutely manic. Their psychological makeup is different. How they relate is different. The ways that they suffer, the ways they cope, the ways they relate to others, are different. When this human dimension is discarded, psychiatry has lost its humanity.

So, the way that psychiatry diagnoses has serious flaws, in my opinion. Of course, the major thrust of this book has been how to tell our miracles from our madness, and this is an area in which psychiatry must become educated.

For the reader, I want to clarify what we've learned so far about distinguishing miracles from madness.

How to Tell Miracles from Madness
Guideline #15

1.   If you think you have seen an angel, or a ghost, you probably have, and you are not going crazy.
2.   If you think you were visited by Jesus, and the experience left you with a sense of indescribable peace, joy, and love, you probably were visited by Jesus, and you are not going crazy. Of course, maybe you were visited instead by Krishna, Sai Baba, Ramana Maharshi, Nicholas Black Elk, Tara, Quan Yin, Mary, Paramahamsa Ramakrishna, or others whose names you don't even know. Just because you don't know their name, does not mean you are going crazy.
3.   There is a huge gap between what average Americans are experiencing and what psychiatry regards as real or relevant, and how the media portrays these issues. The media generally acts as if a vision of a great saint is an extraordinary, rare, and probably absurd, notion. Remember that your paranormal, or spiritual experience has been experienced by millions of people today and

throughout history, and that you are not alone with what you have seen, heard, felt, or perceived.

4.   People with serious mental/emotional problems are still human beings, and as human beings, they too have paranormal and spiritual experiences. You can be depressed AND be visited by Jesus. Sometimes, the dark night of the soul is the very time when God visits you and miracles occur.

5.   I have gone into great detail describing the variety of spiritual experience as well as mental disorders for several reasons. If God visited you, and you do not find yourself within these pages of The Lost Mind, you can feel safe that you did see or hear God. If you do find yourself within the pages of The Lost Mind, AND you have seen God, you may need to be brutally honest with yourself, extra careful in your own assessment of the experience. Again, remember this: people with borderline personality disorder and others who are adult survivors of abuse or neglect are MORE prone to paranormal and spiritual experience than is the average "normal" person. This is a situation in which the mental disorder or anguish is associated with more of the paranormal. This can get pretty tricky.

6.   Very few schizophrenics are going to be reading this book. Most paranoid schizophrenics completely believe their delusion, so it will be almost impossible for them to acknowledge that they suffer from schizophrenia, or that their experience was a sign of insanity. However, you the reader may know someone who truly is schizophrenic, and given that .5—1% of the world is schizophrenic, many of you know people with schizophrenia. Schizophrenics have less genuine psychic experience, ESP, or genuine mystical visions than does the average person. If the person in question is schizophrenic and tells you that God spoke to him and told him to stand in the middle of street intersections preaching, in order to save the world, chances are very high that the voice was a psychotic hallucination.

7.   While it is important to identify mental illness and severe mental suffering as it relates to paranormal and spiritual experience, mental distress does not preclude powerful, life-changing spiritual experience. A good example to illustrate this point is the great prophet, Nostradamus, who lived in the 1500s.

While he already had enhanced paranormal abilities, these increased dramatically after his wife and two children died from the plague. Because he was a doctor, his in-laws felt that he should have been able to save his wife, and so they sued him for a return of the dowry money. Nostradamus surely went through a great deal of emotional turmoil. One can only imagine the range of emotions. Perhaps he became clinically depressed. If he were living in the 21st century and sought psychiatric help, he would have been treated with an anti-depressant medication. My point is that mental distress or even mental illness does not preclude paranormal or spiritual experience. In fact, the great losses that Nostradamus suffered were the triggers that dramatically accelerated his spiritual evolution and the development of his enormous prophetic gifts. So, please understand that in life's complexities, miracles and madness can go together. Mental anguish does not preclude the experience of the paranormal and spiritual. Many of us who have just lost a loved one experience a sharp increase in paranormal and spiritual phenomena.

8. In the section on depression, you read about a priest who became very depressed after he prayed to take on the suffering of one of his parishioners who was about to deliver an anencephalic baby. His lesson from this was, "I need to learn my limits. I can't help everyone. I have to turn out the lights at 9 pm and not take phone calls 24 hours a day. And I cannot pray to take on serious suffering. I am simply not equipped to handle that."

Even people without any mental illness need to be careful about what they pray for. They just might get it. You've read about Shama, a gifted psychic. She has visited an Indian holy woman, Ammachi, many times. Ammachi does take on the suffering of many. During one visit with Ammachi, Shama made a silent prayer. "Let me help you by taking on suffering one day a week. I will set aside Mondays." The next Monday came. Shama became very ill, weak, developed skin eruptions, and a fever. The symptoms did not pass on Tuesday, or on Wednesday, or on Thursday. She internally spoke with Ammachi again, and said, "I am sorry. I cannot help you with this. I am not able to, and I cannot work at all since I offered to take on some of the suffering of the world that you take on." There were no more bad Mondays for

Shama. As the title of one of Dr. Larry Dossey's books says, *Be Careful What You Pray For: You Just Might Get It.*

9.   As you are sorting out your experiences, or simply listening to interesting stories on late night radio, there are a few guidelines that will greatly help you. First, determine if the issue in question was a one-time, brief perception (a discrete event), such as seeing a ghost or the Virgin Mary. Then you can say, "I saw a ghost, or Jesus." Or, "I did have a strong ESP experience in which I saw two planes flying into two very tall towers." These are discrete, time-limited experiences.

10.   Did your experience include a major change in consciousness? Did you feel a shift in time and space and a new sense of your own being? Did you feel as if your consciousness expanded, or that you merged with all of Nature or even the Universe? If so, you experienced an altered state of consciousness (ASC), and these often last for more than a minute or two.

11.   To review items 9 and 10, was your event in question a "discrete event" or an "ASC?"

12.   You can have several things going on at once. Many ASCs include discrete events. In other words, you may have had a near-death experience, a major shift in consciousness, during which you experienced many discrete events, such as visitation by angels and "knowings" of the future.

13.   Was your experience paranormal or spiritual? You may have seen a ghost. That is a paranormal phenomenon if it did not change you for the better in any way. Spiritual qualities include feelings of joy, peace, love, bliss, serenity, the urge to serve others, the sense of the unity of all life, and closeness with God. Spiritual qualities include the five core human values, namely truth, right action, peace, love, and non-violence. Did the experience improve your character? Are you a better person? Did the experience uplift you? Or was your "ghost-sighting" more like going to the movies? Was it fun, but when it was over, did nothing in your life or soul change?

14.   It is possible to have a spiritual experience that does not uplift you, but leaves you scared. If you are a novice to unusual experience, a type A personality, and suddenly Jesus or Krishna walks into your office on Wall Street, while you're busy day-trading

on the Internet, you may get scared. That kind of experience may not be part of your understanding of reality, and you may think you're going crazy. And you're sure your wife will think you're crazy. So, you tell yourself that it never happened, and you bury it as far back in your mind as you can. So, Jesus' or Krishna's intentions were to bring you a gift, a gift of divine love, but you just weren't ready or willing to play with them. But, as you lie on your deathbed, that experience will come rushing back to you, and if someone helps you liberate that memory, re-live it, and understand it for what it was, your passing into the next world will be easy and blissful.

15.   Did your experience last a long time, or a very short time? This is very important to decide, in terms of knowing how to understand and label your experience. For example, in 2004 I had a past-life memory that lasted about a week. Almost every day I would dip back in to experiencing a complex drama that involved the Battle of the Little Big Horn, and the death of General Custer. The experience lasted a long time, about a week (but not non-stop). This was: 1) an ASC, that, 2) lasted a long time, 3) had numerous discrete paranormal events as part of the whole experience (visions of the actual battle, Crazy Horse and many other Lakota Indians) and included, 4) spiritual components, including absolutely knowing that General Custer had reincarnated into my current life. The experience was intense, and at times emotionally painful.

Here's how one can make the "experiential diagnosis" even simpler to read.

1.   ASC.
2.   Long duration.
3.   Discrete, time-limited paranormal phenomena.
4.   Spiritual Visions of Native American medicine men.

I hope you embrace all of your miracles, even if they don't have a name you can find in this book. I hope you embrace the paranormal as an invitation to look at a new dimension of reality, for these experiences "give you notice" that the mind is not confined to the space between your ears. Ask for advice from people you trust. Speak to your priest or rabbi, but understand they may be coming to see me, because they don't understand their own mystical experience. Read other books. Realize that scripture from every religion validates the existence of miracles and visions in everyday life. And then pray and meditate so that you can come to your own, personal conclusion. I want you to "own" your experience as a free man or a free woman, whose decisions and conclusions are not simply the end-result of conditioning by child-hood and society.

Dare to embrace your miracle. Whether you choose to talk about it or not is your own business. I can't advise you what to do once you have claimed your miracle. It's yours. No one can ever take it away from you. And that, my friend, is where I want to leave you in this section of the book. I want you to claim your unusual, paranormal, spiritual, Godly experience as your very own. Make sense of it. Or let it make sense of you. Allow yourself to be changed by the light of the miraculous. Life is fleeting and goes by much too quickly. Our moments with the miraculous are the most important in our lives. If you have ten unusual experiences in your life, they will serve as lampposts along the way, as the most powerful, burning memories that are your true inner guides. At the end of your life, whether you pushed away the miraculous or let it in, those ten lights will glow for you, and you will look back on your life and see that your whole life was miraculous.

Choose to see your life as miraculous now, rather than waiting for the final, last-breath miracle. By so choosing, you invite God into your life at a more profound level. Why should he hang out with you, showering you with visions over and over again, if you don't believe them? Finally, please understand that as the divine reveals itself to you, these visions, these knowings, are leading you to know yourself, to discover that you are much more than this physical body, that your true self is not unlike God. While God's light burns infinitely bright, the light within you is a spark of the Total Light. It takes work and some faith to be led by the inner light. Allowing yourself to accept the paranormal and the spiritual experiences into your heart will help lead you home.

PART IV

TOOLS FOR TRANSFORMATION:
MAKING YOUR OWN MIRACLES

Chapter 15

Spiritual First Aid

Because more and more people are having genuine spiritual experiences, a whole new category of questions and problems has arisen, such as: How do I know if the angel I saw was a genuine spiritual experience or a sign of insanity? How do I cope with kundalini energy once it's been unleashed? How do I know if I'm hearing the "real" inner voice or if it's just my imagination? How can I overcome a crisis in faith?

Western civilization neatly compartmentalized body, mind, spirit, and energy. However, these artificial walls have begun to crumble, and, as a result, we are facing new questions. Medicine of the 21st century must begin to tackle these tough problems, rather than pretending that they do not exist. The times are calling, not only for each of us to heal the split, but also for medicine to heal the split.

In order for us to better handle our spiritual emergencies, we must go through several steps:

1.	Begin to recognize the inner voice more clearly. In so doing, we will be more certain about what to call our experience and what to do about it.
2.	Learn to evaluate your own experience, by expanding the limited vocabulary of consciousness, expanding our awareness of "awareness," and discovering ways to diagnose ourselves systematically, even without visiting a doctor.
3.	Develop specific strategies for each particular kind of spiritual emergency.[1]

It is important to remember that reactions to spiritual experience range from mild distractions to genuine emergencies—from mild anxiety to overwhelming panic, from mild relationship problems to impending divorce. Because of the range and diversity of these responses to spiritual experience, different approaches must be used for each kind of response, reaction, or spiritual emergency.

How to Recognize the Real Inner Voice
Guideline #16

The more clear, the more silent, your mind is, the easier it becomes to recognize the "real" inner voice, the voice of conscience, or sometimes, the voice of God. The practice of meditation, by quieting the mind, makes it easier to recognize the inner voice. The better able you are at recognizing that voice, the easier right action or moral conduct will become, and the easier it will be for you to turn spiritual experience from an emergency into an opportunity for transformation. Here are some guidelines to help you determine if the voice you hear or heard is real:

1.   Did the voice give advice that is in keeping with the five core human values? Did it suggest you do something that would lead to more peace, love, truth, non-violence, or right action? If so, it's probably the genuine inner voice.

If, on the other hand, the inner (or outer) voice told you to kill yourself or somebody else, it definitely was not the genuine inner voice but rather was the voice of psychosis, imagination, or a racing mind. The only instance in which violence may be the dharmic, the correct thing to do is when one is defending one's nation, city, family, or oneself against obvious unprovoked attack.

2.   Does the inner voice provide a consistent message? Let's say you're considering quitting your current job and aren't sure about the decision. You quiet your mind and ask for guidance. Your inner voice says, "Quit your job." However, you ask again five minutes later, and your inner voice says, "Stay at this job." Five minutes later, your inner voice says, "Move to Ohio."

When the inner voice provides a high moral message that remains consistent over time, it is likely that it is the genuine inner voice of conscience.

3.   Does the inner voice prompt action that is for the highest good of all concerned, that promotes unity rather than separation? If so, that's the voice of conscience. If the inner voice is directing you to take action in ways that are violent or divisive, what you are hearing is not your real inner voice.

Practice listening to your inner voice. After awhile, you'll develop a sense for what is the genuine inner voice and what is simply mental clutter. Here's a brief illustration. Over the years, it has become easier for me to "hear" the voice of Sai Baba inside myself. His answers are almost always one word, such as, "Come," "Done," "Yes," or "Wait." When I ask the same question, I get the same answer on a repeated basis. Therefore, I have come to trust that voice. However, when the voice says one thing one minute and something else the next, I know that my mind is fooling me and that I can't rely on that inner voice.

How to Diagnose Your Own Miracles
Guideline #17

If you've had an unusual experience, which you suspect may be a genuine spiritual experience, but you're still not sure, follow these steps in order to have greater clarity and peace of mind. After you've read each question, answer, "yes," or "no" to that question:

1.   Is your brain O.K.?
You want to make sure that your altered state of consciousness or your vision of an angel was not caused by a problem with your brain. Let's say you had an experience that you believe was samadhi, or unity consciousness.

During, or after, the altered state did you notice any problems that were more prevalent on one side of your body than another? For example, did you become weak on your left side? Did you develop numbness in your lower right leg? Such one-sided physical problems may indicate a brain problem.

Have you had problems remembering things since you experienced the altered state? Have you, in particular, had problems remembering things that happened recently? If so, you may have a brain problem.

Was your altered state accompanied by severe mental confusion, so severe that you didn't know if it was day or night? If so, you might have been experiencing a delirium, a disorder of brain chemistry.

If any of these symptoms ring a bell for you, you should see a neurologist to make sure your brain is O.K.

Is your brain O.K.? ____Yes ____No

2.   Is your mind O.K.?

If in doubt, review the chapters in Part III, The Lost Mind, in order to find out if your altered state was really a case of mania, schizophrenia, depression, anxiety, or borderline personality.

Is your mind O.K.? ____Yes ____No

3.   Can you name your own spiritual experience?

If you think you experienced samadhi, review Chapter 8 on Higher States of Consciousness. See if you can find a description of your altered state of consciousness in one of those chapters.

If your strange experience was a visual phenomenon, simply review Chapter 9 on Visual Paranormal Phenomena, to discover what to call your experience.

Can you name your own spiritual experience? ____Yes ____No

What is the name of your experience? _____

4.   Did the experience improve your life?

Did your experience leave you feeling uplifted, more peaceful, or more loving? Do you now feel closer to nature and to your fellow men and women? If so, you probably had a genuine spiritual experience.

If, on the other hand, you became more frightened, even paranoid, found it harder to interact with others, became increasingly anxious, or began staying home from work, it is less likely that you had a genuine spiritual experience.

Did the experience improve your life? ____Yes ____No

5.   Does your experience stand the test of time?

Is your experience consistent with the teachings of the Vedas, the Bible, or the Koran? If so, you probably had a genuine spiritual experience. However, some religions have gone into greater detail in describing spiritual experience than have others, even though all teach the core principles of right living. You may want to explore some of the more esoteric, mystical writings from your religion in order to have a more complete picture.

Does your experience stand the test of time? ____Yes ____No

Now, simply add up the total in the "Yes" column and the total in the "No" column.

Total "Yes"_____

Total "No"_____

If you scored 0, you did not have a genuine spiritual experience.

If you scored 1, you probably did not have a genuine spiritual experience.

If you scored 2, you may have had a genuine spiritual experience.

If you scored 3, you probably had a genuine spiritual experience.

If you scored 4, you almost certainly had a genuine spiritual experience.

If you scored 5, you definitely had a genuine spiritual experience.

Steps for Managing Spiritual Emergencies
Guideline #18

Before proceeding to the actual management of spiritual emergencies, let's review some general steps and some general principles.

1.   What is the name of your spiritual experience? After you've named the experience, use the tools of Psycho-Spiritual Assessment.

2.   What is your *main concern* regarding the spiritual experience that is causing the emergency? In the next sections, we'll look at ways of dealing with the major problems caused by spiritual emergencies: anxiety, depression, pain, marital problems, energy problems, confusion and panic, crisis in faith.

3.   How do you *feel* emotionally about your main concern?

4.   How does your main concern affect your *belief systems* or sense of meaning in life?

5.   Talk about your experience. Powerful spiritual experiences can unleash intense emotion, sometimes emotion that has been held inside for a lifetime. If you know you're not crazy, but your friends,

spouse, priest, rabbi, or psychiatrist are trying to convince you that you're wrong, keep looking until you can find a sympathetic ear. Yes, it is possible that all of those people could be wrong and that you could be right.

If the one nearest and dearest to you can't stand to hear you utter a word about your "angel sighting" or your "near-death experience," please ask them to read this book. You've got to feel heard, and not just "tolerantly" listened to.

Goals of Dealing with Spiritual Emergencies
Guideline #19

1.   Move away from the idea that everything you don't yet understand is a disease. Modern medicine looks at just about everything through the disease model even treating pregnancy, labor, and delivery that way. With spiritual experience, you need to learn to give birth to a new kind of process, a new way of thinking, feeling, perceiving, and believing. But first, you need to get rid of the idea that spiritual experience is a sign of disease.

2.   Strive to find the healing potential within spiritual experience and realize that a spiritual emergency is the way of your "inner wisdom" to force you to grow.

3.   Realize that spiritual growth and ego death go hand in hand. The greater the intensity of the spiritual emergency, the greater the loss of that part of us we had been holding onto as a false safety net. Spiritual experience may nudge us in the direction of giving up arrogant self-aggrandizement, or angry, righteous indignation. We need to learn to grieve the small ego deaths while we are giving birth to our new, truer Higher Selves.

4.   Keep going. Don't give up. Even if your spiritual emergency is impending death, keep going. You're alive until you're dead: use each spiritual experience to bring you closer to love, truth, and God.

Communicating with Your Symptom
Mental Fitness Technique #28

The "mental fitness" techniques you've already read about are "first-line" interventions. They are simple, direct, and powerful, but generally do not have as much transformative power as does the next technique, in which you'll learn how to "go deeper," by working with symbols.

Mental imagery is the language of the imagination, as well as the language of the unconscious. It is also the language that allows the mind and body to communicate with each other. To illustrate this latter aspect of imagery, the use of imagery to cure warts is a good example. Visualizing warts disappearing often makes them disappear.

Carl Jung was the first of the modern psychologists to work extensively with symbols. Later on, Roberto Assagioli, M.D., developed a complete healing system called Psychosynthesis, which is based on mental imagery. Oncologist O. Carl Simonton, M.D., was the first to use imagery with cancer patients.[2] Over the past 30 years, Martin Rossman, M.D. (co-director of the Academy for Guided Imagery and author of *Healing Yourself: A Step-by-Step Program for Better Health Through Imagery*),[3] David Bresler, Ph.D. (co-director of the Academy for Guided Imagery), Rachel Naomi Remen, M.D., Irving Oyle, M.D., and other pioneers helped system-atize imagery work, so that symbols could be more easily accessed and used for personal growth and healing.

Now let's move on to the actual use of symbolic imagery. The technique being introduced here (Communicating with Your Symptom) can help you develop every human value. You can use symbolic imagery to assist you with any problem, symptom, experience, or goal. You may want to refer back to Psycho-Spiritual Assessment to refresh your memory about what your main concern is. Once you've identified your main concern, here is how to proceed. (This is a modification of a technique developed by Martin Rossman, M.D., and Rachel Naomi Remen, M.D.):

Close your eyes, take a few deep breaths, and just let yourself let go and relax. Get in touch with all the thoughts, feelings, and sensations associated with your main concern.

Imagine that you have a volume control like one on a radio or television. Turn up the volume on the entire experience of your main concern.

Now, allow an image that represents your main concern to emerge outside yourself. That image may be anything—a person, animal, plant, rock, or any object. It may be made of any material or be as fine as a mist. Notice the color and texture of the image.

You'll want to bring all of your senses into play. What are the sights, sounds, smells, and sensations associated with your image? If you are a kinesthetic person, you may not "see" an image, but rather may feel or sense it.

The image that appears to you may seem silly at first, but try not to judge the experience. Your unconscious mind automatically provides you with the right image.

Observe the qualities of the image. Is it powerful, gentle, frightening, soothing?

Now, imagine that the image has a voice. This is your imagination, so you can give anything a voice, even a rock. Tell the image how you feel about it. You can speak "silently" and don't need to speak out loud. If you want the image to go away, tell it that. If you're angry with it, tell it that. Whatever you're feeling about the image, tell it.

Now that you've experienced and expressed your initial feelings, see if there are any deeper feelings. Share those.

Ask the image what it wants from you. Give it time to answer. Then ask what it needs from you. Why does it need that? Is the image protecting you from anything? Ask the image if it has anything it wants to teach you.

Now, imagine that you switch places with the image. You are the image, looking back at yourself through the eyes of the image. How does it feel to be the image? How does the "real" you look through the eyes of the image?

Switch places again so that you're looking directly at the image. Notice if anything has changed about the image. Is there anything you hadn't noticed before?

You may wish that the image would just leave you alone and disappear forever, but asking it to leave is not likely to help. What you need to do now is to "negotiate a settlement." You want something from the image (perhaps that it lightens up on a symptom or problem), and it wants something from you.

Ask the image what you need to do to begin to meet its needs. If you meet that need, will it meet you half way and let up on your symptom or problem? Keep talking to the image until your negotiation is successful, leading to a full resolution for you and for the image.

If you're tape-recording this imagery script, take a break for a minute, so that I can explain a little more about the process of negotiation. Let's say your main concern is chronic headaches. After beginning to negotiate, your image of pain has "told" you that it feels neglected by you and would like you to check in with it for a few minutes every day. If you're comfortable with spending a few minutes every day, you're close to "closing the deal." However, if you feel that daily visits are too frequent, perhaps you'll want to offer three visits a week. Keep negotiating in this way until both you and your image are satisfied.

Now, you'll want to make the negotiation as clear as possible, so that you could actually write out a contract with a series of three or four points. Here's an example of how a negotiated contract might look:

1.   I will check in with you, the image, every other day for five minutes before I go to sleep.
2.   You will lighten up on my symptom or problem.
3.   If I fail to live up to my end of the agreement, you, the image, have the right to increase my symptom or problem.
4.   If you, the image, do not let up on my symptom or problem, I will re-negotiate with you and have the right not to visit you so frequently.

In your notebook, draw a picture of your image, using paint, crayons, pencils, pens, or whatever you like. But please don't be shy. Getting it down on paper is a powerful step. Write down your negotiation as well as your thoughts and feelings about this imagery experience.

If this kind of work is new to you, please try to suspend judgment. This work is extremely likely to help you with any problem imaginable. Sometimes the results are truly miraculous as was the case of the man who was cured of 55 years of asthma after two imagery sessions, or the young lady who was cured of severe PMS after one session.

By communicating with your symptom, you begin to break up old habit patterns. Let's say you have chronic pain. That pain becomes a complex habit. It's woven into the fabric of your life. You begin to eat, sleep, walk, and talk pain. After a while, it becomes difficult to separate the pain from yourself. By working with the symbol, the image of your main concern, you begin to break up long-standing habit patterns.

And here's one more very nice piece of information. Because symbolic imagery works on so many levels, it will open up parts of your life that you weren't even focusing on. Even if pain is your main concern, you may find that suddenly you're calmer, sleeping better, feeling more connected to God, and feeling more comfortable in all of your relationships.

Here's a brief story, which illustrates the power of communicating with your symptom:

I was asked to see Edie, a 73-year-old woman, six days before she was scheduled for major back surgery. Although she had had a whole host of medical problems over the years, she didn't seem able to cope with this one. Her oncologist asked me to see Edie because her fear was overwhelming.

Indeed, overwhelming fear was what Edie spoke to me about. She had a strong feeling that she would die during surgery. Allowing Edie to ventilate her fears didn't help so I asked her to picture her fear and helped her communicate with her symbol of fear. Edie pictured her fear as "a bum. I detest him. He doesn't care for himself. But I do feel sorry for him." Edie negotiated an agreement with Jim, the bum: she was to give him sympathy by checking in with him every day. He, in turn, was to give her understanding and let up on her fear.

Despite the depth and power of this imagery experience, I remained deeply concerned. I called Edie's surgeon and was happy to find out that he and I were on the same wavelength. We were both scared about whether she was really ready for the operation.

The following morning I reviewed Edie's hospital chart before visiting her. Her surgeon's note read: "Patient amazingly clearer today. She fully understands options and risks of surgery and wants to proceed." Not only was her fear 90% gone, the patient also stated, "Today is the first day in six months that that dark black cloud of despair has lifted."

During the remaining three visits before surgery, I asked Edie to continue *listening to Jim*. By the second day, Jim needed some help from her, and "required" a place to take a bath. The next day "Jim had moved off the streets and had a place to live."

As a result of this imagery, Edie did a full 180-degree turn, from terror and despair, to hope, tranquility, and faith in the surgical treatment ahead. The surgery went well.

Profound Self-Acceptance — Embracing Overwhelming Pain and Fear
Mental Fitness Technique #29

Sometimes human suffering is so great that imagery techniques alone don't make a dent. The pain or fear goes on and on even after utilizing symptomatic kinds of treatments, after meditating, after communicating with your symptom, after examining your resistance.

This technique is inspired by the work of Stephen Levine, author of *Who Dies,*[4] and *Meetings at the Edge.* For several years Stephen and Ondrea Levine offered free 24-hour-a-day counseling by telephone for those with terminal illness

It is human nature to push away pain and fear and to try to hold on to pleasure. But sometimes you need to fully embrace the pain, rather than using a technique to diminish the pain. The technique I use is a modification of one Stephen Levine developed. What follows is perhaps the most powerful of all the tools of transformation at my disposal. Whereas, "mental fitness" techniques are my first line strategy, and "communicating with your symptom," a symbolic imagery, which is even more powerful, are my second line, "profound self-acceptance/embracing overwhelming pain and fear," the most powerful of techniques, is my third line. This technique helps one overcome any overwhelming experience, emotion, or sensation:

Begin by getting in touch with the variety of bodily sensations you have — the feeling of your body on the chair, couch, bed or floor, the feeling

of your clothing on your skin, the temperature of the air, the rising and falling of your diaphragm. Notice areas of comfort and areas of discomfort.

Allow all these different physical sensations to arise, and to dissolve. As you bring your awareness to these sensations, you will see that they change. Even the pain or fear sensations will arise, change, and dissolve when you bring your awareness to it.

Most of us have a way of closing around the pain. Imagine that there is a fist closed around the pain or fear. Examine the fist and then begin to allow the fingers to open one at a time until the pain is resting in the palm of that hand, until you are really down to the original pain. The body reacts to pain. Muscles cramp around it. But now allow yourself to feel the original pain, the original fear, the one at the center before you tightened around it.

Now, allow those sensations to arise, change, and dissolve. Simply observe. Make no effort to make the pain go away. As the pain sensations arise and dissolve, notice the thoughts, feelings, and images that pass through your consciousness. Observe them also in the same way. Your awareness is simply penetrating and exploring the pain.

After a while, the pain or fear may just seem to float or take on a new characteristic. Continue to observe the sensations. Imagine that you are continuing to open to the pain over and over again.

Now become aware that pain or fear has two qualities: 1) discomfort and 2) energy. Yes, pain is a form of energy. Allow the energy of the pain to move up into your head as if it is charging the batteries of your mind or spirit. Continue to observe the pain. Continue to let the energy part of the pain rise out of it. Notice how you may want to utilize this pain energy. Perhaps you can use it to sharpen your concentration or to take you into a deep meditation.

One might call "embracing overwhelming pain or fear" a "non-technique" technique. Nonetheless, it is quite powerful. The pain or fear will almost always change. And when one observes pain in this way, a whole barrage of feelings may begin to arise. People realize that pain is a signal to them, often a fearful signal. People may realize that when they have pain, they're afraid it will never stop, that it will ruin their lives, that they will end up helpless invalids. This technique is ideal for people with cancer who have survived the first round of treatment and are now experiencing the overwhelming fear of recurrence.

I have used a variety of techniques to help alleviate fear in cancer patients. But the fear is often so enormous that it transcends techniques. Cancer and AIDS are diagnoses that trigger enormous fear. With cancer, the initial diagnosis triggers overwhelming fear. But even after someone has been treated and the cancer is gone, a deep fear of recurrence is often present.

So in the case of overwhelming fear, I often ask people simply to observe the fear without trying to push it away. Let your mind explore the fear.

Where is the fear in your body? What are the fearful thoughts and images? Just observe, allowing the fear to arise, change and dissolve. Let the fear float. Let it break free from the clutches of your mind. Let yourself be fully immersed in the fear. Embrace the fear. Breathe in and out of the fear, allowing your breath to massage the fear gently.

The results are powerful. Sometimes the fear seems to float out of people's bodies, or it gradually disperses. But the experience of embracing the fear, immersing oneself in the fear allows for transformation of the fear. Even the fear of death is alleviated by using this approach. Whether someone is suffering from intense pain, fear, or any other overwhelming feeling or symptom, embracing the pain is a powerful tool that everyone should be aware of, and, as you will see, is part of the "treatment program" for many spiritual emergencies.

---

1. Stanislav Grof, M.D., and Christina Grof, *Spiritual Emergency: When Personal Transformation Becomes a Crisis* (Los Angeles: Jeremy Tarcher, 1989).
2. O. Carl Simonton, M.D., Stephanie Matthews-Simonton, and James Creighton, *Getting Well Again: A Step-by-Step Self-Help Guide to Overcoming Cancer for Patients and Their Families* (New York: Bantam Books, 1978).
3. Martin Rossman, M.D., *Healing Yourself: A Step-by-Step Program for Better Health Through Imagery* (New York: Walker and Company, 1987).
4. Stephen Levine, *Who Dies: An Investigation of Conscious Living and Conscious Dying* (New York: Anchor Books, 1982).

Chapter 16

Spiritual Emergency: Opening the Door to Change

This chapter begins with Guidelines and Mental Fitness Techniques to deal with spiritual emergencies. You'll be reading about ways of managing feelings and problems that you will read about again, later on in this chapter, in the One-Minute Imagery Rituals. The various Guidelines and Techniques address various specific emotions specifically triggered in one spiritual experience or another.

There is a very important point to be made about spiritual emergencies. I encourage you to embrace these so-called "emergencies" as blessings in disguise, opportunities for change. Your genuine spiritual experience may seem dangerous. It may shake the foundation of your beliefs. It may make you depressed or anxious, or even overwhelmed with panic. But within that danger, lies the opportunity—side-by-side. Spiritual emergencies are really better seen as "transitions," times of evolution. Life is not static. If an angel has gotten your attention, it's a good thing. In fact, it's a great thing. It's not a disease. It's a gift, a blessing, and a wake-up call for change and perhaps even radical transformation.

Anxiety as Spiritual Emergency
Guideline #20

Practice this one-minute-imagery ritual for anxiety four times a day. For all One-Minute Imagery Rituals the first two steps are the same. (We begin with these first two here, as well.)

Step 1   Breath Work for Mental Clearing (20 seconds)
a.   Close your eyes, and then inhale to the count of 4.
b.   Hold your breath to the count of 4.
c.   Exhale to the count of 8.
Allow yourself to let go of tension with each breath. Imagine that a wave of relaxation spreads from your head to your toes with this long breath.

Step 2   Mantra Meditation (20 seconds)

Go back to Mental Fitness Technique #2 (mantra meditation, at p. 63, above) to recall the mantra you've chosen. Breathe normally. Let's say your mantra is "Loving God." As you inhale, silently say, "Loving" and as you exhale, silently say, "God."

After you've mastered the basics of the One-Minute Imagery Ritual, silently recite your mantra along with each breath you take. Allow yourself to sink into the peaceful stillness of your own mind. By so doing, you deepen the experience, centering yourself and temporarily withdrawing from life's distractions. Remember that when you're just beginning to practice, start off by only using the 4-4-8 breath of Step 1, just above.

These first two steps being the same for all One-Minute Imagery Rituals, we now continue with the ritual specifically for anxiety.

Step 3   Specific Relaxation Imagery: The Wave (20 seconds)

There are several relaxation imageries or practices presented in this book (see Guideline #12 and Mental Fitness Technique #18 to #22, above, pp. 296-298). Try them all to see which works best for you, but start with the Wave (Mental Fitness Technique #19).

Imagine you are at the beach, lying on the warm sand. The waves are rolling in and each one comes closer and closer to you, until the waves are starting to wash over your body before they roll back out. As each wave falls away from you and returns to the sea, tension, anxiety and stress are removed in the process. With each wave you feel a little more relaxed. Just feel the wave gently pulling tension out of you.

Step 4   Coming Back: (2 - 5 seconds)

Take one more long, deep breath and completely bring yourself back to normal consciousness. This completes the structure of the One-Minute Imagery Rituals (slightly over 60 seconds).

Let us continue here with the specific Guidelines for Anxiety, which follow these four introductory steps:

1.   Develop your inner voice. Ask yourself what the anxiety is about and why it's being triggered by your spiritual experience.

2.	Communicate with your anxiety, allowing an image to emerge that represents the anxiety.

3.	Practice mantra meditation throughout the day in order to become calmer and to slow down the mind.

4.	As you lie in bed before sleep, spend a longer period of time (10 - 20 minutes) with the Wave, or other relaxation, imagery.

Depression as Spiritual Emergency
Guideline #21

1.	Ask yourself what the meaning of your depression is. Why did seeing an angel or having a near-death experience cause you to become depressed?

2.	Exercise—a lot. Jog, swim, or bike 30 minutes, five days a week. Not only will this lift your depression, but if there is anger buried "beneath the depression," exercise will help mobilize the anger.

3.	If you get in touch with buried anger and it starts to erupt, practice the ABCs of Anger Control (above, p. 307).

4.	Don't look only for spiritual solutions to spiritual problems. There are a host of nutritional supplements and herbs that may assist you. The amino acids tyrosine and tryptophan can be powerful anti-depressants.

5.	Make your diet "lighter." Lighten up on the heavy stuff like red meat and cheese, and shift toward a lighter, vegetarian diet.

6.	Practice the energizing breath technique:
Inhale to the count of 2.
Hold your breath to the count of 2.
Exhale to the count of 1.

Unloading Painful Emotion
Mental Fitness Technique #30

1.	Here's an imagery technique to help you deal with depression and other painful emotions:
Imagine that you're walking in your favorite setting in nature. You come across a hole in the ground, about eight inches wide, which goes clear down to the center of the earth.

Get in touch with all the thoughts, feelings, sensations, and images related to the depression and "dump" them down the hole in the ground. Just let the depression flow out of you.

2.   Communicate with a symbol of depression.

Pain as Spiritual Emergency
Guideline #22

Practice the pain one-minute-imagery ritual four times a day. The first two steps are the same ones you read about for anxiety, starting with one 4-4-8 breath (20 seconds) followed by mantra meditation (20 seconds).

3-Step Pain Imagery
Mental Fitness Technique #31

1.   Specific Imagery: Pain Technique   20 seconds
a.   *Focus your attention on your pain, or discomfort. Imagine your pain has a certain size, shape, and color. What does it feel like? Is it rough or smooth? Does it stay in one place or move around?*
b.   *Allow the pain to turn to liquid. It has the same size, shape, and color as before, but now it's liquid.*
c.   *Roll that liquid down to the nearest arm or leg and let it flow out of your fingertips or toes. Watch it as it flows out of the room, out of the house (or hospital), down the street. Just watch it and see where it goes. Maybe it flows all the way down to the ocean. If your pain was 100% before we started this exercise, what percent is it now?*

In my experience, this simple technique cuts the pain in half in almost all cases, whether dealing with fractured spine, cancer pain, or degenerative arthritis, and it helps 95% of people in pain. It's so simple you might not believe it could work, but please suspend judgment, take five minutes to try this technique, and be prepared to be pleasantly surprised. This simple technique was the one that helped reduce Marci's neck pain to zero, following a head-on collision with a combined impact of 140 miles per hour, an auto accident which resulted in numerous fractures in her spine.

Take one more long, deep breath and completely bring yourself back to normal consciousness.

2.   Practice the technique Embracing the Pain (see Mental Fitness Technique #29, above, pp. 333-334) every day for 30 to 60 minutes. If your physical pain is the result of a kundalini process, you'll want to look at the section on Energy Problems, below, in the next chapter, and see if blocked energy is producing your pain.

If your physical pain is the result of obstructed kundalini energy, all of the techniques in the section on Energy Problems may be used to help decrease your pain.

Marital Problems as Spiritual Emergency
Guideline #23

Marital problems frequently arise when one partner has had an unusual spiritual experience and the other hasn't. Suddenly, the two are on different wave-lengths, thinking, feeling, and believing differently. If you're the one who had the spiritual experience, you may not even be able to put the experience into words, thereby creating a widening gap between you and your spouse.

My experience with spiritual emergencies is that the "normal" spouse will want everything to quickly return to normal. She may think you're crazy and may push you hard to just, "Pull yourself together." You're left feeling alone, misunderstood, and frightened. Your spouse may not understand that you love her as much as before, maybe even more. She may interpret your spiritual experience as an attempt on your part to pull away from her. With these basic problems in mind, here's how to proceed:

1.   Communicate. Sit down face-to-face, share all the details of your spiritual experience with your spouse or partner, and ask him or her to listen, without judging, until you have completely finished.
2.   If you are the partner who did not have the spiritual experience, the best thing you can do is reassure your partner how much you love him/her. Keep listening. Keep loving. The more

"space" you provide for your partner to air his or her feelings, the quicker he or she will move through the spiritual emergency.

3.   Ask your partner or spouse to read this book. If she thinks you're crazy, review the chapters on the Lost Mind (Part III) together, so that you can reassure her that you do not have a genuine mental illness.

4.   Be patient. Remember that a spiritual emergency is a transformative process that almost always leaves you better off. It will pass, so don't act in haste. You may feel the desire to spare your partner the suffering you may be experiencing. Maybe you feel that a divorce would be the best thing for your spouse. You're probably wrong. Hang in there as a team.

5.   Don't try to convert your spouse to your new-found spiritual insights. Expect him or her to listen but don't demand that they follow your path.

6.   If no one else understands you, remember that God does. If you are questioning that, dive into the techniques in the chapter on Crisis in Faith.

Energy Surges as Spiritual Emergency
Guideline #24

Energy surges stirred up by a spiritual experience can generally be assumed to be kundalini. To work with this energy:

1.   Practice the one-minute-imagery ritual for anxiety four times a day.

2.   Practice breathing deeply and slowly throughout the day. This will help stabilize your energy without stirring it up more.

3.   Avoid fasting.

4.   Get plenty of rest. Avoid sleep deprivation. Fasting and sleep deprivation are likely to cause kundalini energy to surge.

5.   Avoid any martial art that stirs up chi, prana, or energy.

6.   Balance your energy with therapeutic, touch, reiki, huna, acupuncture, or yoga. Make sure you find a good practitioner. Yoga postures can increase or decrease kundalini energy, so you'll want to find a yoga instructor who comes highly recommended.

7.   Make dietary changes. If your diet has been "light vegetarian," consider adding cheese, other dairy products, then poultry,
fish, and beef—in that order. Honey can also lower energy.
8.   Find ways to "ground" the energy. Physical exercise,
especially when one is in direct contact with the earth, is helpful.
Gardening is a good way to "ground" the energy.
9.   Use this technique to see where energy may be obstructed:

Letting Energy Flow
Mental Fitness Technique #32

*Close your eyes and relax. Slowly become aware of the flow of
energy within your body. The energy may be a powerful current. At other
times, it may be almost imperceptible. The energy may seem to flow from
toe to head, head to toe, or from the center on out.*

*Identify the flow of energy. Let's say, for example, that you feel
energy moving from your toes up to your head. In your mind, follow the
flow of energy. If you perceive any blockage in the energy, imagine that
there is a door at that point. Open the door and explore the room that lies
behind it. Make necessary adjustments in order to allow the energy to flow
through the room, and then allow it to continue on its upward course.*

An infinite array of images may appear in the blocked
rooms. People from the past, who have been our tormentors, often
appear in the blocked rooms. Perhaps a room will be filled with
memories. If you don't know how to handle the people, places,
things, or symbols that appear in the blocked room, invite your
chosen form of God to appear in that room with you. Ask God for
advice as to how to deal with the obstruction.

Confusion and Panic as Spiritual Emergency
Guideline #25

If your spiritual experience is producing a feeling of
confusion or panic, you're in a serious spiritual emergency. First,
realize why you're confused.

The reason for your confusion is that your old belief system
has been overwhelmed by your new spiritual experience. You have
no context within which to understand the experience. Your beliefs

are no longer in synch with what you know to be genuine spiritual experience. And yet, because you can't explain it, you feel overwhelmed or panicky.

Here's what to do:

1.   Clarify, one more time, the name of your spiritual experience. You need to do this in order to reassure yourself that you're not losing your mind.

2.   In order to bring your belief system up to "speed" with your new experience, practice a symbolic imagery. It will help you discover the meaning of the experience:

Get in touch with your feeling of panic or confusion. Ask yourself, "What is the meaning of the experience?" Allow an image to emerge which represents the meaning of the experience.

After you've gotten in touch with an image of "meaning," you can work with that image in several ways:

a.   Use the Communicating with Your Symptom technique.

b.   *Picture your chosen form of God next to the image of "meaning." Ask God what the image means and what you should think, feel, or do about it.*

c.   Oftentimes, as soon as you visualize an image, a symbol, the meaning will automatically become apparent. Here's an example: I asked a patient of mine, a young man with a chronic sleep disorder, to allow an image to emerge representing the problem of insomnia. He immediately "saw" a Scotsman participating in the sport of tossing heavy 50-pound weights, which were attached to three-foot chains. My patient knew that his insomnia was like that 50-pound weight. He'd had the problem for so long, he felt as if he simply couldn't make any progress. He couldn't lift the heavy weight, but he knew he had to.

Immediately, in his imagination, he began picking up the ball and chain. At first, it felt so heavy he could barely lift it off the ground. He continued to practice in his mind until he could swing the ball and chain around and around, finally letting go and tossing it 40 or 50 feet. By so doing, he immediately felt that he would be able to "move" his sleep problem and make headway.

3.   "Embrace the overwhelming fear or confusion." If you're feeling overwhelmed with confusion, chances are you're really frightened. Don't try to bury the fear or chase it away. Rather, embrace it with this technique.

Crisis in Faith as Spiritual Emergency
Guideline #26

Almost all of us experience a crisis in faith from time to time, although most of the time our faith is relatively stable. If you're having a spiritual emergency of a crisis in faith, you may suddenly feel as if God has totally abandoned you. Or you may feel like you're "going to hell" because "Christians don't have past-life memories." Don't panic. Rather, practice this extensive program to restore faith:

1.   Practice connecting with God using this imagery technique:
Picture your chosen form of God in front of you. Imagine that a hollow tube connects your heart to God's heart. Imagine that divine love flows through that tube into you. Allow it to continue flowing until you are filled with love.
2.   Increase the spiritual practices of mantra meditation (reciting the name of God) and visualizing your chosen form of God. These two techniques help make each moment more sacred and make the Divine more of a living presence in your life, rather than an intellectual abstraction.
3.   Pray—a lot. If you've lost all faith, pray that your faith be restored.
4.   Explore the void.
5.   Go to church or synagogue more often.
6.   Speak to your rabbi, minister, priest, or guru, and ask the tough questions. If their answers don't satisfy you, and don't quench your spiritual thirst, keep looking.
7.   Practice a deeper level of surrender, by using this prayer, "Lord, I know that everything is your will." A crisis in faith arises when you ask yourself, "How can this be happening to me?" If you're asking this question, it means that what you believe is not in

harmony with what is actually happening in your life. Pray that you can surrender at a deeper level.

8.   Examine an image of "resistance to faith."

9.   Reassess whether your religion is the right one for you. Does it answer the "heavy" questions?

10.   If through reassessment, you decide that your current religion is the right one for you, don't retreat from it. Don't retreat from the spiritual practices recommended by your religion. Rather, double your efforts.

11.   Have faith that the spiritual practices of the world's great religions have withstood the test of time. Even if those practices don't make you feel better in the short-run, trust that the long-term benefits are worth the effort.

One-Minute Imagery Rituals

There are more than enough techniques in this book for you to transform every aspect of your life. However, if you're like most people, you'll need to consciously "build" these techniques into your life. You'll need to provide a structure.

Although some people find it easy to do the right things, the healing and loving things for themselves, whether it is meditating, taking walks, or learning to relax, most of us need reminders, or else we slip back into our old ways of doing things.

Because you've read so many techniques, you may feel that transformation of one's life is an impossible task. "It must take too much work." The fact is that all you need to do is take one step in the right direction, and then another, and another.

Most of our lives are hectic, and we tend to believe we don't have time, certainly not the time for all the techniques in this book. And you're right. If you practiced every technique in this book every day of your life, you wouldn't have time for anything else.

That's why I encourage my patients, and you, to create one-minute-imagery rituals, which you can practice three or four times a day. If your doctor told you to take a pill four times a day, at 8, 12, 4, and 8, you'd probably do it. And it would probably take 30 to 60 seconds each time for you to remember to take the pill, get a cup of water, swallow the pill, and then dispose of the cup. One-minute-imagery rituals won't take much longer than will taking a pill, but do not underestimate the transformative power of these rituals.

There is nothing "etched in stone" about these four steps or the duration of 60 seconds allotted for the exercise. This imagery ritual was created in this way because so many people never seem to have the time to relax or practice self-healing rituals. But everyone can find 60 seconds three or four times a day.

Tailor your one-minute-imagery ritual to your own particular needs. Design your own time frame and frequency. Perhaps every hour on the hour. You decide. You also may want to add a physical component to your ritual, such as a stretch, a simple physical exercise, or a yoga posture. Maybe you'll create a full one-minute-imagery ritual and will practice it four times a day for the next year.

Still others will want more. They will want to know how to live every moment to the fullest, how to live their dreams to the fullest, how to experience love in every moment, in every interaction. If you are one of those people, you can use one or more techniques during every waking moment. Please remember that if you choose to practice these tools for transformation every waking moment, you are no better than the person who "only" chooses to relax a little more each day. Each of us must carve our own path in life.

If you want to undertake the "full-on," 100% program, here's what I suggest. Start by practicing your one-minute-imagery ritual four times a day. As your current situation changes, you will definitely want to modify this technique. Because our "main concern" changes over time, so too will your one-minute-imagery ritual.

Practice one symbolic imagery several times a week, in addition to your imagery ritual. For example, if you have chronic pain, use the technique outlined in Communicating with Your Symptom on a regular basis.

Chapter 17

Symptoms, Problems, and Solutions

This book may have already helped solve many problems in your life or helped bring a sense of meaning to an experience that seemed meaningless. Although the list of symptoms and problems is vast, in this chapter, I will provide brief techniques that will provide further guidance for some common problems.

These techniques may be used by themselves, as part of a one-minute-imagery ritual, or as part of Your Complete Mental Fitness Program.

Career

The Art Gallery Imagery
Mental Fitness Technique #33

People experience a couple of major problems regarding their career. Either they 1) dislike their career, or 2) love their career, but hate their current job situation. Many of us prefer to change jobs if we dislike or hate the work, but sometimes changing jobs or careers is not a possibility, at least not at the current time. I do not want to talk you into staying with a miserable job, but I know that almost everyone can be happier at what they do. Here is one way to "re-frame" the situation for yourself.

Picture yourself walking into an art gallery. It's a big gallery and you're the only person in it. As you walk across the gallery floor, you can hear your footsteps echoing loudly.

On a distant wall you will see a series of blank canvases. Walk up to the first canvas and allow a picture to emerge that represents your current career or job. This picture may be "real," "symbolic," or "abstract." Now that you're looking at the picture of your job, notice what kind of frame it has around it.

Change the frame, but leave the picture exactly as it is. Make the frame elegant and beautiful. Notice how different your job looks with a new frame around it.

Now take a few steps until you're standing in front of another blank canvas. Allow a picture to emerge representing how you'd love your career or job to be. Put a frame around this second picture. You will notice that your first and second pictures are quite different and you may feel frustrated about the discrepancy.

Take a few more steps to a third, and final, blank canvas. Allow a picture to emerge that shows how painting number one can be transformed into painting number two. Painting number three is a "morph." Put a beautiful frame around the third picture and then meditate on this picture. Study the colors, the qualities, the textures, the meanings you experience in this painting. Notice how you feel while looking at this third picture. Allow yourself to stay with the feeling generated in you by picture number three.

Allow yourself to believe that this transformation actually can take place. Suspend judgment. After meditating on picture number three for several minutes, imagine that a divine being, your chosen form of God, joins you in the gallery. Ask him or her to help you understand how to transform picture one so that it is more like picture number two. Ask him or her how you can actually create picture number three in the "real world."

Energy

River of Light Imagery
Mental Fitness Technique #34

Low energy is so common it's an epidemic in the Western world. This imagery technique is one part of your total "energy" program. Obviously, a serious energy problem requires a thorough medical and/or psychiatric evaluation.

Imagine yourself walking through a sunlit meadow. You listen to the songs of birds and feel a slight breeze against your skin. You hear the sound of a stream and begin walking in that direction. As you approach the stream, you see that it is a river of light.

Walk into this gentle stream. Imagine that it is only about a foot deep. Lie down in the river with your head pointed upstream. Imagine that the river of light pours through the top of your head, through your body and out your feet. The river is charged with energy and fills every cell in your body with energy as it flows through you. Imagine that all darkness, all sadness, all pain is washed out of you by the river.

The river surges through you as if one wave of light after another passes through you, and with each wave of light, you experience more energy. When you have been fully energized by the river of light, come out of the river and dry yourself off.

Fear (Mild to Moderate)

The Jack Imagery
Mental Fitness Technique #35

The "Jack Imagery" technique (developed by Phyllis Krystal) is very useful for mild to moderate fear.

Remember that childhood game called Jacks? Picture a large Jack about four or five inches across. This jack is made out of light. Imagine that the Jack is being lowered in front of you as if it is suspended by a cord or rope.

The Jack continues descending until it is in front of your solar plexus, several inches away from your body. Now imagine that all your fear pours out of your body into the center of this Jack of Light. Perhaps your fear has a color to it, a texture. Like a colored river allow the fear to pour out and dissolve into the center of the Jack.

Now imagine that pure golden light is pouring in through the top of your head. That light enters the space where the fear had been and fills it up. Continue this process of letting the fear pour out into the Jack, and filling the place where the fear had been with light.

Feeling Trapped

Breaking Out of the Cage
Mental Fitness Technique #35

Picture the cage or prison in which you feel trapped. Feel the walls or bars and stay with the feeling you experience in that cage. How do you feel? Is it warm or cold in there? Is there anybody outside the cage, such as a guard? Is there anybody inside the cage or prison with you? Explore the cage, becoming familiar with all the details of color, texture, and sound.

When you're ready, find a way out of the cage. Maybe you'll need to blast the cage open with a bomb. Or maybe breaking out of the cage will be as easy as gently pushing on a wall until it falls down.

Once you've identified the cage or prison, you'll be one step closer to becoming free. Whether or not your mind built a cage to protect you from someone who was actually attacking you does not ultimately matter. Someone else may have forced you to build your own cage or prison, but only you have the power to "un-build" it.

Finance and Love: Creating Abundance

The Hourglass Imagery
Mental Fitness Technique #37

Many of us limit our lives by our unconscious beliefs: I'm not good enough to have that; I couldn't possibly do that job; I could do that if only ...; I'm not very good at that; Oh, no, I'm not artistic.

We limit what we can do, those we allow ourselves to meet, what experiences we can have. We limit all the good that can flow to us when we could be opening up and letting more of life flow to us, and through us. Here is an imagery that Phyllis Krystal uses to help us open up to life's possibilities. It can help us with finance, romance, friendship, and career:

Imagine that you are sitting in the center of a golden circle. The radius of the circle is your arm's length and only the rim of the circle is golden, the rest being clear. Above you is your Higher Consciousness (the High C) which you may imagine in any form, with any name. Imagine that the High C forms the top of a cone, and the golden circle forms the bottom of the cone.

Another cone emerges from the High C going upward and outward toward the sky, toward the Universe. Thus the entire image is of an hourglass. Get in touch with whatever you are lacking in life. Do you want love, friendship, a better job, or heightened creativity? Become aware of limitations you are placing on yourself. Now ask your Higher Consciousness to allow whatever you need to flow from the Universe into the top of the cone, through the narrow neck of the hourglass, down into the lower cone, into your life.

People often have amazing reactions to this imagery. Some receive new job offers immediately after practicing this imagery. Others have met new people, or had new important experiences. Once people realize how they had been limiting themselves unnecessarily, they begin to open up and receive in ways that they were not previously capable of.

Health

There are quite a number of ways in which imagery can facilitate physical healing. These techniques should be used in conjunction with symbolic imageries (Communicating with Your Symptom) in order to maximize the benefit of this technique.

"Attack" Imagery
Mental Fitness Technique #38

O. Carl Simonton, M.D., first used imagery in the mid '70s to assist cancer patients. Please do not use this technique as a substitute for your oncologist's recommendations!

Picture your cancer in your mind's eye. Imagine that your white blood cells are hungry and ferocious. Perhaps they look like sharks or piranhas. The "shark" white blood cells attack the cancer, eating away at it until it shrinks and then finally disappears.

Imagine the waste product of the cancer disposed of through your kidneys and digestive tract, thereby flushing out the last of the cancer.

Transformational Imagery
Mental Fitness Technique #39

Some people are not comfortable with the aggressive nature of "attack" imagery. Here is an example of transformational imagery, which can be used for any physical problem:

Imagine that light streams in through the top of your head, filling your body as if it were a giant container of light. Finally the light pours through your skin, so that the light is both inside and outside you. Focus your attention on your particular physical problem and allow the light to grow brighter and brighter in that area.

Imagine actual healing taking place within the light. You may imagine bones healing, skin healing, your pancreas secreting the right amount of insulin, etc.

Be creative with this work. Perhaps you'll want to bring in microscopic surgeons with blue lasers to "operate" on that body part. Bring in any tools, any people, any objects, any symbols to assist in the healing process.

In my practice, I have seen several astonishing cures through transformational imagery. One such cure was a 15-year-old boy who had broken a leg at the age of five. At 15, one leg was one-quarter of an inch shorter than the other. He and his mother both wanted to see if I could assist him in making both legs the same length. It took exactly six months to accomplish the feat, as verified by physical measurements and x-rays.

My first experience with mental imagery was in 1977, when I taught a man with multiple sclerosis how to visualize his decubitus ulcers (bed sores) healing. He had three holes in his body that were three inches deep, and had resisted all medical treatment for nine months. Four weeks after he began visualizing the sores healing, two of them were 90% healed. A month later, they had completely "filled in" with normal tissue. A minor surgical operation was necessary to finally close the holes.[1]

Oddly, the third bed sore had not improved at all. I asked him what he thought was going on and he replied, "I haven't worked on that bed sore at all, because I know that the hospital is going to discharge me to a terrible nursing home." I spoke with the social service department, who reassured him that they would find him a very nice home, which they eventually did. In the meantime, he proceeded to heal the third sore.

Relationships
The Figure Eight Imagery
Mental Fitness Technique #40

Relationship problems cannot be solved by reading one technique or even one entire book. However, we can make significant progress by identifying a central problem with many relationships and then working with that particular aspect, namely attachment.

Few of us are capable of being in relationships while remaining totally loving, and totally detached. "Detached" may sound like it means "unloving" but it's not. We develop negative attachments in most intense relationships, whether the role we play is parent, child, friend, spouse, boss, employee, healer, or patient. The Figure Eight imagery, which was developed by Phyllis Krystal, helps us identify the negative aspects of attachment, so that we can let go of those attachments. In so doing, we then can bring more of ourselves to our relationships, and can leave behind anger, greed, envy, and jealousy which result from over-attachment.

What follows is an extremely abbreviated version of the Figure Eight and Cutting the Ties techniques developed by Phyllis Krystal.

Picture yourself sitting on the ground in the center of a golden circle whose radius is the length of your extended arm. An identical circle lies on the ground directly in front of you and just touches your golden circle. Together, the two circles form a figure eight.

Picture the individual with whom you are having difficulty in the other circle, facing you. That person may not still be living, but you can still imagine being seated face to face.

Focus your attention at the point where the two circles meet and then imagine a blue neon light that begins to move around the other circle clockwise. After the blue light goes around the other circle once, it begins to move around your circle, counter-clockwise. Take two or three minutes and watch the blue neon light moving around the figure eight, over and over again.

If, while practicing the figure eight, the other person refuses to stay in their circle, build an imaginary enclosure. You must keep them in their circle in order for this technique to work.

This first step of the Cutting the Ties technique begins to sever the attachment, the energy, the negativity that may have existed for decades between you and the other person. The Figure Eight quickly helps you clarify boundaries and borders. If you find that you're having trouble "keeping someone in their circle," that means that you are feeling overwhelmed by that person. You need to separate your energy, your emotion, your over-attachment. The other person cannot be forced to "let go of you," but you have the power to "let go of him."

---

1.   David Gersten M.D. "[Case Report:] Meditation as an Adjunct to Medical and Psychiatric Treatment," *American Journal of Psychiatry*, 135 (May 1978): 598-599.

Chapter 18

Total Transformation

Mantra meditation and conscious use of the breath create what I call "Mental Home Base." It's your foundation, but let's dive deeper for full transformation. Design your own prayer or use one from your religion and say it each morning as you arise. "Carve" God out of the space around you, and keep him with you all day long. Silently recite your mantra when you are not engaged in work.

When you are working, dedicate each task to God. By so doing, you turn work into a worshipful experience. You can use this prayer before undertaking any kind of work: "Think through me, feel through me, act through me, love through me." Before every session with a patient, I dedicate the session to God. When the session is over and my patient has left the office, I silently conclude with this prayer: "Dear Lord, I surrender the session to you and surrender all fruits of my action to you." In other words, it's all about the work and not about any attachment to anything other than the work (like money or pride, for example).

Every time you interact with another human being, remember to look for the divine spark within him, and then silently say to him, "I love you, Lord."

To bring the 100% transformational program to full fruition, develop the spirit of self-inquiry for every waking moment. For each situation, ask yourself, "What is the deeper truth of this situation? What is real, eternal, unchanging in this situation? What is transient or fleeting?" You'll also be asking yourself, "What is the right thing to do in this given situation?" Sometimes the answers are easy. It's wrong to murder, rape, and steal. But how do you decide whether to go to the office party or stay home with your wife, who doesn't want to go to the party? Each moment in life is full of potential, full of possibilities for growth, courage, love, and correct action. One way to fine-tune your inner voice is to ask yourself, "What would Jesus do in this situation?" I ask myself, "What would Sai Baba do in this situation?"

Keep your spiritual life growing, changing and creative. Don't get stuck in a rut. Being disciplined does not mean being rigid. Use those techniques that leap out at you and grab your attention. And remember to practice every technique with a feeling and spirit of love. When you say your mantra, say it with love. When you look for the spark of divinity in other human beings, do so with love. If you do all of these exercises without love, the results will be radically diminished. After all, the goal of all these techniques is to foster love.

There will be times in life when you are on "cruise control," living easily, practicing your chosen spiritual and mental fitness disciplines without too much thought or effort. At other times, life's challenges will require that you reach deep inside for more faith, just to keep going. When things are really rough, or when you're really feeling stuck, practice dialoguing with your image of resistance, and more importantly practice "embracing the overwhelming pain."

Some of you may regard the proposed approach to life to be terribly restrictive, over-disciplined, rigid, and lacking in spontaneity. My experience over decades using these approaches with my patients and in my own life has proven the opposite to be true. I believe that serious effort must be made in order for us to re-integrate body, mind, energy, and spirit. Western civilization has spent two thousand years separating and dividing, relegating the spirit to the clerics, the mind to psychiatrists and psychologists, the body to medical doctors, and energy to the trash can. It will take some effort for us to learn to live in harmony with ourselves, with our fellow men and women, with nature, and with God. Long ago, we forgot how to live in peace and harmony. However, these tools for transformation will end the split for us. Eventually, life ceases to appear "spiritual" versus "material." Instead, we begin to feel whole. After we practice these techniques for a while, it's like riding a bicycle. At first, we fall off. Later on, we can ride a bike without the slightest fear of falling off. It's the same with a spiritual approach to life.

Imagine what the world would be like if every person reading this book made even a small effort to improve his or her life, to become just a little more peaceful, loving, honest, or non-violent. Let's say, for the sake of illustration that one million people are reading this book. Each of us interacts with approximately 20 other people a day. That translates to 20 million positive interactions if we're all trying to be a little more giving and forgiving, a little calmer, a little less violent and short-tempered. Those 20 million people are also interacting with 20 other people per day. There is a trickle down effect resulting from our interactions. Each of us can "make" or "break" someone else's day. If we "break" their day, the negativity will spill over in subtle ways to all the people in that person's life. So, to elaborate on our calculation: 1 million readers X 20 interactions X 20 interactions = 400 million interactions per day. Over the course of one year, 365 days, that amounts to 14.6 billion interactions, almost triple the current total world population.

It doesn't take that much for the world to change if each individual strives to raise his or her own consciousness. And the positive changes illustrated by 400 million positive interactions per day does not take into account at all anything beyond physical reality. It does not take into account the fact that each of us is part of one world, one mind, one consciousness. Each of us is a being of energy and spirit, not just a body and mind. The global effect on energy and consciousness is tremendous when each of us contributes our small part.

Although it often appears that the world is losing its mind, instead of getting enlightened, we must believe and act in ways that ensure that the game of life can be played to the fullest by all, that the dream of life can be realized by all, that the love of life can be enjoyed by all, and that the challenge of life, can and will be met by all.

Chapter 19

The Tao of Love

Living in the moment is easier said than done. Everybody talks about it, but few of us live that way. The "Tao" or the "path" of love is a long journey, but is the only journey worth taking. In order to get "there" from "here," we need to learn how to let go of the past, as well as the future. And where we're trying to get, namely "there," is actually where we already are, and where we've always been, namely in the moment.

The moment is the only time in which peace, love, and joy exist, for when we're stuck in the past, we are not free. All of our actions are conditioned by past experiences. Therefore, only by fully letting go of the past, can one fully live in the present. And, of course, peace does not exist in the future, for when we "live" in the future, we live in a state of worry, anxiety, or fear.

The moment is not necessarily a "place" free from pain, but if we can fully embrace our pain fully in the moment, we become free from neurotic suffering, free from suffering over our suffering. We can feel the deepest pain, and then move on, so that we can feel the greatest peace and the most profound love. There is one other incredibly important "feature" of the moment. It's the place where God is found.

Letting Go of the Past
Guideline #27

Most of us have a difficult time living in the moment and repeatedly have thoughts, such as: I feel so guilty about ...; I'll never forgive her for leaving me; I keep thinking about my ex and it makes me sad.

If your mind works like that, you tend toward depression, and need to work on forgiveness, releasing guilt, letting go of resentment, and overcoming blame. All of these qualities keep us anchored in the past and prevent us from living more fully in the moment.

Let's start with an imagery technique which helps release us from guilt. The "Temple of Forgiveness Imagery"[1] was developed by Mary Jayne Carlson, Ph.D., and is immensely powerful:

Overcoming Guilt: The Temple of Forgiveness
Mental Fitness Technique #41

The burden of guilt you are carrying is very heavy, and you struggle step by step up a mountain path, looking for the Temple of Forgiveness. You see ahead a large wall covered with ivy, and you know that behind the wall is the place you have been seeking. A massive gate is the entrance. The guard of the Temple steps forward to greet you. To enter, you must truly desire forgiveness. Search your heart for this desire.

The guard nods and opens the gate. You walk on and struggle through. Looking up, you see the Temple, simple, yet an impressive sight. You are very aware of how heavy your burden of guilt is. Stepping through the opening of the Temple, you feel the sacredness of this holy place. Look around and listen.

You sit in the back, feeling the peace and comfort of this holy place. You have with you a plain box. Into the box you place your guilt and shame, all that you wish to be forgiven for.

And now you take your plain wooden box to the altar. Notice what it's made of. On the altar there are many symbols of release and forgiveness. Place your box on the altar. Take one of the candles, and light the box on fire. Kneeling, you pray for your guilt to be replaced with forgiveness. Watch the box burn, noticing any feelings you might have. Watch until only ashes are left.

As you rise, leaving the Temple to go into the sun with the ashes, you notice how light you feel, relieved of your burden, free. Finally, forgiven. Joyfully you draw a circle on the ground, then mix the ashes with the dirt. Everything seems bright and new. The colors are brighter, the sounds crisper and more soothing. When the soil is prepared, plant the seeds of the new ideas, attitudes and direction. Then water what you have planted. When you are finished, someone will appear who will watch over your planting while you aren't there. This will be a caretaker who will water, weed and protect the new growth.

Letting Go of Resentment
Guideline #28

Letting go of resentment is no small task. It seems easier to continue to blame and feel resentful.

Before going into specific techniques, here are a few guidelines:

1.   Understand that fear lies buried underneath your anger and resentment.

2.   Realize that underneath the fear is pure, raw pain. When you reach raw pain, you can fully experience it, let go of it, and begin to live more fully in the present. Blame is a cover-up for pure pain.

3.   You can't pretend to be free of resentment. You can't fake it. You have to go through the hard work of honest soul-searching, examining what may seem ugly within yourself.

4.   In your notebook, write down all the things you resent about a particular person. After you've done that, picture that person in your mind, as if he or she were in the room with you, and read out loud those words of resentment you've just written down.

5.   If you believe you can speak directly to the person in question without hurting him or her, without seeking revenge, speak to that person face-to-face, or on the phone. Avoid blaming that person. Try using phrases like, "I know there is another side to this, but I'd like to tell you how I felt when you did such-and-such. I'm still angry and hurting because of that incident, that remark."

6.   Remember that the brutal, honest truth is not always the best policy. If the "brutal" truth will forever destroy a relationship that you want to foster, choose your "truthful" words carefully.

7.   It's never too late to clear the air, even if you're dealing with a parent who abused you 50 years ago.

8.   Once you have expressed the negativity, don't wallow in the anger. There is a time to express anger, hurt, and resentment, and there is a time to let go.

Cutting the Ties
Mental Fitness Technique #42

Cut the ties to any person, any event, or any symbol from the past to which you are still bound, using the following imagery technique:

Imagine there is an actual physical bond connecting your body to her body. This bond symbolizes the negative aspects of your attachment to that person.

The bond may be made of any substance—ropes or chains, ribbon or string, wood or metal, tar or taffy, smoke or light—and may run from any part of her body to any part of yours. Look closer. There may be more than one bond.

How does the bond feel? How does energy flow in and out of the bond? What energy do you send in to the bond? What kind of energy does she send into the bond?

Using whatever tools are needed (scissors, saws, power tools, explosives, anything that works), remove the negative bond between you and the other person. When you have removed it, dispose of it. Burn it, bury it, or throw it into a deep canyon, but get rid of it.

By removing the bond, you are not necessarily ending the relationship.

Removing the negative part of attachment makes room for a relationship in which both of you are independent beings. Cutting the ties that bind makes room for love to move back into a relationship.

"Cutting the Ties" is a technique which has been thoroughly developed by Phyllis Krystal and which she has written about in *Cutting the Ties that Bind* and *Cutting More Ties that Bind.*[2] My extremely abbreviated version is not intended as even a close translation of her work and I would strongly encourage anyone doing this work to study Mrs. Krystal's technique. There are books, tapes, and Cutting the Ties groups all over the world.

In order to be capable of giving and receiving love, including God's love, it's critical to become aware of one's judgments, and then begin letting go of them. You might reread the Judgment Review (Mental Fitness Technique #10, above, p. 115).

Otherwise, life will be about "you against them" instead of feeling love and oneness for others.

Practicing Forgiveness
Guideline #29

You can't begin to forgive until you've gone through the previous steps, until you've gotten in touch with your anger and resentment, expressed it, and finally cut the ties. Then proceed:

1.   In your notebook, review your list of resentments. In your mind's eye, forgive that person for each and every "offense." Say the words out loud.

2.   When you're ready, speak to that person face-to-face and forgive them, one item at a time.

3.   Finally, you'll want to ask them for forgiveness. That's right. The person whom you have seen as your abuser, your tormentor, you now need to forgive. If the thought of forgiving them shocks you, you're still dealing with resentment. You may want to ask for forgiveness for never having fully understood their side of the story, or for knowing no other way of reacting to them other than through anger and blame.

4.   If you're having trouble forgiving, pray that you may forgive.

5.   Once you've weeded the garden of your mind, rid it of negativity and begin to sow the seeds of love. Love needs help in order to grow. The more you work on developing love, the further resentment will recede into the past, the more you will become free from the past, and more able to live in the moment.

Letting Go of the Future
Guideline #30

Many of us who aren't stuck in the past are "stuck" in the future. If you're one of those people, your mind has thousands of thoughts a day, something like this: "I'm so worried about ..." "What if I don't have time to finish work, pick up the kids, and then fix dinner?" "I'm afraid I'm going to get killed by the IRS at tax time next year." If your mind works like that, you're in the future, and not in the present. From a spiritual standpoint, you need to work on faith, trust, and surrender. If you have complete faith in God, you will have absolutely no anxiety or worry. You will deeply trust that your life is "handled." That doesn't mean that you don't have to take action and make things happen. You still have to take appropriate action, even though you may believe that everything is a sign of God's grace and will.

There are two paths to faith. By taking the first path, one seeks, explores, looks for evidence, is finally convinced and then has faith. By taking the second path, the spiritual seeker jumps into the unknown. He makes that leap of faith and discovers that that leap brings more faith.

If you're living in the future, review the section "Crisis in Faith as Spiritual Emergency" and practice those techniques. Anything that inspires faith will, in turn, decrease worry and anxiety and will keep one anchored in the present. Here are some starting points to keep you out of the future:

1.   Remember that worry is the number one kind of mental imagery. All day long many of us are picturing bad things that may or may not happen to us. Begin to observe how your mind worries about the future. Once you're aware of the fact that you're probably having more than 10,000 thoughts a day, and that thousands of them are worries, you may want to start to do something about it.

2.   Practice your mantra every time you find yourself worrying.

3.   Every time you imagine something bad happening to you or to a loved one, mentally rehearse the same scene with a happy ending. If you're imagining coming home from work and having an unpleasant argument with your husband, tell your mind, "Stop." Now, close your eyes, have that conversation with your husband in your head, and make it a good conversation. Forget about "how it's always been." Picture the two of you working out your differences with sweetness and tolerance.

Practice this mental rehearsal technique every time you worry about anything. The fact is that the more you imagine yourself having a fight with your husband the more likely it is that the fight will go exactly as you've mentally rehearsed it, exactly the way you feared it would turn out.

4.   Practice Already-thereness, a concept that Jack Hawley writes about in *Reawakening the Spirit in Work: the Power of Dharmic Management.*[3] Many of us are "strivers," always trying to get "there." When we get "there," we start up the hill to get "somewhere else." Already-thereness means that you're already O.K. as you are right now. One needs goals, so that Already-thereness does not become an excuse for inaction. When we can love and accept ourselves as we are, we are already there, already here. Forget the idea that if you work for the next ten years toward your ultimate goal, you will finally be happy. Be happy now, and work toward your goal.

5.   Practice Instantaneousness, another of Jack Hawley's concepts. This means that we are capable of radical change immediately. Traditional psychiatry teaches that change is slow and takes 10, 20, or 30 years. If you expect your transformation to take 30 years, it will, and you will "live" in the future. However, through my years as a psychiatrist, practicing the techniques you've read about in this book, I have witnessed nearly instantaneous transformation about once a month. In the 1980s, I worked a lot with children and adolescents, often very disturbed kids who required treatment in a psychiatric hospital. After working there for many years, the head nurse approached me and said, "Doctor Gersten, it's amazing, but every one of your kids here gets better." "Betty," I replied, "I thought they were *supposed* to get better."

That's the truth. I honestly thought they were supposed to get better. If they weren't improving, I assumed that I was doing something wrong, or that the right technique or approach simply hadn't been invented yet. I'm telling you the same thing. "You are supposed to get better, and I know you can change—now."

6.   Close your eyes and say to yourself, "I can change right now, this moment."

Be assured that there is always a way to change, a way to be transformed, and even ways to be radically transformed immediately. It requires a lot of courage, but by practicing the techniques you've just read, you will begin to live in the moment and not be a prisoner of the future.

Surrender is the other major lesson that all of us, but especially worriers, need to learn. It's difficult to surrender if your faith is shaky, and if you have no faith at all, it is impossible to surrender. By surrendering, we do not turn over our power to someone else, but rather become more of who we really are. In the Eastern sense, there really is no one to surrender to. In early stages of spiritual practice, we pray and meditate to God. When we become enlightened, or experience nirvana or samadhi, we have the experience of being one with everything, even one with God. At that point, there is no God to surrender to, and there is no self left to surrender. This divine state is reached when one's own inner voice, one's own will becomes so fully imbued with truth, right action, peace, love, non-violence that our voice of conscience is the same as God's voice.

Surrendering to Right Action
Guideline #34

1.   Surrender to the truth of a given situation. Discover for yourself what is the truth and what is the Truth.
2.   Once you know the truth of a situation, muster the courage to carry out the dharma, the correct action for that situation.
3.   If you don't know what the correct action is, pray for 15 minutes, asking for guidance about what to do. If you've kept your mind still for 15 minutes, you will almost certainly hear your true inner voice clearly, and will know what to do.
4.   Once certain about the truth of a situation and the correct course of action, take that course of action.
5.   Make a vow to yourself this very moment that you will always strive to know the truth of every situation and will muster the courage to take the right course of action.

By following these steps, one surrenders to right action. One does what one must do, no matter what anyone else thinks about you. People may praise you for your "courage" or blame you for your "stupidity" depending on their vantage point. However, once you have made this commitment, you have surrendered to a powerful path. You no longer need to worry about the future, for you realize that you will do what is right, no matter what. The "no matter what" is important, for if you qualify your decisions and your actions, and make "small compromises" in human values, you will never conquer fear and worry, and will always live in the future, rather than in the present. Make the bold, courageous decision this very moment so that you don't spend the rest of your life worrying about whether you're going to be courageous in a particular situation.

The ultimate example of this kind of courageous surrender is the crucifixion of Jesus. Jesus knew ahead of time how his physical life would end. He knew he would be betrayed. And he knew that even the betrayal was a necessary part of the drama, without which his lesson could not be taught. Surely, the enlightened Jesus could have disappeared into thin air, vanished from the jail, or used any of the miraculous powers which were at his wish and command. But the lesson for him was not about using his miraculous powers. The lesson was in surrendering to the moment and to right action. Because he knew that the crucifixion was God's will, and because he was one with God's will, his final challenge was to muster the immense courage to do what was right. It wasn't fancy and it wasn't pretty. It was painfully agonizing. People have explored the meaning of the crucifixion in many ways. For now, consider that Jesus taught us how to live in the moment, how to steer free from worry and anxiety by simply deciding to know the truth and by courageously following right action. If we can muster a small fraction of that kind of courage in our day-to-day affairs, we will become free from the future, for, in fact, the future only exists in our imaginations. Only the moment is here—now.

Loving in the Moment
Guideline #32

In order to develop love, first we must understand the nature of love. Love is more than a feeling or emotion. It is more than romance or infatuation, even more than the profound affection we have for our children. Love is our true nature. It is the very nature of the soul. Just as the soul has no limits, so too love can be unbounded. Love is expansion. Fear is contraction. "Love lives by giving and forgiving. Self lives by getting and forgetting."—Sathya Sai Baba.

There are two main ways to cultivate love:
1. Remove the obstacles to love, and 2. Encourage the expansion of love.

Remove Obstacles to Love
Guideline #33

1.   Identify ways in which you are greedy, selfish, judgmental, angry, jealous, or envious. These are all obstructions to love. By identifying these obstacles, you can accomplish the first step in developing love.
2.   Practice mantra meditation to slow down the mind. When the mind owns you, less of your heart is available for love.
3.   *Allow an image to emerge that represents resistance to love.*
4.   Practice the ABCs of Anger Control. The more your anger is under control, the more love will flow.
5.   Practice forgiveness. Pray that you may forgive everyone whom you feel wronged you in any way. Your own resentment is a great obstacle to love.
6.   Excessive material desire decreases our "love capacity." By cutting down on our desires, we can continue to remove obstacles to love. Identify areas of excessive material desire.

Ceiling on Desires
Mental Fitness Technique #43

Here is an imagery technique to help you let go of excessive attachments:
1.   *Allow an image to emerge representing ways in which you are wasting money.*
2.   *Allow an image to emerge representing ways in which you are wasting food.*
3.   *Allow an image to emerge representing ways in which you are wasting time.*

4.   *Allow an image to emerge representing ways in which you are wasting energy.*

By putting a ceiling on our desires, by identifying ways in which we waste money, food, time, and energy, more love begins to flow.

Encourage the Expansion of Love
Guideline #34

1.   Take up selfless service. Serve each individual by using the technique of "Divine Vision," of looking for the spark of the divine within everyone. In other words, don't just go through the motions of service. Rather, perform acts of service that are soaked with love. Remember that the more love you give, the more love you will have to give. Love without attachment does not run out. When we love, but expect something in return, our egos grow and our hearts contract.

2.   Write Letters of Love and Gratitude.
Imagine that you only had one more week to live. During that week, you would want to convey, at the deepest level, how much you love the people in your life whom you really care about. But you don't have to be on your deathbed to express this kind of love. Make believe you're going to die next week, and live today as if it were the last day of your life. If you were about to die, you would overcome all fears about expressing love at the deepest level. So don't wait until you're dying. Be bold and courageous and express your love openly—today. Write letters to those whom you deeply love and tell them why you love them so much. And tell people directly. Speak to them. Say those words that so many of us find so difficult. "I love you."

3.   Sometimes, people find it so hard to love that they need a divine assist, especially when they're dealing with so-called "unlovable" people. Phyllis Krystal, author of *Cutting the Ties that Bind*, practiced "asking God to love through her" when she had the dreadful experience of being hijacked by terrorists on a plane.

When the terrorists first stormed her plane, Phyllis was aghast at the hateful expressions on the terrorists' faces. She remembered Sai Baba's teaching to "love all, serve all," but felt there was no way she could love those people. Mentally, she asked, "Baba, how can I love these people?" Phyllis realized that she had to allow God to love through her, for even though she did not feel capable of loving the terrorists, she believed that God could love them. So she prayed that God would love them through her, that she might be used as an instrument of love. Miraculously, the terrorists calmed down, no one was injured, and when the plane landed, the terrorists surrendered without incident. Practice this technique when your own capacity to love has been tapped dry.

4.   Pray every day that you will be able to love more people, and love them more and more deeply.

6.   Practice random acts of loving kindness. Start with one more act of love, generosity, or service per day than you are used to. Allow yourself to be surprised by situations that call for love, service, or sacrifice. Don't reserve loving acts only for those whom you love, nor for those times when you feel "prepared" to love.

7.   Do not forget to love yourself. Your ability to love yourself is equal to your ability to love others. In fact love "is our self." When we remove the obstacles to love, when we practice love, ultimately we "become" love.

8.   Here is an imagery technique to deepen divine love.

Filling Up with God's Love
Mental Fitness Technique #44

Picture your chosen form of God in front of you. Imagine that you are a container waiting to be filled with God's love and light. God places his hands above your head and his love and light pour out of his hands, slowly filling you up. You are now a container filled with love and light.

Spiritual Connection—the Maypole Imagery
Mental Fitness Technique #45

The Maypole Imagery helps us get in touch with God or a Higher Power. Use this simple imagery to heal your body, mind and spirit. For those seeking a deeper spiritual connection or for those who feel spiritually disconnected, this imagery will help you get reconnected.

Picture a maypole and imagine that God, a Higher Power, or Universal Intelligence is sitting on top of the maypole. Dangling from one of God's hands is a ribbon. Walk up to the maypole, pick up one of the colored ribbons and sit back down. Tug gently on the ribbon so that you can feel resistance or a tug on the other end of the ribbon, the end that God is holding. Allow God's love, joy and healing energy to flow into you. Allow each quality to fill every cell in your body, then filling your mind and spirit. After love, joy, and healing have flowed into you, ask yourself if there are any other qualities you want or need, and then ask God to allow those qualities to flow down the ribbon into you.

Remember that healing and spiritual connection do not have to be difficult and arduous.

---

1. Mary Jayne Carlson, "Temple of Forgiveness Imagery," *Atlantis the Imagery Newsletter* (Oct. 1989).
2. Phyllis Krystal, *Cutting the Ties that Bind: Growing Up and Moving On* (York Beach, ME: Samuel Weiser, 1993); and Phyllis Krystal, *Cutting More Ties that Bind* (Longmead, England: Element Books, 1990).
3 Jack Hawley, *Reawakening the Spirit in Work: The Power of Dharmic Management* (San Francisco: Berrett-Koehler Publishers, 1993).

Chapter 20

Facing the Void:
How Profound Emptiness is Cured

Few of us grew up under ideal circumstances, and many of us suffered some degree of abuse or neglect while growing up. Those of you who suffered severe abuse or neglect, whether physical or psychological, know how hard it is to leave the past behind. You may have gone to therapy for 20 years, joined 12-step programs, practiced meditation, guided imagery, emotional release work, or even shamanic healing. Still there is a good chance that you do not yet feel whole, for psychological damage in our early years leaves an incredibly deep wound.

Most of us know about "inner child work," which is aimed at reparenting that part of us which was wounded as a child.[1] What most people do not yet know is that "inner child work" does not fully heal a heart that was broken in childhood. For almost three decades, I have worked extensively with the abused and have identified several persisting inner ·states, which are invariably associated with abuse and neglect. The "wounded inner child" is one such inner state. The other states that I have identified are: the "inner abuser," the "inner battlefield," and the "void."

A simple technique will assist you in "diagnosing" your own condition. If you were abused or neglected as a child, try this exercise:

Close your eyes. Notice if you feel as if you are standing at the edge of a great void, a great chasm, or canyon. If you do experience the void, notice how far across it extends and how deep it goes. Notice how you feel standing at the edge of the void. Then open your eyes.

The void is the huge psycho-spiritual gap created within us when trust is radically shaken as a child. The void can be healed, but do not attempt to do this work on your own. It is much too dangerous. And do not begin to explore the "inner abuser" until you have sought out professional help and have first begun to heal the void. The void is not only present in people who were severely abused or neglected as children, but also in people who are in the middle of an existential crisis—people whose world has just fallen apart. Maybe they've just been diagnosed with cancer. Maybe they just got divorced, or fired from work. Maybe they're experiencing a radical shift in their worldview, of what they consider to be important or real.

Maybe they are wondering about the meaning of life—or if their life has meaning at all. Maybe they are having a crisis in faith, a dark night of the soul, or just a good old-fashioned "mid-life crisis." These problems can also be transformed immensely by exploring the void.

What follows is an imagery protocol for healing the void. Do not do this work on your own. Find a good imagery therapist, one who has experience with abuse. Bring him or her the following script, and ask if he or she will guide you through the void imagery:

Exploring the Void
Mental Fitness Technique #46

The void can be a terrifying place. You'll need a good deal of guidance to make the "descent."

Close your eyes. If you feel an inner void, picture that void now. Stand back from the edge. Gaze across the void and see how far across it stretches. How deep is it? Now, turn around so your back is to the void. Notice the scenery, both near and far.

People who were abused as children usually have similar experiences of the void. It is often described as "wider than the grand canyon" and "deeper than anything imaginable."

It is almost always a bottomless pit. Many people tell me they "live" at the edge of the void every day of their life. Once they have pictured the void, they need help preparing for the leap of faith into the void.

Imagine you have a parachute on your back. It's one of those high-tech parachutes that gives you lots of control. You'll be able to turn right or left as you choose. Picture your parachute and feel it on your back. Are you ready to jump into the void?

Divine Assistance

By now you are ready to "jump" but there is one more element of the imagery that needs to be introduced at this point—the spiritual dimension.

Imagine that a Divine Being joins you at the top of the void, a being full of light and love, a being you can fully trust. This Divine Being may be male or female; both or neither. Make contact with this being in any way you like. Hold his hands. Look into his eyes.

Now I'd like you to carry one more thing with you. Imagine you're carrying a powerful flashlight.

When you feel ready, jump off the edge into the void. Feel yourself slowly drifting down. Pull on the strings of your parachute, guiding yourself this way and that.

At this point, I will generally suggest that people fall or drift into the void uninterrupted for five or ten minutes. Then I will ask them to describe their experience thus far. I'll ask them to "shine their flashlight" on the walls of the void in order to see what it looks like. And I may ask them to touch the sides of the void in order to know what it feels like. By visualizing the sides of the void in this way, I am encouraging them to begin to observe differences. The void is no longer one giant bottomless pit. People begin to observe changes in the walls—perhaps from hard rock to sandstone. They begin to feel differences in the "weather," changes in temperature. The void begins to differentiate.

Continue to feel the presence of the Divine Being beside you, making your journey safe.

Without my having introduced the Divine Being, no patient of mine has been able to successfully traverse the void, reach the bottom, and make it back to the top. It is only through years of "parachuting" with my patients that I have come to believe in the necessity of introducing the Divine Being during every phase of traversing the void.

After about ten minutes into the "jump," I will ask my patient to look for the bottom. And almost invariably they reply, "There is no bottom. It just goes on forever." As you will soon discover, there are ways of bringing the bottom of the void into view. In most cases the bottom will not come into focus without my making some further suggestions:

Continue your descent with the Divine Being by your side, with your parachute catching the wind. Now imagine you're holding a flashlight.

Shine it on the walls of the void and notice the texture, color and hardness. Shine your flashlight across the void. And now shine your flashlight directly below. What do you see?

As my patients descend further and further into the void, they almost always observe that the walls of the void, which are dry at the top, become damp. When they shine their light across the void, they see that the other side is not very far away. By utilizing the flashlight in this way, the void no longer feels like a bottomless pit.

Reaching the Bottom of the Void

Imagine that there is a ledge jutting out from the side of the void. Land on the ledge and rest for a minute, gain your bearings — and then pick up a rock and toss it into the void. Listen for the sound of the rock hitting the bottom of the void. How long did it take to hit the bottom? Now, stand up on the ledge and jump again. In most cases the bottom of the void is now near and it won't take long for you to reach the bottom.

At this point, most people begin to see the bottom of the void. Before they first jumped into the void, their fear was so great that the void felt like a bottomless pit, ever-waiting to swallow them up.

After a couple of jumps into the void, the fear dramatically decreases.

The void is no longer one giant problem. It has now been explored safely, and has been examined with curiosity. Finally, as the fear diminishes, the bottom comes into view. Sometimes people will begin to see the void narrowing before they reach bottom. On rare occasion, I need to make further suggestions if my patient is unable to see the bottom.

Transforming the Bottom of the Void
Mental Fitness Technique #47

Be aware of the Divine Being who accompanies you into the void—your angel, or God. Imagine you have a magic wand in your hand. Before you transform the muck, become aware of how deep it is. Maybe you'll want to throw a stone into the muck to see how far down it goes. Now it's time to begin to transform the quicksand (or oil). Ask your angel for advice as to how to transform the quicksand, or use your magic wand.

In most cases the murky depths turns into crystal clear water. In one situation I asked a woman if her void came to a point at the bottom. She had been struggling to see the bottom below the oily muck. It just seemed to go on forever. But when I asked if the void came to a point, she began to sob uncontrollably. "Yes, it does. It does come to a point. I thought it went on forever. And, and, there's a huge glowing diamond at the bottom of the void. The diamond turned the oil into clear water."

At the moment when the murky depths finally are transformed, radical shifts in both mind and body take place. People say, "I can breathe again. The air is so clear." And the quality of their breath changes. One woman experienced the water as a healing spring full of energy, or prana. "I feel heat rising up my spine. I feel oxygen entering every cell in my body. It's as if my cells have never been able to fully let oxygen in. This is the kundalini energy. It's rising up my spine. I am in total peace and bliss."

After you have stood in the muck, and transformed it, begin to set up an altar at the bottom of the void. Put whatever you like on the altar—photographs, candles, incense, a Crucifix, a Star of David—whatever you like. And bring your angel to the altar with you.

Sit at your altar and pray or meditate. As you become more and more peaceful, the void will finally begin to heal. It is no longer the place you feared you would fall into, and from which you would never return. Paradoxically, the bottom of the void will become a place of total safety and comfort, a place far away from the worries of the world—a place where you have finally conquered your worst fear and discovered that your enemy is actually your vehicle for transformation.

Several images appear at the bottom of the void over and over again. Images of creation and destruction are common. One woman saw molten lava pouring out of the earth into the bottom of the void, a burning, dangerous lava that was giving birth to new land as soon as it cooled down. The molten lava was at the very center of the bottom of the void, and around that was water, a second image that is usually present.

Circular imagery is common—a ring of fire at the bottom, or a ring of angels. One lady, a devotee of Sathya Sai Baba, "saw" a ring of Baba's around her. The most common universal symbols present at the bottom of the void are: water, fire, and a circle.

Once people have transformed the void, I ask them to return to the top and then stand with their back to the void, looking at the scenery. Before the "jump" the scenery is like a desert, with sand and rocks but almost no vegetation. After they've descended, transformed the bottom of the void, and returned to the top, the scenery always changes. At the end of the session the scenery has started growing. Usually, there are many trees, and shrubs. If they were far in the distance at the beginning of the session, now the new growth is very close to the void.

Now, they are finally ready to explore the void on their own, at home, without a guide. They have gone through the crucible of transformation, almost like a shaman's initiation ritual. They have been burned by the fire, and immersed in the nothingness of the void. They have gotten stuck in the quicksand at the bottom and almost "suffocated" and, at last, they have begun to heal.

Sometimes this work is so powerful that people are physically-ill for several days after "transforming the bottom." One woman was sick to her stomach, had dry heaves for days, and developed hives. Many people report that their breathing changed the day after this experience. One patient told me, "I noticed today that my breathing has become much more regular and deeper. I also realized for the first time that whenever I get stressed out, I hold my breath and stop breathing. But now, I recognize that I'm doing that and I resume breathing." This same person, who suffers from chronic fatigue syndrome, reported that her physical energy went way up after transforming the void.

It is truly difficult to convey in words the power of the experience I have been witnessing with my patients. Although I have had no intention of trying to take my patients through a "birth" experience, their physical and emotional reactions are not unlike the process of birth. When they complain that they are stuck in the muck, that they feel like they're suffocating, and that suddenly oxygen rushes into their body when the bottom of the void is finally transformed—it sounds similar to the birth process.

In time the void will slowly close. It will begin to fill in on its own, but the process takes years—years of traveling to the bottom of the void, setting up the altar, and meditating or praying. There is no need to fill the void, for once it is no longer feared, it becomes a place of personal discovery, a true inner treasure, like a vein of gold.

The Inner Abuser

He's lurking in the shadows, lurking in the depths of the void. He's been stalking people from the inside of their minds all their lives, sabotaging their lives.

As I cautioned earlier, the inner abuser should lie undisturbed until the void has been thoroughly explored and transformed. Only then, and with caution, should one tackle the inner abuser, that remnant of abuse that continues to terrorize people, continues to sabotage their best plans, hopes, and dreams, continues to set them back a step every time they take one step forward. But now the ground is fertile for healing. The void is no longer a place of death, fear, and despair. Fear has been conquered, and the void has become a place of refuge and safety.

After the bottom of the void is clearly and definitely transformed, the inner abuser will usually spontaneously present himself/herself. The inner abuser "lives" in the void. It's his home and he wants to keep it that way. He does not like having his home disturbed and he can become menacing after the void is transformed.

Once the inner abuser has been visualized, all the tools available to the imagery therapist must be called on, for this is a very difficult condition to modify. The damage of early child abuse is so deep that it is as if the abuse is recorded or programmed completely into every cell in the body-mind. People who are survivors of childhood abuse often suffer from compromised immune systems, and are much more prone to chronic fatigue syndrome than is the general public. One must be very patient with this work and prepared to be quite inventive.

You will want to use an inner advisor or a Divine Being to help you interact with the inner abuser. Once you've identified the inner abuser, use the "communicating with your symptom" protocol in order to begin to come to terms with it.

What I have seen to be so critical to this process is the recognition of the void and the inner abuser's relationship to the void. As the void is transformed, the inner abuser is transformed. This is dangerous work, for the inner abuser carries an immense charge. He carries the rage, the destructive urges. If these urges are unleashed prematurely or in a chaotic fashion, the person is likely to get worse, not better.

Recovering from Abuse
Guideline #35

Here is an overview of the steps required to recover from abuse or neglect. No matter what phase of healing you are undertaking, always bring in a spiritual component. Always imagine that God is by your side and visualize him or her:

1.   Work with the wounded inner child, providing it comfort, safety, and nurturing.
2.   Explore and transform the void.
3.   Transform the inner abuser by dialoguing with this image, keeping in mind that it "lives" in and around the void.
4.   Do whatever work is necessary to clear up feelings about people who committed the abuse. Cut the ties to everyone who was abusive.
5.   Use the cutting the ties technique to cut the tie to a symbol of abuse.
6.   Re-enact the abuse scene in imagery, but be very gentle and don't try to dredge up powerful, buried emotion.

7.   Do everything in your power to bring more love into your life. The void came into existence due to a failure of love. By exploring the void and working with the inner abuser, you will have removed the major part of your shadow side. You will have let go the darkness. Now you need to "fill" that void with love. Dive into the moment, seeking to find love in every interaction, seeking to absorb the beauty of every flower you see. Practice all the techniques on developing love from the chapter The Tao of Love (Chapter 19) and strive to deepen your spiritual connection, for it is only through the purest, most unconditional love that the deepest wounds can be fully healed.

8.   Please remember that you are not the cause of your abuse. You are not bad, but people who've been abused, especially children, believe that the abuse must have been their fault.

Recovering from abuse requires great commitment. The long-term effects don't disappear with just a few months of inner work.

Life is a game, play it.
Life is a dream, realize it
Life is love, enjoy it
Life is a challenge, meet it.

Sathya Sai Baba

---

1.   Charles Whitfield, M.D., *Healing The Child Within: Discovery and Recovery for Adult Children of Dysfunctional Families* (Deerfield Beach, FL: Health Communications, 1987).

EPILOGUE

THE ANSWER TO THE QUESTION IN THE BOOK'S TITLE: ARE YOU GETTING ENLIGHTENED?

When people first see, or hear about, the title of this book, *Are You Getting Enlightened Or Losing Your Mind?*, there are several initial responses. Some people simply answer, "Yes," and then they laugh. Others say to themselves, "If I'm losing my mind, I don't want to find out."

The fact is that at least two-thirds of us have had a paranormal or spiritual experience. About one-third have had a life-changing spiritual experience. About 70% of us have had ESP; nearly 50% have experienced contact with the dead. 82% of us believe in miracles.

Hidden within the title is the unwritten message, "Almost everyone has had a paranormal or spiritual experience, and you're normal! You're not losing your mind." I wanted to write about every paranormal and spiritual experience I could so that you would be able to identify your experience and know what to call it.

I don't demean the importance of understanding mental illness. Many people are getting enlightened and also are struggling with anxiety, depression, or something more challenging. In describing the main mental illnesses, I have several goals in mind: 1) I want you to be able to embrace your miracle and know what to call it, 2) I want you to be able to distinguish your paranormal and spiritual experience from mental illness, 3) I want to broaden our understanding of mental illness and include the spiritual component of each mental illness. Those of you with a major psychiatric disorder should be able to find yourself within these pages, and get a new perspective on your problem. If you are suffering from a mental disorder, hopefully, this book will have provided you a very different understanding than you've previously had, and 4) I want to begin to integrate spirituality into the very fabric of psychiatry. Healing is not simply about being treated with the right medication, nutritional supplement, or mental imagery technique. Healing begins the moment a doctor shakes a new patient's hand for the first time.

Very few people feel safe telling a doctor about a spiritual or paranormal experience, and so that silence, that secret will limit the depth and trust of the healing relationship. The fact is that by sharing your miracle story, by being heard, and perhaps even gaining some understanding about what to call your unusual experience, the doctor-patient relationship takes on a new healing quality. Because I've been open to the mysterious, the spiritual, the experience with no name, my patients somehow know within the first half hour of our initial consultation that they can share paranormal and spiritual experience. More than that, frequently people just blurt out these experiences. When they see that I'm not judging or diagnosing them, our connection becomes powerful quickly. I evaluated a woman for abdominal pain (I do also work as a holistic physician). After about five minutes she said to me, "I think the pain is karmic." I replied, "So, you think it's tied to a past-life?" That is what she was saying. While I do want to know the physical cause of her pain, my sense was that there was a karmic component.

Are You Getting Enlightened?

"Enlightenment" is a word, a concept, a state of consciousness that many people and spiritual traditions understand differently. If I'm speaking with a patient about God, their first response is often, "I don't believe in the old man in the sky with a beard." My response is, "I don't recall mentioning that old man. Let me share my view, which has its roots in ancient Eastern religion. God and soul are made of the same 'stuff.' If we think of God as the ocean, our individual souls are all rivers, that are running back to eventually merge with the ocean."

If we've spent decades on a conscious spiritual path, hopefully we are more aware, more conscious, more enlightened than when we began. We are more committed to truth and integrity. We have let go of resentment, because we've learned that without forgiveness, we hold onto anger forever. As we become enlightened, we are able to love more and more people, and love them more deeply. In fact, we come to even do what Jesus taught—to love our enemies.

One simple Mind Map helps us understand the process of enlightenment. We are like an onion, with the soul at the center, and five layers surrounding the center. The outer layer, or sheath, is the physical body, followed by the energy body, the mind (or mental body), the intelligence, the bliss sheath and finally the soul, spirit, or atma. Spiritual progress involves dis-identifying with one layer after another. If you were in an accident and lost a hand, the essence of "you" remains the same. So you *are not* your body. The body is a thing! So is the energy body, and the mind.

I've worked with a lot of surfers here in Encinitas, California. If they are spiritually-challenged, I'll share this: "Think about when you're surfing. You are one with the wave, right?"

"Right."

In order to be one with the wave, you cannot have a single distracting thought. When you're in the curl of the wave, you're in the zone, and you have to be tuned into all the moment-to-moment changes of the wave. If your mind wanders, the wave will toss you in a heartbeat. So the mind is not something that helps you in becoming one with the wave. It's what interferes with that sense of oneness.

The same is quite evident for athletes, entertainers, and musicians. If a musician is on-stage performing, and is thinking about what he's doing, he's really doing two things. He's playing his instrument, and he's thinking about playing his instrument, and just like the surfer, thinking about playing an instrument will lead to performance falling apart. It's important to let people know that the mind and the intelligence are quite different. The intelligence is involved in discrimination, wisdom, and higher problem solving. If we pay attention to our intelligence, it tells us what is right and what is wrong. It tells us the right course of action to take, the moral course of action.

As you read early in the book, the mind churns out in excess of 5,000 random thoughts a day. Our thoughts scan the environment for things we like and things we dislike. If we really like something, and really want it, it becomes a desire. Desires are not bad, but when our mind sinks its mental teeth into our object of desire, it doesn't take long before that object or person seems to own us. We've lost our freedom.

The process of enlightenment requires the taming of the mind and ultimately the total silencing of the mind. The sun shines every day, but if it were cloudy every day, we might conclude that there is no sun. The cloud that blocks the light of the soul is the mind. When the mind slows down and those mental clouds start to part, we see the soul shining through. You can't hear God talking if your mind is always chattering.

Ultimately, spiritual progress involves: 1) taming the mind, and 2) strengthening your soul/God connection. At the end of the spiritual road, we discover that our soul connection is one and the same as our God connection. Someone who is moving closer to enlightenment feels "lighter." They laugh a lot, like the Dalai Lama. They love everyone and are profoundly peaceful. For these reasons, these people are magnetic, and their love is the magnet. People are attracted to them and want to be in their presence, simply because it feels so good to be so close to their light.

The paradox of "Are You Getting Enlightened Or Losing Your Mind?" is that we do have to lose our mind (in a good way) in order to become enlightened. But, we have to have become spiritually strong so that we can choose to weaken the grip of the mind. Someone with psychosis, like schizophrenia or mania, has lost their mind involuntarily. The psychotic loss of the mind does not lead to peace and love. It leads to mental agony. But at both ends of the spectrum, enlightenment and psychosis, we lose our minds. The psychotic person on a spiritual path, has to grow strong enough to tame his mind, so that he can eventually begin to consciously let go of it, in the service of something higher.

How can you identify an enlightened person? You can't! You might think someone is a saint, but he or she might just "look" spiritual. The reality might be quite different. Similarly, you might be sitting next to someone in any setting, thinking, "He's really an un-evolved bum." The fact is that that person who appears very negative in your eyes just might be quite evolved on his spiritual quest.

In my spiritual organization, the Sathya Sai Baba Organization, I was friends with the first president of the organization, Jack Hislop. Jack had previously been head of Krishnamurti's organization, then Maharishi Mahesh Yogi's organization, then Yogananda's organization—and finally the American division of the Sai Baba Organization. Jack passed on in 1995. Everyone who knew Jack believed he was very evolved. I certainly did and still do. I was sitting next to Jack, having lunch, after we'd both given presentations at a retreat in Santa Barbara. I turned and playfully asked him, "So, Jack, what's it like to be enlightened?" He laughed and said, "Nonsense, my boy. I've got as many problems as anyone else."

It's impossible to know another person's spiritual evolution." Jack's words are important because there are so many people who publicize themselves as being gurus, spiritual counselors, or "highly evolved." You might hold a spiritual teacher in very high regard, which is certainly not a bad thing, but it's quite possible that you are more highly evolved, closer to enlightenment, closer to the light than they are. Spirituality is not about how psychic you are. Enlightenment is not about how many angels you've seen or how many times you've experienced nirvana. Some very spiritual people see angels and some don't. Which one is better? Neither.

Let me come back down to earth. If you have become 100% committed to truth, you're on the right path. If you keep practicing doing the right thing *no matter what*, it becomes easier to do that. "Doing the right thing" is dharma, and it's a muscle that gets stronger the more you flex that muscle. As dharma grows, you become more peaceful, loving, and non-violent. You should be able to ask yourself if you are growing stronger in the five core human values—truth, right action, peace, love, and non-violence. That's enlightenment—for the sake of this book's goals and limitations.

If you have attained spiritual enlightenment, the mind no longer exists. Your real experience is that there is only one moment (now) and only one being. Like the surfer in the curl of the wave, the enlightened person's boundaries between Self and God have disappeared, and he lives in the flow of oneness. He's the spiritual Michael Jordan, who played basketball in the zone almost all the time. Maybe all the time.

To return to the title, "Are You Getting Enlightened Or Losing Your Mind?" I'm not writing as a guru whose intention is to help you attain enlightenment. I hope you now have become friends with your paranormal and spiritual experience. I hope you love and embrace those experiences and take the next step, namely to use those experiences to become a more whole and happy person. I hope you can integrate these experiences into your life so that you can begin to share with those close to you. We all want to be heard and seen. We want to matter. We want at least one person with whom we can share our most important secrets, someone who will listen with an open mind without trying to make us wrong or crazy. We want to feel worthy and worthwhile. I hope this book has helped you understand and accept your experience so much that you can take the risk and begin to talk about your unique paranormal and spiritual experience. For when you share, when you are heard, you no longer live in hiding. Your vision can be a light that you can share with more and more people, if you choose. And perhaps the experience you've been afraid to confide in others will provide the light, the spark to transform someone else's life.

APPENDIX A: MENTAL FITNESS TECHNIQUES
Simple, single techniques

APPENDIX B: GUIDELINES

These are lists, or guidelines, some as many as 10 steps long.

CPSIA information can be obtained
at www.ICGtesting.com
Printed in the USA
BVOW03s2132170217

476517BV00001B/19/P